SANTA ANNA

The Story of an Enigma Who Once

Was Mexico

Ant. Lopez de Sta Anna

Santa Anna

*The Story of an Enigma Who Once
Was Mexico*

WILFRID HARDY CALLCOTT

ARCHON BOOKS
HAMDEN, CONNECTICUT
1964

F1232
S2312
1964

92
S23c

Library of Congress Catalog Card Number 64-13173
Printed in the United States of America

TO REBECCA

PREFACE

SANTA ANNA'S career is filled with superlative climaxes which culminate in a tragedy so complete as to provide an ideal theme for either poet or dramatist. When a mere lad the headstrong and impetuous Antonio entered the army and was promptly assigned to duty in the brutal frontier warfare of the day. Thus he was given the very training that would most accentuate his faults. Yet, by ability, bravery and a remarkable personality, he rose until he became the storm center of Mexico's history for thirty-five years. Though possessed of a very moderate social background he was a superb egotist and was so confident of his own ability that he was thoroughly convinced his nation's best interests demanded that he dictate its policies.

After once joining the liberal cause he loyally supported it for a decade though his military training and his own inclinations carried him steadily toward that centralism which he later claimed the logic of events justified and demanded. Had he died during the War with the United States, or even during his dictatorship of the 1850's, history would have treated him far more kindly. Unfortunately, the desperate old man nearing his three score and ten tried to regain power by any means, regardless of whether it was through the support of the French interventionists who were establishing an empire, the United States which urged republicanism, or even his recently denounced liberal opponent, Benito Juárez. The result was to make his name anathema to his countrymen at the time and for succeeding generations.

From the very beginning, his life presents a strange resemblance to the course of a turbulent summer's day. First, there was the brilliant daybreak with only occasional clouds to mar the early prospects. Next came the long period of the morning as clouds and humidity increased, though periodically the sun broke through with its ever increasing power and splendor. By mid-day the spectacle was magnificent but the air was sultry and oppressive. After an interval, while Nature threatened but all good Mexicans enjoyed their *siestas* (Santa Anna in exile), began the fast and furious activity of the tropic afternoon. The blinding glory of the sun was obscured by angry storm clouds tossing and writhing in agony as the lightning gleamed and flashed.

Suddenly, both the fury of the storm and the heat of the day were spent, and there followed a long and peaceful twilight that seemed to have no end. Clouds still lowered over the mountain tops and occasionally there was the glimmer of distant lightning and the mutter of almost unheard thunder. The fearful could still scent danger in the air; the optimists looked forward to a calm and peaceful rest. Imperceptibly, the dusk deepened into night and no one could indicate the exact moment when the day ceased to be (poetically enough, the old man of eighty-two passed on so quietly that only his wife was present when he breathed his last at about 1:30 A.M. June 21, 1876).

TABLE OF CONTENTS

I—DAYBREAK

II—MORNING

III—AFTERNOON

IV—DUSK

V—DARK

LIST OF ILLUSTRATIONS

ACKNOWLEDGMENT

TO write a definitive biography of Antonio López de Santa Anna in one volume is an impossibility, for that would involve little less than a political and military history of Mexico for more than half a century following 1810. To make the task more difficult is the fact that material for the study is widely scattered, there being no outstanding collection of the man's manuscripts and documents. Never a methodical man, Santa Anna kept his papers poorly, so that they were repeatedly destroyed or scattered by the vicissitudes of domestic war and foreign invasion. One set is reported to have been held together for a time but was ordered destroyed when the owner (the mother of Santa Anna's son José) died of a serious communicable disease. As a result, there are now comparatively few letters available of the thousands that must have been addressed to him. On the other hand his own flare for writing letters and proclamations has provided the student of a century later with hundreds of these documents scattered in all kinds of places in Mexico, the United States and Europe; many doubtless being in private hands still.

The author in the following study simply endeavors to use source material in order to give a balanced picture of the times against which appears the career of this stormy petrel of both Mexican and international politics; a man with no impartial observer of his conduct for all became ardent friends or bitter enemies. Entertaining stories and legends of the man are legion. They have been gladly recorded when they have been found to rest on historical evidence but have been consistently suppressed when their accuracy remained in doubt.

Of necessity many controversial matters in both Mexican history and the foreign relations of the country are touched upon. These are especially noticeable to English readers in connection with the period of the troubles with Texas and the Mexican War with the United States. In such cases the effort has been made to state frankly the issue and the author's opinion of the part played by Santa Anna without lengthy technical discussions. The alternative would be a two to four volume work with as much footnote material as text.

Extensive indeed has been the assistance so courteously extended to the author on every side. Especial thanks are due to the University of South Carolina for a revised teaching schedule to allow as much time as possible for the preparation of this manuscript, and to the Social Science Research Council, of New York City, for a grant-in-aid to provide money for a final trip to Mexico to check certain facts and impressions as to local material. Others who have materially assisted are: the University of Texas Library, especially Miss Winnie Allen, Archivist; the staff of the National Library of Mexico, and the custodians of the archives in the State Department, Washington, D. C., as well as in the National Archives of Mexico. Among the numerous individuals to whom thanks are due only the following are mentioned: three gentlemen living in Jalapa, Veracruz; Mr. W. K. Boone, Sr. Alberto Gutiérrez J., and Sr. José Trigos; the reverend Father Mariano Cuevas, S. J., who kindly placed his library in Mexico City at the author's disposal; and Mrs. W. D. Melton, and Mr. Joseph A. Brandt for their cheerful and constant assistance in the painful process of preparing the manuscript for the press.

Columbia, S. C.　　　　　　　　　Wilfrid Hardy Callcott

CORRECTIONS IN TEXT*

Page 6, line 32, for "Costillo" read "Costilla"

Page 34, line 14, for "1882" read "1822"

Page 37, line 9, for "1882" read "1822"

Page 44, line 6, for "Reverend" read "Revered"

Page 47, line 1, for "February" read "March"

Page 53, note 2, for *"a"* read *"la"*

Page 58, line 16, for "recommended" read "continued"

Page 59, lines 2, 6, for "Vázques" read "Vázquez"

Page 60, note 7, for "Aviranteta" read "Aviraneta"

Page 72, line 19, for "been" read "be"

Page 79, lines 7, 8, for "Alcibides" read "Alcibiades"

Page 83, line 3, for "are generally" read "is generally"

Page 89, line 30, for "meditation" read "mediation"

Page 94, line 8, for "of the" read "on the"

Page 102, note 12, for "Boncanegra" read "Bocanegra"

Page 125, line 10, for "provinces" read "province"

Page 126, line 21, for "Mosquite" read "Mosquito"

Page 129, line 35, for "negroes" read "Negroes"

Page 131, line 5, for "negro" read "Negro"

Page 131, lines 23, 24, for "Matamorous" read "Matamoros"

Page 142, line 23, for "Rush" read "Rusk"

Page 146, line 4, for "communication" read "communications"

Page 167, line 2, for "1841" read "1840"

Page 173, line 34, for "proclamed" read "proclaimed"

Page 174, line 10, for "give" read "que"

Page 185, line 24, for "omnious" read "ominous"

Page 192, line 1, for "270,000,000" read "270,000"

Page 196, line 13, for "Laragua" read "Lafragua"

Page 197, line 19, for "gallaries" read "gallaries"

Page 206, line 10, for "daily" read "duty of"

Page 208, line 25, for "Querétarto" read "Querétaro"

*The corrections of the original printing are included in this reprint edition at the request of the author.

Page 219, line 17, for "politic" read "political"

Page 225, line 35, for "proclaimed" read "proclaiming"

Page 232, line 27, for "Ullo" read "Ulloa"

Page 237, line 27, for "asked to tranship four passengers" read ", either because of inefficiency or drink, did not do."

Page 249, line 17, for "security reported" read "security was reported"

Page 262, line 29, for "treaty" read "agreement"

Page 268, line 37, for "Molina" read "Molino"

Page 278, line 18, for "to" read "in"

Page 280, line 23, for "centralists" read "centralist"

Page 282, line 37, for "custom" read "customs"

Page 287, line 16, for "Veláquez" read "Velázquez"

Page 289, line 15, for "journals" read "journalists"

Page 289, line 28, for "Buenrosro" read "Buenrostro"

Page 293. The figures given in lines 9 through 12 follow reports of the time though the reports themselves may have been padded.

Page 330, line 11, for "embyro" read "embryo"

Page 333, line 5, for "up" read "with"

Page 339, note 6, for "tercea" read "tercera"

Page 344, line 24, for "desparing" read "despairing"

Page 359, line 5, for "Hs" read "His"

Page 374, line 2, for "lugar" read "lugaro"

Page 379, line 12, for "1919" read "1911"

Page 379, line 12, add: Smith, Justin H., *War With Mexico,* New York, 1919, 2 vols. (Excellent.)

Page 379, line 25, for "historica" read "historia"

Page 388, line 3, for "Saladas" read "Salas"

I

DAYBREAK

[1794-1830]

A wind came up out of the sea,
And said, "O Mists, make room for me."

It hailed the ships, and cried, "Sail on,
Ye mariners, the night is gone."

And hurried landward far away,
Crying, "Awake, it is the day."

—HENRY WADSWORTH LONGFELLOW

BEGINNINGS

JALAPA, "Water on the Sands," has ever occupied a prominent position in the life of Mexico. Nestling at a height of four thousand feet above the pestilential tropics that made Veracruz so feared for long periods each year, it became a place of refuge and a site for the permanent homes of the wealthier classes. It was so tucked into the folds of the mountains, that storms could hardly strike it, while it boasted of such an idyllic climate that corn could be planted every month of the year. Coffee fincas, orange groves and banana fields now may be seen from the public square, while the chirimoya and mango grow on all sides. Yet, from only a few miles away but higher up the plateau's edge, come successively peaches, and then apples and the cereal belt of the temperate zone.

In addition to fruits, Nature poured out other riches for the inhabitants and gorged them with a riot of color and grandeur. The flaunting red or purple bougainvilla, the brilliant azalea and beautiful dahlia, as well as the humbler geranium, rose, zinnia, carnation and begonia, and the exotic orchid, grew in a natural state or with a minimum of cultivation. And all of these were thrown against a background of wild and imposing magnificence. There were steep cut mountain gorges and the ominous truncated cones of recently extinct volcanoes which had poured out their molten lava to create here and there the fantastic "evil land" (*malpaís*) which seemed to reflect the capers of the children of the old Aztec gods in a mischievous mood. Then towering over all and dazzling in its snow-capped majesty at a height of eighteen thousand feet was Mt. Orizaba.

Amid such surroundings of natural beauty and safety, but so near to the storms and wild forces of nature, Antonio

López de Santa-Anna Pérez de Lebrón was born on February 21, 1794. The child was named after his father, who for many years held the office of sub-delegate for the old Spanish province of Veracruz. He was of a well-established and respectable Spanish family, thought by present descendants to have come from Aramayona in Alava Province, the region of the Basques.[1] The López name was such a common one in old Castillian Spain that this family carried the identification of "Santa Anna," which is said to have originated from the fact that in old Aramayona there was a chapel dedicated to Saint Anne so this family identified themselves as being the López of Santa Anna.

The name of the mother's family, Lebrón, seems to have a French origin, but the connection is vague. She is reported to have been an excellent woman, but with no especial social standing. Most claim that she was of pure creole stock, though others assert that there was some Indian blood in her veins.

From all accounts, the vagaries of nature entered into the very being of the boy. His school life was short, but even at that early date the word "quarrelsome" appeared in a description of his relations with his schoolmates. As he was obviously not a student, it was quite natural for people in his parents' social and economic position (his father was a mortgage broker in Veracruz) to seek an opening for the lad in some business. Probably through his father's connections, arrangements were made for Antonio to work for one Señor Cos, a merchant of Veracruz. Years later, when the boy was an old man, he still boastfully remarked that he was not born to be a "counter-jumper."

After long and painful discussion with his parents Antonio's short merchandising career came to an end. He first won over his mother to his plan for a military career and then the two combined and secured the reluctant consent of Antonio, Sr., for the momentous step. All family pressure and con-

1. Manuel Rivera, *Historia de Jalapa,* Tomo I, p. 308. Rivera states that the family had its origin in Limisa in the Diocese of Limia where it enjoyed excellent connections, but existing members of the family give the origin as indicated above.

nections were at once brought to bear with local officials and finally the coveted position of cadet in the *Fijo de Veracruz* Regiment of Infantry was secured on June 9, 1810. This required proof as to reasonable social standing as well as misrepresentation of the boy's age, for he was as yet too young to be legally enrolled.[2]

Meanwhile conditions in the Spanish Empire were developing which were to affect seriously the entirely unsuspecting cadet. The intelligent reforms of King Charles III of Spain had been followed by the disastrous reign of Charles IV (1788-1808). The administration became a public scandal with the malodorous Manuel Godoy dominating affairs in spite of a reputation based on a shrewd and blatant immorality in both public and private life. In many cases the colonies and their revenue became happy hunting grounds for fortune seekers of an office holding class, men who expressed contempt for the colonials and who cared little for royal orders and decrees, old or new, unless they could be used for selfish purposes.

The European stage as a whole was dominated by the spectacular Napoleon Bonaparte who overthrew the French Directory in 1799. He used Spain as a pawn on the European chessboard, taking Louisiana on his own terms and then driving the southern nation into war with England in 1804. During his later northern campaigns there was such obvious unrest and dissatisfaction in Spain that the Frenchman felt the country ought to be chastised. This also provided an excellent opportunity to bring Spain and the recalcitrant Portugal under the Napoleonic political and economic system. The weak Charles, the incompetent Ferdinand who was heir to the throne, and the unscrupulous Godoy, were all brushed aside while Napoleonic legions

2. In his *Historia Militar y Política* (hereafter referred to as his *Memoirs*), Santa Anna says that he secured the appointment when he was barely fourteen years old. In commenting on this Sr. Genaro García in his manuscript notes for a biography of Santa Anna naïvely remarks: "In writing this, Santa Anna not only forgot the date of his birth, but that he stated in his proclamation of August 10, 1823, that he had begun to serve the Spanish King at the age of sixteen."

marched over the peninsula and proclaimed Joseph Bonaparte as king of Spain in 1808 in spite of the gallant resistance of the Spanish people who bitterly hated the invader.

In Mexico, as in Spain, the French were hated and Charles IV and Godoy were blamed for the corruption in the administration. However, nearly all felt a profound sympathy for Ferdinand so it was not surprising that the colony proclaimed its loyalty to the Prince. Unfortunately, Viceroy José de Iturrigaray (1803-1808) was an opportunist like his protector Godoy. He could not make up his mind whether to remain loyal to Ferdinand, to leap on the Napoleonic bandwagon, or to lead Mexico to that independence that some restless folk were talking about. Tired of this shilly-shallying, a group of Spaniards overpowered the palace guards, seized the Viceroy and hustled him off to prison on September 15, 1808. They then named the seventy-nine year old Pedro de Garibay in his place. For the ensuing year the senility of the Executive only added to the confusion so that Mexico City became a gigantic whispering gallery and rumor factory. In July, 1809, the Archbishop of Mexico, Francisco Xavier de Lizana y Beaumont, became viceroy for ten months and succeeded in antagonising additional local leaders. In fact, a rather serious plot out in the province of Guanajuato was so feared that the administration did not dare to allow severe penalties to be inflicted on the convicted leaders because of the possible effect on popular discontent. At last, the make-shift Spanish government, which had been forced to flee from place to place by Napoleon's forces, named Francisco Xavier Vanegas as Viceroy of Mexico. He assumed office in September, 1810, but was soon to irritate many influential Mexicans and had scarcely assumed office when challenged by the hordes of Father Miguel Hidalgo y Costillo.

In Santa Anna's home town of Jalapa there were stirrings of discontent as early as 1808, and there is good reason to believe that not a few of the local inhabitants were actually using the dread word "independence" as the inept conduct of the rulers of Spain became more and more apparent. Such theories, however, if they ever came to the ears of the boy of sixteen, could not have been expected to have much weight when he was struggling with might and main to secure a foothold in the glorious career that he had envisioned for himself as a dashing officer in the grand old Spanish army.

Quiet training in barracks was short indeed for the young soldier, and early in the year 1811 orders were issued for him to march north for the arduous service of Indian fighting in the arid frontier provinces. The great patriot leader, Hidalgo, had just been defeated in the battle of Calderón and was reported to be fleeing overland to the United States. To prevent this and to restrain the restless northern Indians, Señor Joaquín de Arredondo was ordered to organize an expedition of five hundred men to proceed to the Texas coast. Included in the number was Cadet Antonio. The expedition left Veracruz March 13 by sea, but on account of transportation difficulties, landed at Tampico.

This was doubtless the first sea voyage undertaken by the young soldier. On the twentieth, the men disembarked for a week's stay in Pueblo Viejo. Early in April, after organizing the local troops, Arredondo started his campaign to the interior only to hear of the capture of Hidalgo. This, however, did not long deter the ambitious soldier for there were several hundred insurgents, semi-patriots and semi-bandits, in small groups in the vicinity.

To follow the petty details of ensuing actions is infinitely boring. In his *Memoirs* Santa Anna says: "The first battalion of my regiment was destined for the pacification of the Eastern Internal Provinces under the orders of Colonel Don Joaquín Arredondo, it being my fortune to take part in that five year campaign." The disturbances seem to have taken on a rather serious character and the number of government troops was increased to two thousand. Antonio immediately began to show his real love of campaigning and Arredondo reported on June 3, that he was one of the cadets "who had enough constancy to suffer the inconveniences of continuous marches, giving an example in this way to the troops, and demonstrating the most *vivid desires to give credit to their valor."*[3] About this time, a change was made that must have been pleasing to a youth so ambitious and devoted to the picturesque. He was transferred to the cavalry and thus enabled to gratify that inborn desire to follow in the steps of the Spanish horseman, who, for so long, had struck terror in the hearts of the humble native folk.

During this first campaign of a high-strung, ambitious and impetuous youth the destruction, death and terrorization of all actual or possible enemies was held to constitute success for the government forces. The innocent were imprisoned (one might almost as well say tortured) for "months and years, till a sufficient number of false witnesses were found to give an appearance of justice to the caprice, hatred and animosity of the commander." After one defeat of the rebels, in which many supplies were captured "some of the prisoners were killed, others horsewhipped, and the rest turned loose"— to keep a large number of ignorant Indians as prisoners would have been a nuisance. On another occasion, the Spanish officers "swept off all they found, confusing the peaceful inhabitants with fighting men .... some were shot and others sent to work in the fortress of Altamira with little effort made to separate one group from the other.[4] Such was the school in which Santa Anna was an eager pupil and learned all too well, but it should be remembered that this was typical of Indian warfare as it had been carried on for generations, both north and south of the Río Grande and by descendants of Anglo-Saxons as well as by those of Spaniards.

In July, Santa Anna was ordered to report to brevet Colonel Cayetano Quintero, who was going to the state of San Luis Potosí to "pacify" that section. Here the same story was repeated as the fighting extended through the Sierra Madre range of mountains. On August 29, in an active skirmish or battle with Indians at Amoladeras, Santa Anna received an arrow wound in his left arm or hand. This was the first

3. Walter Edgar Hancock, *The Career of General Antonio López de Santa Anna* (MS., Ph. D., thesis in the University of Texas library), p. 10 note.
4. José María Luis Mora, *Méjico y sus revoluciones,* Tomo IV, pp. 264-65, 447-48.

blood he shed for his country but Mexico was to hear of it for many years to come. His consistency and activity—and this life of change and movement just suited his nature—continued and on January 5, 1812, he was recommended for promotion to the rank of second lieutenant. The recommendation was approved and his commission issued with the date of February 6, only to be followed on October 7 of the same year, with a further promotion to the rank of first lieutenant. Beyond doubt, an enthusiastic young man was meeting with the approval of his superior officers. But success in this reckless and bloody warfare for a lad of eighteen presaged ill for old Mexico if the lad, become a man, should employ the same principles on a national scale.

By this time he was often entrusted with minor commands on his own account. On one occasion, he was reported as leading a band of thirty troops and defeating 320 Indians, strongly located in a gorge. A number of such successes were to be attributed in part to recklessness and bravery, but even more to subtle maneuvering and stratagems that took the enemy by surprise.

Meanwhile the Viceroy was trying to get Arredondo to return, but that wily commander proved peculiarly desirous of avoiding headquarters for he feared an audit of his accounts. To the delight of the Brigadier (Arredondo had been promoted) word came that Texas was being overrun with republicans and republican ideas from the United States. This, of course, demanded investigation. The joyous preparations of Arredondo were legalized when he received orders from the new Viceroy, Calleja, to take the post of Commanding General of the Interior Provinces and to proceed with the conquest of Texas. One Colonel Ignacio Elizondo was instructed to co-operate, but he apparently wished to secure all credit for himself. He did not wait for his commanding officer but hastily collected some two thousand men and dashed off—only to be soundly defeated by the rebels.[5]

5. Ignacio Elizondo was the worthy who played the traitor to the patriot, Hidalgo, in 1811. He ambushed his chief and then surrendered him to the royal forces for execution.

The situation was now becoming critical as Coahuila and other north Mexican provinces insisted on adherence to the fantastic idea (or so the regular army officer thought) of independence that had been popularized by the harebrained Miguel Hidalgo and his rabble that had been so soundly threshed two years before. Arredondo quickly completed his plan and set out for Laredo, on the Río Grande, in the early part of June, 1813. Then began an arduous march indeed. The fertile valleys with mountainsides, checkered and patterned by solid rock walls, surrounding a quarter or half acre of cultivated land with the stones that patient labor had dug out of the scanty soil, gave place to dusty valleys and barren slopes as the edge of the desert was reached. The dazzling glare of the sun and choking dust from the advancing column were only occasionally relieved as scanty shadows hastily chased each other across the bare mountain sides, but seemed to hide the scorching sun for only a moment before the clouds were gone.

Elizondo received orders from General Arredondo to join the remnants of his troops with the main column as it advanced to the north from Laredo. Only four hundred men were left with Elizondo, but, added to the main army, they raised this force to about two thousand, of which 735 were reported as infantry, the rest being mounted.

The rebels were a motley crew of adventurers and Indians from the so-called "Neutral Ground," that free-booter's paradise between the United States and Spanish jurisdictions. The total was probably about twenty-five hundred or more though only some 850 are reported to have actually taken part in the Battle of the Medina. Arredondo arranged his men in ambush in a V-shape, taking advantage of the growth of chaparral, mesquite and other bushes. The attack of the rebels was not long delayed. Following their prey (really decoys placed in position only to retreat) they dashed into the ambush. Bancroft comments: "Then burst forth on right and left of them a blaze of fire, leaping from levelled muskets and pointed cannon, which struck them down by scores.... For four hours, they maintained the unequal fight, and strove in vain to turn the enemies' flank. When nearly all were slain, a remnant of the obstinate band escaped from the field of slaughter—when their ammunition was spent! Out of the eight hundred and fifty Americans, who entered that gorge of death, only ninety-three effected their escape to Nachitoche."[6]

To the Mexicans, however, this was a victory over a superior force. Arredondo reported fifty-five dead, one hundred and seventy-eight wounded, and one hundred and sixty-five with contusions (*contusos*), though all figures were probably under-estimates. The 112 prisoners taken were shot that day and the next, whereupon the victorious troops moved on to San Antonio. In this town were captured 215 more rebels, of whom most of those from the United States and many others were shot.

The whole campaign built up in the mind of Santa Anna (still a boy of nineteen, but again warmly commended in official reports of the Battle of Medina for gallant conduct under fire) two illusions that were to cost him dearly at a later date. One of these was that the way to handle Texas rebels was by terrorization, and the other was that the said rebels were ineffective fighters and could easily be defeated by Mexican troops.

After the capture of San Antonio, the canons of frontier warfare were naturally applied. In the suburbs of the town a large number of women, some of them the wives and daughters of the best people, were forced to work in the preparation of military supplies. At the same time, they were subjected to the insolent and brutal abuse of an immoral and cruel soldiery.[7]

For his bravery in action Santa Anna was to receive a special decoration (*escudo*), but of that he probably knew nothing for a time. Be that as it may, one of the weaknesses of his character came near to getting him into serious difficul-

6. Hubert Howe Bancroft, *History of the Pacific States of North America*, XI, 29, 30.

7. Vicente Filisola, *Memoria para la historia de la Guerra de Tejas*, p. 75.

ties. Having lost heavily at the gambling table, he forged the signatures of Colonel Quintero and General Arredondo on drafts drawn on the company's funds. His defense was that he was helping out a brother officer who was in distress, and that he was trying to maintain the honor of his regiment. D. Jaime Garza, the surgeon of his regiment, came to the rescue and advanced the sum of three hundred *pesos* to help the young officer make restitution. To further make up the deficit, Santa Anna's personal property, "even to his sabre," was confiscated. In fact, according to his own statement, he was left only two old suits of clothes. The rest of his property, said to have been worth one thousand *pesos,* was sold to satisfy the total amount due of less than half that sum. This hushed up the matter for the time, but it was to be dragged out in the open repeatedly in the future.

As soon as spring arrived, Arredondo felt that he should be nearer the center of his district, which was composed of the provinces of Nuevo León, Nuevo Santander, Coahuila and Texas. He set out for Monterrey with his army and from that headquarters resumed the old and apparently endless job of chasing rebels and bandits.

Meanwhile news of the nation stirring events in the rest of the country must have filtered through to the frontier garrison very slowly indeed. To the rising young officer, Santa Anna, Hidalgo had merely received his just deserts when his mob of 80,000 was routed by 7,000 government troops. The Inquisition had shown the attitude of the "best" people clearly by de-frocking the rebel priest on the charge of heresy, whereupon he had been promptly executed by the civil authorities. Later reports probably indicated that there was still some little trouble in the far away mountains of the South where another priest by the name of José María Morelos y Pavón, a friend and old student of Hidalgo, was reported to be giving trouble on a small scale. In fact, the report was that he had actually announced the adoption of a Constitution in 1814 and had gone so far as to endorse the idea of independence, a proceeding utterly fantastic in the eyes of the young bloods of the *Fijo de Veracruz.*

[12]

What these young fellows did not realize was that a much sturdier group of folk were supporting Morelos and that this very publication of a constitution indicated an organized thinking that was new among Mexican rebels. Conditions had reached the point where abuse of administrative power and especially long continued uncertainty, had forced many people to begin to think for themselves. If the United States could secure independence from England and successfully manage their own affairs, why could not Mexicans do the same, ran the increasingly popular argument. But such logic was lost on the uneducated officer of the frontier regiment who only knew that the rebels he had met were a contemptible rabble. Furthermore, he had just heard that the imposter Napoleon had been overthrown in March, 1814 and the old Spanish kings had been restored in the person of the popular Ferdinand VII.

Hard on the receipt of this excellent news, in the latter part of 1814, Lieutenant Santa Anna left the frontier for Veracruz. He carried warm recommendations from his old General, for whom he always expressed the highest regard, to General José Dávila, Governor of the port. At his new post his first assignment was that of chasing rebels and bandits who were operating against the trade routes leading from the port into the interior. This was most congenial employment for the Lieutenant, even though it was certainly more strenuous and dangerous than garrison duty.

Thus passed another year and a half, though probably a rather lengthy furlough had intervened between his arduous northern campaign and the beginning of his activities around Veracruz. During these eighteen months national events moved rapidly. The Morelos movement dwindled and almost disappeared with the death of its leader (Morelos was executed December 22, 1815), and Bourbon power seemed firmly in the saddle once more. However, the reactionary policy so quickly announced by the new King of Spain rapidly alienated substantial numbers of that stubborn class of his Mexican subjects who had begun to think for themselves.

The general situation is well illustrated by an interesting report of Santa Anna, dated September 8, 1816, and addressed to General Dávila. In it the writer stated that he had just defeated a band of rebels, capturing the leader and two other men. These were part of the group that had seized control of the highway and were charging half a *peso* of anyone who wished to pass through. This was surely a modest sum for which to risk one's neck and lends much color to the presumption that these were "customs collectors" of the organized rebel government. This is all the more likely in view of the fact that one of Santa Anna's announced duties was to destroy rebel custom houses (*aduanas*) wherever found.

On the last day of October, 1816, Lieutenant Santa Anna sent a report to the Governor of more serious activities which had involved him in active campaigning from the twentieth to the twenty-second of the month against one Francisco de Paula and other insurgents. Several of the rebels were killed and wounded and a quantity of arms captured. The report so pleased the Viceroy that Santa Anna was promoted to a captaincy, while his brother, Manuel, who was also on the expedition, was made a first lieutenant.

During the next two years, it would seem that the young officer continued his duties as a result of which he had acquired a reputation for leading "terrible excursions" and of striking "terrific blows."[8] No particular actions are worth noting except that in June, 1818, he was reported as defeating a group of rebels at Boca del Rio.

While this was going on and the young captain was enjoying the favor of General Dávila one *contretemps* threatened to end all for him. He had just been out on a flying trip to

8. C. W. Raines, "Life of Antonio López de Santa Anna," *The Texas Magazine,* I, 49, in his article says that Santa Anna was with Arredondo when he captured the Mina expedition. True, Arredondo was still using some of the Veracruz troops and this is probably the source of the error, but it is strange that no Mexican historians note this fact when they mention less important acts of Santa Anna. Also, he was certainly back at his old rebel hunting outside Veracruz in 1818. Too, such an excursion as that against Mina would have required a rather definite change in the Veracruz organization and no such change is noted by local historians.

Venta Arriba on September 7. Four days later, Valentino Guzmán and Marcos Benavides at the head of two hundred horsemen retaliated with a daring raid to the very walls of Veracruz. The royalists fell back at first, Santa Anna trying to rally them at two different points. This was not to be done, however. One of his officers was killed, together with seven of his men. While the citizens looked on from the housetops of the city, Santa Anna, with his hat gone, had to swallow his pride and in full view dash madly for the city; his safety depending solely on the swiftness of his horse. The raiders presumably retired at their own convenience after helping themselves to such livestock and other movables as struck their fancy.

Needless to say, his pride cried aloud for vengeance and Santa Anna could not rest till this was accomplished. Two months later, however, he could report that on the night of November 8, he had secretly entered Venta Arriba where Francisco de Asis was at the head of some rebels. This man, one of those on the raid of September 11, was captured and forthwith ordered to be shot. No explanation was given, and in truth none was needed when one recalls the preceding events. Santa Anna always had difficulty in recognizing enemy bravery if displayed against himself, and, if accompanied by a personal insult or humiliation, forgiveness was not to be expected. Beyond doubt his services were appreciated, for the Viceroy in the name of the King, asked that "due thanks" be extended to the victor and accompanied his message with the sincere wish, "Let his useful services continue." So it was, and early in January, 1819, he led an expedition through a number of neighboring towns and reported that three chieftains and one hundred and sixty men had accepted the terms of pardon being offered. The rebel movement around Veracruz appeared to be on the wane.

Meanwhile the young officer was instructed to devote most of his efforts to the building of villages for the terrorized folk scattered through the foothills of the plateau. At least eight such villages were soon in process of construction in the neighborhood of Veracruz. Santa Anna had been especially interested in one of them and personally directed the building of the church, which was dedicated June 23, 1820. In his report, he modestly conveyed the request of the villagers that the name of the place be changed to San Antonio in his own honor. This the Governor did not approve.

In his report of July 12, 1820,[9] Santa Anna claimed special credit for his work in connection with four of the villages and went into detail as to his accomplishments. In three villages churches worth over one thousand *pesos* each were built, together with homes for the priests. In one, a fort for fifty soldiers had been constructed, and in several were places of detention for prisoners. The families settled there had to build their own homes but they were given lands at not more than four miles from the villages. Each family had, at least, enough land to plant a half pint of corn, beans and rice, as well as room for sugar cane, bananas and vegetables. The four villages were: Medellin, with 112 families; Jamapa, with 140; San Diego, with 237; and Tamarindo, with 54. In each of these was placed a school teacher to make the inhabitants "good citizens" and to teach them "Christian doctrines." "All this," he said, "is due to my activity, zeal and hard work and has not cost the treasury a cent even for minor expenses, because I have paid for them personally. Likewise I did not spare myself work, fatigue or danger however great provided only that I could be useful to my country and loyal to my superiors." Here began to appear that egotism which was later to be so marked a feature of his pronouncements. He closed with a word of commendation for the assistance of some of his men, including his brother Manuel, who had worked faithfully in spite of the trials of "climate, insects and other animals."

The present day investigator cannot help but wonder if this long and bombastic report was not calculated to act as an offset to the very uncomfortable details just then being published in connection with the old forgery charge made

9. E. Méndez, "Santa Anna, el anormal," *Todo*, April 17, 1934.

against him while in Texas. The surgeon, Jaime Garza, in the early part of 1820, had petitioned the Secretary of the Viceroy to force collection of the three hundred *pesos,* which he said Santa Anna had not repaid him after the trouble in San Antonio. His protest was duly forwarded through General Dávila, in May, 1820, and was answered by Santa Anna on June 8. He claimed that far more than the sum due had been taken in the form of property, and that the present move was plain viciousness and vindictiveness on the part of Garza. The surgeon's rejoinder, dated April 24, 1821, was forwarded directly to the Viceroy six days later. Apparently no more was heard of the case at this time. Incidentally, as will be seen in the next chapter, the last days of April, 1821, were no time for the authorities to be penalizing a brilliant and loyal officer even though the case against him were stronger than this one, which had been allowed to lapse for so long.

This long report also showed the stirrings of ambition as the writer was about to step onto a larger stage. His service record already listed over ten and a half years of actual service by the end of 1820. Active campaigning, as is common in many armies, counted for extra time so that he had credit for the surprising total of eighteen years, nine months and five days in the royal armies—and that when he was a man of only twenty-six!

By this time, boyhood was definitely left behind. Experience, hardship, the desert heat of the north and the noxious coasts and jungles of Veracruz province had made him a man. In addition, he was a man trained in a ruthless and brutal school where fear was the chief taskmaster, where morality and ethics were largely unknown and where the end was held to justify the means. With such a training and an experience far beyond his years, the record of the ensuing decades should not be so surprising.

ROYALIST—PATRIOT

MEANWHILE events beyond the ken of a mere captain chasing petty bandits near Veracruz were sweeping Mexico into its revolution against the Mother Country. The rebellions of Hidalgo and Morelos had failed and few refused to admit the fact. Indeed, Spanish control appeared somewhat difficult to challenge for it was supported by 8,500 regular soldiers from the Old Country, as well as by upwards of thirty-two thousand Mexican troops. But here was a serious weakness. Of the Mexican troops a third were veteran regulars, but the 22,000 provincial militia were not so reliable for in general they were willing to turn a dishonest penny by banditry now and then and were "open to reason" politically anyway.

In 1820, however, the ultra-liberals and Masons in Spain secured political control and promptly applied severe restrictions to the heretofore highly privileged clergy and army officers. Among the privileges threatened were substantial tax exemptions and the right to try all cases affecting the clergy and army officers before special courts. As a result two Mexican groups that had been especially loyal to the Mother Country during the early disturbances and whose hold over the masses was incalculable, were incensed. To remain loyal meant a real personal sacrifice.

This situation provided the heretofore poorly led and half-starved insurgents with the trained officers of the regular army and the funds of the church. Such a combination practically guaranteed success to the new leaders while it offered them the opportunity to make their own government. In brief, the masses could easily be aroused to drive out the Spaniard and make Mexico independent. Once this was done

[18]

the new leaders would have little further use for the principles of equality and fraternity as advocated by the liberals.

A brilliant, dashing young spokesman named Agustín Iturbide soon appeared to lead the revolt. He asked to be sent to the mountainous regions of the south to chase rebels, but soon reported a serious need for more arms and men and then for still more. Having secured all the government supplies he could, he announced, on February 24, 1821, the famous Plan of Iguala. This guaranteed the rights of the Church, for clerical cash was essential. It demanded independence under a prince of the Spanish Royal House, for these men only thought in terms of monarchy and had no objections to, but only respect for, the Bourbons. Finally, it demanded the elimination of racial distinctions or discriminations—"molasses to catch flies." As just seen, the abolition of social and political distinctions was one of the last of the real desires of the new leaders, but some guarantee to secure the support of the masses was essential.

But what about Santa Anna? His services were clearly appreciated for he had just received the Shield of Honor and Certificate of the Royal and Distinguished Order of Isabella the Catholic. His family was not of the old bluebloods, and naturally the honors secured in the grand old Spanish army seemed very real to his bourgeois origin. Doubtless he played the grand cavalier in merchandising Veracruz, but he instinctively felt the subtle distinction between the local respect and the attitude of the officers drawn from the old families of the capital. He was not one of them and he naturally hesitated to join them.

As the revolution grew on all sides, supported by the sturdy reputation of Guadalupe Victoria and the popular Agustín Iturbide, the aggressive and locally renowned rebel-fighter Santa Anna became more and more sought after. Santa Anna's old home town, Jalapa, had welcomed the Plan of Iguala and formally joined the movement. Soon after, the neighboring towns of Orizaba and Córdoba joined in. The answer of loyal old General Dávila down in Veracruz was promptly to order Santa Anna to cease his village building and to take up the more congenial task of conquest, even though it must ultimately be directed at his old home town.

He set out for Orizaba in March, 1821. Here, on the twenty-third, the rebels boldly suggested that he join them. His response was to open fire at once. He fortified himself in the Carmen Convent, and ordered the inhabitants of the town, with arms and horses, to report in two hours. After fortifying his position, he was ready on the twenty-ninth for a vigorous sortie on the unsuspecting rebels at 4 A.M. Having killed some, and captured horses, arms, supplies and most of the enemy, the royalists withdrew to celebrate and report their victory.

However, the rebels were closing in from all sides and a substantial number under José Joaquín de Herrera arrived the same day. Now there took place the first of those lightning-like changes that left both the enemies and friends of Santa Anna aghast. At 2 P.M., Santa Anna joined the rebellion. Just like that!

Had he been negotiating with the rebels and was this a carefully planned step? Then why the early morning attack? Possibly the arrival of Herrera showed him the whole country was arising and that one could wear himself out and never crush the opposition. Santa Anna's own statement was that "I wished to aid with my grain of sand the great work of our political regeneration." The difficulty in accepting this as the whole truth is that it is hard to see how such a reasoned decision could have been reached during those few hours between the successful sortie in the morning and 2 P.M.— hours when he would normally have been very busy caring for the details of his victory.

It is also to be noted that he was to get a promotion of one full rank in joining the rebels. As a reward for the morning victory and before hearing of his defection, the Viceroy promoted him to the rank of lieutenant colonel. This, Santa Anna insisted, was his rank at the time he joined the rebels so he forthwith insisted that he had become a full fledged colonel. Two promotions in one day! Not so bad!

Beyond doubt his action was a serious blow to the royalist cause on the east coast. C. M. Bustamante commented: "Finally, Santa Anna embraced the cause of independence. Such conduct was not expected of this officer and it had no little influence on the victories that the patriots began to secure from that time on."[1]

Whatever the reasons for the *volte-face,* our colonel was now just as active as a rebel as he had ever been as a royalist. His troops, united with those of Herrera, forthwith marched on Córdoba which surrendered without a struggle. There was little use for so many men at this point, so, having returned to Orizaba and secured a forced loan of seventeen thousand *pesos,* Herrera and Santa Anna agreed that Herrera should go to Puebla while the latter should proceed to the coast where his influence was so great. He first took five hundred men to Temascal, and then proceeded to the port of Alvarado, about forty-five miles south of Veracruz. He reached there with six hundred men on April 25. The Com mander prepared to defend the place, but gave up the idea when he heard "some cries for independence among his troops." Instead he retired to Veracruz with a passport graciously provided by his enemy.

It was a reckless, dangerous game that was being played. Treachery was on all sides as may be seen from the simple remark of Rivera: "Santa Anna avoided assassination here [at Alvarado] for some wished to avenge themselves for the many cruelties that he had committed thereabouts."[2]

Feeling all along the coast was reaching the panic stage. "Terror seized the people of Veracruz" and at 12:30 P.M. on April 3, a general alarm was sounded by the alcalde, who became terrified when he mistook an affray between two Negroes for the noise caused by the approaching rebels. Because of the ensuing confusion, the Governor ordered 220 sailors to leave their vessels in the harbor and to help maintain peace in the city. On the night of April 11, some of

1. Carlos María Bustamante, *Cuadro Histórico de la revolución de la América Mexicana,* Tomo V, p. 184.
2. Rivera, *op. cit.,* Tomo III, p. 153.

these sailors heard a noise and gave the usual challenge. Not receiving a response, they opened fire—on two hungry pigs that were rustling for food. It is all ridiculous enough in the telling, but such a state of nerves tells its own story. In fact, all the gates of the city, except that of la Merced, were closed after the victory of Santa Anna at Alvarado.

Veracruz, however, was not to be attacked lightly and Santa Anna turned once more to the interior when he heard that the recently captured Córdoba was besieged by royalists. He reached the town on May 17 or 18 at the head of five hundred men. He at once offered battle, but this was refused on two successive days. Patriot reinforcements continued to arrive and, on May 20, the royalists retreated with Santa Anna in hot pursuit. The patriot partisan, Bustamante, reported that the patriots lost only seventeen killed, but that the enemy suffered casualties amounting to over thirty killed, eighty wounded and fourteen taken prisoners. Zamacois, however, states that the patriots secured no particular advantage from this pursuit.

It was now feared that the royalists would strike across country to Jalapa, so Santa Anna immediately set out for his old home, arriving the night of May 26. Two days later, with the aid of Joaquín Leño, who had joined him, he attacked the city and, after desultory fighting lasting some hours, captured the place. The defenders were allowed to go to Puebla, but greatly needed artillery and large quantities of muskets and powder were captured by the victors. Also the city had to pay for its rescue by a forced loan of twelve thousand *pesos* to help clothe and arm the patriots. Only about three-fourths of this was collected, but even that amount of cash was gladly received. A number of reinforcements were added to the ranks, among them the historian C. M. Bustamante, who was to teach Santa Anna to add classical references to the egotism and bombast of the day in his future proclamations.

The actual accomplishments of these three months can be better appreciated when one considers the natural conditions involved. In the first place, the campaigning was across and along the edge of the plateau. Córdoba and Orizaba were only about nine miles apart on the map, but the shortest road between the two more than doubled the distance. Also, to move from Córdoba to Jalapa meant a trip not to be lightly undertaken even in the 1930's. In fact, the general traveler is regularly advised to go down toward Veracruz and come back on the other road, even though this involves a journey of five times the distance that separates the two places. The reason is that the highways from Veracruz to the interior still mount the plateau, the one through Córdoba and Orizaba, and the other through Jalapa and Perote. Then there was the daily expected rain, that seldom indeed failed to drench this precipitous slope the year° around. Finally, the temperature had to be considered. In 1847, Captain Kirby Smith reported: "Our march on the twenty-first [of April] commenced [from Santa Fé, about ten miles from Vera Cruz] at three o'clock in the morning and was over a hilly country, but on a tolerably good road....we labored on under a burning tropical sun, some of the men breaking down from the intense heat, till nine o'clock in the morning when we halted near some water where there was a fine shade, and rested six hours.... We could not march during the middle of the day for there was a breathless calm and the sun would have melted men and horses in an hour."[3]

Before Santa Anna left the city of his birth, bitterness between him and the Jalapa city fathers began to develop. Possibly it was due to his being a prophet without honor in his own country, or possibly it was the forced loan that had not rested well on their pocket books. Jalapa had never been too fond of soldiers anyway for, as early as 1802, the city voluntarily had built a barracks to get thieving officers out of the homes of private citizens. Now, the ostensible cause of the quarrel was over the recognition of Santa Anna as Military Governor of the State of Veracruz. This, the City Council flatly refused, and Santa Anna as vociferously demanded.

3. Emma Jerome Blackwood, *To Mexico with Scott*, p. 134.

However, little time could be wasted on such a question just then. Veracruz was beckoning and Santa Anna was eager to respond but could not do so because word came that royalists were threatening Perote. In response he left June 11 for that place, only some twenty miles farther inland as a bird flies, but double that distance by road and four thousand feet higher than Jalapa. The royalists had completed their raid before he arrived so he at once made contact with Herrera and they agreed that the latter should return to the State of Puebla while Santa Anna gladly turned to Veracruz with his string of victories unbroken.[4]

To capture this port was a formidable undertaking. Through the three centuries of Spanish control, it had been the place of deposit for billions of treasure sent to the Mother Country, so every precaution in the way of defense had been taken. In fact, in all the civil wars of Mexico, Santa Anna was the only chieftain who had the temerity to attack the plaza of Veracruz by land.

The preliminary steps were skillfully calculated to play upon the feelings of troops and people already seen to be on the verge of hysteria. Ever since taking Jalapa, he had allowed the mails to go from Veracruz to the interior as a courtesy. For some time, the royal authorities indignantly rejected the offer, but finally swallowed their pride, probably due to the demands of the merchants, who thus were made to feel the rebel's power.

On June 24 he issued the famous proclamation addressed to his men from the hacienda of el Lancero (better known as el Encero). This was doubtless written by Bustamante,[5] who served as secretary to Santa Anna at the time. Though these ignorant soldiers—and probably Santa Anna himself—had

4. For the Córdoba victory he was authorized to wear the "Córdoba Cross," while for the Jalapa and Perote campaign he was given the Cross of the First Epoch (*Primera Epoca*) as it was called. This began to make a rather imposing array when added to the Spanish decorations already conferred upon him.

5. Lucas Alamán, *Historia de Méjico*, Tomo V, p. 190. In his biography Bustamante claims authorship for this, but in his better known *Cuadro Histórico*, he modestly includes all of it and refers to it as "outstanding" among such proclamations.

never before heard of the events referred to, they sounded good on paper so the proclamation went forth:

"Comrades! You are going to put an end to the great work of reconquering our liberty. You are going to plant the eagle of the Mexican empire, humiliated three centuries ago on the plains of the Valley of Otumba, on the banks of the humble Tenoya, where the Castillian flag was first unfurled. The soul of Quauhpopoca, burned alive in the great square of Mexico City, because he avenged the iniquitous act of Juan Escalante, pleads for justice; and the victims of the horrible massacre of Cholula, whose cries have startled two worlds, filling both with horror, will not be satisfied unless you restore to your oppressed native land the liberty which they lost."

The proclamation closed with a plea to the men to be good soldiers and true liberators so that history would refer to the glory of this Eleventh Imperial Division as greater than that of the Corteses and Alvarados of the Conquest.

On June 27, Santa Anna reached the hacienda of Santa Fé, a few miles from Veracruz, where he met reinforcements from the coast. General Dávila, Santa Anna's old friend and protector, called in the crews of Spanish vessels in the harbor and mobilized the available young men of the city for the defense. Lieutenant Colonel José Rincón was ordered to go outside of the city walls with six hundred men and destroy all buildings or other objects that might serve as cover for the advancing enemy. This work continued for two days, when Santa Anna put an end to it by a sharp attack on the wrecking party. Friend and enemy were so confused in the ensuing mêlée that troops on the walls could not fire, fearing lest they injure as many of their own men as of the rebels.

Santa Anna seems to have experienced real regret at having thus to attack his old and good friend, Dávila. But, as is usual when such things happen, the friendship soon turned to bitterness and reproach.

To delay longer would only give the royalists added advantages so, on July 7, 1821, the order to attack was given. The advance began well enough, but the rebel troops soon broke and fled before the Spanish regulars, leaving Santa Anna with a handful of men in such an exposed position that even to retreat meant crossing in front of the batteries manned by the Spanish marines. But this was finally accomplished, after the Spaniards had inflicted losses of thirty killed and taken about eighty prisoners. Santa Anna's personal bravery was outstanding for he had led the attack and was the last to retire.

Though the royalists did not dare, or were not able, to pursue the patriots, despondency at once began to play havoc as desertions took place even among troops that had arrived after the conflict. Fearing that an effort would be made to open communication with the interior, Santa Anna ordered part of his men to hold the Jalapa road while he fell back on the other highway to Córdoba, to recoup his losses.[6] From here, five days after his defeat, he wrote a simple account of the affair, giving distinct praise to several of his officers for gallantry.

Just a week later there appeared another bombastic and oratorical flourish that smacked strongly of the pen of Bustamante:

"Veracruz! the cry for your extermination will be from this time on the watchword of our men going into battle: in all juntas and senates the demand for your ruin will be added to all deliberations. The memory of Carthage, from whose grandeur you are as far removed as the humble grass (*grama*) from the stately oak, should make you tremble. Mexicans! Carthage never offended Rome as Veracruz has Mexico. But Rome had its Scipios. God help you."[7] Such bombast could only inspire fear and hatred in those in Veracruz who might otherwise have welcomed Santa Anna. This at-

6. Dávila was not averse to trying a little "strategy" himself as may be seen by the fact that he sent the Spanish brigantine *Diligente,* under a United States flag to Boca del Rio, thinking that Santa Anna would be sure to go on board to secure arms and munitions. The Colonel, however, shrewdly sent a Captain Nemesis Iberri, who pretended to wish to sail to Veracruz as a private individual. Having found that the vessel was Spanish, he forthwith notified his chief, who thus avoided the trap.

7. Alamán, *op. cit.,* Tomo V, p. 193.

titude was reflected by General Dávila when Iturbide invited him to adhere to the Plan of Iguala. He responded that he might consider giving the city up to some other man, but not to Santa Anna.

Santa Anna now went to Puebla, which had been captured by the rebels, and talked over plans with Iturbide. It was agreed that the coastal chieftain was to leave Veracruz alone during the fever season and to try to oust the royalists from the powerful old fort of Perote up on the plateau. This, in the midst of its plain, had long been a menace and terror to evildoers in general and especially to the bandits accustomed to dash down from the mountains upon the valued treasure trains destined for Veracruz and the Mother Country. By the time this had been captured, the yellow fever season would probably be over and another attack on Veracruz could be considered.

Some time was spent in and around Jalapa, but on July 30, General O'Donojú, the new Spanish Viceroy, reached Veracruz. Unable to move outside the city walls because of the rebels, yet eager to get out of the fever zone, he soon asked Santa Anna, as the local rebel chieftain of importance, to come down for an interview. Other despatches were sent to Iturbide at Puebla. On August 5, Santa Anna entered the city for the interview. He promptly reported to Iturbide and made arrangements for his chief to meet the Viceroy at Córdoba. In spite of later criticism, Iturbide warmly commended Santa Anna for his handling of this affair.

Two weeks later the Viceroy gladly left the port, being met at the city gates by a "brilliant cavalry escort" from Santa Anna's division. On August 23, the Spaniard was in the New World namesake of the famous city of sword makers. Iturbide soon arrived and was widely applauded by the people who unhitched the mules from his coach in order to pull it to the inn themselves.

The next day, an accord was reached whereby the Viceroy practically approved the Plan of Iguala. In his *Memoirs,* Santa Anna recorded: "I attended the conferences called by them and took a very active part in the happy result which they reached." A regency of three (Iturbide and O'Donojú being two) was agreed upon to control the country pending its complete pacification and the selection of a sovereign. The Plan of Iguala was modified so that a king might be selected from the Spanish royal house or "such person as the Imperial Cortes may designate."

Again Santa Anna turned his attention to the attack on Perote and the general supervision of the coast province of which Iturbide had made him Military Governor. Toward the end of September, an incident at Jalapa showed his contempt for civil authorities and the increasing antagonism that was developing toward him there. A baker was accused of making bread for the prisoners of war out of rotten flour. The City Council confiscated the flour and imposed a fine of one hundred *pesos*. The man's wife appealed to Santa Anna, who was in the neighborhood. He ordered suspension of the sentence "because it was not right to condemn any man unheard." The regidor proceeded to carry out the Council's orders whereupon the Military Governor hotly remarked in the hearing of many "respectable" people: "If I had been there at the time, I would have arrested him [the official] and tied him to the tail of a horse." The insulted city authorities now refused to recognize Santa Anna's authority unless he proved to their satisfaction his right to his position. He ordered them to meet, saying he would face them in person. They refused until the documents had been sent them. Finally, the matter was compromised with the Council meeting to hear him, and his promising to respect their rights.

As late as the first of October, there was still some haggling over the Colonel's presenting a written apology but attention was now directed to a wrangle over a "voluntary" contribution of three thousand *pesos,* of which only seven hundred *pesos* had been paid. Santa Anna then asked for twenty thousand rations of beans and other supplies. This provoked more correspondence, with Santa Anna praising his own sacrifices for his country and condemning the Jalapeños for their niggardliness and lack of patriotism.

[28]

At last, on October 7, came the joyful news that the fortress of Perote had surrendered when word came that Mexico City was in the hands of Iturbide.[8] This meant that Santa Anna could again proceed against Veracruz, while Iturbide was consolidating his control over Mexico City in accordance with the terms of the treaty of Córdoba. Further to aid Iturbide's ambitions, his Spanish associate on the Regency, O'Donojú, died. Thus the able and tremendously ambitious man had another obstacle removed from his path to the crown, for the Viceroy had steadily insisted on the idea of a Spanish prince for Mexico.

As Santa Anna approached Veracruz, he entered into negotiations with Dávila October 18, and at once sent word to Iturbide that he was sure of the surrender of the city and the fortress of San Juan de Ulloa in a week or ten days. However, Dávila would not give up without a struggle and, on October 26, quietly left the city, moving his men and public funds to the castle which had been built on an island in the bay and so fortified that it was considered impregnable. Dávila now had sweet revenge on his one time protegé for the people so feared Santa Anna that they had petitioned Iturbide to send some other man to take over the city. Santa Anna may have anticipated something of that kind for, six days earlier, he wrote to the Town Council of Veracruz urging capitulation. He said that he had more than enough troops to take the city by assault and that after the hardships of the campaign his troops were clamoring for the attack. Of course, this would mean pillage but he was trying his best to restrain them because "Vera Cruz is my country and there is no sacrifice too great for me in order to save it from the evils which threaten it, and which will be inevitable if it persists in its vain and senseless resistance." This, in addition to the earlier

8. Alamán, *op. cit.,* p. 341, states that Iturbide rewarded Santa Anna shortly after this with the rank of brigadier general, thus raising him from a first lieutenant with the brevet of captain, to a brigadier general in six months. However, Santa Anna's service record (*Historia de Jalapa,* Tomo I, p. 317) states that he received his brigadier's commission by action of October 31, 1822, but that it was dated as of May 8 preceding.

proclamation crying for vengeance, readily accounted for the uneasiness of the people.

Probably as a result of the petitions of the Veracruzanos, Iturbide sent Colonel Manuel Rincón from Jalapa on October 23 to negotiate. Two days later, he entered the city and agreements were made for the surrender to take place October 27. On that date, Santa Anna marched through the gates to take charge, but, under Iturbide's orders, Rincón remained as Governor, to the great chagrin of the man who was really responsible for the victory.

On taking over the city, a joint proclamation was issued by Santa Anna and Rincón:

"Rest tranquilly then, citizens of Veracruz, putting away all fear and suspicion. Those of you who are wandering outside of the city return to your homes. Let confidence be reborn and become permanent under the protection of the Mexican eagle.

"We guarantee the brave troops of the Empire will maintain the strictest discipline and will observe the most fraternal conduct, for this has been, and is, our glorious motto."

To add a last wound to the pride of his brigadier, Iturbide sent an order which was received on November 5 for Santa Anna to retire from the city and "rest from his labors." Thus were sown the seeds of distrust and suspicion between the two men.

Fate was already indicating the future, for Mexico City was just becoming conscious of the new hero and had joyously celebrated the news of the fall of Veracruz with toasts to the name of Santa Anna. Of course, the citizens of the capital were too far away to realize what Jalapa and Veracruz had already learned: personal contact with Santa Anna produced friction, but to see him at a distance was to be dazzled by a picture of splendor and brilliance. Iturbide was of the same type and the capital was becoming acquainted with him. The country was not large enough for the two of them.

AMBITIONS

IN the National Capital, Iturbide was skillfully maneuvering amidst wavering political currents while, through numerous promotions, he assured the temporary support of most of the military. By a little judicious management, he arranged that the elections of members to the Congress which was to meet February 4, 1822, should be on the basis of social classes. The representation was so distributed between army, clergy and other delegations that the Iturbidists (those who wanted him as emperor) outnumbered both the simon-pure republicans and those who favored a Bourbon for the crown. To aid him further, the Spanish Cortes (parliament) speedily repudiated the Treaty of Córdoba, so that those who had wanted a European prince now had to choose between Iturbide and republicanism.

Unfortunately for himself, Santa Anna had almost no social or literary training. Shrewdness applied with violence, bluster and the crudities of harsh campaigns against the savages had taken the place of organized and systematic education. Now, with his tremendous energy and rough-shod methods, he was about to clash with a man as ambitious as himself, but who had far more social background and training. To secure a fair picture of the man from this time on becomes increasingly difficult because of the torrent of abuse which poured upon him for the next century. Beyond doubt he was vulnerable, but much of the criticism was the tirade of unreasoning enemies. Typical of the sweeping attacks is the statement of his one-time supporter, Bustamante: "We knew that he passed the preceding days [about 1822-23] in cockfighting, and the nights in dancing and gambling." Possibly true, but the implication is rather extreme for, if these were his main occupations, he yet found time to overturn an empire as a side line.

One of the most agitated questions of the day was the inevitable persecution of Spaniards that accompanied any revolution against Spain. Even the Treaty of Córdoba did but little to abate this. As early as October, 1821, Colonel Manuel Concha, on passing through Jalapa toward Veracruz with the idea of taking ship there, was offered an escort by Santa Anna. He declined it, but, on leaving the town on the fifth, was attacked and killed. This terrified the Spaniards all the more because the authorities made ostensible efforts to catch the culprits, said to have been well known, but seemed unable to find them. By February, 1822, great difficulty was experienced in Jalapa by Santa Anna in securing lodgings among the townspeople for captured Spanish officers. As one writer commented: "It seemed that no bond of blood united them [the Spaniards and Mexicans] any longer."

As the year 1822 opened, Santa Anna was found in the National Capital for the first time, so far as the records show. One may be sure it was a gay occasion for this dashing young officer, whose reputation for having endured hardships on the frontier and for heroism with a touch of brutality was already known. His rank granted entrée to wealthy social circles where he could cultivate his love of pleasure among people who were talking of their boxes at the opera, leased at five hundred dollars a year. Even the less pretentious folk among the elect leased seats in the orchestra by the month. Evidently his Veracruz brogue and his cultural crudities were condoned for in a society built around Iturbide and his family Santa Anna did not hesitate to seek out the sister of the future emperor and pay her marked attentions.

By the middle of January, the vacation was over and Santa Anna had returned to Jalapa as Military Commander. Soon the old difficulties with the citizens flamed anew when he sent orders by two of his officers to a rich merchant named Bernabe Elías. The townsman declined to open the orders whereupon the two officers severely upbraided him and, insulting the civil officer present, threatened to use force. Elías promptly appealed to the City Council, which asked the Captain General of the Province of Veracruz to call Santa

Anna to account. It would seem that the Captain General, Domingo Loaces, had no great love for his impetuous and stormy young officer and reported to Iturbide in a fashion that reflected seriously upon Santa Anna. This was at least the second complaint Iturbide had received so he may well have begun to be somewhat critical of his agent. However, the enthusiasm of Santa Anna for his chief was still unabated and on April 23 he was instrumental in holding a notable celebration in Jalapa for the formal taking of the oath to support the new order by the local authorities. Then, the next month, he had the pleasure of announcing personally to the Jalapeños that Iturbide had won out in his struggle with a recalcitrant congress and by a *coup d'état* had made himself emperor. Santa Anna at once ordered the singing of a solemn *Te Deum* with all officials present.

For some time the young commander had been assiduously cultivating Iturbide, and on February 28 had written congratulating him on the successful opening of the Congress and denouncing the "machinations of many evildoers, who are trying to bring about bad results." He then wrote: "My illness continues [this is the first time he is highly enough placed to be able to indulge in those ailments that later became so common in his correspondence], but in all things I am entirely at the disposition of your Highness. I received your last letter with the greatest [pleasure] and am as grateful as pleased [*esperanzado*] at your generous offer."

On April 24, he again wrote from Jalapa: "My beloved General: I include to Your Highness the attached Petition to the Regency requesting the position of Commanding General of the Province of Veracruz and that of Military Governor of the City.... The reason for rushing this at the present time is that the Captain General leaves tomorrow for Tehuacan and Sr. Rincón is left at Veracruz in complete charge of the Province, a situation that mortifies my pride greatly for the many reasons that I have already given your Highness.

"However, if this Officer is thought the better man for the position, I must present my resignation. I would regret this since this part of the Empire is at the present time most interesting and for that reason I wish to remain here, but with the command that my delicacy demands."[1]

This certainly indicated considerable confidence in his position because Santa Anna was never a man to throw away opportunities. Some say that he realized Iturbide was afraid of him, but this would not seem probable. On the other hand, Santa Anna well knew that he was a man of influence and a power in Veracruz and was determined to make the most of it. The response of the Regency was to call him to the Capital the next month and to promote him to the rank of Brigadier General. From this time on the oft-quoted words are increasingly correct: "The History of Mexico from the period we are now taking up [end of 1882] could be properly called the History of the Revolutions of Santa Anna."[2]

After Iturbide had seized the national government nothing but praise and flattery were to be heard for a time. The whole nation appeared enthusiastic at the idea of a Mexican product for the Mexican throne. José María Bocanegra, who was to serve in the cabinet repeatedly and later as President *ad interim* of the Republic, commented on the enthusiasm and asserted that it could be said without exaggeration that scarcely one in a thousand of the people of Mexico would have failed to approve the step.[3] Even the old patriot Vicente Guerrero, joined in the popular acclaim and pledged his support. Santa Anna's effusions, therefore, can hardly be considered surprising. On announcing the event to his men at Jalapa he said: "I cannot restrain my excessive joy for this step is the most suitable possible to bring about the prosperity of all. It is the thing we sighed and longed for, and although it may be necessary to exterminate some discordant and disturbing elements, which do not possess the true virtues of citizens, let us hope that we can hasten to proclaim and take an oath to support the immortal Iturbide as emperor...."

1. Originals of both these letters are found in the *Riva Palacio Papers* in the García Collection of the University of Texas.
2. Alamán, *op. cit.*, p. 686.
3. José María Bocanegra, *Memorias para la historia de Méjico independiente*, 1822-1846, Tomo I, p. 67.

He likewise wrote to Iturbide referring to his elevation to the throne as a "worthy recompense for sublime merit; and a most powerful dyke with which to oppose the furious attack of reckless passions." He further pledged the support of his regiment, saying it would be glad to shed its blood for its emperor.[4]

To the student of Mexican history there is more than a little food for thought in these references to the shedding of blood and to the "discordant and disturbing elements" here so contemptuously dismissed. Even the contemporary excitement and enthusiasm of the coronation days did not sweep all of the republicans-by-conviction off their feet, and this small nucleus were quick to take advantage of the despotism and arrogance of the Emperor to extend steadily their power and influence.

On the other hand, though Iturbide was proud, arrogant and foolish, he was not unskillful in his handling of the glamor-loving masses and the army men. The coronation ceremonies were elaborate, even though a bit gaudy; the robes were gorgeous at a distance, even though some malicious ones whispered that the unseen parts were shoddy and not silk; the jewels glistened right bravely, even though some were borrowed at the National Pawnshop, and busybodies insinuated that others originated in glass factories and not through the inscrutable processes of nature.

Military promotions continued to be dealt out so lavishly that in the Capital there were 1,802 officers from colonel to ensign, and 3,161 sergeants, corporals and musicians, but only 8,308 soldiers. This meant that there were less than two privates for each commissioned or non-commissioned officer.

To inaugurate a nobility and cement the support of the upper classes, the Order of Guadalupe was founded. There were various awards for different grades of eminence. The highest was the grand cross, given to selected archbishops, generals and bishops. Santa Anna was not forgotten, but received a cross "*de numero,*" one of the second order.

4. Alamán, *op. cit.,* pp. 606-7.

Santa Anna's acknowledgment of this honor is not available, but his letter of thanks to Iturbide for his promotion was evidently written just at this time and after the Regency had given place to the Empire. The letter was undated, but was addressed to: "My most worthy and especially beloved Emperor." It praised Iturbide for freeing the Mexicans from slavery and stated that he was the logical man for the position of Emperor because of his outstanding ability and patriotism. The writer then especially recommended his brother, Captain Manuel Santa Anna as well as a number of other officers for exceptional ability. An analysis of the letter shows about seven hundred words of flattery and expressions of loyalty ending thus:

"I close begging your Majesty that you do not ignore my request concerning the position of Commanding General of this Province, for to say nothing of the special interest which your Majesty knows that I have, it will produce palpable advantages to the service as I shall be able to prove and as I have already stated.

"Your Majesty knows that I am and will be throughout life and till death your loyal Defender and Subject.

Sir,

At the Illustrious Feet of Your Majesty,

(Signed)   Ant° López de Santa Anna.

(rubic.)"[5]

All through this period are found denunciations of Santa Anna's personal excesses, but such conduct is hardly surprising in an unmarried army officer with his background and in a society which Mr. J. R. Poinsett described with the surprise and quite probable exaggeration of a foreigner:

"There are certainly some young ladies (very few I am afraid) who do not smoke; some married women (many I hope) who have no lover, or if this would be interpreted to derogate from their charms, who consider him only as a convenient dangler, and are fondly and faithfully attached to

5. Original in *Gómez Farías Papers* in the García Collection of the University of Texas.

[36]

their husbands; and there are certainly many gentlemen who are not gamesters."[6] However, Mr. Poinsett had already remarked that if Mexicans "meet to dine together, they sit down to play before dinner and no reunion takes place in the evening without gaming."[7] It might be said at this point that while Santa Anna frequently played with women and was an inveterate gambler, still his most vicious critics, at this or later dates, seldom accused him of drunkenness.

It was on his visit to the Capital in 1882 that our young Brigadier, now about twenty-eight, was pressing his suit for the hand of Iturbide's sister, Doña Nicolasa—a lady of sixty years of age. The Emperor is said to have made sport of such a suggestion with sneering sarcasm (*amarga burla*) and to have ordered Santa Anna to attend to his military duties. To this incident, some attribute the beginning of the final break between the two men.

But even though personal reasons contributed to the break, it was noticeable that a general reaction against the Empire was affecting the whole nation. On August 1, 1822, stern old Guadalupe Victoria, with principles and characteristics reminding one of the gnarled heroes of the days glorified by Plutarch, issued a ringing proclamation to the people. He denounced Iturbide as a self-seeking tyrant, who had betrayed his principles for the sake of power. Others too were disgusted as it became evident that Iturbide was more and more influenced by flattery and by the idea of "playing the emperor" when only steady and hard work could establish the nation. Also congress was complaining of the Emperor's constant invasion of its rights.

On September 9, Santa Anna reported to Iturbide, addressing him as "My always beloved Monarch." After some minor details about his own men, he stated that the day before he had sent in a report on the rebel movement among the coast Negroes concerning which "perhaps Governor Rincón will have sent you details." He said that he thought Victoria

6. J. R. Poinsett, *Notes on Mexico*, p. 160.
7. *Ibid.*, p. 78.

was behind this, but was awaiting word from those he had sent to investigate, then continued:

"My spirit is restless, worrying about the revolutions against your Majesty in these sections, though the confidence I have that your Majesty knows how to take the proper steps and that you will never allow my honor to be abused cheers me...."[8] He reiterated his old dissatisfaction over Rincón's position but the questioning note went so far as to use the dread word "revolutions," instead of the earlier casual dismissal of "disturbing elements."

Possibly Iturbide detected the new note in the letter for, in spite of renewed complaints from the City Council of Jalapa over local matters, Santa Anna received the long sought for appointment of Military Commander of Veracruz on September 25. This was followed by political control on October 12. Iturbide later claimed that he gave Santa Anna the post in spite of all the complaints "because he was brave, a quality that I greatly esteemed in a military man, hoping furthermore that his position and responsibilities would help to correct his faults."

At Veracruz, Santa Anna went to work with his usual activity. So long as San Juan de Ulloa remained in the hands of Spaniards the trade of the city was seriously handicapped. Furthermore, to drive out the Spanish would stamp the victor as the hero of the day. Santa Anna informed the central government that he had a plan on foot to capture the fortress which was now commanded by Brigadier General Francisco Lemaur. At once, orders came down to José Antonio de Echávarri, the new Captain General of the province, to cooperate. Echávarri arrived October 25 and was told by Santa Anna that he had tricked the Spaniards into believing that the city would be surrendered to them if they would send landing parties at night. Then using the reinforcements of the Captain General, the depleted fortress was to be captured while the landing parties were to be ambushed as they reached the shore.

8. *Gómez Farías Papers,* García Collection.

The Captain General agreed to co-operate and went to the point assigned him to meet one of the landing parties. There he found so few Mexican troops to assist him that he narrowly escaped capture or death at the hands of the Spaniards. Also it would seem that little or no effort was made to follow the original plan to destroy the retreating landing parties or to attack the fortress in any way.

Echávarri was highly indignant and reported confidentially to Iturbide that Santa Anna had by this trick attempted to have him killed because of spite at his recent elevation to the post of Captain General, which Santa Anna coveted. Mexican historians are uncertain in trying to pass judgment here. Some consider it was a plain case of blundering; some that Echávarri's report was correct, and others that he was the one who was jealous of the rapid rise of Santa Anna.

Iturbide was obviously alarmed at the turn of events and immediately decided to investigate in person. Here were the two highest officials in what was probably the most important military district outside of the Capital hurling mutual recriminations and charges of attempted murder. Pending his investigation, the Emperor determined to flatter all concerned and promoted both Echávarri and Santa Anna as well as most of the other officers in Veracruz for their "brilliant defense" of the city against the Spanish attack. Also the two chief officers were given special medals.[9]

On November 10, Iturbide set out for the coast in spite of the fact that the Empress was expected to give birth to a child any day.[10] Six days later, he arrived at Jalapa to which point Santa Anna had been ordered to report, presumably to talk

9. Santa Anna, in his *Memoirs,* says simply: "The Spaniards in possession of the Castle of Ulua, attempted one night to capture the plaza of Veracruz in order to destroy the bulwarks of Santiago and Concepción so as to avoid further attacks from them. The vigilance of the garrison prevented the attempted surprise, but a combat of over two hours which ensued cost the invaders considerable losses. They left one *jefe,* three officers and one hundred and forty-six soldiers of the Battalion at Catalina as prisoners in our hands. The Imperial Government described this triumph as 'glorious for the defenders of the plaza' and sent me a commission as Brigadier *con letras."*

10. The child, a boy, was born while the father was away.

over new plans for the attacking of San Juan de Ulloa. The Brigadier arrived with great pomp as the conquering hero and with an escort rivaling that of the Emperor in splendor.

At this meeting, two shrewd and unscrupulous men were pitted against each other. The Emperor felt that his officer must be removed to a place where he would be less dangerous: Santa Anna was determined to brook no interference with his ambitions. Iturbide took the initiative and notified the General that his outstanding talents were so recognized by the Government (had he not recently been promoted and decorated?) that his services were needed in a broader field. He was to be transferred at once to the Capital. Santa Anna was not deceived and well knew that Iturbide would not have left Mexico City merely to tell him this. He demurred at leaving his post so quickly, saying that he was in debt. This was brushed aside with a grand gesture as Iturbide ordered one of his staff to give the General five hundred *pesos* in cash. Santa Anna now hastily assured the Emperor that he had many private affairs to attend to, but that he would be glad to report to the Capital in a day or so. This, after all, was so plausible that Iturbide felt his trip had been eminently successful and so the delicate interview ended on a note of apparent harmony.

Santa Anna himself told a good story, that is given credence by many of the best historians, in regard to this interview. He said that in the course of conversation he sat down. Soon the Captain of the Guard entered and brusquely said to him: "Señor Brigadier, no one sits in the presence of the Emperor." Santa Anna restrained his feelings and the next morning accompanied Iturbide on his journey for a few miles in a most friendly fashion. He then turned around muttering to himself: "We shall soon see, Señor Brigadier, if no one sits down in the presence of the Emperor."

Iturbide blamed the trouble on Santa Anna's ambitions, irregular conduct, treachery against Echávarri, and his "volcanic passions." Such arguments have been largely *ex post facto,* but the east coast situation was obviously critical and the fact that Santa Anna was ordered to the Capital clearly showed

*House where Santa Anna was born (photograph taken by
Dr. Gustavo A. Rodriguez, April, 1934)*

*El Encero, home of Santa Anna near Jalapa (photograph taken by
Dr. Gustavo A. Rodriguez, April, 1934)*

that Iturbide was watching him carefully. The Emperor was not one to hesitate at disciplining a young and comparatively minor officer, but the rebels were gaining ground, and this was a time to use diplomacy if it were possible to save the services of such an able, though probably over-ambitious, subordinate.

While the Emperor made haste to return to Mexico City, the Brigadier set out at break-neck speed for Veracruz. With a late start on December 1—after seeing Iturbide off he rode all night with scarcely a pause and reached the port next day. He summoned what soldiers he could find, and harangued them in the name of liberty. Then, placing himself at the head of some four hundred men, he rode through the streets proclaiming a republic. Meanwhile the church bells were ringing, bands playing and people shouting.

Santa Anna's brain had not been idle on that long night ride. His plans were shrewdly calculated to provoke this hullabaloo approval of the masses while not neglecting other essentials. In addition to the froth and foam of public applause, sinews of war were provided by appropriating funds said to have amounted to 117,000 *pesos*. Troops were simultaneously despatched to hold the passes and strategic points on both roads to the interior.

The future course of *the* movement was less obvious even to the mind of Santa Anna than reasons for *a* movement. He knew that he was none too popular in the province of Veracruz, but that the Emperor was even less so. The popularity of the rebel Victoria, the arguments of such theorists as Bustamante, the trouble between the Emperor and Congress, and the coast jealousy of the Mexico City product as Emperor, all contributed to this. Then there was the powerful influence of the Scottish Rite Masons. Suárez y Navarro stated that the majority of the army officers were members of this organization and that it was uniformly hostile to Iturbide.[11] In addition, the still influential Spaniards of the coast region blamed the Emperor for much of the persecution they had suffered.

11. Juan Suárez y Navarro, *Historia de Méjico*, Tomo I, p. 26.

Santa Anna had just witnessed an expression of this feeling in Jalapa. When the royal party was ready to return to the Capital, orders were issued for pack-mules to be secured from the merchant Bernabé Elías, a "respectable" Spaniard of prominence and wealth. When response was made that the animals were not available, the Emperor lost his temper and in a towering rage insulted Elías "not only with words, but actually struck him in the face" and ordered that he and certain others involved should be imprisoned. Friends intervened and secured the release of the merchant, but not before the local Spaniards had become highly incensed. In fact, some assert that Elías went directly from prison to Santa Anna, and gave him drafts on Veracruz with which to start a rebellion.

Up to this point in his career, Santa Anna seems never to have thought seriously of a republic as a system of government. Years later, he is said to have remarked that all he knew about republics at the time was what a lawyer in Jalapa had told him. By a whim of chance, however, the Minister of the Republic of Colombia, Miguel Santa María, had recently been dismissed from Mexico by Iturbide because of his apparent endorsement of a plan to overthrow the Empire and had just arrived at Veracruz on his way out of the country as the revolt began.

Santa Anna went to see the Minister who at once agreed to draw up a "plan" for a republic and a proclamation to accompany it. The "plan," consisting of seventeen articles, was dated December 6, 1822. It was significant that the first article was a guarantee of security to all Spaniards and foreigners who were not opposed to true liberty, while the second guaranteed citizenship to all native-born and to all naturalized Spaniards and foreigners. Among the later articles was a provision that a distinction was to be made between the patriots who joined the cause after, and those who had fought for it before the Plan of Iguala.

The movement spread alarmingly. Generals Guerrero and Nicolás Bravo who had been in Mexico City, promptly left to join the rebels in the south. Captured by a royalist officer, they bribed him with ten ounces of gold and some jewels and continued on their way. The highly respected Guadalupe Victoria[12] offered his services to Santa Anna, but the latter was wise enough to know that Victoria's name was one to conjure with. Here was a man who had left a student's career at the age of twenty-five to join the patriot cause in 1811. Though the early liberal movements had been defeated he had refused to surrender his principles but became a fugitive in the mountains instead. By 1820 his name had become synonymous with fabulous escapes and raids in the name of liberty. Refusing to recognize Iturbide he had been arrested, only to escape and be elected to Congress from Durango. Instead of inviting arrest by taking his seat he remained in hiding until Santa Anna's proclamation gave the signal he so eagerly awaited.

On December 27 Santa Anna formally recognized Victoria as the official leader of the rebellion and called upon all civil and military leaders to respect and obey him as such.[13] Meanwhile appeals were being made to all persons of influence who could be approached; each was assured that the others were co-operating while Iturbide was denounced for his unconstitutional conduct, absolutism and extravagance.

The Emperor realized the seriousness of the situation when the news of the events in Veracruz overtook him at Puebla on his return journey to the Capital. He hastened to Mexico ahead of schedule, thus deliberately avoiding the official welcome that had been prepared. Santa Anna was declared a traitor and his property ordered confiscated, while an inspired press referred to him as childish, stupid and plain crazy. Amnesty was offered to those who would desert the rebels, and orders went out to Government officers to report on the behavior of all officials for suspicious conduct: the Archbishop was even asked to excommunicate all republi-

12. Manuel Felix Fernández was this man's name, but he dropped it in the revolution against Spain and adopted the name of Guadalupe Victoria, commemorative of victory in the name of the great national shrine, Guadalupe.

13. Suárez y Navarro, *op. cit.*, p. 25, note.

cans. Simultaneously, troops were ordered to the coast under Brigadiers Cortazar and Lobato.

A letter of Santa Anna to Iturbide, dated from Veracruz on December 6, was a shrewd statement. It is too long to quote in full, but a few sentences provide a key to the whole:

"Reverend Sir: You are well aware how much I labored for, and contributed to, your being crowned and proclaimed emperor; you are aware of my zealous endeavors to perpetuate the diadem in your family, encountering cheerfully fatigue and sacrificing everything for that object, so much so as to have become odious to my fellow citizens, who thought me servile and a flatterer....

"To senior Dávila, I was bound by gratitude and friendship, from which I severed on account of that sacred duty [love of country]. Thus it is that I have felt myself under the necessity of separating myself from under your command...."

He continued, promising a congress of real representatives of the nation to form a constitution on the basis of "religion, independence and union." He then pledged himself to reward Iturbide's services with a "distinguished place in the nation," but insisted that he renounce the crown.[14]

At this point, Santa Anna's relations with the Spanish force in San Juan de Ulloa became interesting. Iturbide's persecution of Spaniards and confiscation of their property led Lemaur, the Commander of San Juan, to send his private secretary to see Santa Anna as soon as he heard of the rebellion. The Spaniard offered an armistice and military support to the rebels with the idea of creating a situation in which he would hold the balance of power among the Mexican factions. The rebels needed all the aid they could get and so agreed to the armistice with the approval of the provincial delegation and of Victoria himself. While this agreement was to demand frequent "explanations" in the future, it should be noted that "religion, independence and union" were the principles he was fighting for. What was said in the private interview

14. *Niles Register*, XXIII, 344.

with Lemaur's Secretary is not known, but Zamacois[15] flatly asserted Santa Anna was not a tool of the Spaniards.[16]

With his customary activity, Santa Anna now set out to meet the imperial troops that were advancing and demoralizing the rebels. At Plan del Río, about three-fourths of the distance between Veracruz and Jalapa, he captured a detachment of the Imperial Grenadiers, freeing the officers and adding the men to his own forces. Victoria remained at this strong and important point while Santa Anna continued to Jalapa which he attacked at daybreak on December 21. His recently acquired Grenadiers deserted in a body and a part of his men who had fortified themselves in San José (the Church in which Santa Anna had been baptized) were forced to surrender. Seeing that his force was thoroughly demoralized, Santa Anna fled hurriedly with a mere bodyguard of cavalry. The rebels were in such disorder that there is little doubt the Imperialists by prompt action could have marched into Veracruz and ended the rebellion speedily.

Santa Anna's mental processes had been reversed suddenly and he was panic stricken. On passing through Puente del Rey, he met Victoria and suggested that they hasten to the port and take ship for the United States. But that Chieftain had been through too many disappointments to lose his head over this one. He is said to have responded: "Companion, go to Veracruz and fortify your post; when they present you my head will be the time to set sail. But so long as I live your honor demands that you remain at my side, defending the cause of liberty."

On January 24, 1823, the formal taking of the oath to Iturbide was performed with appropriate pomp and cere-

15. Niceto de Zamacois, *Historia de Méjico*, Tomo II, p. 453.
16. The famous letter of Tornel published in the *Gaceta del Gobierno Imperial* of December 21, 1822, lamented the course of Santa Anna as the result of a trick of his enemies. The support of Lemaur was characterized as worse for Mexican liberty than the Greek horse was for Troy. A republic was praised as the finest form of government, but as one for which the Mexicans were not ready. In addition, the attitude of Iturbide to his Congress was justified because of the wrangling of Congress; and his confiscation of cash and property was explained on the basis of necessity and the equivocal conduct of the persons concerned.

mony in the Capital. General surface appearances were auspicious though a strange lack of energy was to be noted in the prosecution of the campaign against the Veracruz rebels. The administration probably relied upon Echávarri's old hatred of Santa Anna and did not seriously consider the possibility that the two might join forces.

The disillusionment took place February 1, when the Plan of Casa Mata was published. It soon became evident that the motive power behind the new movement, which was to sweep the moribund Santa Anna rebellion to victory, was the Scottish Rite Masons who had long been affiliated with the Spanish branch of the Order and who hated Iturbide as an opportunist and one who had violated the Plan of Iguala. They skillfully approached Echávarri and persuaded him to take the lead in the matter. The new plan did not reject Iturbide outright, but called for the meeting of a new congress under the protection of the "Liberating Army" as the combined troops now characterized themselves.[17]

This was an actual continuation of the Veracruz effort to overthrow Iturbide, but the Emperor did not openly denounce it at once. In truth, the statements of neither rebels nor imperialists were clear though intentions were obvious. Tornel commented later[18] that Santa Anna had at least rested his case upon the will of the people, but that Echávarri had deliberately demanded the reorganization of a congress known to have been hostile to Iturbide.

When commissioners were sent by the Emperor to talk matters over with the quasi-rebels no agreement was reached. Instead, the Captain General of Puebla, José Morán, soon adhered to the Plan of Casa Mata and the City Council of Veracruz endorsed it. By February 26, the troops in far away Guadalajara seconded the move and the Emperor's house of cards had obviously crumpled in confusion. He tried to stem the tide by calling for a newly selected congress of his own, but this idea was rejected so he sadly appeared before his old

17. The similarity of this proposal to that made in Santa Anna's letter of December 6, 1822, to Iturbide is obvious.
18. Tornel, *Breve Renseña Histórica*, p. 11.

obstreperous Congress on February 19 and abdicated the throne. In return, that body ordered him into exile in Italy, where he was to be paid twenty-five thousand *pesos* as an annual pension. On March 27, the Liberating Army marched into the Capital.

If pique and a desire for vengeance against Iturbide were his impelling motives, Santa Anna had been gloriously successful. But, if personal ambition was the mainspring of his conduct, he was left queerly in the lurch. As the movement abruptly changed from failure to success, it swept beyond his control. Others mastered it and by it were carried on to power, but he remained a popular army officer only.

PROBLEMS AND PRINCIPLES

CONGRESS was now to consider the Plan of Casa Mata under whose vague terms a republic could have been established, or a monarchy set up with anyone from a Spanish prince to Iturbide as king or emperor. In fact, a triumvirate composed of three generals, Nicolás Bravo, Guadalupe Victoria and Pedro Celestino Negrete, was given *ad interim* powers till a constitution could be drawn up. This task was finally completed and the document published October 4, 1824. It provided for a republican form of government many of whose features were drawn from the Constitution of the United States even though the people were not conscious of the duties and responsibilities thus devolved upon them.

The fields of legislation and constitution making were never ones that appealed to Santa Anna. Surprising as it may seem, in his long public career he never served a day in a legislative body or a national cabinet. It was the army camp or the executive's chair for him. His personal preference called for the former, but his vanity demanded the latter. He enjoyed luxury and even voluptuousness, but a rising excitement swept these aside whenever the nostrils of the old war horse caught the scent of battle.

For a short period in March, 1823, Santa Anna was President of the Provincial Junta of Veracruz (probably as near to legislative activity as he ever came), but he craved more excitement than this. On the nineteenth, the very day of Iturbide's abdication, he set sail from Veracruz with the announced purpose of carrying the revolution to San Luis Potosí. This reason appears somewhat inadequate for that northern area was entirely sympathetic and could have been relied upon to support the cause voluntarily. A real incentive for the expedition probably lay in the fact that Santa Anna realized that he would be overshadowed if he remained close to the Capital. Bravo, Guerrero and Victoria had precedence over him from the military standpoint so he could not hope to be very prominent in that field and both his temperament and lack of training left him unfitted for constitution making or legislative work. Rather than appear in a secondary rôle, he was off to his old stamping ground in the north where he had first tasted hardships and glory.

He set sail in four vessels with about five hundred infantry and fifty cavalry. After a rough trip, the expedition landed at Tampico April 1. The next day, he set out for the interior, stopping only to secure horses and supplies from time to time. At the hacienda of Peotillos, various officials and a committee of the citizens of San Luis Potosí came out to greet him as the new Commanding General. The people, however, did not seem to have reassuring memories of this returning officer and the local troops were openly hostile. To make matters worse, violent quarrels broke out between Santa Anna's infantry and cavalry outfits, with local sentiment supporting the cavalry. Also there was trouble in securing supplies since some of the drafts brought by the General were protested by those on whom they were drawn. This left him short of provisions so he appropriated the bar silver in the local treasury. Such conduct was not surprising but a violent quarrel broke out when he refused to pay the coinage costs for the minting of the bullion.

To straighten matters out between his infantry and cavalry units, the Commander gave a peace and harmony banquet in the Alameda de Bracamonte, a large city park in San Luis. Officers addressed the men and all started off smoothly enough. After the meal, the men began to wander through the park together while the officers still chatted around the tables. Suddenly a quarrel broke out among the men, hidden knives were drawn and stones flew. The officers struggled to control their troops and finally separated the two groups, but not before half a dozen were killed and a large number bruised and wounded.

Muro[1] says that Santa Anna was spending his days in cock-fighting and his nights in roistering conduct with a few select cronies. The statement is quite circumstantial but is probably exaggerated as a part of the gossip spread by the busybodies of the times. Be that as it may, it substantially encouraged the antipathy of the townspeople who were none too pleased at the presence of these troops anyway.

One opportunity to employ his men against rebels did arise, but this was ignored. On April 28, word arrived from Mexico City to the delegation of the State of Nuevo León, the State directly north of the city of San Luis, saying that Santa Anna was to co-operate in suppressing rebels up in Texas. Those northern deserts probably had little attraction for him. However, it is only fair to say that it is quite likely the message reached him after he had taken his next significant step so his failure to march to Texas was not entirely due to his love of the flesh pots of San Luis. On the other hand, it is obvious that he had failed to secure the support of the Potosians and that the local situation was steadily growing worse.

Some say that Santa Anna now revealed his real purpose in coming north, others think his conduct was simply another effort to secure national recognition, and still others that the new step only went to prove his consistency in following up his Veracruz Plan. Certain it is that on June 5 he fully armed his loyal troops and marched them into the principal plaza of the city. There one of his officers read a proclamation endorsing a federal republic before the results of the labors of the Constitutional Convention could have been known. Another officer then went to the barracks of the Twelfth Regiment (and there lay the opposition) to read the same document. The men of the Twelfth promptly rejected the idea and seizing control of church towers and local strong points defied their Commanding Officer.

The townspeople supported the Twelfth and the whole city prepared for street fighting. Stores were closed and the people kept indoors though whenever the Commanding General

1. Manuel Muro, *Historia de San Luis Potosí,* Tomo I, pp. 365-66.

went abroad cries of "Death to Santa Anna!" "Death to the Veracruz Jews!" and "Long live the Twelfth!" were to be heard from the shuttered and barred houses which extended their solid front walls for block after block along the streets. After a day or so, the members of the Twelfth who lacked strong leadership were won over to support a republic, but the hatred of the townspeople continued and quarrels among the troops were frequent. When some of Santa Anna's men went out into the country, they were attacked in the Indian villages of Santiago and Tlaxcala. On hearing of this, the General ordered the Eighth to go out and punish the villages, bringing in all Indians found. Vigorous protest of the city authorities barely averted the catastrophe of wholesale destruction of the country folk.

It was clear that the local situation was largely due to the personal unpopularity of Santa Anna. This was just another indication that a close view of the man, at this early date especially, was unpleasant. He needed to be at a distance for his maneuvers to dazzle without his personality repelling. When news of the disorders reached Mexico City, Negrete and Bravo marched to the north with government troops. Santa Anna promptly withdrew from San Luis on July 10, 1823, protesting his loyalty to the national government. He then left his command at Querétaro while he went to the Capital to answer the charges violently attacking his personal conduct and his patriotism that had been brought against him.

Meanwhile the San Luis episode was having repercussions in Mexico City. As early as June 12, a special session of congress had considered his proclamation of a week before. Then, after further deliberation, Congress determined to organize the new government on a federal basis. Victoria himself frankly considered the San Luis movement as immature and unwise and deplored any action not in obedience to the central authority—but he obviously sympathized with the idea of a republic. In other words, the action of Santa Anna crystallized sentiment on all sides.

When the court martial met to consider the case there were all kinds of political influences to consider, as well as pleas such as the following by the accused: "National independence and liberty were always the sweetest object of my desires. Pursued by misfortune, defamed by the masses, my reputation attacked without mercy, I, with a serene countenance shall cry: *Sat patriæ datum* (enough has been given to my country)—Oh, beloved and most dear Native Land! It is sufficient that I have loved you in the days of my disturbed life. You are free and happy; only let me dig myself an humble grave so that my ashes may perish with my memory." This appealed to the emotional masses who only knew of Santa Anna through his exploits. The case dragged on for some time but to have prosecuted an indictment against a man for attempting to establish a republic at the time Congress was organizing that very form of government would have approached the realms of persecution, to say the least.

While the suit was still pending, General J. M. Lobato started a revolt in January, 1824, demanding the immediate dismissal of all Spaniards in office. Many thought that Santa Anna was merely using Lobato as a cat's paw to start the movement so as to test public sentiment before committing himself. Such criticism seems somewhat unfair, for, in the first place, Santa Anna had been a friend rather than an enemy of Spaniards in Mexico up to this time. Also, he promptly issued a public protest at such implications and forcefully denied them. On the twenty-ninth, Lobato published a manifesto and failed to contradict Santa Anna's protest as he would have been sure to have done had Santa Anna betrayed him. Still later, Lobato tried to implicate Santa Anna, but his action was hardly convincing. Meanwhile, on the twenty-fourth, the General offered "his sword and his life" to the government authorities to crush the rebellion. The offer was accepted, but the rebellion soon collapsed anyway. The fact that he was to be entrusted with troops while still under indictment showed that the authorities considered him loyal. As was natural, little more was heard of the court martial.

The next two or three months were quietly spent at Jalapa where Santa Anna had been acquiring property. Then, in the latter part of April, he received orders to go as Military Governor to one of the very difficult and distant parts of the nation, Yucatán. Was this a reward to a courageous and worthy officer or an excuse to place a dangerous man at a safe distance?

Whatever the reason for the orders, Santa Anna left Jalapa on April 29, and plunged into his new work with a will. The conditions in that isolated southern peninsula of the Mexican republic were enough to test the ability of any man. The chief trouble lay in the rivalries and conflicting interests of the two chief cities, Mérida and Campeche. Nearly all the trade of Mérida was with Havana and the old Spanish empire, while that of Campeche was with Mexico. While Mérida desired to remain in the Spanish empire, or else to be the capital of an independent Yucatan republic, Campeche wished full union with Mexico.

As was natural, Santa Anna landed at Campeche and there showed great interest in the people, who welcomed him gladly. Soon after, he went to Mérida and found considerable merit in their protests. His report, dated July 9, 1824, gives a good picture of conditions. He stated that he was trying to unite the factions in the war against Spain. He frankly stated that in the conflict of "ideas, opinions and rights" he had been forced to suspend judgment and simply had reported the facts. He asked for funds to strengthen military posts and public works.[2] When he tried to prosecute the war with Spain trouble developed and the civil authorities resigned. Santa Anna was then given civil power also only to find that it was one thing to criticise the other person and quite another to do the thing well himself.

The national government had paid little attention to his report except to order the prosecution of the war against Spain. This meant the ruin of the Mérida trade and aroused such bitter protest that the Yucatán legislature condemned the Military and Civil Governor in secret session on Septem-

2. Tomás Aznar and Juan Garbó, *Memoria Sobre a conveniencia....*, documents.

ber 30. It accused him of tampering with the Declaration of War, of misusing funds sent for recruiting troops and of having more troops under arms than necessary.

In the meantime, the General was planning another typically Santa Anna move—none other than the invasion of Cuba, the key to the Caribbean. This had much of the appearance of a fool rushing in for Mr. Canning, the British statesman, had bluntly stated that neither England, France or the United States would permit one of the others to obtain it. To keep it from being revolutionized by a Latin American country was the desire of all of these, but just the same Santa Anna was proposing the step and the government of Colombia showed decided interest. Mr. J. R. Poinsett, the United States envoy to Mexico, was quite perturbed by the situation as may be seen from his numerous and detailed reports sent back to the State Department. His conduct opposing such a move was endorsed when word was sent to Mexico from Washington that the geographical location of Cuba indicated the United States should be the recipient in case ownership of the island passed to a New World power.

A secret society, by the name of the *Aguila Negra,* had been organized as early as 1823 to help free Cuba. In the United States this was centered in New Orleans, while no less a person than Guadalupe Victoria was the official leader in Mexico. Efforts to secure co-operation from Colombia failed because of a local revolution, but it is obvious that Santa Anna was simply undertaking what many had been considering but had not dared to start.

The Governor of Yucatán reported August 18, 1824, that the time was most auspicious because of serious discontent in Cuba arising from crop failures, pirate invasions and government exactions. He added that Spanish troops in the island were too few to leave the fortresses and advised that the invasion start the following spring or sooner. Though not authorized to proceed, he certainly was not discouraged and, when spring came, he actually embarked some five hundred men, awaiting orders to sail.

At this point, for the first time, the blunt soldier was to

feel the exasperating power of the wiles of the diplomat. As already seen, foreign powers with Caribbean interests were far from ready for this question to be precipitated. Before their protests Mexican authorities suddenly needed a scapegoat. Santa Anna was the most convenient victim, as is seen from the letters of P. D. F. to Pablo Obregón, the Mexican Minister in Washington:

"N. 142.

Mexico, August 3, 1825;

Through Note No. 104 of Your Excellency, the President of the Republic has learned of the rumors current in the States concerning the expedition planned against Havana by General Santa Anna.... Your Excellency has been notified repeatedly of the ideas of the Government concerning Cuba, and now I must say to you that General Santa Anna acted without instructions or orders whatever and strictly upon his own authority. This with other reasons made it necessary to remove him as Commanding General of Yucatán. However, it is advisable not to give this too great publicity because of the opinions that might be formed of the Government. The independence with which this General has acted might provide arguments to our detractors as to the lack of loyalty of our leaders at a distance from the center of government."[3]

Victoria who was the newly elected president under the Constitution of 1824, recalled Santa Anna to Mexico City with cautiously worded private explanations as to the inadvisability of the movement. However, it is a well known fact that the whole affair had been carefully watched from the Capital and that the Minister of War had bluntly encouraged it with the cynical statement that if it were a success, it would be fine for the nation; while, if Santa Anna were killed or ruined in the affair, the Republic would still be the winner.

To carry out the semblance of punishment, Santa Anna was ordered to appear before another court martial. However,

---

3. Luis Chávez Orozco, *Un esfuerzo de Méjico por la independencia de Cuba*, p. 9.

this was a mere technicality for the court never met. On the contrary, the recalled officer was rewarded with the nomination to the post of Director of Engineers. Once more lack of a proper education was seriously felt and the enviable position was reluctantly declined because of obvious lack of qualifications. There can be little doubt though of Santa Anna's substantial success in the difficult post of Governor of Yucatán. He left the peninsula in peace, no mean feat given the rivalry of the two chief cities, while the local legislature conferred on him the title of "a citizen well deserving" of the State. His resignation as both Civil and Military Governor took effect on April 25, 1825, just after he had promulgated the new and liberal constitution, which provided for popular suffrage, freedom of the press except for censorship of religious publications, no extension of slavery, etc. He probably had little to do with the formation of this document, but he certainly did not oppose it, for he could easily have postponed its promulgation till after he left office had he so desired.

On his return home, Santa Anna was a man of thirty-one. After fifteen years of active campaigning, he probably was wearied of it all. His apologist, Suárez of Navarro, says he was a sick man, but there seems little evidence that there was much wrong with him. A kind of disheartened world-weariness can easily be understood after the rude dashing of his hopes for the conquest of Cuba. To him, disillusioned, it must have seemed that he had been victimized just as he was dreaming of the glories of a conquest that would have made him talked of in the capitals of the world. So now he retired to play the country gentleman on his hacienda of Manga de Clavo[4] located on the road from Jalapa to Veracruz.

It would appear that he had married just before he left for Yucatán, for the British *Chargé d'affaires,* H. G. Ward, spoke

4. The hacienda of Manga de Clavo (Clove Spike) was the center of Santa Anna's holdings. Probably the name originated in the Chinese trade of colonial days and may have been given in memory of an attempt to raise cloves in Mexico. Those acquainted with Old Mexico know that numerous relics of trade with the Far East are still encountered on every hand.

of being "luxuriously lodged in the house of Madame Santa Anna" on the night of March 16, 1825. Quite possibly this was a marriage of convenience, but there can be no doubt of the sincere respect of each of the parties for the other. The father of the bride was a Spaniard of some means, for, in his last will and testament, written in 1867, Santa Anna stated that the dowry of his wife, Doña Inés García, was six thousand *pesos* in country property. He added that his own property consisted of his hacienda worth twenty-five thousand *pesos*. Doña Inés was highly praised by contemporaries for her sturdy virtues, while a modern student refers to her as a "classic example of Veracruz womanhood."[5] She was described as a "tall, thin woman" without much physical beauty, but she was devoted to her home and family of several children. In his will, Santa Anna gives the names of the children as: María Guadalupe, and María del Carmen, his two daughters; and two sons Manuel and Antonio (who died at the age of five). In addition, there are reports of an afflicted child, a boy, to whom the mother was devoted. Legend has it that when Santa Anna reached the presidency he was ashamed of the child and did not want him in Mexico City, but that the mother would not leave him and spent much of her time on the hacienda as a result.

It was also obvious that Doña Inés was hardly the type to shine in Capital society because of her self-consciousness among those other poorly educated but haughty and condescending dames. Santa Anna himself said in his will that he had little property at the time of his second marriage, in 1844, "when one considers that my beloved wife, Inés de García, was very economical and that she was almost always on our country properties advancing their interests, preferring this work to being in Mexico City, where she could have taken advantage of all the pleasures and delight which that beautiful capital offers."

On his return from Yucatán the former Governor retired to home life for a couple of years. Social intercourse was scant

5. Mendez, *op. cit.*, July 3, 1934.

between the haciendas in the 1820's, and each was forced to stand as a self sufficing unit. Conditions were especially bad in the State of Veracruz for the presence of the Spanish garrison in San Juan up to the end of 1825 had thoroughly disrupted trade. The merchants of the port in desperation had moved their businesses to Alvarado, about sixty miles to the southward. This small town, as a result, was unable to care for the congested population. In May, 1825, just as Santa Anna returned home, an epidemic of yellow fever increased the death rate in the little port to one hundred a day even though the summer had barely started.

Travel of all kinds was severely reduced and that for pleasure not to be indulged in. Ward commented in 1823 that a full day's journey for passengers on the old Royal Road to Puente del Rey, actually located on Santa Anna's property, was twelve leagues a day only. He recommended: "We found the greatest difficulty in advancing, from the extreme badness of the road, which was in many places a wilderness of sand." Again, speaking of traveling conditions in 1825, he said:

"A Mexican inn, or even a second-rate Hacienda, contains little or nothing beside bare walls. If the traveler be very much fatigued, he may stretch himself at full length upon the floor, or perhaps he may obtain the luxury of a table, which, as presenting a less uneven surface, forms a better substitute for a couch. To anything beyond this, he must not aspire, nor must he expect to find, except in the towns, any other provisions than tortillas (a thin, tough variety of hoe-cake) and chile. He therefore depends, both for rest and food, upon his own supplies, and of these he ought never to lose sight."[6]

Details of Santa Anna's country life are lacking at this point, but the following description of a country dinner gives a very good idea of the somewhat crude but lavish hospitality of the country gentleman of Veracruz province:

"At one-thirty Sanabria came to wake me and take me to dinner in one of the eating places on the plaza. The table

6. H. G. Ward, *Mexico*, II, 104.

was set for fourteen persons who formed the company of Vázques; all Jarocho officers [that is, officers from the country outside Veracruz] who had served in the War of Independence against the Spaniards, but not one of them wore any insignia whatsoever. They were dressed simply as Jarochos and were in shirt sleeves, as was the Colonel Vásques.

"There were no table cloths or napkins though the table was clean. They brought out two large bowls filled with moniatos [a kind of sweet potato], cabbages, potatoes, jerked beef, sausages and bacon, and two servants began distributing the food in some jícaras [vessels made from wood or gourds] and ordinary plates, giving to each person his portion. We each had a wooden fork and began to eat, some with their forks, others with their fingers. They then brought out some big baskets of tortillas enchiladas [a concoction made of chiles and meat served with corn meal hoe cakes] that burned like the devil, so much that I could not eat them. They served the tortillas in the same vessels and plates that they had used for the stew. Next they brought on some small roast pigs, cooked in underground ovens, as is their custom here. They served these with a pepper sauce which was put on after the animals were cooked. This is a delicious dish. One of the guests, armed with a long knife, began to carve the roast pigs, and the servants distributed the portions on the same vessels and plates we had used all through the meal and poured the sauce over the meat from a pot. After this came a quarter of venison roast in the same manner as the porkers, but served with a different sauce, and with this two large wash-basins of lettuce salad. There was no bread, only tortillas calientes [a kind of pepper pancake made of corn meal]. For dessert they served us large plates of rice pudding, small portions of custard, and a kind of cottage cheese made from curds. One portion was served to four persons, and was eaten from ordinary plates with wooden spoons.

"Coffee was served in abundance in clean gourd cups. There were also liquors. All of the guests were remarkably silent, because the Jarocho in general is silent, grave, and

[59]

modest in his deportment. Such is the country dinner Colonel Vázquez gave in our honor."[7]

Country sports of the day were as robust as the dietary accomplishments and the gentry and army men greatly enjoyed such activities as the *colea de toros* (bull tailing). In this two or more riders dashed full speed after a bull, each attempting to grasp the fugitive by the tail. The first one successful then spurred his mount forward and by a hard jerk, applied just as the animal's hindquarters were raised in running, turned him heels over head. With the erratic running of a frightened animal and the jostling of several horsemen, this demanded both skill and strength. Another sport was *el gallo* (the cock). The first step was to tie a live cock to a tree by a string. Then several horsemen attempted to catch the bird and carry it off to a certain point. After the bird was caught, the rest of the men tried to prevent the apparent victor from making his get-away. In the melée the bird was frequently torn to pieces. In addition, there was the still more dangerous sport of men wrestling on horseback.

Incidentally it was while in the midst of just such sports that Santa Anna began to build up his yard of fighting cocks. The skill, caprices, and whims of chance displayed in the cock-pit peculiarly appealed to the love of gambling, to the appreciation of activity and skill, and to the profound streak of fatalism in this man who was spending his life in gambling on his own agility and skill, and on the whims of fate.

Before long, however, rustic virtues and activities and even city life in Jalapa began to pall on Santa Anna, who, from the age of sixteen, had probably spent no single three months period in which he had slept in the same room each night. As a result it is not surprising that he was interested in the social clash developing in Mexican society. This was between the old heroes of independence, such as Guerrero, Victoria and Lobato all of whom were *mestizos* (part Indian and part Spanish) and who controlled the administration, and the pure

---

7. Eugenio de Aviranteta e Ibargoyen, *Mis memorias intimas, 1825-1829,* p. 20.

white former officers of the old Spanish army, such as Miguel Barragán, Manuel Gómez Pedraza and Santa Anna. This antagonism had developed to the point of frequent newspaper abuse and personal criticism.

A more momentous development was the bitter rivalry between the Masonic orders; the old Scottish Rite Lodge and the more recent importation, the York Rite Lodge. The latter, sponsored by Mr. J. R. Poinsett, representative of the United States, stood for liberalism and a full republican organization while the old lodge favored centralism. Soon the rivalry waxed so bitter as to become a matter of national importance with the Scottish Rite lodges and the Spaniards scheming for the overthrow of President Victoria.

Manuel Santa Anna, brother of Antonio, was one of the editors of the *Veracruzano Libre,* a Scottish Rite paper, and there was much speculation as to whether the General was behind him. Certainly Santa Anna's father-in-law, a Spaniard, gave that impression to his countrymen in Veracruz. However, Santa Anna had been a Yorkino in 1825 and now bought the *Mercurio,* one of the chief Yorkino newspapers. Surprisingly enough, he appeared to take little part in editing the paper or in directing its policy. In other words, he was biding his time and was not yet willing to have his hand forced.

A mob sacked the press of the *Veracruzano Libre* with the apparent approval of the Military Commander, Santa Anna's old rival, Rincón. The Governor of the State at once arrested him and sent Santa Anna, though not in active service, to take charge. The solution of the whole matter was finally turned over to General Guerrero, who proceeded to his post impressed with the necessity for "the most mild and conciliatory measures," as Poinsett reported to the United States Secretary of State, Henry Clay.[8]

Slowly, Santa Anna was more and more committed to the Scottish Rite faction. Alamán states that he actually saw the

8. *Mexico, Despatches,* State Department Archives, Letter of September 5, 1827, III (Poinsett, No. 99).

proofs of Santa Anna's membership in the order when he was Governor of Yucatán. He was elected Vice-Governor of Veracruz September 6, 1827, by a Scottish Rite Legislature and Governor, while in the three months Guerrero was in Jalapa (August-October, 1827) he was a frequent visitor of Rincón, on which occasions a favorite topic of conversation was said to be Guerrero's disapproval of Santa Anna. Bancroft clearly states that Santa Anna was affiliated with the party demanding the expulsion of Poinsett, who had been a kind of god-father of the Yorkists ever since he installed their Grand Lodge.

At this point events broke rapidly. The Vice-President, Nicolás Bravo, rose in revolt, demanding certain cabinet changes, the expulsion of Poinsett as United States representative and the abolition of all secret societies. This became known as the Plan of Montaño with the State legislature and Governor of Veracruz supporting the move, and with Manuel Santa Anna as an active participant. Strangely enough, on January 2, 1828, General Santa Anna wrote from Huamantla condemning the movement and offering his services to the Government and simultaneously notifying Guerrero, a confessed Yorkist,[9] of his support. Promptly the movement collapsed. Santa Anna himself went on to Mexico City and then returned to Jalapa early in January, 1828. The local legislature was panic stricken at having supported the Plan of Montaño and hastened to give the Governor, Barragán, permission to retire. This left Santa Anna in charge temporarily. Guerrero was promptly elected to fill the place but due to his absence Santa Anna continued to serve.

Many think that Santa Anna was simply cautious here and took no stand at all till he could see which side had the stronger battalions. The facts are that it was a badly garbled and confused political, fraternal and social situation with all parties boasting of their liberalism. For some time Santa Anna's position had been increasingly doubtful and it must

9. Guerrero's letter of November 1, 1827, to J. R. Poinsett shows this clearly. See Justin H. Smith, *Notes on United States-Mexican Relations*, University of Texas Library.

be remembered that his professed republican principles and Yorkino membership were at varience with the actual program of the Scottish Rite Lodge and the sympathy of his family. After some hesitation, he stayed with the York Rite faction. He may have been the plain and unvarnished opportunist that he was later to become, but there is also a chance that he was still living consistently and in accordance with his professed liberal principles. Beyond doubt, his support of the government was a case of endorsing the same republican ideas that he had supported ever since his move to overthrow Iturbide.

POPULAR HERO

THE political pot began to bubble right merrily as Victoria's presidential term drew to a close. The abortive revolt of Bravo had definitely eliminated the Scottish Rite Spanish faction, so it became a contest between the two Yorkists, Vicente Guerrero and M. Gómez Pedraza. Guerrero, the old Mestizo hero of the Revolution, had the support of the masses, but the "correct, proper and better" people threw government support to Gómez Pedraza with his pure creole background. Under such circumstances, the reported returns naturally showed the election of the creole.

Mutterings of discontent were to be heard on all sides and it is not at all surprising that Santa Anna was soon drawn into the dispute. He had many ties with the creole faction, but Gómez Pedraza was the Minister of War who had so cynically wished to send Santa Anna to his ruin in Cuba, and ere this the remark had got back to the intended victim. In addition, the Minister of War had failed to have the regular courtesies extended to Santa Anna that were due his rank on official occasions. The General could stand almost anything except an attack on his pride so his support of Guerrero in the campaign was to be expected.

While he was Acting Governor of the state of Veracruz, he exerted pressure on the legislature to secure its vote for Guerrero. When this failed, the Jalapa Town Council, controlled by Santa Anna, officially declined to recognize the legislature. The law makers responded by deposing the Acting Governor on September 5, 1828.

He gave up the position peacefully in spite of much popular support, but soon found that charges were being preferred against him for attempting to control the votes of his troops and for other irregular conduct. The justices selected to try the case would so gladly have officiated as hangmen also that Santa Anna had to choose between a possible death on the battlefield and the one on the scaffold that Gómez Pedraza and his partisans were preparing. Tornel said: "The certain fact is that Santa Anna, Zavala, Cumplido, Salgado and other officials opposed to Pedraza were selected for a malicious and immediate expiation [for their conduct], and ignoring the influence of their positions and personalities, the persecution began before they were disarmed."[1]

Under such circumstances, Santa Anna was never a man to await the attack. On September 11, warning no man, he suddenly left Jalapa with a handful of infantry, a squadron of cavalry and two light field pieces. The next day, he appeared before the strong fortress of Perote, some forty miles away, and took it over. His band was thus swelled by the local troops plus four hundred deserters who promptly joined him from the Government forces. These were really prisoners of the Government, now condemned to serve with the national troops at Veracruz. Hearing of the rebellion the wretched men overpowered their guards and joined the rebels.

President Victoria determined to do his duty and crush the rebels so as to end his administration in peace. He summoned his cabinet and with the whole group present had the War Minister (the President-elect) notify General Rincón that he had been selected to march at once for Perote. Even before the details of the revolt were known, Congress was asked to give the Executive "extraordinary powers" for the emergency. Both Senate and Chamber of Deputies agreed, and on September 14, 1828, issued a decree of outlawry against Santa Anna and provided heavy penalties against his officers if they did not surrender within such a period as the Executive should fix. However, seven senators and a number of the deputies refused to agree to such drastic action and were even accused of being friends of Santa Anna. Bustamante commented that when the decree was published three days later it was accompanied by so "insignificant and languid" a manifesto

1. Tornel, *op. cit.,* p. 344.

that its effects were seriously weakened. Santa Anna's men and officers were urged to desert him, but there could be no doubt that many officials were "whistling to keep their courage up."

J. R. Poinsett[2] reported to Henry Clay on the seventeenth, saying that Santa Anna was in arms "for, as he says, the preservation of the Federal Government, the sovereign rights of the people, the immortal General Guerrero and for the total expulsion of the European Spaniards."[3] The heart of the new pronouncement was that Guerrero must be the next president, while Gómez Pedraza was declared to be an enemy of federal institutions. The Government meanwhile tried to force Guerrero to declare his position by issuing a forged proclamation over his name denouncing the rebels. The old warrior would be understood to endorse it if he kept silent, so he simply stated that: "The proclamation is not mine for I have no public position from which to issue such. I love peace and the laws." This was interpreted to mean sympathy for the rebellion.

Disaffection spread rapidly. The sympathizers of the movement of the preceding spring soon joined in when the hardships of those defeated and unfortunate leaders became known. In fact, General Bravo and sixteen others had had their lives spared, but had been sent into exile from Acapulco, on the west coast, to Guayaquil, Ecuador. The hardships of the journey were such that Bravo's only son and Manuel López de Santa Anna (Antonio's brother) both died. Lorenzo de Zavala, later to be so prominent in the early Texas Republic, suddenly fled from his position as Governor of the most powerful of all the states of the republic, that of the State of Mexico, when he was impeached on exceedingly flimsy evidence largely secured from anonymous letters. Poinsett reported on October 22, 1828: "In this manner, a man of talents and of great energy of character, and justly beloved by the people, has been forced to become a rebel to the Gov-

2. *Mexico, Despatches*, IV (Poinsett, No. 151).
3. For Santa Anna's Proclamation *see* Bocanegra, *op. cit.*, pp. 473-75.

ernment. He is in the neighborhood of this City, with a small body of partisans where he presents a rallying point for the discontented."

Meanwhile, General Rincón had started for Perote. At Puebla, he found out that the military units he was to use were much weaker than he had anticipated. To complicate matters for him his methodical character was in marked contrast to that of his dashing enemy. His cautious approach to Perote gave Santa Anna a fine chance to dazzle the country even though his pyrotechnics gave little real advantage to the besieged.

He first spread the rumor of an advance or raid toward Puebla. Then, on the night of October 6, he actually set out and marched about three miles in the direction announced, but circled and re-entered the fort from the rear. Santa Anna hoped the enemy would divide his forces to pursue the raiders while he, actually back in the fortress, could demolish one or both of the reduced bodies of troops. All started on schedule, but in the darkness, rain and fog, three pieces of artillery were lost. By the time these were recovered and brought into the fort, the whole scheme was obvious. However, with such an uncomfortably active opponent there is little wonder that Rincón was cautious.

Two days later, Santa Anna went out to the *"malpaís"* (lava flow), which crossed the old Royal Highway, about ten miles east of Perote. This is a wide strip of country where gas formed under the lava as it cooled. The resulting bubbles burst and the crust crashed into piles of broken jagged stone sometimes as much as twelve or fifteen feet in height. A few sharpshooters here could keep a regiment at bay—and this Santa Anna determined to capitalize upon by fortifying a selected spot across the one road through the "evil land."[4] Here he intercepted Government orders which showed

4. In 1934, local inhabitants of Jalapa told the author of this old breastworks of Santa Anna, attributing it to the efforts of the Mexicans to prepare a defense against the United States advance in 1847. A trip in company with Mr. W. K. Boone of Jalapa found the breastworks in a good state of preservation, but it faced west toward Perote with the firing step for the

that General Calderón and other reinforcements amounting to eight hundred men were advancing to join Rincón.

These were too many for him to attempt to meet, for he lacked supplies with which to stand a seige, so he hastily returned to Perote and then showed that he considered discretion the better part of valor. He started a retreat with some 625 men in the direction of Oaxaca, where he hoped to combine with other rebel forces in the mountainous district of the south. Rincón followed slowly, having no desire to come in contact with the lightning-like thrusts and sorties for which Santa Anna was so notorious. Also, there was always the chance that some strong position might be held by loyal troops so that the wily fox would be caught between two forces. His fame and prestige coupled with the reputation of Guerrero were such, however, that they opened the way ahead of the fleeing rebels.[5]

Tentative negotiations were opened between the generals in early November for a truce to be observed till word could be received from Mexico. But in spite of the truce Santa Anna seized the city of Oaxaca. This Rincón claimed was a violation of the armistice terms, so the correspondence took on a much more acrimonious note. General Calderón now superseded Rincón in command of the Government troops, and soon had a concrete sample of his enemy's tactics. By night, some of Santa Anna's men scaled the walls and quietly took possession of the convent of San Francisco where Calderón usually attended mass. On the morning of November 29, the faithful appeared as usual. The large number of the priests present excited little suspicion until the robes were

---

defenders on the Veracruz side. There is no other possible approach over the laboriously made Camino Real so there is no reasonable doubt that this is the actual Santa Anna breastwork thrown up in 1828.

5. Bustamante, *Voz de la Patria,* Tomo III, Núm. 8 (July 3, 1830), p. 3. Bustamante claimed that President Victoria secretly ordered Rincón not to defeat Santa Anna. By way of proof, he says that certain events were announced in the Capital by the Yorkists the day they took place two hundred miles away. In the same periodical for July 28, Bustamante maintained that Rincón's conduct consistently showed his obedience to such orders for he made no effort to use his cavalry against Santa Anna who was forced to rely upon infantry alone.

suddenly thrown aside and the congregation, including many wealthy citizens, found themselves prisoners. General Calderón by chance was not present that morning, but a large "voluntary" contribution was paid "very promptly" to the unholy fathers who withdrew the following night to their old quarters, incidentally taking the alms box of the convent with them.

Calderón steadily drew his siege lines closer and closer till Santa Anna was in extreme difficulties. His men stayed with him with remarkable loyalty but there was no disguising the serious situation for Calderón refused to enter into negotiations except for unconditional surrender. In desperation, Santa Anna suggested that the hatchet be buried while all turn against the Spaniards, who were said to be planning to invade Mexico, but still Calderón refused to rise to the bait.

Just as the end was in sight fate took a hand. A garrison outside the National Capital at the barracks of the Acordada "pronounced" on November 30. They were probably inspired by Zavala, who, with Guerrero, soon joined them. Three days later, the President-elect fled from the Capital and the revolution had triumphed. Unfortunately, the rebels in the Capital were supported by the undisciplined masses, who under the pretense of attacking Spaniards, demolished one of the finest shopping centers of the city.

On December 5, Guerrero sent the glad news to Santa Anna who responded on the eleventh from Oaxaca:

"My beloved friend and companion: What thing can be asked of me in the name of my country and by my worthy friend, the patriot Vicente Guerrero, that I will not do? Your command has been carried out and we are busy working out the armistice the supreme government directs. I judge that these negotiations will have a prompt and happy ending when I see you concerned in them and in accord with our friend Sr. Victoria, whom a handful of ambitious fellows without love of country, without heart and without virtue, will no longer make the plaything of their passions as they have done in the past, shedding the blood of our brothers."[6]

6, Bocanegra, *op. cit.*, pp. 485-88.

The armistice here referred to was forthwith agreed upon, so that by the end of the month Santa Anna practically had control of the city. In January, 1829, Congress met and declared Guerrero president-elect and proceeded with the inauguration. This, of course, was entirely illegal and set a most unfortunate precedent. It gave the impression that the proper thing for a defeated candidate was to protest the election by force of arms. The victors, however, had convinced themselves that they had been cheated in the election, and that they had only secured justice by force when it had been denied through fraud.

Pending the inauguration the following April, Guerrero was made Minister of War and forthwith withdrew Calderón from Oaxaca. On becoming President, he further showed his gratitude by promoting Santa Anna on August 29, 1829, to the rank of General of Division for "extraordinary ability."

The few months after the armistice passed quietly and, in January, 1829, Santa Anna went to Mexico City where he attended a banquet with Guerrero. The President-elect wished him to retire from active command of his troops but this he flatly refused to do. After some discussion it was decided that Santa Anna should return to the State of Veracruz with his men, where he was to reassume his position as Governor. In March, Congress formally cancelled the decree of outlawry.

When the renegade, now a hero, reached Jalapa in February, he was met and welcomed by a committee of the Town Council. These good men were surprised, if not alarmed, to find that he had no less than a thousand men with him. To reassure the people, he issued a proclamation, saying: "Santa Anna, proscribed, persecuted and villified a short time ago, returns after the storm to the bosom of his beloved native land, *not as he left it, nor as Marius and Sulla returned to Rome, but with an olive branch in his hand.*" But, just the same, his men had to be fed so the leading citizens were asked for the usual voluntary loan, this time of seven thousand *pesos.* The sum was not subscribed so the city fathers asked what he intended to do about it. His mild response was that this was a "voluntary" loan, so he did not wish to use force, but, if they would make out a list, showing those who had paid and those who had refused, he would be able to determine the most suitable course to pursue. The suggestion worked like a charm and the recalcitrants hastened to subscribe their sums in full. Santa Anna was known in the old home town!

Meanwhile events outside of Mexico were developing to carry still further the popularity of this man, whom many considered the hero of the day and one who had received no actual reward (his promotion had not yet been announced). As may be seen from Aviraneta's *Memoirs* the Spaniards had been carefully watching Mexican factionalism for months, hoping to reassume control of the country by offering the people peace and security. Spies reported each step in the complicated events of the country and insisted that reconquest was entirely plausible. Cuban and Spanish officials eagerly absorbed these reports and before long the much discussed invasion was prepared.

Santa Anna was just as eagerly watching developments and in May decided to go to Veracruz to be as near the scene of expected trouble as possible. Without instructions from headquarters, but as Governor of the State, he had mobilized the local militia and ordered that all surplus arms be collected from public and private sources. He had asked to be allowed to attack the Spaniards wherever they might land, and, not having received instructions, was making his plans anyway. Roads were almost impassable and the Jalapa-Veracruz highway was in such condition that in many places only empty coaches could hope to get through.[7] In spite of these handicaps and even though this was the yellow fever season, Santa Anna collected two thousand men under arms in the port as well as a fair supply of munitions scraped together from here, there and yonder.

Just as he was about ready for them, the invaders landed close to Tampico on July 16. The same day, word reached

7. Even so, the toll rates charged for a carriage were twenty-one *pesos* for a round trip from Veracruz to Jalapa.

Veracruz that the expedition had left Cuba. Though the news arrived at 10:00 P.M., Santa Anna ordered the church and barrack bells to be rung. When the people had crowded the central plaza, he addressed them: "Friends, the Spaniards have disembarked in Cabo Rojo. We are so far from fearing them that, on the contrary, I want you from this minute to start celebrating the triumph of our arms. I have to march against them, and I do not doubt that I shall quickly send you good news."[8]

Certainly he received no orders to justify his activities, but that was a minor matter. If anything was to be accomplished, it had to be by private initiative for Congress was engaged in "noisy debates on trifling subjects and in mutual accusations and recriminations."

Santa Anna did not hesitate. Here at last was a possible chance to appear on the international stage. He imposed and secured the payment in three days of a forced loan of some twenty thousand *pesos* on the business interests of Veracruz. All available boats were mobilized, as may been seen by the names of the transports: *Louisiana, Trinidad, William,* and *Splendid* of obvious Anglo-Saxon origin, as well as the *Felix* and *Iris,* and several others with Spanish names. These carried the infantry while the cavalry, nearly half the total force of two thousand men, were sent by land.

As Commanding General of Veracruz, Santa Anna has been severely criticized for setting off on this reckless adventure while he left the chief seaport of the country practically unguarded from the Spanish fleet known to be in that vicinity. Also it should be noted that he had no naval strength with which to resist an attack at sea that might easily have wrecked his whole enterprise. To make matters still worse, he was opposing a hostile force reported to be composed of four thousand regular troops though he had only half that number of poorly equipped and hastily assembled men, about half of whom belonged to the militia. It

8. Bustamante, *Memoria . . . . de la Invasión Española . . . . en el año 1829,* p. 3.

was another of the foolhardy and reckless moves which made the man so beloved by the masses and so feared by his enemies. He gladly relied upon boldness, strategy—and chance—to make him a hero or to send him to his grave.

But, if Santa Anna was reckless and foolish, the Spaniards were equally reckless and seriously misinformed. The officials of the Mother Country had listened so eagerly to reports of disorders in Mexico that they had convinced themselves that the Mexicans were disgusted with their experiment in self-government, and that the mere presence of a Spanish force on their shores would cause the people to rise *en masse* to return to their old allegiance. To make matters worse, inadequate preparations were made in outfitting the expedition in the naval support given it. As the Spaniards sailed from Cuba, the Governor of the island ordered that the fleet should return for other duties as soon as the troops were landed. This materially reduced the effectiveness of the expedition.

Yucatán was the logical place for the Spaniards to land both because of its trade interests with Cuba and because of its antagonism to Mexico. Even the commander, Brigadier Isidro Barradas, became convinced of this after the expedition was under way for the port of Tampico with its pestilential coast and its desert hinterland. The strain and uncertainties of the trip were so great that Barradas and Rear-Admiral Angel Laborde, in command of the fleet, quarrelled bitterly and are said, on one occasion, to have become so incensed as to have thrown chinaware at each other while at the dinner table.

About three thousand men actually sailed from Cuba, but one vessel was wrecked on the Louisiana coast in a storm and only about two thousand six hundred actually landed at Cabo Rojo, fifty or sixty miles south of Tampico. With no ambulances, which had been overlooked in embarking the expedition, and in the midst of a blazing hot summer, the Spaniards then toiled overland to the yellow fever ridden port. Their food supplies were inadequate and the country could provide little. However, the town had most ineffective defenses so no opposition was provided as the Spaniards marched into their death trap.

A week after Santa Anna set out for Tampico, Congress authorized his expedition by allowing Veracruz troops to be used in another State. (The constitution forbade this without special permission.) Troops from the northern interior provinces were also ordered to the coast, so Santa Anna found himself with a steadily growing body of troops, while the Spanish force was constantly depleted by the ravages of sickness.

Without going into the details of military maneuvering in which Santa Anna is praised by his friends for ingenuity and ability, and censured by opponents for recklessly exposing his men, it may be said that he delivered a vigorous attack on August 21. At this time, the Spanish forces were divided, over one-half of them having been taken by Barradas to a healthier point, Altamira, about twenty miles north of Tampico. The next day, the Spaniards asked for an interview to consider a truce.

Aviraneta, the ranking officer left in the city, recorded that the meeting was in the English consulate. At the request of the commander the consul "gave the orders, and the servants brought in a large table with ham, smoked tongue, sweet cakes, various kinds of wine, Jamaica rum and other liquors." He commented that Santa Anna soon appeared with his staff of over thirty persons and then added:

"Santana received us very well. It was supposed that they would come in hungry and that the majority of them were great drunkards (*borrachines*). I gave them ham and tongue and made them drink Jerez and Port in small and large quantities. They ate and drank at a great rate, and somewhat more than usual, and talked about everything except the terms of surrender. The consul ordered them to be served with tea and coffee in abundance and they drank rum and Bordeaux anisette as if they were water, till many of the Mexicans were embracing me. I observed that Santa Anna was eating little and that he drank nothing but water and wine."[9]

9. Aviraneta, *op. cit.*, p. 218.

[74]

After an hour and a half, Santa Anna brought up the subject of a capitulation, but the Spaniard stood out for a truce only. They were interrupted by an officer dashing in with the report that Barradas had returned with the balance of the Spanish forces, thus in effect trapping Santa Anna and his staff. However, Santa Anna was present under a flag of truce and the Spaniard was too honorable a man to violate this even though he had the chance. In an interview with Santa Anna, he assured him that the purpose of the invaders was not to make war upon Mexico, but to establish a point around which Mexicans desiring peace could rally.

Each body of troops had learned something. The Spaniards were convinced for the first time that the Mexicans could fight and that they were under the command of a man of bravery and resources. The Mexicans now knew that the Spanish regulars were not invincible and that they were badly weakened by disease. During two more weeks of considerable fighting, there were numerous notes sent back and forth, the Spaniards wishing to discuss terms, but Santa Anna insisting (probably falsely) that he had instructions from the Mexican Government to consider nothing short of absolute surrender.[10]

On the 10th of September, following a heavy rain, Santa Anna attacked so late in the afternoon that fighting extended into the night. The next day, Barradas asked for a consultation which Santa Anna granted. The Spaniards had lost nine hundred or more men, but were still in fairly strong positions. To eliminate all details it may be said that an agreement was reached by which the invaders, except the sick in hospitals, were to evacuate Tampico and surrender all arms and supplies. In exchange they were to be allowed to secure transports to leave the country (about 1,800 did this) and were to retain all personal property.

10. Copies of this correspondence may be found in Aviraneta, *op. cit.*, and Zamacois, *op. cit.* These letters when read at the present time reflect credit on the Spaniard for his conservatism and restraint. Of course, he was the suppliant, but, even so, there is a marked contrast in the dignity of his letters with the bombast and gasconade in which the Mexican indulged, with his references to the sacred soil of Mexico invaded by barbarians, and to slaves driven to combat, etc.

After the capitulation, the terms were observed by both forces. Officers fraternized freely and the Mexican officers entertained the Spaniards with a banquet. It is true that Santa Anna may have caused needless bloodshed by his last attack for he could probably have secured the same terms some days earlier. Before criticising too severely, however, it should be remembered that in a European general, this might have been subject to criticism, but in Mexico the popular demand for surrender "at discretion" was great. It should also be remembered that severity to an enemy was not considered to detract from glory in the school in which the Mexican general had been trained.

Behold the conquering hero comes! As early as the opening of July, Santa Anna's name had been freely coupled with those of Guerrero and Zavala as a public toast, but now public enthusiasm knew no bounds. One report has it that President Guerrero and his family were at the Teatro Principal for the evening performance when a tired and dusty courier, in leather clothing, entered the presidential box and handed him a message. Tension seized the audience, which rose to its feet hoping for an announcement as the word spread that the courier came from Tampico. Guerrero then rose and said:

"Mexicans, I am going to give you some splendid news which will fill your hearts with rejoicing. Brigadier Santa Anna has forced Barradas to surrender in Tampico, he has conquered him, saving the honor of the nation. As a just recompense I am going to send him this general's belt which I am wearing, in order that he shall put it on with all solemnity and as a just reward in his camp and before his soldiers."[11]

Pandemonium broke loose and the production was stopped as the hysterical crowd rushed out to carry the news to the city. In his own *Memoirs,* the public idol remarked:

"As is customary in Mexico, applause to the victor, ovations on all sides. The General Congress saw fit to give me the title of "Well deserving of the Native Land" (*Benemérito de la Patria*); the government promoted me to the rank of Gen-

11. Juan de Dios Peza, *Recuerdos*, pp. 51-53.

eral of Division, sending me the insignia to be conferred upon me, a thing which my assistant General Manuel Mier y Terán, did with his own hands in the place where the invaders surrendered their arms. Some legislatures gave me swords of honor and the people called me the Victor of Tampico."

This was not an exaggeration except for the fact that the promotion was accorded by Congress before the surrender of the Spaniards and so could not have been a reward for it. The States of Veracruz and Puebla declared him "Well Deserving" while Jalisco and Zacatecas conferred citizenship upon him, the latter sending him a gold medal also. Guanajuato sent a sword of honor, while the National Congress conferred the title above mentioned, together with a medal to the victorious officers, and in 1833 ordered a handsome monument to be built (this was never done) on the site of the victory. Also the city of Tampico had its name officially changed to Santa Anna de Tamaulipas.

The hero was glorified in prose and verse while Mexico City went into raptures at the time of the reception of two Spanish standards and a flag he had captured. On October 4th, these were placed on a balcony of the National Palace amid salvos of artillery. Here appeared the National Constitution, amid a rich setting of handsome draperies, with the Mexican flag proudly flaunting above the whole.

The most vociferous greetings were accorded the hero in person. He left Tampico September 20, and reached Veracruz five days later. A wildly enthusiastic crowd carried him in triumph to the church for the singing of a *Te Deum;* Bustamante spitefully remarking that he paraded around "through the whole city till eight o'clock at night." On October 2, a magnificent ball was given in his honor at the Municipal Palace. A few days later, he proceeded to Jalapa and took up his headquarters at his estate, *El Encero.* This city now vied with Veracruz in paying him homage. In fact, the committee of the city fathers who rode in the formal reception, actually used a coach "rented at twenty-two *pesos*"— when the man who had been asked to loan his vehicle "was not willing to do so."

Old President Guerrero considered Santa Anna had been too liberal in the terms granted to the Spaniards and was beginning to fear this man so proudly playing the hero, but all he could do was to acquiesce in the honors paid while he dryly remarked that he would probably have to hang him yet.

The uncertainties of the daybreak were now passed. The sun in its full splendor shone upon the man of destiny as he strode forth with confidence to mold—for good or ill—his country's future.

II

MORNING
[1830-1845]

Go on boldly, my son, and increase in credit with the people, for thou wilt one day bring them calamities enough.

—*Timon the Misanthrope to Alcibides,*

PLUTARCH'S LIVES AND WRITINGS, ALCIBIDES

POLITICS

AT the age of thirty-five, Santa Anna was a man whose every act was of significance to the nation. In appearance he was about five feet ten inches in height, quite tall for a Mexican. His frequent campaigns along the tropical coasts had left him with a sallow complexion, but his figure was of lithe and athletic build with little or no surplus flesh and indicated unusual hardiness and good health. His face was lined by experience, and his whole bearing indicated that he was a man accustomed to command and who would brook no opposition. Rather melancholy of countenance, at first glance he was easily mistaken by a stranger for a member of the scholarly class or of the learned professions. One of his most important possessions was a marvelously flexible voice: he could roar the order to charge, or so modulate and inflect it as to play upon the tenderest emotions of his hearers. When conversation drifted to topics of interest to him, his eyes would light up into a kindly expression of interest; gleam momentarily with the quickly-veiled sly cunning of the wild animal, or flash fire as the demon in his nature tore his features into a snarl that betokened a man beside himself with rage. In short, he was a man of striking personality and marvelous gifts, but of such contradictory characteristics that his closest friends would have hesitated at this early date to predict his future course.

When Guerrero was seated in the President's chair a serious blunder was made in selecting Anastasio Bustamante as Vice-President. He was a man much better known as a conservative than as a liberal so before long he was suspected of plotting against his chief by taking advantage of the old dislike between Creoles and Mestizos. Due to the alignment of a few years before, it was natural to suspect that Santa

Anna would support him. The clamor and enthusiasm of the hero worship was dying down, and country life had never appealed to the Hero of Tampico anyway. In answer to the repeated rumors of collusion between them, the two men issued a joint statement October 29, 1829, denying revolutionary ideas or plans. They urged that the Constitution be strictly adhered to and legal means be invoked in the coming elections to secure the changes which so many desired. This was something of a surprise and caused Poinsett to feel that the danger of rebellion was so definitely over that he asked to be allowed to return to the United States.[1]

For Bustamante, at least, the proclamation was simply a "red herring" to deceive the authorities and on December 4, 1829, he inspired the Plan of Jalapa. This pleaded for the reinstatement of the Constitution of 1824, which it maintained had been violated by the selection of Guerrero as President, and for the installation of Gómez Pedraza in the executive's office. Of course the last provision was chiefly for effect as Bustamante really wanted the position himself. Numerous sections sent word of their support, but Santa Anna held aloof in spite of several invitations that had been sent by the Jalapa rebels asking him to lead the movement.

The truth was that the hero had been hankering for political influence for some time. While still in Tampico, under the date of August 26, he had written a letter to the President in which he practically demanded cabinet changes, saying that the incumbents had little political influence or personal merit. This was followed by a threat to the effect that, if his request were not granted, he would most assuredly retire at the end of the campaign to his own estate, which he never again would leave.[2]

To the invitations that he take charge of the rebel campaign, however, he responded that his health was so bad he could not think of it. He wrote that he thoroughly approved

1. *Mexico, Despatches,* Poinsett to Van Buren, November 4, 1829, IV (Poinsett, No. 187).
2. For this letter see *Voz de la Patria,* Tomo IV, Núm. 26 (March 2, 1831).

the demands presented in the Plan of Jalapa, but urged that legal procedure be followed since the employment of irregular measures "are generally the source of unfortunate clashes which inflame excited minds and end in civil war."[3]

The legislature of Veracruz remained loyal to Guerrero and hastily placed the civil and military governorship of the State in the hands of Santa Anna. These offices he accepted and, on the fifteenth day of December, declared that he would allow the overthrow of the President only over his own dead body. He maintained that Guerrero had been elected by the constituted authorities with no single delegate protesting the legality of the proceedings, and that to start a revolution on the ground of illegality when the Executive had already served for a year was preposterous.

It is difficult to believe that Santa Anna was not consistent still for he had just refused to sponsor a revolt in Yucatán and it is well known that the whole country was clamoring for a change. If he were merely playing the opportunist he certainly lacked the political acumen for which he became famous shortly thereafter. It was quite obvious to all that old Guerrero was a tragic misfit among the ceremonies and in the high society of the Capital. With something of a sigh of relief one imagines he placed himself at the head of a small force and turned to his beloved south to fight the rebels. He made no effort to attack Jalapa, but went to the mountains where through years of toil and hardship he had been so justly famous as a hero of independence. He was never accused of cowardice, but he knew when a city was untenable. When he left the Capital all knew that the rebels had triumphed.[4]

3. Suárez y Navarra, *op. cit.*, p. 176 note.
4. The *Voz de la Patria,* Tomo XX, Núm. 3 (January 21, 1830), p. 8, gave this popular description of Guerrero's government:
Guerrero did the thinking; Herrera helped him; Zavala contradicted him; Bocanegra put their thoughts in Spanish and Moctezuma carried them out.

> For the above mentioned affair
> Two were more than enough;
> But they being such as they were
> Four were necessary.
> —Fable of the Four Cripples.

Santa Anna meanwhile had started to Mexico City to aid the President. Many of his men, even the veterans of the Tampico campaign, deserted him by the time he reached Perote. Then word came that Guerrero had fled, thus acknowledging defeat. Chagrined and somewhat of a laughing stock in the eyes of the people, Santa Anna turned his steps back to his estate, Manga de Clavo. He formally gave up his political and military positions on January 3, 1830, and decided to bide a better time to secure political influence.

Congress duly assembled and declared Guerrero, whom they had raised to the presidency only a year before, morally unworthy of the office which was then conferred upon Vice-President Bustamante. Thus after each of the first two elections under the new Constitution the man selected for the vice presidency had engaged in revolution! If Santa Anna's conduct had appeared to his friends as a blunder they were soon pleased with the turn of affairs, for against the background of Bustamante's not-to-attractive personality, the dash and consistency of the Hero of Tampico were to be greatly praised. In the streets of the Capital, as early as January, 1830, cries of "Viva Santa Anna!" and "El Vencedor de Tampico" could frequently be heard.

In a letter to the Minister of Foreign Relations on January 3, 1830, Santa Anna sent in his resignation as Governor of Veracruz. He then added: "So far as I am concerned, I find myself the victim of renewed attacks of illness, and must retire to the midst of my family to recuperate, a thing I can never do while involved in public affairs."[5] It is impossible to state whether this was a political ailment, or some type of malaria or dysentery of which he was periodically a victim.

Whatever the cause, he again spent about two years on his country properties at Manga de Clavo and El Encero. Though given to excesses at times, his activity was such as to enable him to enjoy the age-old charm of the mountains for the early riser. By looking to the south and west in the early dawn, he could see the approach of the new day as the sun gilded

5. Súarez y Navarro, *op. cit.*, p. 187 note.

Orizaba and other peaks with its early shafts though the valleys remained in shadow. Meanwhile, as day advanced, what had first appeared to be broad paths on the mountain sides turned into ravines, cut in the slopes by the torrential rains to which that region was constantly subjected with its local rainfall of about one hundred inches a year. Not surprisingly, such contemplation of the beauties of nature only seemed to stimulate his land hunger abnormally. He had certainly acquired El Encero by this date, and furiously set to work to gratify his lust for power by amassing new properties only to be estimated in tens of square miles.

In national politics there were numerous conflicting currents. Alamán felt that a real conservative party was forming around a program that would mean prosperity for the country. However, many rallied around those who cried out for popular rights and privileges, and who demanded a reduction of the power and influence of the army and clergy. Colonization problems too were pressing for solution as the Texans became more and more restless, and other northern provinces demanded protection from Indian raids. Smuggling was rampant on all sides, with United States and European citizens the most active offenders. Whenever such a culprit was arrested a messenger was "despatched posthaste to the foreign minister in the City of Mexico, generally English, with a flaming account of highhanded outrages against the person and property of a foreign citizen by the barbarous Mexicans."[6]

Incidentally, the overthrow of Guerrero meant that Poinsett left the country at once. He was replaced by the unscrupulous and much less able Anthony Butler whose early reports are interesting in that they clearly reflected the thinking of an influential group with whom he came in contact. He was, of course, critical of the administration, but his comments to Secretary of State Martin Van Buren, under date of August 26, are worth noting:

"It is impossible to foresee how all this may end—but should the discontent lead to the elevation of Genl. Santa Anna, I

6. C. Lempriere, *Notes in Mexico,* p. 178.

should hope for tranquillity:—His talents, his energy, his eminent public services united to great prudence promises fairer to restore order, inspire confidence and unite public opinion than any other man in the Republic; and many of the army (who are every thing here) begin to look to Gen. Santa Anna as that man." After calling attention to the fact that Santa Anna had kept his pledge to support Guerrero even when that meant a contest with the bulk of his friends in the army, Butler remarked that since that time he had "kept aloof from all public employment. Hence he stands fair with both sides."[7]

In October, the regular elections were held for all deputies and for half the senators of the Republic. All was reasonably quiet but when the results were known, it was obvious that there had been some efficient "management," to say the least, for almost half the deputies were clergymen and a large number were military men and large land holders. This meant that Bustamante was to depend upon the army and clergy for his support. Opponents received scant consideration and Zavala fled to the United States from where he defended his course in a pamphlet distributed in Mexico. Immediately the *Voz de la Patria* commented (November 3, 1830) that this was the result of ill-considered clemency and clearly recommended the death penalty for all such political opponents so as to stop pernicious propaganda.

Such, in truth, was the attitude taken toward Guerrero himself. His followers dwindled and fled. Finally, the old hero went on board a Genoese boat, commanded by Captain Francisco Picaluga, where he thought he was among friends. The renegade Captain, however, captured him and surrendered him to the national officers. After a trial for treason (!) he was executed February 14, 1831.

The cry of indignation which arose was spontaneous but not profound so Santa Anna remained quietly on his estate. This is not so surprising in view of the financial condition of the treasury and of the fact that the only two sections really dissatisfied were Jalisco and Zacatecas. On the other

7. *Mexico, Despatches,* V.

hand, Santa Anna refused to take service under the administration though the opportunity was offered him. A letter of April 9 to a friend, Santangelo, showed a general discouragement with public life—and this probably quite accurately reflected his emotions of the moment. He said: "In regard to my country, I cannot tell you anything, because it is now sixteen months since I have abandoned public affairs and retired to this farm, which is my own property, where I desire nothing but the peace and welfare of the country, and my own tranquility. I never enjoyed more satisfaction than during the time of my retirement, in the bosom of my adored family. I enjoy the necessary comforts of life, and *look with horror upon high stations;* so it is that in this corner I am nothing else than a spectator of what is passing in the world."[8]

By late summer, however, his ambitions were awakening and he was cautiously feeling out the situation and organizing support. This could be seen in September when S. F. Austin addressed a meeting at far away Brasoria, Texas, and said:

"It is my duty to state that General Santa Anna verbally and expressly authorized me to say to the people of Texas, that he was their friend, that he wished for their prosperity, and would do all he could to promote it; and that, in the new constitution, he would use his influence to give to the people of Texas a special organization suited to their education, habits and situation."[9]

Another indication of his awakening ambition is seen in a second letter written to Santangelo, dated November 11, 1831. He wrote: "....I do not know of any other question of public interest now in agitation, than the approaching *elections of President* and Vice President. When that period shall arrive, should I obtain a majority of suffrages, I am *ready to accept* the honor, and to sacrifice, for the benefit of the nation, my repose and the charms of private life. My fixed system is *to be called,* resembling in this a modest maid, *who rather expects to be desired, than to show herself to be*

8. Santa Anna to Santangelo, April 9, 1831, in Orazio D. G. A. Santangelo, *Statement of facts....,* p. 59.
9. H. S. Foote, *Texas and Texans,* II, 63.

desiring. I think that my position justifies me in this respect. Nevertheless, as what is written in a foreign country has much influence at home, especially among us, in your city I think it proper *to make a great step on this subject;* and by fixing the true aspect, in which such or such services should be regarded, as respects the various candidates, one could undoubtedly contribute to *fix here public opinion, which is at present extremely wavering and uncertain.*"[10] Clearly, his hat was in the ring.

Unfortunately, no one had any faith in the actual chances for a free election. Both Guerrero and Bustamante had acquired office by controlling the polls and Gómez Pedraza had been named in the same manner. Santa Anna could only hope for success by a show of force for he could never be elected when a rival manipulated the machinery. Knowing this, he quietly began collecting troops near Jalapa.

Events were now skillfully managed by the hero of Tampico. Just as the administration was boasting of the splendid financial record of 1831 and of the fine outlook for peace, Colonel Pedro Landero, in charge of the Veracruz garrison was having financial troubles. His accounts were some eighteen thousand *pesos* short, for he had lost the money in gambling and was now nearly desperate, fearing discovery. He had probably been selected for the Veracruz post because of his known personal dislike of Santa Anna. But "needs must when the devil drives" so he asked Santa Anna for a loan, which was extended on condition that Landero launch a revolution.

Whether this agreement inspired Landero's subsequent conduct, or whether it was one of several motives may be open to discussion, but the outstanding fact is that on January 2, 1832, he called the officers of the garrison of San Juan de Ulloa to meet at his home. Here a set of four articles were agreed to. These reindorsed the old Plan of Jalapa; asked for changes in the President's cabinet; invited Santa Anna to take charge of the movement, and agreed to do nothing until he saw fit

10. Santa Anna to Santangelo, October 11, 1831, in Santangelo, *The Two or Three Millions.*

to act. That same night, two couriers were despatched to ask the master of Manga de Clavo to leave his retirement. Twenty-four hours later, the General had reached Veracruz where he was joyously acclaimed as the leader.

On January 4 he sent a letter to Bustamante with copies of the pronunciamiento and offered his services as *mediator*. However, it is to be noted that he directly sponsored the one specific demand of the rebels. This was for a change in the ministry, but, so far as his letter went, there was no indication of a move to overthrow the President. He wrote: "I have reason to know the state of public opinion, and on what individuals approval falls; thus it is that I do not hesitate, in case of your removing the present ministers or as I hope that they will voluntarily resign, to propose the following gentlemen to take their places: For Relations, Sr. Camacho; for War, Sr. Muzquiz; for Treasury, Sr. García, the present Governor of Zacatecas; and for Justice and Church affairs, Sr. Dr. Valentín.

"I do not doubt that with this simple change the public desires will be satisfied, that peace will be established and order not disturbed and that everyone will bless you with all their hearts."[11]

Santa Anna was still obviously taking no chances, for without waiting to hear the response of the Government he appropriated a local supply of federal funds, said to amount to 279,000 *pesos*. In addition, he took control of the customs receipts of the port of Veracruz (probably half of all those of the Republic) and secured the support of many merchants by offering special bargains to them on customs due or to be collected. His offer of meditation was ignored and the national authorities prepared for war. It is true that the ministers, who were under fire, went through the form of offering their resignations, but this was done in such a way as to link the fate of the incumbents with that of Bustamante. The houses of congress, therefore, endorsed both the President and his ministers: thus the issue was squarely joined. General José

11. *Gómez Farías Papers*, García Collection.

Calderón was sent down to the coast to attempt once more to humble his old enemy.

Santa Anna himself, however, was none too anxious to resort to force. On January 25, he wrote a six page letter to Bustamante still insisting that he desired to mediate and pointing out that the one point of issue was the elimination of the cabinet. The pointed attack on Lucas Alamán rather indicated that if he were dismissed a compromise might be reached with regard to some of the others. Possibly this mildness was due to the miserable condition of the rebel troops. Even after making due allowance for the surprise of a British gentleman accustomed to efficient European troops, still the following description shows the parlous state of the defenders of Veracruz:

"As the general's men had fought and conquered, they had a right to be called soldiers; but certainly heroes exhibiting so unmilitary and extraordinary an appearance, I never witnessed before. They were attired in shreds and patches formed of every color in the rainbow. Some had no uniforms at all, and many of them, leaving out of consideration altogether this warlike distinction, seemed pretty nearly divested of all clothing whatsoever. The cavalry, so to call them, were a complete mob of half starved peasantry; numbers of them were without either stockings or shoes, others were deprived of both coats and jackets, and their nether garments, torn in rags and tatters, seemed ready to be carried away with the first good breeze that might blow. Their accoutrements corresponded in fanciful variety with the rest of their motley attire; and rusty swords, broken pikes, and worn-out fire locks, apparently kept for show rather than use, constituted the mortal weapons of this ragged cavalcade."[12]

But, when Bustamante declined to negotiate, even such troops as these were to be used. Taking a group of about three hundred of his so-called cavalry, Santa Anna set out the night of February 24. The next morning, he fell on and

12. Tudor, *Narrative of a Tour in North America*, II, 164-65.

[90]

captured a government convoy about fifteen miles from Veracruz, carrying munitions and between thirty and fifty thousand *pesos* in cash to the enemy. Calderón knew nothing of it till Santa Anna was re-entering Veracruz amidst the wild acclaim of the populace, the firing of a salute and the ringing of bells.

About a week later, on March 3, Santa Anna moved his troops out of the city and met Calderón in the battle of Tolumé. His ragamuffins were outnumbered more than two to one, but continued to fight from 10:00 A.M. to 5:00 P.M., only to be disastrously defeated, losing thirty-two officers and over four hundred and fifty killed and wounded. Among those killed was Colonel Pedro Landero who had been the mouthpiece of the rebellion.

Calderón could easily have taken over the port by prompt action, but very leisurely made his plans. This gave Santa Anna a chance to dash back to the city and, with whirlwind activity, to enroll more troops and prepare the walls for an attack. When Calderón did arrive, it was only to find that the defenders had one hundred and twelve guns in place, manned by two thousand five hundred men. He wisely hesitated to attack such fortifications, and instead laid siege to the place regardless of the fact that the yellow fever season was just starting. After he had lost about a thousand of his men, the general decided he had had enough and so retired to the highlands on May 13.

The tempo of events now increased steadily as the tide of discontent rose. The Departments of Zacatecas, Jalisco and Durango had joined the protestants while the ports of Matamoros and Tampico had been taken over by rebel sympathizers. In the national congress itself were numbers who received news of government victories with "expressive silence." A periodical commented that prices of sugar and whiskey, "two articles which can almost be classed among the prime necessities of life," were going up in price rapidly because throughout the south the rebels had deserted their fields or destroyed the growing crops. Meanwhile flood waters were rising in the Capital streets because all funds usually used for drainage had been diverted to finance the contest against Santa Anna.[13]

On May 17, just after news arrived of Calderón's retreat from Veracruz, the much denounced cabinet ministers finally resigned. This might have ended the fray had it occured four months earlier, but, after they had precipitated the struggle and the national government had become so thoroughly identified with them, mere resignations were not sufficient. Santa Anna advanced steadily after his retreating foe and, on June 13, entered into an armistice at Corral Falso, so as to open negotiations. These came to naught, for the rebels were frankly demanding that Bustamante be overthrown and that Gómez Pedraza be recalled to serve out the term for which he had been elected in 1828.

To the rebels it now made little difference that Gómez Pedraza had not been allowed to take office in the first place because Santa Anna had declared the election illegal. They glibly explained, to their own satisfaction at least, by saying that at the time of the election they considered Guerrero as the choice of the people for the presidency, with Gómez Pedraza as the second preference. Now that Guerrero was dead, the second choice should ascend to office, but Bustamante as executive was a plain usurper or interloper.

Chiapas and Oaxaca soon joined the rebels outright and S. F. Austin wrote to Santa Anna on July 6: "I would not be a devotee of the fundamental principles of the constitutional liberty of my adopted country if I failed to respect the Chief, whose arms have always been used to protect and uphold them." On the twenty-eighth, he wrote to Ramón Muzquiz from San Felipe de Austin:

"I suppose that you have received the few lines that I wrote you hurriedly from Brazoria [dated July 18, 1832]. In that letter, I manifested the opinion that under the actual circumstances it was very important for us all to join the plan of Santa Anna....

"A meeting of the Ayuntamiento took place the day before yesterday, and another yesterday, of the people, which was

13. *La Marimba*, Tomo I, Núm. 10 (March 3, 1832), pp. 91-92.

well attended, and in which the plan of Veracruz was unanimously adhered to, the most perfect unity and harmony prevailing in that expression of the public will."[14]

Two weeks before this, Butler had reported that the Mexican government was in serious straits with Santa Anna attacking Orizaba and General Moctezuma advancing upon San Luis Potosí. To make matters worse, an outstanding officer of the government, General Terán, had just died. "The finances of Mexico are completely exhausted, and the Administration literally subsists upon loans from week to week at an interest of four per cent a month."[15]

Santa Anna remained two months in Orizaba drilling his troops, but Bustamante realized that his prestige was declining and so placed himself at the head of the army. A vain effort. The rebels were rapidly growing in numbers and their attacks on all sides were constant. Through the months of August and September these continued till the rebels had opened the road to Puebla and counted a majority of the one-time defenders of that city in their own ranks.

Just as Santa Anna was ready to advance, Gómez Pedraza was writing from exile in Pennsylvania on September 21, 1832, that he would return to serve out his term of office—in other words to be the cat's-paw the Veracruzan so badly needed. This meant that all could be done in the name of legality. On September 28, Butler reported that he understood Puebla had fallen and added: "I hazard nothing in predicting that from the taking of Puebla [a town of probably sixty thousand people at a distance of a little over one hundred miles from Mexico City, with one hundred and fifty-five thousand population] the present administration is put down never to recover."[16] The rumor was premature for Santa Anna did not open fire on the City of Churches, as Puebla was proudly called, till a week later. However, after some little fighting an agreement was made for the national troops to withdraw to Mexico City with their arms. A few

14. E. C. Barker, *The Austin Papers,* II, 811, 825-26.
15. *Mexico, Despatches,* V (Butler, No. 32).
16. *Ibid.,* VI (Butler, No. 39).

days later, the Puebla Commanding Officer reached the Capital and had to confess that during the retreat his men had deserted him and joined the victors.

Mexico City was panic stricken and well it might have been for Santa Anna had the goal in sight and allowed no pause for his men to enjoy the pleasures of the captured provincial capital. He drove them from the Valley of Puebla, at an altitude of seven thousand feet, up to the pass of the shoulders of the two great snow-capped volcanoes, the sentinels of the Capital. For seacoast troops to campaign at an altitude of over ten thousand feet was quite an accomplishment in itself, but there was no time to consider personal comfort or even a few lives. The men dashed along, scarcely seeing the panorama of the Valley of Mexico as it spread out before them because they were so quickly down in the midst of it. Puebla was captured, the holdings consolidated, the army transferred to the suburban towns of the city of the Montezumas, and made ready for the siege within two and a half weeks.

Soon after the investment was begun, Santa Anna realized that Bustamante, who had been campaigning to the northwards around Queretaro, was returning and might cut him off from his supplies. The rebels hastily reversed their front and engaged in several skirmishes and light battles in the Valley of Mexico during November. In all of these, they were victorious, or at least undefeated. This was enough for Bustamante so, after preliminary negotiations, an agreement was reached December 11, 1832. This provided for the cessation of hostilities and a temporary recognition of the existing state and national lawmaking bodies. As soon as elections could be held the new state legislatures were to convene February 15, 1833, and were forthwith to select senators and vote for a president and vice-president. The national congress was to convene March 25 to count the ballots for the two chief offices. Meanwhile Gómez Pedraza was to be lawful President until April 1, while a complete amnesty was to be extended for all political offenses committed on and after February 1, 1828.

Congress stubbornly refused to recognize the agreement which they felt had repudiated them by calling for new elections. Whereupon Santa Anna, Bustamante, Gómez Pedraza and other leaders met at Zavaleta, close to Puebla, on December 21, and reached an accord embodying the provisions already agreed upon. This was signed as a treaty by the leaders concerned. Five days later, Gómez Pedraza while still at Puebla took the oath inducting him into the office for which he had been chosen nearly four years before.

The king-maker, recognized as the king-to-be, now accompanied his cat's-paw to Mexico City to launch properly his own campaign for election at the polls. In his inaugural address, Gómez Pedraza had referred to Santa Anna as that "singular and illustrious military genius of the people," but that was just a faint prelude to the flattery about to follow. On January 3 was the triumphal entry into Mexico City. At last the Hero of Tampico confidently gazed upon the palace crowning the Hill of the Grasshoppers (Chapultepec Palace) as his just reward, the point from which he confidently expected to convince the world of his genius and ability.

The triumphal march entered through the famous Belén Gate. Here four huge floats presenting tableaux and drawn by the people themselves took part in the procession. The first showed the Battle of Tampico with the central figure of the scene that of a young girl carrying a banner on which was a picture of the national hero. The second showed the Homeland (*Patria*) holding the Constitution. In the third, the central figure was a young man, Valor, accompanied by Fame and Abundance. The last carried twenty-one young girls; the central figure being the Mexican Nation which was accompanied by the twenty states of the federation. Here was scant notice indeed of the President, whereas the first and third floats clearly referred to Santa Anna.

Everyone vied with his neighbor in paying tribute to the hero of the hour. That the applause, coming simultaneously from ultra radicals and the ecclesiastical hierachy, was incongruous was apparently noted by no one. Let the future take care of all problems; this was a time for rejoicing and celebration by all except the old stuck-in-the-mud conservatives.

The broker's son had become a full-fledged politician.

EXPERIMENTS

SANTA ANNA enjoyed flattery and hero-worship, but was far too shrewd to allow them to interfere with his chances of election. He well knew that Gómez Pedraza's pride would not permit of his being ignored too long while he was President. Also it was a self-evident fact that the President could guarantee Santa Anna's election while the hero played his rôle of the "modest damsel" sought after rather than seeking, that he had referred to in his letter to Santangelo.

So, impelled by these considerations he retired to Manga de Clavo towards the end of January, 1833. However, he could not resist the temptation to issue a public proclamation, on the nineteenth, in which he pleaded for: "Indulgence with mistakes of opinion, an end to hatreds, and the erasure from memory of the word, 'vengeance.' Thus you will attain the object of your desires and sacrifices, long and happy days for the republic, durable happiness for all. If my dedication and sacrifices for liberty are worth anything, respond to my pleas. My whole ambition is restricted to beating my sword into a plowshare. If any hand should again disturb the public peace and constitutional order, do not forget me. I shall return at your call, and we shall again show the world that the Mexican Republic will not tolerate tyrants and oppressors of the people."[1]

All in all, the administration slate was skillfully made up. Santa Anna was a popular hero with a reasonably consistent record, but even so there were many who feared his connection with the army, the old Spanish element and the Scottish Rite Lodge. To allay suspicion and guarantee a liberal program, Valentín Gómez Farías, a doctor of Zacatecas,

1. Suárez y Navarro, op. cit., pp. 371-72.

was selected for the vice-presidency. He was a man of broad education and culture (which Santa Anna was not), and having been born and educated in Guadalaja he was popular throughout the west where Santa Anna was little known. His inflexible character and purity of principles commanded the respect of all. Some even give him the credit for insisting on the legal procedure of placing Gómez Pedraza in office to complete the unexpired term. Meanwhile he acted as Minister of the Treasury, pending his promotion to the vice-presidency, and thus held the purse strings of the puppet president. Another strong point in his favor for the second executive position was the fact that a civilian might not be so discordant an element in that office as had been the case with the two preceding incumbents. They had been military men and had both led military revolts.

Santa Anna's correspondence shows that he was in close touch with affairs. On February 16, he warmly commended Gómez Farías for taking a place in the cabinet. Three days later, he sent a letter that was typical of the time. In it he asked that two men of Jalapa be paid the sum of 22,378 *pesos,* which they had advanced for the troops there. By way of explanation, Santa Anna wrote: "It is impossible in some cases to fail to take account of the wishes of friends, and for this reason I trust you will forgive my continually bothering you."[2]

When Congress met and the state ballots were counted, it was seen that the Administration candidates had been comfortably elected, Santa Anna received sixteen of the eighteen state votes cast, having failed to receive only those of Chihuahua and Guanajuato. For the vice presidency Gómez Farías received a majority of eleven.

There was, of course, some dissatisfaction and the United States Minister frankly feared another revolution on the part of those who had gone through the form of an election the preceding September and who wanted Bravo to succeed Bustamante. These men greatly feared the ultra-liberal Gómez

2. *Gómez Farías Papers,* García Collection.

Farías and the "red" Congress that was taking office.[3] Possibly it was for the purpose of gauging the strength of the various factions and of quietly watching the situation that Manga de Clavo was so attractive.

In a letter to Gómez Farías, dated March 16, 1833, Santa Anna had written:

"I am writing to my friend Sr. Pedraza, and I repeat to you that it is impossible for me to go up [to the Capital] since I have begun a cure as a result of which I am in such a condition that I cannot even put on my shoes (*calzar votas*), the effects of my recent irritations.

"You, my good friend, can take charge, supposing you will be elected Vice-President, if the [main] election should fall to me. Then the Mexicans will have nothing to wish for, or to fear in regard to their liberties."[4]

On April 1st, a queer spectacle presented itself to the nation. Whether through deliberate craft or because of actual illness, as he insisted in his correspondence, Santa Anna was rapidly developing a technique for holding public attention. The unexpected was interesting, the inscrutable was intriguing. Santa Anna capitalized on this and as the letter just quoted suggested, he did not appear for the inauguration. The keen edge of his appetite for adulation had already been taken off by the reception in January, so now he preferred to nurse his health, especially when this carried the implication that he was a martyr, broken in his country's service.[5] To add further to his popularity, Santa Anna graciously transferred to the public education fund a pension of two thousand *pesos* per year, which the State of Yucatán had just voted him for public services.

So it was that on April 1, Gómes Farías took over the reins

3. *Mexico, Despatches,* Butler to Secretary of State Luis McLane, March 2, 1833, VI, No. 63.

4. *Gómez Farías Papers,* García Collection.

5. Rivera, *op. cit.,* Tomo I, pp. 318-19. It is interesting to note that Santa Anna's service record, by this time, showed a total credit of forty-three years, nine months, and fifteen days, due to extra military service and the extra time allowed to those who had participated in various campaigns.

of office with the cordial approval of Santa Anna, as indicated by his letter:

"Most Excellent Sr. D. Valentín Gómez Farías
Mexico.

Manga de Clavo, April 10, 1833.
My Very Esteemed Friend:

With the greatest satisfaction I have learned from your appreciated letter of the 3rd that on the 1st you took the oath and assume the Executive Power. Also, I send you my sincere thanks for your good wishes regarding my health.

Even though conditions were most opportune, I would not hasten to take over the reins of power because of my confidence that they are in the hands of a citizen suitable both because of his abilities and reputation rather than in those of a poor soldier such as I. However, my health improves slowly, even though I am devoting myself exclusively to its improvement.

.   .   .   .

(signed)   Ant°. Lopez de Santa Anna."[6]
(rubric)

Gómez Farías forthwith launched a broad and effective liberal program. Most of the members of Congress knew little of public affairs and came to the Capital merely insisting that there be changes of some kind—just what they hardly knew. They wished to abolish conservatism and the army-clerical-landlord system of control. As one of the old conservatives later remarked in words reeking with scorn: "the majority of the members of the Congress were new to the political theatre; absolutely unknown in good society....and some put on a dress coat, or a Prince Albert and gloves, for the first time in their lives when they attended the opening of the session."[7]

There is every reason to believe that Santa Anna was a real liberal at this time, or was at least glad to see some new experiments tried. He had been associated with liberals for

6. *Gómez Farías Papers*, García Collection.
7. F. de P. Arrangoiz, *Méjico desde 1808 hasta 1867*, Tomo II, p. 216.

a decade now and had endorsed their principles in both Yucatán and Mexico. Furthermore, it is inconceivable that Gómez Farías would have launched a program without his chief's indorsement. Certainly Santa Anna wrote several letters in March and April in which he spoke of their unity of ideas. Then, in letters of April 10 and 13, he made recommendations as to finances, but avoided the more dangerous topic of restricting army and clerical privileges.[8]

The stand of Gómez Farías on these points had been well known for years. As early as 1826, while senator, he had tried to secure for Congress the right to control church patronage and fees, as well as to regulate many questions of church policy. Minister Butler reported that some considered the Vice President a booby and that others said he was assuming too much power,[9] but there was no reason to believe that he was exceeding the desires of Santa Anna.

Congress considered the new program at some length, but there was little accomplished before May 16 when Santa Anna came to the Capital for a visit that was to last till June 3. Later he took charge from June 18 to July 5, and in October assumed control for two months. Three days after the close of his first visit, during which affairs must have been rather carefully discussed, the clergy were notified not to deal with political matters from their pulpits. On October 27, the very day Santa Anna assumed control, government enforcement of the collection of church tithes was suspended. In November, members of monasteries and nunneries were authorized—if not actually encouraged—to foreswear their vows and re-enter secular life. To complete the reforms, the liberals determined to reduce the size and influence of the army. Even this was done with the apparent approval of Santa Anna, who as late as July 27 had written urging that "we be moderate in the distribution of military promotions and commissions." There was little wonder then that the army joined

8. *Gómez Farías Papers*, García Collection.
9. *Mexico, Despatches*, Butler to Livingston, April 27, 1833, VI (Butler, No. 46).

the clergy in the propaganda for "Religion and Rights" (*Religíon y Fueros*).

It is true that Santa Anna was becoming somewhat fearful of possibilities and, as early as June 3, wrote the Vice President urging that the newspapers be "persuaded" to suspend religious agitation. To this, Gómez Farías responded two days later that the idea was good, but that "one cannot prevent them from answering the charges of impiety which you know are constantly hurled at the government."[10]

There can be no reasonable doubt, however, that Gómez Farías had good reason to believe that he had the essential support of Santa Anna in the early days of his administration. On the other hand, the President must have been equivocal at least in his correspondence with the discontented elements. Possibly, as Zamacois thought, this was in order to calm the opposition that crystallized rapidly after the reform measures were introduced into Congress.[11]

A formal pronouncement of May 26 in Morelia brought the discontent into the open. The protest was led by one Ignacio Escalada and demanded the restoration of rights to the army and clergy; that Santa Anna be proclaimed supreme head of the nation and protector of the cause; that the last elections be declared invalid and that the landholders of the communities select a temporary *jefe político* as executive; and that political opinions be respected and no penalties imposed because of them. With their motto *Religión y Fueros* and their enthusiasm, these rebels not inappropriately called themselves crusaders. Close to the Capital, at Chalco, General Gabriel Durán seconded the pronouncement. Later, General Mariano Arista insisted that Durán had only done this when he understood that the President approved his conduct.

Whatever Santa Anna's private communications with the rebels, on June 1 he issued a clear statement to the soldiers of the nation. After blaming some "turbulent spirits" for attempting to seduce them and of actually invoking the holy

10. *Gómez Farías Papers*, García Collection.
11. Zamacois, *op. cit.*, Tomo X, p. 28.

name of religion for the purpose, he continued: "I swear to you that I oppose all efforts aimed at destruction of the constitution and that I would die before accepting any other power than that designated by it.... My firmest determination is to defend without the slightest hesitation the constitution as our representatives gave it to us in 1824."[12]

The same day, Congress authorized him to take charge of the army, so on the morrow he left the Capital and again deposited executive power in the hands of Gómez Farías. Certainly high office had not yet changed his characteristics or made him cautious. To travel behind an army was more than irksome to a man of his temperament, so it is not surprising that Arista commented that he usually went ahead of his men with an escort of about thirty dragoons. This, of course, was simply one of the little things that gave his men such confidence in him.

Now some really shrewd work ensued. General Arista was with the expeditionary force and on the eleventh pronounced in favor of the enemy and invited Santa Anna to join them with the understanding that he was to be dictator. The President did not accept the proposal and so was "detained" by his men. Arista insisted that he was convinced that this was the desire of Santa Anna and that he was astonished on the next day to receive word that the President had fled the night before. The news of his flight demoralized the rebels and, in a council of officers, the overwhelming majority declared they would support Santa Anna. This let Arista know that he was placed "in the crater of a volcano."

Cæsar, having declined the crown, made his way to Puebla as a refugee and from there sent a blistering letter to Arista. How could the offender have believed Santa Anna would countenance such conduct? How could the culprit have thought that a man of principle would cease to act as chief executive so as to lead such a revolt? How could any man think Santa Anna could become an oppressor of the people? In short, Arista should return to his senses, undeceive those he

12. Boncanegra, *op. cit.*, Tomo II, p. 438.

[102]

was leading, confess his mistake and throw himself entirely on the mercy of the supreme government.[13]

When the news of Arista's action reached the Capital all was confusion, and many prepared to support the rebels. The fearful, however, had overlooked the acting president. Taking extraordinary powers, Gómez Farías promptly arrested all suspects, declared the city in a state of siege, and called to arms all men from eighteen to fifty years of age. A reward of one hundred thousand *pesos* was announced for anyone who would rescue the illustrious prisoner whose escape was not yet known. If more than ten men were in the rescue party, the reward would be raised as high as five hundred thousand *pesos*. Just as all were preparing for heroic action, the escaped hero returned to the Capital from Puebla and at once became the center of a solemn thanksgiving. Was any man ever able to give his people greater emotional variety!

There was so much foolish agitation and uncertainty about the position of all parties that the whole situation took on the atmosphere of a comic opera—except for the unfortunate victims. With the approval of the cabinet, the two houses of Congress, acting irregularly so far as constitutional procedure was concerned, rushed through a new law banishing fifty-one selected opponents of the Administration. In addition, this famous *Ley del Caso* authorized the executive to banish such other enemies as he considered to fall in the same class.

Three weeks in Mexico City was enough for Santa Anna, and, on July 10, he marched out at the head of twenty-four hundred men to crush the remaining rebel forces in the northwest. Meanwhile he was constantly in touch with them, urging that they submit to the Government, and promising them his personal protection. When they did not accept these proposals, he actively prosecuted the campaign and brought on several encounters around Guanajuato, where Arista and his army finally surrendered "at discretion" on October 8. Most of the other rebel bands had withdrawn from the contest, so on the twenty-seventh, the President was back in Mexico City; this time to stay until December 15.

13. M. Arista, *Reseña Histórica de la Revolucion de 1833*, pp. 98-99.

Santa Anna has frequently been accused of leaving the Capital while Gómez Farías tried out new policies. This was doubtless true at times, but the last two absences were to enable him to lead the army. Arista's delusion that Santa Anna would support the rebels is the most difficult phase of the whole situation to explain. Friends of Santa Anna simply said that Arista was gambling on Santa Anna's ambition getting the better of his pronounced principles. Opponents said that Santa Anna was a most accomplished dodger, skillfully using both Gómez Farías and Arista in order to feel out public opinion, and that for the time being he had decided democracy was the best policy.

But new questions had to be met. Though there was little he could do about it, the nation was suffering from a serious yellow fever epidemic along the coast, and also from a terrific scourge of cholera. In a single day, 1,217 deaths were reported in the Capital alone in the late summer. Some said that this was a demonstration of divine wrath and a warning of national destruction if the anti-church laws were enforced. But in spite of popular clamor Gómez Farías had continued his program and now Santa Anna was to "carry on."

On October 19, the University was finally closed and a new centralized General Directory of Education was established for the Federal District and Territories. Certainly such a step would not have been undertaken without the President's approval, so at least a modicum of praise is due him for helping to establish the new body which was to become a definite step in the direction of a more modern educational system.

A more serious problem was that of the northern states. In addition to constant banditry and disorders there were fundamental questions of policy involved. The army had just been substantially reduced by dissolving the units whose loyalty had been contaminated by the recent uprisings. The frontier, however, had to be protected so the missions in the Californias were secularized, the funds confiscated, and the lands distributed to the natives or thrown open to settlement. There were of course other reasons for the secularization of these properties in the anti-church program of the day, but the colonization motive and the desire for ready cash were also motives that lent much cogency to the confiscation plans. Likewise, other public unoccupied lands were declared open to colonization, and earlier restrictions of 1824 and 1830 on foreign settlers were removed.

As all well knew the crux of the frontier problem was Texas. On November 5, Santa Anna called a special meeting of his ministers to which the Texan representative, Stephen A. Austin, was invited. Here the Texan complaints were sympathetically discussed. No action was taken on the request for separate statehood, but Austin was kindly received and was delighted at the new authorization which again permitted United States emigrants to settle north of the Río Grande. The national government also agreed to support the colonization companies and to improve the mail system for Texas. In addition, it was agreed that all encouragement would be given to reforms of the jury system, and to increasing the number of justices of the peace, etc. The plain truth was that Zavala and other Mexicans, including the Vice President, were just as anxious for sweeping governmental reforms as the Texans. So Austin naturally felt that there was no reason for his constituents to be antagonistic to or in fear of Santa Anna. In short, the President's actions were still in harmony with his professed principles of democratic government.

Apparently Santa Anna was on a rising tide of popularity after the rebels were crushed. The Town Council of Jalapa hailed him as "illustrious chieftain, outstanding champion, [one] selected by heaven for the happiness of his fellow-men, conqueror of Spaniards and aristocrats, a most worthy son of Mexico and an unbreakable bulwark for holy liberty."[14] As progress and peace descended over the land, he announced on November 18 that the emergency was over and that he was surrendering the special powers conferred upon him by Congress.

Occasionally there were pleasing interludes in the round of political duties and celebrations. One such was connected with a then unknown youth by the name of Guillermo Valle.

14. Rivera, *op. cit.*, Tomo III, p. 176.

[105]

Back in 1828, when Santa Anna had invaded Oaxaca and was trying to get a message into the Monastery of Santo Domingo, a barefoot youngster asked him what he was doing as he examined the walls. The boy then suggested that he attach a note to a block of wood and let it float in the stream under the wall. The ingenious suggestion so pleased Santa Anna that he told the boy to look him up if he ever needed help. Five years later, on hearing that Santa Anna had been made President, young Valle made his way to the Capital as an assistant to some freighters. He then secured a job in the palace kitchen.

When he was allowed to wait on the table, his chance came. After a good meal, when the President was in a playful mood, the boy asked if he might tell Santa Anna a story. "Oh, yes," said the President, "let's hear that story. You know it quite well, but I do not tell it well. Bread is for children and wine for drunkards. Once upon a time there was a king—now go on." "No, sir," responded the servant, "Once upon a time there was a great general," then he continued with the story of the events of the Oaxaca campaign, telling them with such effect and such skillful compliments to the Commander that Santa Anna was thoroughly captivated. To make the long story short, he took the lad and placed him in the school of San Ildefonso at his own expense, where his education was completed.

Another minor incident was quite significant of the drift of the President's thoughts. Though other events interrupted and the orders were not carried out until 1830, Santa Anna directed that the remains of Iturbide should be disinterred and transferred with special honors to the National Capital. As a matter of fact, the order was issued as a recognition of one of the heroes of independence. However, it was Santa Anna who had overthrown the first Mexican Emperor, and one wonders if he had begun to think that Iturbide was not so far wrong after all.

Early in December, Santa Anna asked Congress for a six months leave of absence for the sake of his health. On the tenth Congress gave its consent and five days later the President once more turned the chief executive office over to the Vice President. On the sixteenth, after issuing a proclamation to the people, he set out for Manga de Clavo.

This was the last official act of Santa Anna, the liberal.

CONSERVATIVE

EARLY in 1834, disquieting rumors began to spread with increasing frequency about the goings and comings from Manga de Clavo. Mail pouches carried large bundles of letters even in those days of little correspondence, and many men journeyed to and fro who seemed to wish to pass unnoticed but who bore unmistakable signs of belonging to the clerical and gentry classes. By this time, the full force of the reform program was being felt and much opposition was being expressed. Now was the time for the hero of the people to come forward with one of his ringing proclamations and a reiteration of his principles—but he was silent.

Such silence could only be interpreted as opposition to the program, and busybodies were gleefully spreading the rumor of a split between the President and Vice President. The truth was that in the four months following the middle of December, 1833, Santa Anna remade his whole announced political philosophy. He said later that he had slowly become convinced of the fact that the people were not ready for self government, hence that democracy was impractical for Mexico. Wharton relates the following incident which is probably as good an apology as any for Santa Anna's views in 1835-36. When Santa Anna was in the midst of his misfortunes in Texas Poinsett sent him the following message:

"Say to General Santa Anna that when I remember how ardent an advocate he was of liberty ten years ago, I have no sympathy for him now, that he has gotten what he deserves."

To this very unkind message, El Presidente made this deliberate reply:

"Say to Mr. Poinsett that it is very true that I threw up my cap for liberty with great ardor, and perfect sincerity, but very soon found the folly of it. A hundred years to come my people will not be fit for liberty. They do not know what it is, unenlightened as they are, and under the influence of a Catholic clergy, a despotism is the proper government for them, but there is no reason why it should not be a wise and virtuous one."[1]

Meanwhile all efforts to deflect the Vice President from his liberal reforms—even the reported offer of a five hundred thousand *pesos* bribe—were unavailing. However, as Santa Anna was willing to "play" with the conservatives, he found plenty who were eager to meet him on his own terms.

The position of the iconoclastic Vice President was steadily more difficult. To begin with, he lacked the prestige of acting in his own right; also his electoral majority had been none too large, and just at this time when the onus of unpopular laws was falling on him, he no longer had the support of the popular hero. Butler wrote: "it will demand all the tact and talent of the President to restore the political state of the country to a healthy condition."[2] Gómez Farías knew what was going on, but determined to continue his program so long as it was legally possible to do so. On March 12, Santa Anna wrote him a severely critical letter, but this had no visible effect.

There can be no doubt that the wholesale reformation of social and political life, as planned by the liberals, was unwise and premature, and that much antagonism was to be expected. The defection of the President from the liberal cause was freely rumored but it was not till April 16 that letters were read before Congress clearly indicating the disagreement between the real and acting executives.

Santa Anna before this had made up his mind to bring matters to a head. On the eighteenth, he passed through Jalapa and on the twenty-fourth reached Mexico City. The Vice President had been amply warned and knew that Santa Anna meant to repudiate his party and election pledges.

1. Clarence R. Wharton, *El Presidente*, p. 64.
2. *Mexico, Despatches*, Butler to McLane, March 27, 1834, VI (Butler, No. 66).

However, he was the legally elected President and had not denounced the Constitution, so the acting President quietly relinquished his office. The result was that the liberal program remained legally sound while the opposition had to assume the burden of proof to justify all change.

And changes came speedily. The Constitution provided that the congressional term should expire on April 15, though, if the deputies thought conditions warranted, they could remain in session another thirty days. Not only was this done, but at the expiration of the thirty days they still considered it needful to remain on duty. At once a curt notice was received stating that if they did not disperse, Santa Anna would turn them out. To a vociferous public protest the President answered that the Vice President and hoodlum congress had exercised a tyranny over the people. Right speedily Gómez Farías went into exile to the accompaniment of such irrelevant and wild charges as: "Yesterday the execrable Gómez Farías finally left the Capital, overwhelmed with the just imprecations of the leading city of Columbus New World on which his terrible acts weighed so heavily ....Gómez Farías attracted, like an ill-fated comet.... cholera and misery; immorality and tyranny; espionage and treason; ignorance and sacrilege; the promotion of delinquents and the demotion of the honorable; the triumph of the worthless canaille and the debasement of the select people; terror and mourning in families; banishment, sorrow and death in a thousand and more horrible forms...."[3]

It was soon evident that the conservative program had been carefully worked out. Between May 11 and 23 "plans" were announced in Puebla, Jalapa, Orizaba, and Oaxaca—all regions with which Santa Anna had been in direct contact. These unanimously opposed the laws for the reform of the Church and called Santa Anna to assume control with special powers. On the twenty-fifth, Cuernavaca declared the liberal

3. Narciso Bassols, *Valentín Gómez Farías,* pp. 36-37. After leaving Mexico, Gómez Farías went to New Orleans, where he seems to have been in contact with the rapidly developing Texas discontent that was also attracting the cordial support of Zavala.

Looking southeast from chapel at El Encero (August, 1934)

Looking north from chapel tower at El Encero (August, 1934)

View of Jalapa looking east from plaza (August, 1934)

Two fig trees in courtyard of Hacienda of El Encero (August, 1934)

legislation had introduced chaos and insisted that constitutional legislation could only be enacted with the approval of the people. The Cuernavacans considered that the objectionable innovations did not have such approval, hence did not legally exist. To clear up the whole situation the President was called upon to annul the new experiments and to act in his own right until a new Congress could be selected.

Here was a frank invitation, which was gratefully accepted, to assume dictatorial powers with the simple provision that the executive merely submit his acts for approval to a Congress hand-picked from his own supporters. Governing under this plan Santa Anna was very careful to have his acts duly ratified, but his enormous power was obvious from the fact that he changed his cabinet at will and was not restrained either by council or congress. He actually went so far as to disband state legislatures and to depose governors and town councils when they opposed the *new* "sovereign will" as expressed in the Plan of Cuernavaca, as opposed to the *old* "sovereign will' which had clearly favored the liberal administration elected in 1832.

The United States Minister expected the opposition to resort to the sword, but said: "For myself, I cannot think the event in the least doubtful, commence how and when they may—Gen. Santa Anna must prevail—everything favors him —He is in the first place an abler, and more of a practical man than can be found in the Ranks of his adversaries; He has the National resources at his command, and this would secure him the Majority of the Troops were there no other Consideration to operate—public sentiment (up to this period at least) is decidedly in his favor—All the great proprietors, the Aristocracy of the Country—look to him as the last hope for the re-establishment of tranquility and Order, and protection for person and property, and throw the whole weight of their wealth and personal influence into the scale with the President;—The Clergy, as you will perceive from the Newspapers couple the cause of Religion with the name of Santa Anna—and solemnly commit to his charge the protection of Religion and the rights of the Church from all of which you must perceive the probabilities of any present struggle terminating in favor of Genl. Santa Anna."[4]

Incidentally, there could be no doubt of the support of the clergy. Bishop Juan Cayetano Portugal of Michoacán was placed in the cabinet while church organizations sang peans of praise to Santa Anna such as: "All generations shall praise his name, old men and young men shall praise him, young men and maidens; because we have all, through the efforts of his religious piety and true catholicism, secured peace and liberty for our Church.... We were perishing but God mercifully turned over a blessed leaf for us and had mercy on our sufferings. At the end of last April there appeared unexpectedly a brilliant star, whose beauty, clarity and splendor announced to us, as in other times to the three Wise Men, that justice and peace were drawing near and were already in our land. This was, speaking respectfully and without any intention of being profane or of confusing the two events, the sudden arrival of the Most Excellant Señor President Don Antonio López de Santa Anna at this capital.... whose religious and patriotic sentiments qualify him eternally as a hero of the love and recognition of the nation...."[5]

Naturally, thinking was far from clear after such a hectic series of events. It was a four-ring circus with the clerico-army group holding the spotlight and in a strategic position by virtue of having taken the initiative. However, they were without an adequate leader and were wooing Santa Anna. In addition, there were the recently overthrown federalists, the also discredited Scottish Rite (*Escocés*) faction and the simon-pure *Santanistas*, who cried with a holy fervor: "Santa Anna, right or wrong! Santa Anna!" The President-dictator could always count on the support of the *Santanistas*, and had long since had much in sympathy with the *Escocés* faction. His problem now was to combine these with the clerico-army group.

4. *Mexico, Despatches*, Butler to McLane, June 2, 1834, VI (Butler, No.71).
5. Bassols, *op. cit.*, pp. 34-35. Announcement of the ecclesiastical cabildo of the cathedral to the people.

He soon launched into his conservative program. The sweeping anti-Church laws were declared of no effect and the special *fueros*[6] returned to the clergy; the University was reopened on the old basis, and the exiles and fugitives of the preceding year welcomed home once more. The change was practically completed in four months. It is not surprising that the situation has been summed up as one in which the executive appeared "to be steadily marching to a throne."[7] Santa Anna, in his *Memoirs* dismissed the matter by denouncing the radical laws which had so disturbed the country and added: "I, obeying my conscience and in order to avoid revolution, refrained from sanctioning and issuing the above [liberal] decrees."

By July, disorders began to be noticeable, but they were not very serious. For one thing, the inscrutable Santa Anna was shrewdly keeping his own council. Though all knew that wholesale governmental changes of some kind were in process the whole pattern had not yet been seen. By refraining from sponsoring any one program he was able to keep the support of nearly all the doubtful elements, while he consolidated his own power. The United States Minister who had anticipated a revolution four and a half months earlier now simply reported that the tendencies were monarchial, but that it would be difficult to get Santa Anna to commit himself. On October 20, he commented that some who favored a federal, as well as those who desired a centralized republic, still thought they had the President's support.

An illustration is found as late as January, 1835, when S. F. Austin, the Texan agent who was attempting to secure special recognition for his people, thought that Santa Anna was still a liberal. In fact, in this month the Dictator helped expedite the litigation which was to free Austin after he had

6. These *fueros* were special privileges or rights extended to an individual or group. Among them were the right to organize courts to settle disputes involving church property and clergymen, exemption from certain tax payments, etc. The record of these extends far back into Spanish history and provides the subject matter for one of the most acrimonious disputes in the account of the stormy relations of Church and State.

7. *Niles Register*, XLVII, 6. September 6, 1834.

been arrested on suspicion of unpatriotic activities. True enough, the student may now suspect that this was done deliberately in order to quiet the fears of Texan and Mexican liberals who could otherwise secure cold comfort from the general tendencies of the executive.

The new Congress met January 4, 1835, and contained a majority of delegates of the military-clerical coalition. Here was a group to do the Dictator's bidding so he was faced with monotony in which the unexpected could no longer be expected, and with the spice of opposition removed. As of old he quickly wearied of administrative routine and before long asked leave to retire from the presidency to "reestablish his health."

His renunciation of the supreme office was of course declined forthwith, though a leave of absence was granted. Since Congress had already disallowed the selection of Gómez Farías as vice president it now chose General Miguel Barragán as President *ad interim* on January 28. The new executive had indicated his subservience to Santa Anna and retained the existing cabinet in full. On all important matters couriers dashed down to the Clove Spike to consult with the master. To act as a guardian over legislative deliberation, and to remind the law makers of his interest, the Dictator was glad to arrange so that a portrait, representing him as the hero of the battlefield of Tampico, was formally presented to Congress just after he left.

One discordant element lay in the fact that the stubborn federalist and pure-blooded Indian, Juan Alvarez, soon started trouble in the south. However, the authorities kept the situation well in hand and there was no need for Santa Anna to give up his rustic meditations. *El Mosquito Mexicano* in the April 10, 1835 issue denounced the democratic supporters of Alvarez thus: "Sacred religion; the venerable clergy; the well-deserving standing army, author of our independence and liberty; the most worthy and virtuous citizens; all were the subjects of attacks of those sons of darkness, perfidy and error."

A more serious situation was developing in Zacatecas. In

that northwestern province, the spirit of democracy had run high for generations. This was the region where an independence loving Indian population had defied the conquerors and had forced the frontiersmen into settlements described as places in which the agriculturist held his plow with one hand and his gun with the other. When the races amalgamated, the love of freedom was not abated. Among such ardent federalists Gómez Farías was a hero. When word reached them that Congress, by an Act of March 31, 1835, had ordered the discharging of nearly all the local militia the Zacatecans rose in revolt. They were exceedingly proud of their local troops and did not wish to be left at the mercy of a regular army, controlled by political enemies who sponsored centralism.

The movement was so threatening that Santa Anna left his estate, and, with the permission of Congress, proceeded from Mexico City on April 9 to the scene of the trouble in the northwest. A month later, he was before the city of Zacatecas where Francisco García, the Governor of the State, had gathered five thousand men for the defense of liberty and democracy. The Governor did not know the first principles of warfare and was entirely befuddled by his opponent, who advanced with only about three thousand five hundred men.

This was the kind of campaign for which his early training had fitted Santa Anna. Here were the same great distances, the same climate and somewhat the same section of the country; so he employed the same tactics that Arredondo had been famed for. Whether because of treachery or plain inefficiency, or both, the result was a crushing defeat of the local troops. Immediately, the town was turned over to the victorious troops as their reward. Plunder was the order of the day with especial hatred shown toward the few English and United States citizens present. Their property was destroyed, some of the men killed, and men and women shamefully treated. A protest to Santa Anna met with the response that he had no jurisdiction in the matter and that another official would have to consider the case. The latter in turn said that if the protestant "knew the persons he would bring

[115]

them to justice if they were in the state." Thus the matter ended.

The character of these seemingly endless rebellions deserves a few general remarks. At first glance it appears strange that a people would so recklessly plunge into a rebellion, only to flee in utter panic after a brief engagement. Equally surprising is the fact that a people who had revolted in behalf of a principle should apparently forget that principle and acquiesce in enemy control after one defeat. The explanation probably is to be found in several factors. For one thing, the Mexican was a new ethnic combination and as such had not become standardized as a product either physically or mentally. No plant or animal breeder will risk his cash or reputation by guaranteeing standard results as to types, color or characteristics of plants or animals secured from a new blend. The more emotional and less stable new racial blend, the new Mestizo, had vague longings for equality and justice, but as a class lacked the stamina and courage of his own convictions. He would start out boldly, but, at the first reverse, his old fear of the "master" would return, and, panic-stricken, he would give up the contest.

To make matters worse, the Spanish adventurers from which the Mestizo originated had had their weakness accentuated through the centuries of the colonial period. The impetuous, reckless and headstrong conquerors had found the wealth of Mexico in its mines. This developed a civilization where gambling was the basis of the economic order. By the whim of chance a casual turn to the right or left for the prospector meant wealth or continued poverty. The drifting, homeless conqueror, with weak family ties, was lord of huge properties by the right of conquest, and, in addition, was entrusted with the "civilization and Christianization" of the Indian. In return he was granted the right to use the Indian as a serf for a period of ten years or more. Needless to say, the system of serfdom soon became indefinite and the owners continued an absolutist dominion over their estates of tens of thousands of acres. The right of the owner to the first

[116]

fruits, as well as later contributions, of man, maiden and crops was seldom if ever challenged.

As for practical training in self-government, there was none for either master or man: they were all cogs in the machine. Such allegiances as developed were purely local ones, based upon local conditions. It was Yucatán for the Yucatecans, Zacatecas for the Zacatecans, Jalisco for the Jaliscans, etc. To the masses the term "Mexico" was an indefinite something vaguely associated with grandeur and magnificence—just as the word "Spain" had once been—though the new term lacked the prestige and heritage of the old. A Viceroy from the Mother Country could count on a glorious reception and cordial support so long as he did not interfere too much with local affairs. So the name of Iturbide, and now that of Santa Anna, were ones of value with the masses up to a certain point. A response was guaranteed; usually applause—but occasionally hisses. Rebellions sprang up freely but to attain success they needed speedy victories.

As yet, few indeed were the Guerrero's, the Alvarez's and the Juáres's who could inspire their men in spite of repeated failures.[8]

Commenting on these characteristics, Bulnes remarked that the Mexicans inherited one ridiculous vice from the emotional Spanish conquerors: "Before a battle, all the Spanish equipment was excellent; artillery, powder, bullets, fortifications, cavalry, arms, and especially the troops, the officers and the general; even the light, the clouds, the earth, the flowers and the beasts. After the defeat it is asserted that the artillery was of wood (*oyamel*), the bayonets of clay, the powder was wet, the bullets would not fit the guns; there was no artillery park or train, nor mules to move it; clouds had made it dark as night; the sun had blinded the eyes of the troops; the earth had opened and swallowed up various outfits, while the very

8. The author is far from wishing to leave the impression that the preceding description applies to all Mestizoes of the twentieth century, for vast strides have been taken through education and racial stabilization. But it does seem that such characteristics go far to explain many events of a century ago.

flowers had breathed out poisonous vapors. Without such untoward developments victory would have been certain for our gallant troops can never be defeated."[9]

When the plundering of Zacatecas was over, the President led his troops from the crushed and bleeding province and once more turned his steps toward the Capital. Again he was hailed on all sides as the savior of his country and the victory acclaimed as a brilliant achievement. It is true that the rebels had lost all sense of morale and discipline after two hours of fighting, but, even so, the capture of twenty-seven hundred prisoners was no mean feat. Those of necessity had been released and soon the officers were pardoned by Santa Anna as a gracious act. Vengeance had been satiated in Zacatecas itself so he could afford to be the gracious and generous foe when the emotional reaction set in. The masses and the man himself both gloried in the smashing victory and in sensuous natures glutted with spoils—and equally in the grand gesture of magnanimity.

After a triumphal entry into Mexico City on May 21, he soon passed on to Manga de Clavo. Congress had remained in session just long enough to welcome him and then adjourned on the twenty-third. First, though, it had joined the public acclaim and declared the President "well-deserving in heroic grade" (*benemérito en grado heroico*) of his country. Likewise Congress neglected to withdraw the office of General-in-Chief conferred for the emergency, so he retired carrying with him these unusual powers, again leaving the puppet Barragán in charge.

The idea of a centralized form of government now made rapid headway. Even Austin, who owed so much to Santa Anna, soon saw that federalism was doomed. On May 19, Orizaba declared itself in favor of a centralized administration, and asked the President to hold a plebiscite on the question. Ten days later, Toluca issued a similar petition in favor of a "popular, representative, central" system, which would guarantee the Roman Catholic religion, national in-

9. Francisco Bulnes, *Las Grandes Mentiras de Nuestra Historia*, p. 772.

[118]

dependence, and a free press under the protection of Santa Anna as "President and Supreme Chief."

This was just what he wanted so the national hero could well afford to retire upon his laurels while the rising tide of popular favor prepared the public for the legal establishment of a despotism. Congress was called to meet in special session on July 19 to consider the state of the nation and the numerous demands for a change in the plan of government.

On October 3, 1835, came the official revolution when Barragán formally proclaimed a congressional act providing: that all state governors should hold office only at the will of the Supreme Government; that all state legislatures should cease to function after selecting a council of five men to assist the governor (in case of a vacancy in the governor's office these men were to select three nominees, of whom the Supreme Government would approve one); that where the state legislatures could not meet in a week's time the town council of the state capital should act in place of the legislature; that the judicial systems should remain unchanged for the time being, and that all vacancies in the ranks of state officers should be filled by appointment of the governors with the approval of the Supreme Government. The clergy supported the new program and are said to have contributed forty thousand *pesos* per month as a "loan" and as an expression of confidence in the government.

The two houses of Congress disregarded the fact that they were elected as a legislative body and formed themselves into a unicameral organization and then proceeded as a constitutional assembly thoroughly to overhaul the whole system. This was not completed till the end of 1836 when the new instrument of government became known as the famous Seven Laws ("Seven Plagues," said the opposition). These provided for a bicameral legislature with property qualifications requiring an annual income of fifteen hundred *pesos* and twenty-five hundred *pesos* for deputies and senators respectively. The President was to be elected by a weird system: the Senate, the Supreme Court and the President's Council were each to nominate three men, each with a minimum annual income of four thousand *pesos*. From this list of nine names, the Chamber of Deputies was to select three from whom the departmental assemblies made the final choice. The man so selected was to serve for an eight year term and to be eligible for re-election.

Such a system was ideally planned for unscrupulous machinations of a would-be despot. The large number of nominations would stop criticism, but judicious control of the Chamber of Deputies would guarantee the fact that no real rival of the favored candidate would be allowed in the list to be submitted to the departments. In addition the departments—no longer states—were so centralized as to be dominated by the national government which was very properly designated the "Supreme Government" in official documents.

The scheme went forward with comparative smoothness and seemed to reflect the new popular desires. It was doubtless directly in line with the wishes of Santa Anna, but the details of the despotism provided for were not due to his supervision since he had left for his ill-fated Texas campaign months before the document was completed. Then too, his Man Friday, Barragán, died and had to be replaced by José Justo Corro who continued to act as president *ad interim* in spite of the fact that Santa Anna had been thoroughly discredited in Texas and had slunk home to temporary oblivion at Manga de Clavo.

Regardless of the hero's eclipse the wave of centralism was so strong that its supporters could openly gloat:

Keep your eyes open, tightrope dancers
    And followers of Anaya
For today the canaille does not rule
Nor do spread-eaglists control affairs.
    Be careful barbers
Of Anaya and Gómez Farías
For if you indulge in trickery
    As with justice I suspect,

'Tis not unlikely that Acapulco
[port of embarcation for Mexico's famous penal colony]
Will see the end of your careers.[10]

The pessimism of the liberals was not surprising. One of them wrote to Gómez Farías now in exile:
"A colossal power which overwhelms everything has been created by the clergy. This has been brought about by the treachery of Santa Anna; the deception of the army by the priests; the approval of the Spaniards who hope that a change might benefit them; and the innumerable parasites, driven on by ambition, which the revolution has produced."
".... the demoralization is general; the corruption of public officials scandalous; the boldness of the clergy is without precedent, and can only be compared with the subservience of the so-called congress, and with the prostitution of the government: in short the nation having been raped sleeps wasting away."[11]
All they could do was to wait and hope.

10. Ojo alerta, maromeros
     y satélites de Anaya,
     Que hoy no mande la canalla
     Ni campan los patrioteros.
          Tened cuidado, barberos
     De Anaya y Gómez Farías,
     Como con justicia aduzco,
     No es dificil que Acapulco
     Ves terminar vuestros dias.
               —*El Mosquito Mexicano*, September 22, 1835.
    11. *Gómez Farías Papers,* García Collection, "El q. lo visitó en Aljopeca" [*sic*] to Gómez Farías, September 4, 1836.

TEXAS CAMPAIGN

EVENTS in the north now crowded fast upon each
other. The Zacatecas campaign ended the rebellion
in that neighborhood for the time being, but across
the desert to the northeast lay Texas. In the land of the blue-
bonnets the Anglo-Saxon traditions of democracy were so
strong and the distance from the rest of Mexico so great
that more or less of self-government was practiced and independent thinking was indulged in regardless of Mexican
laws. Those indefatigable federalists had long considered
Santa Anna as their friend, but now that centralism was
established the colonists determined to take matters into their
own hands in spite of Austin's reassuring statements that
Santa Anna would use his influence to grant them a measure
of self control.

A few ardent liberal spirits from Mexico were lending
moral, if not physical, support to the Texans. Among these
were such old associates of Santa Anna as Lorenzo de Zavala,
Valentín Gómez Farías and J. Antonio Mejía. Gómez
Farías in New Orleans was conferring with Texans and
ardently sponsoring liberal ideas though he was a staunch
Mexican and would not endorse the idea of a division of the
soil of the republic. Would he help to overthrow the government by force of arms? Yes, gladly! Dismember the nation?
Never! Some of the others, however, had no such scruples.

Zavala had been serving as Mexican Minister in France
when the government of his country was centralized. Forthwith he resigned from his post and went to his estate on the
San Jacinto River in Texas. He had written directly to Santa
Anna, bluntly telling him that his earlier successes had been
due to the principles for which he had fought, but that liberalism and justice would overthrow opportunism in the end.

[122]

In an address, published in Texas, August 7, 1835, Zavala directly accused Santa Anna of treason and stated that such acts as the dissolution of the state legislatures were so irregular as to "destroy all claims to obedience" on the part of the people. Such attacks from an old associate really hurt Santa Anna's pride so there is little wonder that he was so eager to get his hands on Zavala all during the northern campaign. Bulnes thought that Zavala's action in joining the revolution was due to his hatred of centralism in general but especially to his personal detestation of Santa Anna,[1] while General Vicente Filisola said the activities of Zavala "were one of the principal causes of the unfortunate Texas campaign."[2]

Mejía was more active still and embarked an expedition composed of colonists and adventurers in New Orleans. On the sixth day out from port the men were notified that their destination was Tampico and that they were to launch a movement to overthrow the Mexican despotism. About fifty of the men agreed to the scheme and the rest were driven below decks. The vessel was wrecked on a bar at the entrance of the harbor, but the handful of adventurers managed to land. To their surprise, for they expected to receive active support, the inhabitants arose with cries of "Death to the Foreigners" mingled with "Vivas" for Santa Anna: a temporary success soon became a complete failure. Most of the men escaped in a small vessel to the Texas coast but thirty-one were captured. Of these, three died of their wounds while the rest were shot on December 14, 1835. Doctor Barker comments:

"Thus ended, in relation to Texas, the Tampico Expedition. Succeeding, it would have concentrated federalist opposition in the eastern states, would have diverted Santa Anna's attention from Texas, and eventually, no doubt, after the capitulation of Cos, would have drawn Texas into active co-operation with the liberals; the dictator might have been overthrown

---

1. Bulnes, *op. cit.,* p. 845.
2. Filisola, *op. cit.,* Part II, p. 577.

on his own soil, the 'republican principles' of the constitution of 1824 preserved, and the Texas declaration of independence obviated thereby."[3]

The Texans, however, were far from dependent for inspiration upon such men as the above three. The spirit of discontent had found vigorous expression in a protest meeting at San Felipe de Austin. R. M. Williamson, the Chairman of this meeting, declared July 4, 1835: "Gen. Santa Anna, instead of being your president, has been invested by the general congress with the absolute powers of the Dictator. Elected President by the Republican Party, he no sooner took his seat than he threw off the veil of disguise, and to the amazement and consternation of the Republic Party he exhibited himself the friend and supporter of the aristocrats and defender of the Clergy." He insisted that General Martín P. Cos, brother-in-law of Santa Anna, had been ordered to Texas with 3,400 men, many of whom were from the Zacatecas expedition, and then added:

"For what Fellow-Citizens are they coming, in the name of God say not speculation; they are coming to compel you into obedience to the new form of Government; to compel you to give up your arms; to compel you to have your country garrisoned; to compel you to liberate your slaves; to compel you to swear to support and sustain the government of the Dictator; to compel you to submit to the imperial rule of the aristocracy, to pay tithes and adoration to the clergy."[4]

The agitation culminated on November 3 in a declaration of independence. This was published four days later and proved to be a direct attack on Santa Anna. Its opening words were "Whereas, General Antonio López de Santa Anna and other military chieftains have by force of arms overthrown the federal constitution" and dissolved the social compact be-

3. E. C. Barker, "The Tampico Expedition," *Texas Historical Association Quarterly*, VI, 186.

4. Barker, "Pioneer Municipalities in Texas Revolution—Mina and San Felipe. Documents, 1835," *Publications of the Southern History Association*, VIII, 9, 13.

tween the states, therefore the people of Texas establish their independence.

While these events were taking place, the Dictator was far from idle. As Yoakum commented, with most of Mexico acclaiming centralism, Texas appeared to Santa Anna like "Mordecai sitting in the king's gate." The Dictator's personal opinion of Texas, gained on his boyhood campaign, had been a very sorry one, but his friend, Juan N. Almonte, had just published a most enthusiastic report in which he boasted of the climate of the northern provinces, its enormous resources, its importance to Mexico, and the danger of its absorption by the rapidly expanding foreigners.[5]

The Dictator's conciliatory attitude to Austin's request was speedily changed. Troops later ordered to Texas had first been used in Zacatecas, but even before this Martín P. Cos, brother-in-law of Santa Anna, was ordered to Coahuila and Texas, and on August 31 the Dictator notified all departmental governors of his intention to lead a force to crush the spirit of rebellion there.

Cos reached Texas with less than a thousand men. These were divided to make as impressive a show as possible, but were promptly devoured piecemeal by the rebels. The Dictator paid little attention to this warning. Had he not been successful repeatedly where others had failed? Did he not know from boyhood experiences on the Medina and from recent efforts in Zacatecas that all northern rebels were poltroons and cowards? Little wonder then that he was in a boasting mood when visited by the French and British Ministers at Tacubaya. With flashing eye he indulged in modest hyperbole saying that he would sweep all before him, and,

5. Juan N. Almonte, *Noticia Estadística sobre Tejas;* Almonte was the son of the patriot priest Morelos and Doña Brigida Almonte. Legend says that the name was derived from the fact that when the father went on his campaign, he took the mother and child to the mountains (*al monte*) for safety, but this cannot be verified. Certainly the young man, about twenty-seven years of age at the time of the invasion of Texas, was loyal as aide-de-camp to Santa Anna during the reverses of the campaign, and was later to be able and prominent—though somewhat variable in his political affiliations—in his country's history.

if he found that the United States Government was aiding the rebels, that "he would continue the march of his army to Washington and place upon its *Capitol* the Mexican *Flag*."[6]

On receiving authorization from Congress, he set out for the front and reached San Luis Potosí on December 5. After a brief delay he continued to Saltillo which was to be used as the base of operations. This point was some three hundred desert miles from the Río Grande, while from the Río Grande to San Antonio de Bejar (San Antonio) was another 150 miles, only slightly less inviting than the first stage.

At Saltillo, his flare for organization was employed to the full for about a month, though he was handicapped, according to his *Memoirs,* by being sick in bed two weeks. Service in this section was far from popular, but the frontier states contributed with fair generosity, stimulated by speeches, proclamations and promises. These frontier garrisons, which had had so little opportunity to shine before the eyes of the glorious Santa Anna, felt that their chance had come at last.

Further to stimulate recruiting a decree was issued through the Minister of War and published in *El Mosquite Mexicano* on January 22, 1836. This declared, in the savage words of this brutal frontier warfare that, though "civil wars are always bloody," this especially ought to be a war "without remorse." It provided for a special Legion of Honor for those fighting in the contest or in other wars against a *foreign* foe. There was provided an elaborate ceremony of decoration for those receiving the honor:

"The insignia of the Legion of Honor shall be a cross or a star with five radiants. The center shall be surrounded by a crown of laurel; at one side shall be the national arms, on the other the motto, *Honor, Valor, and Country.* On the reverse side of the medal in the center shall be the name of the campaign or action for which this decoration is awarded with the words *Republica Mexicana.* This cross shall be of

6. *Consular Letters, Mexico,* Vol. II, No. 36. Report of United States Consul W. S. Parott, December 14, 1835.

silver for the cavalrymen, but of gold for all officers. The grand crosses will wear a band with red border on each edge across the right and left shoulders. This is purely a military order and shall be considered the highest honor the Mexican soldier can merit. None besides soldiers ought to obtain it."[7]

To raise and reorganize the troops was a considerable undertaking in itself, but there was much more to the task than this. The National Government was desperately resorting to forced loans since it could only secure niggardly sums of 500,000 *pesos* and 200,000 *pesos* in the open market, and that by promising to pay 45 to 48 per cent interest a year. As for forced loans the best of the four northern departments, San Luis Potosí, contributed "576 *pesos, 4 reales, 3 cuartillas,*" thus leaving a deficit of 3,979 *pesos* of the sum asked. The Commander, at his wit's end, finally entered into a contract for rations on a deferred payment plan at rates more than double those usually paid. By way of partial explanation of the exorbitant prices agreed upon it may be said that the supplies were to be delivered to the men in the field and not at stated depots. Furthermore, it was this or nothing.

It is true that some of the most favorable contracts went to friends or kinsmen of the General-in-Chief, and bond issues bearing the highest rates of interest were subscribed to by his associates. In fact, there is the very uncomfortable report that some of these bonds were kept in the possession of the President. One wonders if he actually paid the full face value in the first place, or if they were just a few left-overs.

Whatever questionable means were employed in raising men and money, the fact remained that the men were wretchedly equipped. Mules were not to be had, so oxen were employed as draft animals. Medicines and surgical equipment were almost non-existent, while surgeons and doctors were lacking to the point that frequently the officers could get no attention when sick.

Finally, eight thousand poorly equipped men set out, but

7. Amelia Williams, "Critical Study of the Siege of the Alamo," *Southwestern Historical Quarterly*, XXXVII, 5. To this study the author is substantially indebted for parts of the account that follows.

they had scarcely started across the desert when supplies became so short that the daily rations issued had to be reduced by half. Even worse were the hardships due to lack of water. As usual, many women and children accompanied the forces. The suffering among these was intense and on one day thirty of them were said to have died of thirst. The General himself was reported as suffering from an "inflamation of the stomach," and disease was rampant throughout the whole force.

The countryside itself offered no assistance. In this harsh and arid land were no food crops, only scattered chaparral and other desert bushes. The chief vegetation was composed of prickly pears aspiring to the dignity of trees as they reared themselves on fibrous trunks to a height of ten or twelve feet. Above these, at intervals, were the Spanish Daggers rising to fifteen or twenty feet with writhing and twisted branches, reminding a person of the contorted limbs of a soul in torment. The very mountains seemed wearied from the fierceness of the contest with the forces of nature. With scant covering of shrubs—for of trees there were none—they had given up the struggle to maintain individuality. Their long, sloping sides of two thousand or even three thousand feet were about all that was left, with only here and there on the summit the lingering frown of a crumbling cliff or peak that once had defied the elements with imperious majesty and haughty contempt.

The journey to the Río Grande was a heartbreaking ordeal for man and beast. In fact, many of the ranking officers had protested against using this route and had urged an attack by sea. This, Santa Anna was utterly opposed to. Word had just come that Cos had been defeated at San Antonio so he determined to strike directly for that point. To land on the coast meant some fighting there before he could reach the focal point in the center of the rebel settlements. It is true enough that an attack from the coast would have cut off the supplies being landed for his enemies, but that was a minor point to a man who held his opponents in such contempt. He fondly dreamed of one glorious dash across the known hardships of the desert and one crushing victory at the point where others had failed, then the rebellion would be over *á la Zacatecas*.

The Texans had had ample warning of the coming of the Mexicans, but this too was discounted by Santa Anna, for he naturally felt they would not expect him in midwinter. Also he felt that there were many loyal Mexicans in the region to provide him with information, and that there were the Indians to be relied upon as enemies of the settlers who had taken their lands. Incidentally, this last was another fond delusion, for the Texas plains' Indian had no intention of fighting for anyone but himself.

So it was that in the dead of winter Santa Anna advanced upon the frontier and reached Laredo long before he was expected by the rebels. Peremptory orders were issued for Cos to violate his word of honor (given to the Texans that he would not again fight them) to join the relief expedition. This raised the Mexican force to about six thousand men for the actual invasion of Texas.

The Texan population had changed greatly since the raw recruit had learned to despise them at the Battle of the Medina. Santa Anna, however, still considered them barbarians to be terrorized. All leaders captured were to be executed; all foreigners landing in armed bands since 1828 were to be considered pirates; all who had taken part in the war were to be exiled, and all peaceful foreigners were to be segregated in the interior of Mexico and far from the coast or the United States border. The property regulations were no less drastic: all expenses and losses due to the insurrection (including custom duties past due) were to be reimbursed by confiscation of property; no Anglo-American was to be allowed to settle in Texas, while land grants and sales to non-residents were to be nullified (the best lands were to go to Mexican soldiers, the balance to be sold at one dollar per acre, though the quantity allowed to English, French and German settlers was severely limited). Finally, all negroes were to be freed forthwith. There is every indication that this whole program was a deliberate policy: the one that had been regularly pursued in this northern region.

To go into details as to the military movements from Laredo to San Antonio, and then to San Jacinto would be to repeat that which has been carefully and amply studied and made available for both the scholar and general reader. To leave out the military details, it may be said that Santa Anna advanced over pretty much the same route followed in 1813 till he reached San Antonio at the end of February, 1836. By March 4, he had about five thousand men on hand.

In the fort, the Alamo, were probably one hundred and sixty men in all. This included officers and men, sick and well. Samuel Houston, the Texan commander, had ordered these men to give up the fort and withdraw. They, however, responded that they "had rather die in these ditches than give them up to the enemy." They, with Santa Anna and many other Texans, felt that this point was the key to the province. After some skirmishing, the siege lines were drawn. In communications which passed between the lines, Santa Anna let it be definitely understood that he would grant no terms other than for the garrison to surrender "at discretion." In spite of scant supplies and ammunition, Travis lost his temper, assembled his men, "harangued them and administered .... the oath of 'never surrender.'"

Santa Anna gave his final orders on the afternoon of March 5, and early next morning the men were in their places when there rang out in the early morning hush one long, clear note from a bugle. This was followed by the most dreadful and horror inspiring of all army calls of the day —the *deguello*. Far back through the centuries of the Moorish wars this call had been employed from time to time. It had been named the "fire and death" call and always signified to the enemy that no quarter would be given: that utter destruction and ruin were the only war dogs to be loosed by Mars for this battle.

The next hour saw sheer weight of numbers crush the foolhardy but gallant band. The outer and sustaining walls of the Alamo reduced, the old mission building was captured room by room, with each cell displaying its cordon of slain Mexicans at the door and one or two corpses within. Five miserable fugitives were found hiding and were brought to the Commander-in-Chief. Upbraiding the captors for chicken-heartedness and cowardice, he turned his back and left the captives to their fate. Six only in the whole fortress were spared, three women, two children and a negro servant-boy. The rest, sick, wounded or well, had been sent to meet their God. Little wonder that the cry rang through the United States: "Thermopylæ had its messenger of defeat, the Alamo had none!"

The Mexican losses can only be estimated. Santa Anna admitted seventy killed and about three hundred wounded though his Secretary, R. Martínez Coro (who later wrote a severely critical account of the whole campaign), reported three hundred killed outright plus one hundred more who died of their wounds. Clearly, the Mexicans could stand few such victories. On the other hand, the focal point of the rebellion was captured and if the whole had collapsed as in the case of Zacatecas the victory would not have been too expensively bought. Santa Anna felt that the contest was really over and was anxious to complete the details quickly. His idea was to advance through the settled parts of Texas with three bodies of troops: two to march generally eastward from San Antonio while a third under Urrea was to proceed along the coast from Matamorous, the port at the mouth of the Río Grande. In this way he could pursue the fleeing Texans under Houston and impress all the Anglo-Saxon settlements with the utter futility of future rebellions.

According to military canons of most ages, victors were entitled to a bit of relaxation and Santa Anna was seldom one to deny his men or himself such enjoyment. In some way he met a pretty girl in San Antonio and a bogus marriage ceremony is said to have been witnessed by some of his leading officers. By early April, however, it was time for him to be about more serious business, so his personal coach started the long and weary journey with a small escort, plenty of cash and a disillusioned and lonely girl back to Mexico. Somewhat later, she was duly installed as his mistress in a very good dwelling just a few doors from the public square of Jalapa, where legend still has it that she lived, childless, for many years.

Meanwhile the glad tidings of rebel defeat continued to roll in. As the month of March passed by, General José Urrea was still steadily advancing as ordered. He showed some hesitation about the execution of all prisoners, but again had been notified on the third that all foreigners captured with arms in their hands were to be considered as pirates, while all Mexicans so captured were traitors. Death to all of them!

At Goliad was a force under Commander James W. Fanning. They were surrounded by Urrea and parleys took place. To fight it out would probably mean extermination for the Texans and heavy losses for the Mexicans, so a surrender was agreed upon. Whether this was "at discretion" or with positive assurance that the lives of the Texans would be spared has been a bitterly debated point. However, these men knew the type of warfare they were engaged in, and it is incredible that they would have laid down their arms without a positive guarantee. In addition, there are the unqualified statements of a few survivors. Certain it is that Urrea ordered no executions of these prisoners and recommended clemency to his Chief.

The following letter of Santa Anna, dated March 23, 1830, on the subject explains itself:

"To General Urrea &c:—

Under date of the present, I have stated to the commandant of the post of Goliad, as follows:—

By a communication made to me by Colonel D. F. Garay, of that place, I am informed that there have been sent to you by General Urrea, *two hundred and thirty-four prisoners,* taken in the action of *Encinal del Perdido (Coleta)*, on the nineteenth and twentieth of the present month; and as the supreme government has ordered that all foreigners taken with arms in their hands, making war upon the nation, shall be treated as pirates, I have been surprised that the circular of the said supreme government has not been fully complied with in this particular; *I therefore order, that you should give immediate effect to the said ordinance in respect to all*

[132]

those foreigners who have yielded to the force of arms, having had the audacity to come and insult the republic, to devastate with fire and sword, as has been the case in Goliad, causing vast detriment to our citizens; in a word, shedding the precious blood of Mexican citizens, whose only crime has been their fidelity to their country. I trust that, in *reply* to this, you will inform me that *public vengeance has been satisfied* by the punishment of such detestable delinquents."[8]

Urrea himself later insisted that the men surrendered at discretion, but stated that "every soldier in my division was confounded at the news; *all was amazement and consternation*" at receipt of news of the diabolical order. The actual order for the execution was sent by Santa Anna to Colonel J. M. Portilla, who was in charge of the unfortunate prisoners, and reached him on the twenty-sixth. At daybreak the next morning the garrison and prisoners (Portilla said 445) were awakened. Eight of the Texans were to be spared for they had been captured when not under arms. The others were marched out into the clear spring morning, many thinking this was the first step toward liberty. As the sun shed its early rays on a bright landscape there were a few sharp, nervous military orders. Volley after volley of rifle fire poured into the helpless victims till all that remained was a group of Mexican soldiers holding their smoking guns, and a mass of still warm corpses so numerous that the only feasible way to dispose of them was by means of a gigantic funeral pyre. When the firing started a number of men took a desperate chance and dashed for the nearby bushes and trees. About thirty-five escaped, but the dead were variously estimated at from three hundred and thirty to three hundred and eighty-five.

The responsibility for this ghastly deed must rest squarely upon Santa Anna. This was no man trained in so-called civilized warfare where deviltry at least masqueraded behind a code, and such conduct was a definite part of the military art as he knew it. Had he later marched back to Mexico in

8. H. Yoakum, *History of Texas from its first settlement in 1685 to its annexation to the United States in 1846*, II, 517.

triumph, beyond doubt he would have been hailed as a great conqueror who had promptly punished traitors. Captured by the enemy and his expedition a failure however, he was to be violently denounced as a cruel, bloodthirsty wretch, who did not have the elements of humanity in his make-up. The criticism had all the more effect when the storm of indignation throughout the United States became known and when the British and French Ministers at Mexico protested formally against such severities.

Meanwhile the campaign went merrily on with Houston steadily retreating. "Universal consternation" had seized the coast country and there was open talk of displacing Houston and trying another leader, even if mutiny had to be resorted to. The Mexicans, of course, were all the more confident that the war was over. The one ominous fact for them was that Houston's men, though bitterly disappointed and discouraged, had not disbanded and given up the contest.

In early April, the Mexican Commander himself accompanied part of the troops on the march to east Texas. His idea was to advance through the heart of the country, make a demonstration close to the United States border, and then to return to Mexico by sea. For this purpose, a boat had already been ordered to the coast. General Vicente Filisola was to be left in charge of affairs when the President returned to Mexico. This officer did not like the looks of the situation and, supported by some other officers, protested so effectively that Santa Anna agreed to stay awhile longer and to leave behind most of the troops when he did depart.

Soon after this, word reached the Mexican camp that the Texas government was at Harrisburg, down on the coast and close to Galveston. A dash to the village revealed a score of wooden houses, but no able bodied men in the town. Santa Anna then went over to New Washington where Colonel Almonte had captured a few military supplies. This dreary campaign amidst swamps and lagoons where the chief enemies were mosquitoes and an occasional sharp-shooter, was getting on the Commander's nerves. Also, there was no sizeable towns to stop in. The luxuries of life and lady friends, which he had learned to appreciate so much in the last few years, were lacking. True, he was always glad to give these up for excitement and military glory; but where was either excitement or glory in these swamps? What kind of enemy was this that was forever being defeated and cut to pieces, and who always retreated, but did not know when he was licked? Was it possible that the great Military Commander of Mexico was being made a fool of by being led into chasing a ghost—or by being led into a trap?

The morning of April 20 found the somewhat worried and taut Commander in the single narrow street of New Washington when a courier brought the news that Houston had suddenly appeared a few miles away at Lynchburg and killed some Mexicans. What did this mean? The Texans were supposed to be more than fifty miles away! Was the trap about to be sprung? Was he in it? His excitement rising at the mere thought, Santa Anna's self control snapped and spurring his horse he dashed down the street yelling "The enemy is on us! The enemy is on us!" Though he probably would have explained this as prompt issuance of orders to prepare for possibilities, the effect on the men must have been disconcerting to say the least.

The truth was that Houston, goaded on all sides had determined to act and was moving quickly. On the nineteenth, he had written that he was "in preparation to meet Santa Anna. It is the only chance of saving Texas.... We go to conquer. It is wisdom growing out of necessity to meet the enemy now; every consideration enforces it."[9] Both bodies of troops were about equal in size for Houston admitted that he had 783 men and Santa Anna had between 750 and 800. Some say that the Texan should have struck just as soon as he made contact, i.e., on the twentieth. However, his men were tired from strenuous marching so he saw fit to wait.

Santa Anna was delighted on the morning of the twenty-first to receive about four hundred reinforcements under General Cos. This restored his numerical advantage, his equanimity and his contempt for the foe. The new arrivals needed

9. *Ibid.*, II, 498.

rest, however, so casual orders were issued to place sentinels while the troops were allowed to eat and take a *siesta,* in spite of the fact that the enemy was nearby and the location of the Mexicans anything but well suited for a battle. The President himself retired to his tent and surrendered to the wooings of Morpheus.

Houston's men advanced silently through the woods and prepared to spring upon their prey. All romance, however, demanded a band to fill the air with martial strains and cheer the cohorts into battle. The Texans unfortunately at this time seemed able to boast of one lone flute or fife but this bravely did its duty and piped away at the popular love song of the day: "Will You Come to my Bower I Have Shaded for You?"[10] The falsetto notes were soon drowned in the roar of the dreaded war whoops and blood-curdling yells of: "Remember the Alamo!" "Remember Goliad!" and "Death to Santa Anna." Like men possessed the Texans dashed upon the startled enemy. In the Mexican camp all was turmoil and confusion, Houston reporting: "The conflict lasted about eighteen minutes from the time of close action until we were in possession of the enemy's encampment." Then followed sporadic single shots or little flurries of firing as the pursuit was continued by grim frontiersmen who were determined to avenge the earlier tragedies of the war.

The Texans lost six killed and twenty-four wounded. Among the latter was Houston, who had his right leg shattered just above the ankle. Houston reported that the Mexicans had lost 630 killed, 208 wounded and 730 prisoners. The number of prisoners is probably more or less correct, but the other figures were simply estimates which were obvious exaggerations since there were only about 1,150 Mexicans present

10. Professor Samuel E. Asbury, an authority on Texas Revolutionary music, informs me that the author was Tom Moore of *Llalla Rhook* fame. He also calls attention to the fact that Mr. Moore had the song omitted from most of his collections, probably because of the salacious character of one of the stanzas. This very character, of course, would practically guarantee its popularity with Houston's men and made it not entirely inappropriate to be sung to Santa Anna.

when the battle began. Whatever the exact figures, however, the rout was complete.

Just after the alarm was given, Santa Anna rushed from his tent to find the situation hopeless. One of his aides pictured him as bewildered, wringing his hands and not knowing what to do. If orders were issued, they fell upon dazed brains and deaf ears. The Commander secured a horse from an aide and with two companions dashed off, hoping, as he said, to join General Filisola who was some forty or fifty miles away. On reaching the place where a bridge had been built over the San Jacinto, he found the structure burned. His horse bogged down in the mud and his companions fled, so he hid among some small pine trees. Later under cover of night, he waded across the stream.

The next morning he found some cast off garments in a deserted cabin. He promptly took off his uniform, changed clothes and thus continued on his way in blue cotton jacket, linen trousers, cap, and red morocco slippers. About noon on the twenty-second, the mud plastered fugitive had reached a bit of level and fairly open ground just as a party of five Texans, hunting fugitives, spied him. He at once fell in the grass and tried to cover himself with a blanket. When ordered to rise, he reluctantly did so.

Ingratiatingly he advanced and shook hands, then asked for General Houston. When asked who he was, he first answered that he was a common soldier. However, his bearing and fine shirt studs obviously belied the claim, so he finally said he was an aide to Santa Anna. When he insisted that he could walk no further, one of the men took him up and the two rode toward camp on the same horse. His captors considered him just another Mexican and paid so little attention to him that James A. Sylvester, who first saw him, did not even return to camp with the party. On reaching camp, however, some of the other prisoners at once acclaimed the captive as "The President!"

Thus, the Texas campaign, and in fact the Texas war, was ended. The grand triumphal march had collapsed in complete disaster. Before Santa Anna was to leave this land he had so haughtily entered, the branding iron of the contempt, scorn and hatred of the Texans was to sear an indelible mark upon his very being. He might later muster fair words for individual generous leaders, but hatred of Texans as a whole was to become part and parcel of his very thinking.

ECLIPSE

THE captive general was at once taken to Houston, who was seated under a tree attempting to ease the pain in his badly wounded foot. "Houston," says Santa Anna, "on recognizing me, shook hands and spoke courteously," while word was sent to Almonte, also a prisoner, to come and act as interpreter. Santa Anna, who was almost exhausted, sat down on a tool chest. According to common belief in Texas, he gave the Masonic distress signal which was said to have been recognized by J. A. Wharton who later used his influence to save the prisoner's life.

The Mexican was highly nervous and excited till his request for opium with which to calm his nerves was granted. Then once more master of himself, he with the frankest egotism skillfully flattered Houston as the conqueror of the Napoleon of the West, and entered into negotiations forthwith. The Texan demurred, saying that this was the prerogative of the civil government. In response, Santa Anna, who probably knew something and suspected more of the friction that had developed on the Houston retreat, characteristically answered: "I dislike to have anything to do with civilians, and would much rather treat with the general of the army."

When Houston took him to task about the Alamo massacre, Santa Anna readily answered that the lives of the defenders were sacrificed by the men themselves who, when they obviously could not hold the fortress, had nevertheless insisted on defending it for the chief reason that they could thereby slaughter a large number of the enemy. As for the Goliad butchery, Santa Anna cooly stated that he knew nothing whatever of any terms of surrender and that he had merely ordered that the commands of the national government be carried out. It has already been seen that this man

[139]

would occasionally lose control of himself and become panic stricken or fly into a passion, but, for the most part, his facile brain and fluent tongue were far more than a match for his opponents.

The most surprising development at this stage of the proceedings was the foresight of the classically trained adventurer and former governor of Tennessee, Samuel Houston. While his men were clamoring for revenge and the blood of Santa Anna, Houston steadily insisted that the prisoner was worth more to Texas alive than dead. Executed, there were still over four thousand Mexican troops under the quite able Filisola to be met, as well as additional thousands, who would almost certainly be sent up from Mexico. Alive and a prisoner, there was an excellent chance to hold him as a hostage in order to secure a satisfactory treaty as well as the withdrawal of the Mexican forces without more bloodshed. Houston was now the victor, but the memory of that long retreat was still fresh in his mind. The god of battles had only reluctantly smiled after many a weary day for the Texans: it would be foolish to tempt him again.

As the Texans moved their camp from the decomposing bodies on the battlefield, the negotiations opened. T. J. Rusk, the Texan Secretary of War, made certain proposals, which were somewhat softened and then agreed to in the form of two treaties, signed May 14, 1836: the one to please the bloodthirsty Texan soldiers, and the other for practical use—and, not surprisingly, to be kept secret. By the public treaty, all fighting was to cease; and the Mexicans agreed to retreat beyond the Río Grande as speedily as possible, acquiring by purchase only such supplies as they needed on the way. In addition, all materials captured by the Mexicans were to be returned and prisoners were to be exchanged. Meanwhile, Santa Anna was to be sent to Veracruz "as soon as it is thought advisable (*conveniente*)," though he was not again to take up arms against Texas.

The secret treaty was a personal triumph for the uneducated Santa Anna as a negotiator. It provided: "Antonio López de Santa Anna, General-in-Chief of the Army of

Operations and President of the Mexican Republic, pledges himself [not his nation] solemnly before the Government established in Texas, to the fulfillment of the following articles." Then followed the provisions: that he would not again take up arms or aid in the war against Texan independence, but would take steps to remove Mexican troops from Texan soil; that he would "prepare the Mexican Cabinet to receive a peace commission" from Texas, *though Texas was not to extend beyond the Río Grande* (this skillfully reversed the emphasis as found in the public treaty); and that Texas was to send him to Veracruz "without loss of time."

These provisions were sufficiently different and vague for Santa Anna to be able to boast later:

"In short, I offered nothing in the name of the Nation: in my own only did I agree to provisions which my Government had the right to nullify, and I received in return the promise of being placed at liberty without delay. Where is there treason in this? Where the cowardly pusillanimity which I was accused of?"[1]

But all was not going well. Many Texans wanted vengeance and could only be restrained with some concrete proof of immediate results. So Santa Anna instructed his second in command, Filisola, to order all Mexican troops to retreat since an armistice had been agreed upon (it had not). The latter Commander was now in a most difficult position. Was a prisoner of war in position to send orders? Would obedience in ordering a retreat not mean almost certain criticism and court martial?[2] Would not failure to retreat mean almost certain death for Santa Anna with a resulting storm of popular wrath that would probably ruin the unlucky Filisola?

1. Santa Anna, *Las Guerras de Mexico con Tejas y los Estados Unidos,* p. 58.

2. Filisola was actually called back from Texas to answer charges before a court martial in spite of the fact that Tornel, the Minister of War, wrote on May 15 that he should proceed "with great prudence so as not to compromise in any manner the life of the illustrious general Santa Anna." Finally, after the passage of an anxious year, Filisola did justify himself and was reinstated in his command.

So, while resenting the tone of Santa Anna's letter and in spite of the protests of General Urrea, Filisola ordered his troops to retire beyond the Río Grande. Heavy rains had set in and the retreat became a nightmare of horrors for the dispirited and broken troops whose morale was fast disappearing. The famous black mud of the Texas prairies was able enough to weaken the spirits of the best troops, to say nothing of men half clothed, poorly disciplined, on half or no rations, who had just had their dreams of victory rudely snatched away, and had been told they were defeated and must retreat. The stragglers are pictured as plodding along, carrying whatever plunder they could secure: one man with a load of smoothing irons, his wife with a burden of crockery ware, all tea pots; others with kegs of lard or boxes of candles to be carried four hundred miles through a summer's sun out of the mud and across a semi-desert to distant Monterrey or beyond.

So far so good, but the situation was still complicated for Santa Anna. Partly to get him away from the rabble the Texan officials took their prisoner on board the *Yellowstone* and set out for Velasco, near Galveston, on May 5. It was on this trip that his personality had a chance to mitigate the harsh terms that Rush had first proposed for the treaty. The prisoner's brilliant conversation on history and politics, on the beauties of nature in the Texas swamps and on women as the "gravy of society" quite captivated his hearers, most of whom found themselves very inferior in the graceful turning of compliments and in the social amenities to their hostage.

Houston now went on to New Orleans to secure medical treatment for his quite troublesome wound. This was a severe setback to Santa Anna's hopes of an early return to Mexico for while President Burnet, W. H. Wharton and others felt as Houston did still they did not have the influence of the Victor of San Jacinto. On the other hand, M. B. Lamar, of the Texan Cabinet, was only expressing popular clamor when he denounced Santa Anna as the "Nero of his day" and the "foe of all virtue" who would not and could not carry out the terms of the treaty.

Only a few days after Lamar's outburst, plans were completed and Santa Anna and three of his staff were transferred on board the armed schooner *Invincible* which was to transport them and two Texan commissioners to Veracruz. But chance took a hand this same day, June 1, when 230 volunteers for the Texan cause arrived at Velasco from New Orleans. They had arrived just too late to be heroes, so they had to prove their mettle by heaping insults on the fallen Mexicans and by howling for blood. Their courage grew with the noise they made and imprecations were soon hurled at the Texan President for making the treaty. Burnet did not know what to do and asked advice of the commander of the newcomers. The response was unhesitating: "in accordance with the overwhelming public will of the citizens of the country, he should remand the prisoner ashore and await the public will to determine his fate." The President replied he would do so, and an order to that effect was promptly issued. Meanwhile Santa Anna thought that he was safely on his way home and had just issued a surprising farewell to the Texan army as follows:

"My Friends: I have been a witness to your courage in the field of battle, and know you to be generous. Rely with confidence on my sincerity, and you shall never have cause to regret the kindness shown me. In returning to my native land, I beg you will receive the thanks of your grateful friend. Farewell!

Ant°. Lopez de Santa Anna

Velasco, June 1, 1836."

The plunge from joyous anticipation and scheming as to how he could best camouflage the Texan disaster and create new political capital at home, to the immediate facing of death was too much. Black despair seized upon the Hero of Tampico and again his self control snapped. He blustered, pled, and protested hysterically. He was fully convinced that if he left the vessel for the shore that he would go to certain death. In his own account, he says he earnestly begged to be killed on board rather than to be taken back to his enemies. Finally, after some two hours of frenzied expostulation, the threat to place him in-irons and carry him ashore (plus, probably, the effect of more opium) had the desired effect, and he consented to go peaceably.

On nearing the shore, he agreed to wave the Texan flag to pacify the crowd that had collected. The "whole company cheered [jeered?] while the prisoner attempted tremulously to wave it, in which [act] he had to be assisted by Captain Brown, so physically unnerved was he for the task."[3]

On June 9, he sent a forceful protest to President Burnet against various alleged violations of the treaty. Yoakum commented that the President was powerless due to the state of public opinion, but that the protest was well founded insofar as it referred to the treatment of the prisoner.

In the excited state of mind of many Texans, almost any tale as to the finery (some of his jewelry, silver plate and monogramed china were said to have been captured at San Jacinto), rascality and debauchery of Santa Anna was believed and the clamor for revenge continued. There are still current in Texas reasonably authentic accounts that at least one stout colonial dame had her private plans to shoot the prisoner—and came perilously close to success. Then on June 27, a drunken soldier actually rushed by the guard and fired through the window into the small room where Santa Anna and two companions were confined. Rumors of assassination were more or less constant so it is not surprising that the Mexican became melancholy what with his own violent emotions and passions, the experience of being placed in irons from time to time, and the actual danger that existed.

An abortive attempt by a young Spaniard named Bartholomew Pagés to aid Santa Anna to escape only made matters worse.[4] However, really powerful influences were at work on the prisoner's behalf. Time is a marvelous soothing syrup for inflamed passions. Every day that passed made the prisoner's

3. Raines, *op. cit.*, p. 376. Quoted from the account of General T. J. Green.
4. R. M. Caro, *Verdadera Idea*, p. 57 ff.

life materially safer. Burnet, who after all was the President; S. F. Austin, the long recognized spokesman for the Texans; and blunt Sam Houston, who soon returned to Texas, all used their powerful influence to secure the release of the captive.

Soon Houston was elected President of Texas and took office anxious to settle matters. When his congress placed control of all prisoners except Santa Anna and Almonte in his hands, he vetoed the act as unconstitutional and proceeded to take charge of all of them for he was satisfied that he could use Santa Anna to good advantage. As early as June 4, the prisoner had written to President Jackson of the United States, asking that he use his prestige to have the provisions of the general agreements, signed just after the Battle of Jacinto, carried out in full. This letter was supported by one from S. F. Austin (who may have suggested to Santa Anna that Jackson could be a powerful friend) showing the value of returning Santa Anna to Mexico and of Jackson taking a definite hand in the Texas situation. Old Hickory responded two months later that the Mexican Minister in Washington informed him that the Mexican Government had officially repudiated the Dictator who now had no political or military standing, and that consequently the United States could not deal with him. However, the United States President continued, his government would be glad to have Mexico accept its good offices to end the civil war. Then, on the same day, Jackson wrote to Houston saying of Santa Anna: "His person is still of much consequence to you. He is the pride of the Mexican soldiers, and the favorite of the priesthood. While he is in your power, the difficulties of your enemy, in raising another army, will continue to be great. The soldiers of Mexico will not willingly march into Texas, when they know that their advance may cost their favorite general his life. Let not his blood be shed, unless imperious necessity demands it as a retaliation for future Mexican massacres. Both wisdom and humanity enjoin this course in relation to Santa Anna."[5]

5. Yoakum, *op. cit.*, II, 195 note.

By this time, Houston had about decided on his plan of action. To speed matters somewhat, Santa Anna wrote Houston on October 24, pointing out that his repudiation by the Mexican Cabinet in communication to Washington only made his return to Mexico the more essential. He stated that if he remained a prisoner the treaty agreements would certainly not be carried out, but that if he returned to Mexico he might be able to help the situation. On November 5, he frankly admitted that Texas would never reunite with Mexico and that attempts at reconquest would be "imprudent." He considered the outstanding issue to be one of boundaries and one that could best be settled by direct conversations in Washington.[6] After conferring with his prisoner at some length, Houston issued the orders so Santa Anna and Almonte set out for the United States Capital at the end of November in company with the Inspector-General of Texas, George W. Hockley, Colonel Bernard E. Bee, and Major William H. Patton.

The journey was no minor matter for it meant a trip by stagecoach across Texas and Louisiana to the Mississippi. Winter weather was coming on and roads were bad indeed, but this way lay freedom. On December 14, Bee wrote to Houston, saying that for twelve days they had traveled "more through water than on land" and added that Santa Anna had remarked that he thought they "would have made better progress in the Independence [vessel] Commodore Hawkins —than on our ponys." However, they pushed on steadily by coach, horseback or boat until they reached Plaquemine. From there, they proceded to Natchez by boat and on up the Father of Waters and the Ohio to Louisville, Kentucky, which they reached Christmas Day, 1836.[7]

The journey was through the heart of a region where Santa Anna was looked upon as a fiend incarnate. One observer commented on him as "tolerably pleasant of countenance and speech (which is exclusively Spanish), very po-

6. *Ibid.*, pp. 530-31.
7. George P. Garrison, *Diplomatic Correspondence of the Republic of Texas*, II, Part I, 427.

lite, and using stately compliments." However, it is noticed that he kept out of sight in his stateroom because of a well understood fear that he might be attacked by friends of the Alamo and Goliad victims who had come from this section. The long strain and the hardships and exposures of traveling had given him a severe cold and it was feared that serious complications might develop. After a few days, a physician by the name of Doctor Dudley said he could continue the journey on January 5, but insisted that it would be wise to secure a special conveyance so as to avoid night travel. Two fine four-horse coaches were reported to have been obtained at a cost of $500.00 for the trip from Lexington to Wheeling, West Virginia. Before the party left Lexington, however, a large number of the members of the state legislature then in session at Frankfort, Kentucky, came over to pay their respects. This was probably more morbid curiosity than anything else, but it was significant and something of a compliment to his personality that there was no effort to injure the prisoner at any point on the trip.

On passing through Frederick, Maryland, Santa Anna called on General E. P. Gaines, who had for so long been engaged along the southwestern frontier in suppressing Indian raids and in tantalizing Mexico. Colonel Almonte had meanwhile gone ahead to Washington to make preparations for the visit of his Chief. Some apprehension was naturally felt, for Santa Anna had no official standing, and Jackson was known to sympathize ardently with the Texans and his old friend, Houston. The Mexican Minister had reported, on May 30, 1836, on the attitude of the general public in Washington. He said everyone had given up the Texas cause as practically hopeless when the astounding news of San Jacinto arrived. He continued: "Never have I seen greater surprise, nor more indecent joy than that which the news produced in these people, who believed it implicitly as an article of faith without stopping to examine its origin, circumstances and the numerous contradictions. Men and women, large and small, educated and ignorant, all congratulated each other as though their own salvations were in volved, and they all felt that now they could freely express their own hatred of Mexico. On that day nothing else was talked of in the Senate and certainly the expressions employed were not those due to the decorum and gravity of that body."[8]

Most of the bitterness had now passed, however, and a spirit of reaction provided a very pleasant round of receptions and entertainments for the handsome and unusual stranger. Congressmen and other officials called upon him and, before long, a meeting was arranged with the President and his cabinet in spite of the fact that the Mexican Chargé d'affaires refused to have anything to do with the arrangements and even declined to be in Washington at the time.

President Jackson gave a dinner at the White House, "attended by noble persons, both national and foreigners," says Santa Anna. However, there is no word as to ceremony or formality, so one rather suspects that the visitor from the Halls of the Montezumas was not overly impressed by the surroundings of Old Hickory. Nevertheless a very clear understanding was obviously reached. The Texan Commissioner in Washington, W. H. Wharton, carefully reported his conversations with both Santa Anna and Jackson just after the two had met, and gave a remarkably concrete account of the agreement, both as to the provisions the Texan approved and those he disagreed with.

In spite of Wharton's protest that his country had gained its independence, it was obvious that the President and the former Dictator had discussed what amounted to a balancing of United States claims against Mexico with what the northern republic would pay for a quit claim to Texas. Jackson mollified the protesting Texas Commissioner who insisted that Texas had won its independence already by saying that this was a matter of form only and that the United States "obtained no claim or shadow of jurisdiction over Texas without her full and free assent." Santa Anna in turn told the Texan that the United States had once offered Mexico $13,000,000 for Texas, but that, of course, he would not think of asking

8. Antonio de la Peña y Reyes, *Don Manuel Eduardo de Gorostiza y la cuestión de Texas,* pp. 148-49.

[148]

that much now that Texas had declared its independence (The sum actually under discussion was $3,500,000). His only reason, he insisted, was to satisfy the Mexican people and make the cessions more palatable to them under the guise of a sale. "He [Santa Anna] concluded, by jocularly saying, that the United States had an overflowing treasury, about which there was much debate and squabbling, and he hoped that I as the Minister of Texas would not oppose any obstacles to his obtaining a few millions from this Govt. for a quit claim to Texas...."[9]

That Jackson expected Santa Anna to regain power and carry these tentative agreements into effect was obvious. The actual negotiations, however, as Professor Barker suggests,[10] were hardly more than a jockeying for position with each of the parties securing about all that he had expected. Santa Anna secured his freedom; Jackson and the Texans the "admission from the Mexican statesman best qualified to know that Mexico could not conquer Texas and ought therefore to recognize its independence."

Some accounts have it that Jackson was captivated by the courteous and gallant Mexican. Certainly he was never one to express love for Spaniard or Mexican, yet he issued orders for the United States frigate *Pioneer* to carry Santa Anna and Almonte to Veracruz. The passengers boarded the vessel February 2. Santa Anna had been to Washington—not to plant the Mexican flag on the Capitol, as he had so proudly boasted, but practically as a prisoner to endorse the planting of the Texan, if not the United States flag, on what had been Mexican soil to the Río Grande. And, when it was all over, he had left there as the guest of the northern Republic.

The *Pioneer* enjoyed such light winds that Veracruz was not reached until the twenty-first. During the trip, the former Dictator, now repudiated and a mere private citizen, had time to think and plan how to meet the home situation that had so changed in the year of his absence. The death of acting

9. Garrison, *op. cit.,* pp. 187-90. Reports of W. H. Wharton, the Texan Commissioner for February 1, 1837, and February 16, 1837.
10. Eugene C. Barker, *The Life of Stephen F. Austin,* pp. 518-19.

President Barragán on March 1, 1836, from typhoid fever had removed one staunch friend and supporter. Congress had then promptly selected the somewhat colorless José Justo Corro to take over the administration but the defeat of the expeditionary force at San Jacinto was a serious blow both to the pride and popularity of those in office. The heavy expenditures and the reckless contracts undertaken by the treasury had left the new executive with his best army officers removed, his prestige weakened and his financial affairs in chaos. Thus it is not surprising that numerous revolts had broken out in Guadalajara, Guanajuato, Oaxaca and elsewhere when word of the San Jacinto debâcle reached the country. It is true the rebels had made little headway but more and more of the people wished for the return of Anastasio Bustamante to take the president's office. His administration of a few years before had been financially efficient and genuinely conservative so that he could readily fit into the new constitutional set-up. Likewise his consistency strongly recommended him over the spectacular plunger who had disappeared in the north.

A military hero defeated is a hero no longer, unless perchance he dies in the wreck of his movement and so becomes a martyr. When acting President Corro heard of Santa Anna's capture he at once ordered all national flags to half mast and all military standards to be draped in mourning till the prisoner was released This, however, only advertised the fact that the hero was no more—and that he was no martyr.

In the scramble for power in process just before Santa Anna reached Mexico, the former Dictator's few friends were too wise to be very conspicuous. *El Mosquito Mexicano* and some individuals supported him, but, as rumors of the Texan negotiations were bruited about, these supporters had less and less to say. The administration officially forgot him as soon as possible, taking the stand that he was simply a captured military officer who had no civil status. The United States Minister, Powhatan Ellis, reported October 11, 1836: "Those in power are exceedingly fearful lest Santa Anna return. The official disclaimers which they have made of his acts since he became a prisoner of war, leave them no hope of place or preferment."[11]

No one knew Mexican psychology better than Santa Anna and his reported statement on leaving Texas reflected his ideas when he said: "You have kept me too long. The Presidency will have passed into other hands; and on my return I shall have to retire to my *hacienda* shorn of all power, and incapable, however desirous, of carrying out my pledges."[12] The elections, it is true, were postponed until January, 1837. But, when the electoral machine ground out its returns, Bustamante received fifty-seven votes and the former hero, two!

As has been noted above, Santa Anna might lose control of his nerves and passions when caught unprepared, but with a short notice he was a magnificent gambler. He knew quite well that there might easily be a violent demonstration against him on landing at Veracruz, and that physical violence might even be attempted. Though he grimly kept silent, the offer of Lieutenant J. Tattnall to land with him, thus lending the support of a United States uniform, was gratefully accepted.

Word rapidly spread through the city that Santa Anna was about to land. Crowds hurriedly collected on the mole, and several regiments of troops were called out for the "unstable elements were in violent commotion and no one could foretell the results." As Tattnall and Santa Anna "stepped from the barge upon the wharf and walked up, arm in arm, there ensued a profound silence in the multitude of late so vociferous and swayed by conflicting emotions. As they approached the soldiery, a change appeared to come over their thoughts and purposes. The salute was given, the band struck up, the colors drooped amidst the most enthusiastic vivas from soldiers, citizens and rabble."[13] Tattnall extended his protection for several days and actually accompanied Santa Anna to his estate to be sure that all was well.

11. *Mexico, Despatches,* Ellis to Forsythe, VII (Ellis, No. 27).
12. Raines, *op. cit.,* II, 444.
13. Charles C. Jones, *The Life and Services of Commodore Josiah Tattnall,* p. 45.

Before long, the veteran was planning his "come back." He was too shrewd to bid for office openly, but quietly bided his time. Beyond publishing a vigorous report on the Texas campaign he simply relied upon the normal reaction of the people against the prosaic Bustamante. His report was an eight thousand word defense addressed to the Minister of War in which he insisted that he "would have suffered a thousand deaths before subscribing" to any agreement in Texas containing the remotest reflection upon the honor of Mexico. At the same time, he so severely condemned Filisola and others for their failures and weaknesses on the northern campaign as to lay himself open to the accusation that he was trying to make others suffer for his own poor judgment and mistakes. However, he was not entirely without gratitude for he warmly commended Colonel Almonte for his consistency and fidelity, and declared General Woll worthy of all praise.

All talk of bringing Santa Anna to trial for the events of the northern campaign was soon dropped (a most wise action for his political opponents), and Congress simply asked him to explain his conduct while a prisoner and on the Washington trip. His answer appeared in a 108 page pamphlet, published in May, but this contained no new material worthy of note. He remained quietly at Manga de Clavo for about eighteen months of country life. During this period some wanted him to protest the election of Bustamante but he promptly declined. Instead he took the oath to support the new constitution on March 9, 1837, adding: "God and my honor, all that is most sacred in Heaven and on earth, bear witness forever to this duty, so pleasant to me. May it be thus to all Mexicans; and may the constitution thus affirm peace and happiness to the nation eternally."[14] He also published an open letter dated July 7, in which he approved the constitution except as amended by legal procedure, and definitely condemned all revolutionary activity, saying that his own public career was forever ended.

Though revolts and dissatisfaction were widespread on the part of both federalists and those who could be classed as

14. Rivera, *op. cit.*, Tomo III, p. 313.

[152]

Santanistas, still Santa Anna continued the rôle of gentleman farmer. His estate of Manga de Clavo extended from within a few miles of Veracruz to the edge of the plateau, with its peons by the hundreds and its livestock by the thousands. From whence? 'Tis probably best to answer with the famous Mexican gesture composed of raising the eyebrows, innocently shrugging the shoulders, tossing the hands gently outward with the palms up, accompanied by the gently breathed query: *"Quien sabe?"* (Who knows?)

Thus passed in peace and quiet the remainder of 1837, and spring, summer and autumn of 1838. Many fancied that the brilliant star of the Hero of Tampico had been only a meteor that had flown its course and had been permanently extinguished. The truth was that the Texas episode was merely an eclipse whose umbra had already passed and whose penumbra was just about to vanish with that breath-taking suddenness so characteristic of Mexican politics, which leave the inhabitants dazed, and the sober historian convinced that his *cold* facts excel the acknowledged fantasies of fiction.

VINDICATION

THE management of an estate (princely though it might be) was dreary work for a man in his prime who had been engaged in active military or political campaigns for a quarter of a century. Manga de Clavo could provide little excitement beyond periodical quarrels with neighboring landlords over a few head of cattle or over grazing rights. On the estate itself occasional interest would attach to some jealous lovelorn swain who saw fit to dispose of a rival for serenading his sweetheart, with the resulting complications to be straightened out. But such affairs were petty indeed to the man who had been dictator of the nation and who had so fondly thought that he was becoming a figure of world renown.

In the broader field of national affairs conditions were badly confused. Gómez Farías returned from exile in February, 1838, and still had assurances of considerable support for his liberal principles. However, the whole liberal movement was seriously discredited because of the fact that the Texan liberals had maintained their principles to the point of declaring their independence, hence were to be classified as little better than traitors. Too, certain old associates of Gómez Farías, such as Zavala and Mejía, had thrown in their lot with the Texans. It is not surprising then that Santa Anna was now a confirmed conservative who strongly disapproved of those whom he termed the *sansculottes.*[1]

The gravity of the situation was also strikingly obvious in connection with the army. In spite of the increased number of regulars due to the Texan War the army was more disorganized than ever before. Guillermo Prieto, with delight-

1. Rough, ragged fellows unable to afford breeches; hence, the popular party.

[154]

ful humor and sarcasm, remarked upon his youthful experience as a soldier at this time. When he appeared on the drill field, he had never fired a gun and was frankly afraid of one. However, he found himself in the rear rank with a druggist's clerk in front of him. The orders were given to load and fire. By his own account: "I closed my eyes....and said under my breath to the druggist "God help you!"....When I opened my eyes, the druggist was getting up off the ground badly frightened and bruised. I had singed his bushy hair and he wished to devour me....On returning to the barracks expecting arrest or some such thing I found I had been made a sergeant—so as to prevent me from firing any more guns ....Now you can see what a fool I was for not following the glorious career of arms in which I had secured such a quick and unexpected promotion."[2]

To make matters worse, the continued military and financial inefficiency had aroused the indignation and cupidity, if not the expansionist sentiment, of the French. Some roistering Mexican soldiers had destroyed a bakery, inflicting possibly a thousand *pesos* damage on the owner, a Frenchman. As some five years passed, distance had lent such enchantment to the view that now a demand for the neat little sum of sixty thousand *pesos* damages was presented through diplomatic channels. This, together with claims from other sources, gave a total of six hundred thousand *pesos* that the French wished to collect. Little wonder that the trouble which ensued was dubbed "The Pastry War" (*Guerra de los Pasteles*). The French demands were blandly ignored or met with evasive answers till the Minister of that country asked for his passports on April 20, 1838. These were duly forwarded to him two days later.

Of course, any man and people are entitled to reasonable recreation, but, with such matters pending and intervention a strong probability, it seems rather ridiculous to find the President, Bustamante, all wrought up over a bull and tiger fight. The incident would not be worth noting except for the fact that it helps to explain the situation of

2. Guillermo Prieto, *Memorias de mis Tiempos, 1828 a 1840,* pp. 277-78.

which Santa Anna was to take advantage shortly. A forlorn Bengal tiger, far from his native haunts, was dumped into the bull ring to fight a Mexican bull. The President graced the spectacle, and, together with the masses of the people, went into ecstasies of joy as the bull, symbolizing his native land, gored and tossed the foreign invader in the contest. Flowers were showered upon the victorious animal, whose life was spared from further jeopardy in the bull ring, while the President and others clamored for the privilege of buying him.

From such vicarious demonstrations of patriotism the nation was abruptly aroused when a French fleet appeared in April and declared a blockade of the Mexican ports. It demanded a settlement of the protested claims and guarantees for the protection of Frenchmen in the future. Naturally enough, the French were glad to foster the rebel activities and announced that their quarrel was with the administration and not with the people. However, the months dragged by and little was done toward making payment. Meanwhile the French were suffering badly from fevers and were not anxious for coastal service during the summer, but with the coming of cool weather they determined to attack Veracruz with its fortress of San Juan de Ulloa. After careful and businesslike preparations, Admiral Baudin opened fire on November 27. The guns of the fort were woefully inadequate, being either obsolete, mounted on improper carriages, or not having proper ammunition. The French, well equipped, saw the old fortress crumbling after each hit. The limestone (coral) walls, which had been thought to be impregnable, were torn from top to bottom by the shells of the fleet. It is easy to summarize the potential strength of the fortress as does Bulnes, but that helps soldiers little when walls are crumbling, powder magazines exploding, and their powder so weak it will not propel their own bullets to the enemy vessels.[3]

The faintest whiff of burnt powder was enough for Santa Anna. He dashed off to Veracruz post haste and got there just after Generals Gaona and Rincón, commanders of the

3. Bulnes, *op. cit.*, p. 781 ff.

[156]

Fortress and of the Department of Veracruz respectively, had made a truce with the French. Rincón was glad to escape final responsibility for giving up the fort and eagerly received his quondam enemy, rival and friend. As the hero of the last foreign invasion, the Victor of Tampico was asked to examine the fortress and decide as to the best plan of action. Santa Anna reached the fortress at 8:00 P.M. on the twenty-seventh. His examination and a conferrence with the officers lasted until 2:00 A.M. the next morning when it was agreed to surrender the fortress and neutralize the city. Of course, the nation was duly informed by Santa Anna that this was to save Mexican lives, with the clear implication that the condition had developed through incompetence of others, i.e., of the administration and the officers directly responsible for the fortress.

As a matter of fact, the masses needed little prompting to believe this. On the thirtieth, the news reached the Capital, and on December 1, the Congress before crowded galleries met to discuss steps to be taken. News that Rincón and Gaona were to be recalled and Santa Anna placed in command met with vociferous applause and cries of: "That's the man we want!" and "He is the savior of the country!"

Probably Bustamante had few regrets in assigning to his old rival, whose fame again seemed to be rising, the well-nigh impossible task of defending Veracruz after the protecting fortress had been lost. Be that as it may, Santa Anna received the new orders at Manga de Clavo (he had retired there immediately after performing the inspection of the fortress and giving his report) and at once reported to Veracruz, reaching the port at 11:00 A.M. on December 4. He at once notified Baudin that the Central Government had disapproved the proposal to neutralize the city, and simultaneously called his own ranking officers for a council of war at 2:00 P.M. These men insisted that the city could not be held, but the new Commander promptly overruled them and issued orders for all precautions to be taken while General Mariano Arista in the interior was urged to rush reinforcements to the city.

The French did not give the new Commander much re-

[157]

spite. In response to the notice of Santa Anna, the Admiral had stated that he could capture Veracruz at will, but did not wish to endanger the life of the populace. Probably this did not deceive Santa Anna though the Frenchman's conduct early the next morning was somewhat surprising. Arista came on into the city the night of the fourth, and the two generals stayed up until one or two o'clock, making their plans. Then they both decided to get some sleep. Meanwhile, Baudin had planned a raid to dash into the city at 5:30 A.M. to seize the person of Santa Anna, while two supporting parties captured the chief city forts, Santiago and Concepción.

The forts were rather easily taken, but the force sent to capture Santa Anna led by the Prince de Joinville, son of the French king, had to force open the city gate with a petard. This awoke Santa Anna, who seized a part of his clothes and dashed downstairs at full speed. The French, entering the house, laughingly let the frightened man pass after asking him which was Santa Anna's room, little dreaming that he was the prize they sought. Arista, who took a little more time to maintain his dignity (he had not recently been a captive of the Texans) was captured, and Santa Anna's aide, M. M. Giménez, quite badly cut up with eight wounds from pistol bullets and sword cuts.

Firmly believing that discretion was the better part of valor, Santa Anna rushed outside the city to a place called the Matadero, which was close to a woods. Here a number of refugees slowly gathered. Meanwhile Baudin had looked over the situation and decided that the movement was useless and ordered a retreat.

Santa Anna seems not to have been near the barracks where something like active resistance was offered the French, but after a time he was ready to act. He gathered together a few refugee troops and rushed into the city while the French were re-embarking. The invaders had placed a captured cannon at the end of the street to cover the embarkation. As Santa Anna galloped up at the head of his men, this gun, which had been loaded with grape, was discharged. The General's horse was killed and he himself wounded in the left hand and leg. In addition to some others wounded, two officers and seven men were killed. This completely disorganized the attack, so the French entered their boats and left at their convenience.

The leg wound proved to be quite serious, and a conference of three physicians agreed that amputation was necessary. The operation was set for the next day, while Santa Anna turned his energies to the composition of a magnificent report to the Minister of War. In this he related that he had charged the enemy at the head of his men and had driven them into their boats at the point of the bayonet.

"*We conquered, yes, we conquered*: Mexican arms secured a glorious victory in the plaza; and the flag of Mexico remained triumphant: I was wounded in this last effort and probably this will be the last victory that I shall offer my native land.

"On closing my career, I cannot refrain from expressing my joy at seeing the beginnings of reconciliation among the Mexican factions. . . . .

"I ask also of the government of my country that my body be buried in this same soil (*medanos*) so that my companions in arms may know that this is the line of battle I leave marked out for them: that from this day forward the most unjust of Mexican enemies shall not dare to place their feet on our soil. I demand of my fellow countrymen also that they do not stain our victory by attacking the indefensible Frenchmen, who live among us under the protection of our laws . . . .

"May all Mexicans, forgetting my political mistakes, not deny me the only title which I wish to leave my children: that of a 'good Mexican.' "[4]

In a postscript, he said he had lost some twenty-five men killed and wounded, while the enemy had lost over a hundred dead on the streets "and a multitude of wounded."[5] Also, he

4. This was printed as a broadside and widely circulated around the Capital.
5. P. Blanchard, and A. Dauzats, *San Juan de Ulúa*, pp. 381-82. The French reported their total casualties at sixty-eight.

claimed that a large number, including Baudin himself, had been literally driven into the water and drowned. A second postscript said his condition was such that he had forgotten to state that he had left Colonel Ramón Hernandez in charge as the senior officer. The man lived so entirely with his own enthusiasm that he doubtless believed every word of this. He was thoroughly enjoying this orgy of emotion and his own glorious death-bed scene.

Santa Anna had been taken out to Pozitos on the afternoon of the fifth, and the next day his left leg was blunderingly amputated. The work was so poorly done that he suffered considerable pain on and off for the rest of his life. The patient and the amputated member were both carefully transferred as soon as he was able to move to Manga de Clavo so that he could convalesce under the efficient ministrations of Doña Inés.

The nation once more had its hero. Santa Anna's report was published on all sides. "In the drawing room, cafés and plazas; in the midst of people who crowded together the manifesto was read while tears washed away all recollections of San Jacinto and enthusiasm for the Hero of Tampico was reborn." Special prayers were offered for his life and all were convinced that a great victory had been gained at a cost which had verged upon a national tragedy.

Meanwhile, the Bustamante government was bordering on collapse. On December 7, United States Consul W. D. Jones reported "a complete state of anarchy" with constant cries for dictatorship. However, there were some patriots in Mexico like old Gómez Farías. Though he was held in prison as a suspect still he flatly refused to countenance any revolution at the time. Also, after the events of December 5, the many who wished to make Santa Anna the object of a popular uprising were restrained because of the state of his wound.

After a slow convalescence, the hero started for Mexico City in a litter. He was frankly looked upon as the man to save the nation, but his journey was so slow that some began to suspect he was carefully sounding public opinion so as to gauge his course the better. In mid afternoon of Sunday,

February 17, 1839, he arrived, being preceded and followed by an elaborate military escort and by carriages full of his adherents who went out six miles to meet him. The rabble was enthusiastic, but it was clear to the careful observer that Bustamante was uneasy, if not actually worried.

The rebels in Tampico were rapidly extending their activities so that something had to be done. Here was Bustamante's opportunity. The only way he could hope to remain as President was to offset the reputation of Santa Anna by one of his own. But could he afford to leave his rival alone in the Capital? Finally, this appeared the only possible course, so he reluctantly asked Congress to let him go to the front. Just as the permission was granted it very conveniently happened that the President of the Council, who should have succeeded Bustamante as executive according to the Constitution, was sick so Congress enthusiastically selected Santa Anna as president *ad interim*.

As a matter of fact terms had just been agreed upon with the French, thanks largely to the efforts of the British Minister, Mr. Pakenham.[6] But even with this problem practically solved Bustamante could not make up his mind to leave. C. M. Bustamante relates that, after many days, Santa Anna bluntly said to the waverer: "I did not come here to take your place from you: I have been brought without wishing it. I advise you as a friend to go to Tampico, because if you do not, the evil will grow greatly, and when you wish to do so you will not be able to control it. If you do not go I shall, in spite of my physical condition."[7] Bustamante went, but he was a worried man.

The President *ad interim* announced that he was too weak to appear to take the oath of office in person, so the various department heads did it in his name. Obviously, he thoroughly enjoyed having exceptions and special concessions made to him. It flattered his vanity and was fine advertising.

6. The French treaty was actually agreed to on March 19, with most people agreeing that the influence of Santa Anna was largely responsible for the ratification. Needless to say, most of the French demands were met in spite of the "victory" at Veracruz.

7. Bustamante, *El Gabinete Mexicana*, Tomo I, p. 162.

Santa Anna had been the more anxious to foster the negotiations with France, for the blockade of Veracruz had forced the merchants to import their goods through Tampico, and this meant that the rebels were getting ample supplies and revenue with which to fight the government. Other matters were also demanding attention. To secure revenue for the army, he ordered the military commanders of the departments to use local funds as they saw fit; liberty of the press was abruptly curtailed by suppression of newspapers and imprisonment of objectionable authors; anyone of doubtful loyalty was forthwith dropped as an official, while suspected conspirators were hustled off to safe places.

Bustamante had gone to San Luis Potosí and was there trying to decide what to do when word reached Santa Anna that the rebel General J. A. Mejía was approaching Puebla in an attempt to cut the highway between the Capital and Veracruz. This called for immediate action so the President asked his Council for permission to lead the troops to Puebla in person. When it agreed, he did not stop to ask the consent of Congress and ignored the fact that the Council revoked its approval.

Hastening into his litter, he left Mexico City on April 30 to be carried over the pass where the two snow caps quietly look down upon the heat and turmoil of human life. On this occasion at least, his haste proved highly advantageous for in the City of Angels (*Puebla de los Angeles*) all plans had been perfected for the local garrison to join the rebels. Santa Anna's unexpected arrival was just three hours before the time set for the "pronouncement" and proved to be such a powerful sedative that the about-to-be rebels changed their minds.

With his usual activity, troops were organized and preparations made so that by the morning of May 3, 1839, sixteen hundred men were ready for the rebel attack at Acajete, near the city. After several charges, the rebels broke and fled before the counter attack of the cavalry under General Valencia. The six hundred men killed gave ample evidence of the fierceness of the contest. Santa Anna himself reached the battlefield after the rout had begun, but undoubtedly his activity in the first place had saved Puebla and had inspired the troops to victory.

The gallant Mejía was himself taken prisoner and well knew the fate that awaited him. Various stories are told of his death. One is that Santa Anna sent him word that he would be shot in three hours. His grim reply was: "Tell General Santa Anna that if captor and captive had been reversed in position I would have allowed him only that number of minutes, not hours."

Five days later, the idol of his people returned to Mexico City. Though the Chamber of Deputies had not given him permission to leave, they hastily appointed a special reception committee to repair the oversight. A swarming, yelling mob filled the streets with cries that were punctuated by the hollow boom of cannon and the rhythmic sound of ringing church bells throughout the city. Fireworks popped sporadically, while at night the public buildings were lighted and hung with special draperies.

There were many who expected Santa Anna to proclaim himself dictator, and thus precipitate an inevitable clash with Bustamante. This was not done, but a wholesale reorganization of the army was in progress with generous promotions of his friends and supporters, while likely opponents were relegated to harmless positions. The Texan Commissioner, B. E. Bee, wrote from Veracruz May 24, 1839:

"....but as to Santa Anna, we must give him time,—at this moment he does not *dare* make a move openly in favor of Texas. He is playing a great game. The press is put down. The Militia of the country disarmed. Soldiers are pressed into the Service. Mexia's followers made to fall in the ranks, Captains reduced to privates. Bonaparte's conscription adopted. Despotism covers the land, and until he is firmly seated as *Emperor*, nothing will be done. In the meantime he will *hector* about Texas, (and in *secret* will negotiate with her), keep Bustamante at the head of the Army, etc....

[163]

"Texas must prepare for war, but with little probability of ever being invaded. I would not call a single farmer from his plough...."[8]

This estimate was not far wrong. So far as Texas was concerned James Hamilton rather shrewdly remarked that Santa Anna found his hands tied for the simple reason that he could hardly talk about recognizing Texan independence at the very time that other states were in revolt; and that his talk of conquering the northern rebels was just political hokum for public consumption.

As the summer advanced, the President *ad interim* sent down to Manga de Clavo for his wife to come up and help care for his health. This was a popular move and would pave the way for a future physical breakdown if such proved advisable. The truth was he had done all he could to further his cause in the Capital. To continue the *ad interim* position longer was foolish for it would only create opposition, especially now that Congress was about to meet to discuss the troublesome financial problems of the country.

He sent word to Bustamante to return from his successful but mediocre campaigning to take the President's office since he, Santa Anna, could not stand the strain longer. To emphasize his precarious health he turned the executive power over to Nicolás Bravo, President of the Council, nine days before Bustamante could arrive. On July 11, at 5:00 A.M. he again set out for his estate leaving poor Bustamante to wrestle with the humdrum financial questions and to try to convince a dazzled people that his own rather drab personality was worthy of occupying the presidency for the seven years still remaining of the eight year term. The popular answer was reasonably certain in view of Santa Anna's exploits of the past few months and the enthusiasm they had engendered. Even Congress had joined in the adulation and ordered a magnificent jeweled decoration (*placa*) made for him which was delivered by the Bishop-elect of Oajaca and the *Vicario Capitular* of Mexico as those gentlemen strained vocabularies and oratorical abilities in doing justice to the occasion.

8. George P. Garrison, *op. cit.*, Vol. II, Part I, p. 448.

When the President took charge in his own name once more it is not surprising that many of the acts of Santa Anna were undone. Liberties were restored to the press, the army was again subjected to reorganization, while financial and other acts of Santa Anna were promptly reversed and the cabinet reorganized. The following letter is almost too perfect an illustration of what was going on to be true, but it certainly shows Bustamante's attitude. It was addressed to J. M. Tornel, an ardent friend of Santa Anna.

"*My esteemed friend and companion*: Yesterday I had the pleasure to sign your despatch of general and active brigade, which was remitted to you by the chief officer; and today I have the profound sentiments to dictate this letter to say, that the apoplectic fits to which you are subject being so frequent, I believe it indespensably necessary, to avoid a recurrence of them, that you separate yourself from the immense toil of the ministery, and dedicate yourself exclusively to the reestablishment of your health, which, as your sincere friend, I cannot behold with indifference. Under such circumstances, I hope you will ask your dismissal, which I consider necessary for the reason expressed, and *for others which I will make known to you as soon as you are restored* to health.

In regard to your secretaryship, I have directed that the chief officer sign all the documents for the ordinary mail of today; *and I also request that you remain entirely free from all fatigue that may be prejudicial to your health.*

I thank you for the discharge of your duty during my administration; and you must always reckon me as your sincere friend, who esteems you, and cordially desires to be of service to you.

Anastasio Bustamante."[9]

To cover such cases of plain persecution, Bustamante's friends were talking loudly of the million *pesos* which they said Santa Anna had stolen while acting president. Meanwhile, at Manga de Clavo, the master was watching and guarding the Veracruz road. Along this came the new Spanish Minister and his brilliant wife, Madame Calderón de la

9. *Niles Register*, LVII (November 2, 1839), 150.

Barca, who was so ably to interpret Mexican life through the balanced approach of a girl reared in the United States and married into a proud old Spanish family. She wrote as follows:

"We arrived about five at Manga de Clavo, after passing through leagues of natural garden, the property of Santa Anna.

"The house is pretty, slight-looking, and kept in nice order. We were received by an aide-de-camp in uniform, and by several officers, and conducted to a large, cool, agreeable apartment, with little furniture, into which shortly entered the Señora de Santa Anna, tall, thin, and at that early hour of the morning dressed to receive us in clear, white muslin, with white satin shoes, and with very splendid diamond earrings, brooch, and rings. She was very polite, and introduced her daughter Guadalupe, a miniature of her mamma, in features and costume.

"In a little while entered General Santa Anna himself; a gentlemanly, good-looking, quietly-dressed, rather melancholy-looking person, with one leg, apparently somewhat of an invalid, and to us the most interesting person in the group. He has a sallow complexion, fine dark eyes, soft and penetrating, and an interesting expression of face. Knowing nothing of his past history, one would have said a philosopher, living in dignified retirement—one who had tried the world, and found that all was vanity....

"En attendant, breakfast was announced. The Señora de Santa Anna led me in. C——n [her husband] was placed at the head of the table, I on his right, Santa Anna opposite, the Señora on my right. The breakfast was very handsome, consisting of innumerable Spanish dishes, meat and vegetables, fish and fowl, fruits and sweetmeats, all served in white and gold French porcelain, with coffee, wines, etc. After breakfast, the Señora having despatched an officer for her cigar-case, which was gold, with a diamond latch, offered me a cigar, which I having declined, she lighted her own, a little paper 'cigarito,' and the gentlemen followed her good example."[10]

10. Madame Calderón de la Barca, *Life in Mexico*, pp. 32-33.

The winter season passed and spring gave place to the summer of 1841, while Santa Anna quietly watched the troubles of Bustamante increase. Not only were the prospects of reconquering Texas practically non-existent but the administration was further discredited by the sinister rumor that other dissatisfied northern provinces were considering the advantages to be secured by joining the new republic. In addition, Campeche in the far South, declared for federalism and José Urrea and Gómez Farías became more and more restless in the Capital. The over-shadowed President found matters constantly more confusing to his rather slow moving mind. Mrs. Calderón commented: "There cannot be a greater contrast, both in appearance and reality, than between him and Santa Anna. There is no lurking devil in his eye. All is frank, open, unreserved." And so he blundered on into the revolution.

In truth, once given the President's personality, there seemed to be little that could be done about the discontent, and the little that could have been done he was largely blind to. Society danced, with the ladies wearing their jewels (colored stones being most popular) worth sums of *pesos* running up to the five or even the six figure mark each. Though the entertainments may have been overly lavish, they were brilliant and only the "proper" people present. One ball to the socially elect was reported to have cost the host eleven thousand dollars.

Of an afternoon, all went to drive on the Paseo, where it was quite possible to see a thousand carriages and five thousand horsemen at the same time. The ladies would bow graciously and languidly wave their fans to the flirtatious or serious advances of the gentlemen riders so rigidly forced by custom to do their courting in this stilted fashion. Not only the ladies, but also the gentlemen, were fashion plates of the day; "nothing is regarded more vulgar than to be seen on horseback in a dress coat or any other than a roundabout. These are richly embroidered with silk or with gold and silver lace, and covered all over with buttons. Their cherivalles are equally fine, and generally open from the knee down."

[167]

More elaborate still were the saddles and bridles of the horses, with their masses of hand-wrought silver. The price of such equestrian furnishings alone frequently ranged as high as a thousand dollars, while five thousand was not unheard of.[11]

By late summer, however, the Paseo was deserted while a veritable three-ringed politico-military circus took its place as a public entertainment. On July 15, General José Urrea launched a federalistic revolt in the Capital, supported by the fifty-seven year old liberal patriot, Gómez Farías. Bustamante was captured and invited to lead the movement for governmental reform. He refused, escaped and actively organized the opposition. For nearly two weeks, the contest continued with the liberals slowly losing ground before the unexpectedly determined resistance.

Gunpowder being burned! Again it was Santa Anna's cue, and the heretofore unnoticed third circus ring was suddenly the center of attraction. The Hero of Tampico and Veracruz sent a letter to the President, which stated that he was hurrying to the Capital at the head of a "respectable division." Bustamante could not afford to have his government saved by the national hero a second time. Also there was general talk that Santa Anna was proposing himself as mediator. Both factions knew only too well that in such a case the orange would be neatly halved to all appearances, but that in reality the flesh would be skillfully scooped out of each rind before it was presented to either contesting party. It was not surprising then that Bustamante hurriedly made terms on the twenty-sixth with the failing rebel movement. Word was at once sent to the "loyal" General Santa Anna, thanking him for his support, but ordering him back to the coast. On the twenty-ninth he responded:

"The triumph which the national arms have just obtained over the horrible attempts at anarchy....is very worthy of being celebrated by every citizen who desires the welfare of his country, always supposing that public vengeance (*La vindicta pública*) has been satisfied; and in this case, I offer you a thousand congratulations....I anxiously desire to re-

11. Waddy Thompson, *Recollections of Mexico*, p. 217.

ceive the details which your Excellency offers to communicate to me, so that if the danger has entirely ceased, I may return to my *hacienda,* and may lay down the command of those troops which your Excellency orders me to preserve here.[12]

The hero's position now was vindication enough for the Texas collapse and the indignities suffered since. It was perfectly obvious to all concerned that Santa Anna was master of the country: that when he spoke, all trembled; and that all officials were anxious to please him. On October 29, 1840, the President issued a decree to add another medal to the overloaded chest of the owner of Manga de Clavo on account of the repulse of the Spaniards at Veracruz *eighteen* years before. The country gentleman could play any rôle he desired and either pull the strings while the official marionettes danced; or, in his own good time and in his own way, annex part or all of the political power for himself.

---

12. Madame Calderón de la Barca, *op. cit.,* pp. 252-53. The fighting was actually quite serious as may be seen from the estimate of C. M. Bustamante, *op. cit.,* Tomo II, pp. 78-80, that there were 886 killed and wounded.

MASTER

THE Capital danced while it could. What though the New Orleans mint did announce publicly that some Mexican *pesos* in circulation contained only 65 per cent as much silver as others? When one man was accused of counterfeiting, his wife was said to have exclaimed: "I really wonder why they make so much noise about it. It seems to me that my husband's copper is as good as any other." What though a dozen of the leading brigadier and major generals of the country had carefully stayed away from both government and rebel headquarters during the July revolution of 1840? They were probably no more opportunists than hundreds of other leading citizens.

In the midst of the political uncertainties Capital society received quite a shock when the brilliant Gutiérrez Estrada issued a pamphlet in October, 1840, in which he strongly advocated the establishment of a constitutional monarchy under a foreign prince. To justify the idea he admitted that the United States had prospered as a republic, but stated that France, a Latin country, had been wrecked by the change to that type of administration. The Spanish colonies had been happy under monarchy; why not Mexico a few years later? Furthermore, as proven in the case of Iturbide, a local military leader would only precipitate more bloodshed if selected as king whereas Belgium, on separating from Holland, had chosen a foreign prince and was happy. Thus he drove home his arguments. The master of Manga de Clavo, of course, protested vigorously against such a suggestion though he must have found much of the logic of the monarchists in line with his own thinking.

As the spring of 1841 passed by many of the seven and a half million people of Mexico began to suspect that Santa

Anna was becoming a bit restless. He had been appointed Military Commander of Veracruz that spring so as to organize a force for the subjugation of rebellious Yucatán. This was done with his usual efficiency but he was much too shrewd to go to the south, and suggested that another man make the trip. Something was in the wind and this was no time to be isolated on the southern peninsula.

The unrest was especially noticeable in liberal Zacatecas where García, the victim of Santa Anna in 1835, was still considered a hero. Efforts of the Government to suppress this feeling only added fuel to the flames. The dissatisfaction was also manifest in the Capital and was noticeable on the anniversary of the July revolution of 1840 when General Valencia in fulsome words bestowed a jeweled cross upon the President in the name of Congress. He stated that in those trying days: "Society arose in chaos. Its president is taken. Authorities no longer exist, and those who ought to save them are converted into their oppressors. *'God said let there be light, and there was light.'* The honorable troops .... said 'Let order be re-established—let the supreme magistrate be set at liberty, and let things resume their proper march.' Order *was* re-established, your Excellency was set free, and the political body followed the regular path.... So it is that those worthy troops .... now also resemble the Creator of the world in his content, when satisfied with his work."[1]

Strangely enough the troops, and not Bustamante, seemed the subject of the oration. Quite significant!

Finally matters came to a head out in Guadalajara when General Paredes y Arrillaga issued a pronunciamiento on August 8. This denounced the Government for overtaxing the people while failing to protect them from Indian attack; for neglecting the army; for wrecking industry and impairing the international standing of the country. It called for a special congress to revise the constitution, and pending this for the executive power to be placed in the hands of a "citizen worthy of confidence," who would have "extraordinary" powers. This meant Santa Anna, as all knew. By the end of the month,

1. Madame Calderón de la Barca, *op. cit.*, p. 388.

General Valencia, Manuel Lombardini, and others had joined the movement in the Capital while all eyes turned anxiously to Santa Anna. He had rejected revolutions in his favor before this, would he do so again?

Orders were sent to the Governor of Veracruz to watch him carefully. On the fifteenth, Santa Anna himself wrote the Minister of War, professing entire loyalty. But this was no more convincing than his statement that he would like to act as mediator in the disturbed political conditions. In fact, in Veracruz on the twenty-sixth, a noisy gathering hailed Santa Anna and Paredes as the saviors of the country. Santa Anna still kept his own council but moved his men up onto the plateau and took charge of the old, but very strong, fortress of Perote which stood in the midst of its plain and defied attack. He was still talking about mediation, but his correspondence to the Minister of War was now little less than insubordinate. To him it was ridiculous that Almonte, his ex-private secretary, should presume to send him advice and orders as to the best way to discharge his duties as Commanding General of Veracruz.[2]

Though Bustamante tried to consolidate his position in and around Mexico City, it was well known that the rebellion was growing rapidly. Finally, a plan seconding the revolt in the Capital was proclaimed and signed by Santa Anna on September 9, 1841. A week later he wrote Almonte saying that the Seven Laws had never met his ideas of a desirable form of government, and that they would have to go. At the same time he advanced toward Puebla, where he took charge without opposition on the eighteenth. With scarcely a pause in this city he continued onwards, and on the twenty-fourth, was in the Valley of Mexico at the village of Tesmelucan. He still kept up the farce of acting as mediator and actually had the administration in such a delicate position that though it denied his right to act in such a capacity it sent word that he might use his good offices to bring the erring ones to see their mistakes.

2. For very important correspondence see C. M. Bustamante, *op. cit.,* Tomo II, p. 142 ff.

Paredes, too, had arrived in the Valley of Mexico to lend his aid. On the twenty-seventh, a truce was agreed upon with the understanding that Bustamante should be displaced. As the President left his headquarters near Guadalupe, the sentinel on duty gave the regular call: "Members of the Guard! His Excellency, the President of the Republic," at which all hastily presented arms. Then word came of the new arrangement and the poor sentinel did not know what to do as he saw Bustamante returning. Thoroughly confused, he hissed to the guards nearby: "Members of the Guard, the Old Uncle is here." Bustamante smiled and said to the officer: "Order my nephew to the lock-up." But even so, his sun had set and the order was little more than a gesture.

The next day the three victors, Paredes, Valencia and Santa Anna, met at Guadalupe to divide the spoils. When his companions promptly fell to quarreling Santa Anna held the balance of power. He soon secured the support of the blunt soldier from the west [Paredes] who realized the Veracruzan was the one man with sufficient energy and popularity to control the situation. Thus it was decided that the General-in-Chief, Santa Anna, should name two representatives from each Department to form an Assembly of Notables, and that these should in turn select a provisional president. The new executive was then to call a congress and to re-make the machinery of government. These agreements were sent to the old Minister of War for his indorsement.

Bustamante was down, but felt that he was not yet "out." With a few faithful troops, he went to the great central plaza of the city and formally renounced centralism and proclaimed a federal republic. This was undoubtedly a popular step with many and had it been taken earlier might have changed affairs considerably. However, it was now all too obviously a catching at straws, and was clearly illegal. Santa Anna forthwith proclaimed Bustamante in rebellion against the government of the country of which he claimed to be the chief support, and, in spite of broadsides which appeared upon the streets denouncing "Santa Anna, the Dictator," it was only a matter of days until such poems as the following were published on all sides:

> There is no reason to sing of victory
> Government Thief (Bustamante)
> Glory is for Santa-Anna
> For you, Hell:
> You are entirely evil
> And we shall soon see you
> In a shanty.

> (No hay give cantar victoria
> Ladron Gobierno
> De Santa-Anna es la gloria
> Tuyo el Infierno:
> Todo eres falso
> Y pronto te veremos
> En un cadaholzo.)[3]

The contest was clearly unequal and October 5, Santa Anna wrote to Bustamante, claiming to have nine thousand troops ready for an assault, but suggested that terms be discussed. Bustamante agreed the next day and it was decided than an amnesty should be granted to all political offenders; that all acts of Bustamante and of the new Provisional President were to be submitted to the constituent congress for approval; that officers who desired might withdraw from the army with all pension rights guaranteed, and that the government troops were to remain under orders of Santa Anna. Bustamante forthwith left the country for Europe.

At five o'clock on the afternoon of the seventh Santa Anna made his triumphal entry with all the panoply of a military conqueror. He was duly received by the Governor of Mexico, the Town Council, and the higher clergy with the ceremonies of a *Te Deum*, clashing of bells, salvos of artillery and a formal

---

3. *Mexico, Despatches*, Ellis to Webster, October 2, 1841, Vol. X (No. 47). There are several other stanzas of this literary effort but the above gives an idea of the whole.

review of ten thousand of the combined troops of victor and vanquished.

In providing for the Assembly of Notables, it had been agreed that each Department must be represented by its own natives. At once there ensued a frenzied search through the Capital to find men who had the proper qualifications and who thought "right." Finally a list was made up and the individuals chosen were informed of the high honor done them by Santa Anna. In gratitude they could do no less than select him as Provisional President: of the forty-four possible votes he received thirty-nine.

The inauguration was to be at the Cathedral on October 10. The old building was brilliantly lighted with hundreds of candles for the occasion while troops formed outside and even within the sacred edifice to the sound of trumpets. When all was ready and thousands of people waiting, the Archbishop in cope and mitre, holding a magnificent jeweled crucifix worth a fortune, went to the entrance of the sacred edifice to meet the President-elect. After forty-five minutes had passed and when all realized that he dared keep even the Archbishop waiting the great man approached. He was surrounded by generals and officials in their finest uniforms and robes, but he in deliberate contrast was in a plain frock-coat. Within the Cathedral he was seated on a kind of dais or throne though all others stood for an hour during a splendid rendition of the *Te Deum* led by the Archbishop. The oath of office was: "Do you swear to God to discharge the duties confided to you, for the good of the nation, and reorganizing the republic in all the branches of its administration?"

In addressing the Assembly a few days later he commented in what might be called an inaugural address: "I pledge myself as a citizen and I swear as a soldier, now that I am placed for the third time in this high position, which is also a precipice [who knew it better than he?], that all my efforts shall be directed to the glorification of the nation, to the development of harmony among all its children, and to the establishment of principles worthy of these times in which the human race

[175]

progresses."[4] Vague generalities, but probably as clear as his own thinking on many of the actual questions of the day.

A day later, orders were issued for a great celebration on October 28, to take the place of September 16, the regular Independence Day celebration whose observance had been prevented by the recent disorders. So little enthusiasm was shown that it was evident that emotions were burned out for the time, and that the government had to set itself to the sterner tasks of the day. Santa Anna was obviously determined to play the dictator again, but he had every intention of doing it in such a way as to retain himself in power. He was shrewd enough to know that an administration which was to last, must be built upon something more than a popular excitement subject to violent reactions.

Among the problems faced with energy and effectiveness was the question of copper money. It was the money of the masses so no earlier administration had dared to tackle the problem in spite of the fact that it was often subject to discounts of 40 to 50 per cent. Taking the bull by the horns, Santa Anna ordered all of it to be called in in thirty days. Those who delivered it were to receive its value in new government copper coins within six months. This meant that the masses were without money for a considerable period. In the long run, the move helped somewhat, but the delay brought severe criticism, especially since the movement was not completed because of lack of funds by the government.

National revenues were far from sufficient to meet expenses and pay vouchers were discounted as much as 90 per cent. To secure a little cash, government resources were sold at a tithe of their value. For instance, the Fresnillo Mine was sold for approximately $400,000 (plus perquisites) when the annual government revenue up to this time for the property had been reported as over $500,000. Taxes were laid on every conceivable article of private property, such as the number of gutters that poured water from the tops of houses, the number of coach wheels on a man's vehicles, and many other lux-

4. Bustamante, *apuntes para la historia del gobierno de* ....`Santa Anna,` pp. 1-2.

[176]

uries or mere indications of wealth. All salaries were taxed while a head tax of 1.50 *pesos* a year was laid on all men between sixteen and sixty years of age.

A chief source of ready money was the clergy, who looked upon Santa Anna as their friend, and who were willing to supply a certain amount of cash. Some Church property was surrendered outright, but, on the whole, the protests of the Archbishop were effective in protecting this as in the case of the Inquisition building of Mexico City, which Santa Anna wanted for a barracks, but did not get. The Dictator has been criticized for ordering the sale of some of the old Jesuit property near the Capital, but it is only fair to state that this had been held by the government (first the Spanish and then the Mexican) ever since the expulsion of the Jesuits in 1767 so that ownership by pre-emption had been fairly well established. The outright confiscation of the Pious Fund of the California Missions was a more serious invasion of clerical rights, but as has been seen there were other factors involved here and the hierarchy continued their support. When the Archbishop of Mexico was asked for five hundred thousand *pesos,* he compromised for two-fifths of that sum, but this was far more than any other one source could provide. Other clerical groups contributed smaller amounts. It is true that there are stories that Santa Anna treated the clergy with scant dignity, actually calling for the Archbishop of Mexico, then keeping him waiting for an hour and finally sending out word that he was too busy to see him but would appreciate an immediate payment of fifty thousand *pesos* of money not yet due. This may have happened but it is hardly likely, if for no other reason than because the Dictator needed money too badly to be killing the goose that was capable of laying so many golden eggs.

The new laws and decrees issued were a queer mixture of financial juggling and constructive activity. To appease certain discontented elements real estate taxes and a consumption tax were slightly reduced. English bondholders were persuaded to accept small cash payments only, which also sounded good to Mexicans. At the same time a committee of leading lawyers was appointed to codify the confused laws of the country, while a special merchant's court was organized, and the old miner's courts were given a needed overhauling. A committee on public instruction was intrusted with the task of outlining a national program of education, and adopted the Lancasterian system. Postage rates on newspapers were sharply reduced. Then, in spite of serious opposition and fear on the part of many Mexicans, Santa Anna forced through a law which would permit all foreigners who would subject themselves to Mexican laws, to own land in the country.

Extensive internal improvements were undertaken to impress the public and satisfy the ruler's pride. Sections of the Capital that had long been an eyesore and a health menace were torn down to make way for a Plaza del Volador, a public building, or a great theatre to carry the name of the Dictator. At the same time, he undertook the construction of a railroad from Mexico City to San Angel.

In foreign affairs, there were numerous border problems to consider. Soconusco, a small area on the Guatamalan border, was definitely annexed. Also a contract was entered into for opening the Tehuantepec Isthmus between Yucatán and Mexico to inter-oceanic travel by boat and railroad. This was not carried out because of lack of time and money though it was of great potential significance both as a matter of local development and for the purpose of keeping out the detested Yankee. In Yucatán and Tabasco there had long been trouble. Both regions were finally pacified and, after lengthy negotiations, Yucatán agreed to re-enter the Mexican union in theory though it practically retained its own sovereignty in a treaty signed by Sr. Andrés Quintana Roo. In January, 1842, this treaty was indignantly rejected by the Council of Ministers, and Santa Anna issued a decree, saying that to re-enter the Mexican fold Yucatán must renounce all friendship with the Texan rebels and must subscribe to the agreements reached at Tacubaya (*Bases de Tacubaya*) in full. His next step was to send an expedition of fifteen hundred men to conquer the region.

[178]

On the northern border were the Texas and California questions. To reconquer Texas was out of the question, but to give it up was equally difficult. To make matters worse, Great Britain and the United States were interested in California where the inhabitants were already thinking in terms of independence. To give up one or both of these areas would almost certainly mean to do the same in regard to Yucatán. One way out that was considered was to get cash from Great Britain for a mortgage on or sale of California and to use this cash to fight the United States and consolidate the rest of the country.[5] In the meantime General Woll was sent in September, 1842, to lead a raid on San Antonio for the triple purpose of scaring the Texans, justifying the heavy taxes, and of making political capital in Mexico. He reached his objective and carried off a number of leading citizens as prisoners. However, it is doubtful indeed if the Dictator had any idea of subduing Texas. It was patriotic to talk about it, gave him a fine excuse for his large army and tended to keep the minds of Mexicans off their home troubles.

In this same connection, there occurred an interesting bit of diplomatic trickery. James Hamilton, who had just been to England on a mission for Texas, sent a letter to Santa Anna in a sealed package which Packenham, the British Minister, delivered without suspecting its contents. In it, Hamilton wrote under date of January 13, 1842:

"I take the liberty of proposing to your excellency (if you think it consistent with the honor and interests of Mexico) that a treaty of peace and limitation should be entered into, with Texas, upon the basis of an indemnification of five millions of dollars, which I can place in London, for this object, within three weeks after receipt of the agreement, together with two hundred thousand dollars, which will be secretly placed at the disposal of the Mexican Government."[6]

On February 18, Santa Anna responded:

"Your proposals of five millions of dollars for the renunci-

5. *Mexico, Despatches,* Thompson to Webster, July 30, 1842, (Thompson, No. 4).

6. *Niles Register,* Vol. LXII (March 26, 1842), p. 50.

ation of Texas, is a miscalculation, and an act of audacity; permit me, sir, to add to you, that your offer of two hundred thousand dollars for the secret agents of the government of Mexico, is an insult and infamy unworthy of a gentleman."[7]

To this Hamilton rejoined on March 21, 1842:

"The supplementary offer of two hundred thousand dollars for contingencies and secret service were to defray the cost of running the boundary line, the expenses of the respective legations, and for secret service. You are too disciplined a veteran in the politics of your own country not to know the necessity and value of this last item, yet you have thought proper, it appears, to pay yourself the compliment of supposing that I designed that this money should be insinuated as a *bribe* to yourself. I assure your Excellency that I am too well aware of the spotless integrity of Don Antonio Lopez de Santa Anna, President of the Republic of Mexico, to have hazarded such an experiment on the virgin purity of your Excellency's honor."[8]

It must be said, in spite of Mr. Hamilton's rejoinder of some eighteen hundred words in length, the Mexican seemed to be in the stronger position. It is not likely that a *douceur* would have been objectionable to him, but, just at the time, the strengthening of his home and foreign position was more important than the extra cash.[9]

The Texans returned the Woll raid by one of their own to Santa Fé, New Mexico. This expedition was not so fortunate as that of Woll, and was captured. After a nerve and body racking experience as captives most of them survived the journey to Mexico and were confined in Perote. Some harrowing tales were published as to the hardships they experienced, but the fact is that this was a decided improvement over the treatment received by the captives in 1836, and some of the men admitted that their treatment was very good. "We have plenty to eat, Good clothes to wear, Coffee twice a day

7. *Ibid.*, p. 51.
8. *Charleston Mercury*, March 21, 1842.
9. Houston, the Texan President, disavowed the conduct of his agent as soon as he heard of it.

meat once, good flour bread, I am at work at 25 cts per day Milvern also I am coopering and make about one well bucket a week Play on it pretty fine. All carpenters and tradesmen have the privilege of working at 25 cts per day. The rest are locked up at 4 P. M., let out at 9am."[10] Soon after their arrival the Dictator noticed the name of Phelps on the roster of the survivors. He investigated and found that this was the name of a son of one Dr. Phelps in whose home he had been when a prisoner in Texas. He forthwith sent for the boy, gave him his liberty, entertained him at the palace, and personally paid his expenses back to the United States.

Another young lad, by the name of John Hill, was credited with unusual bravery and with killing several Mexicans before he was himself captured. Santa Anna sent for him, congratulated him on his bravery, and then adopted him as his son and placed him in a Mexican school to finish his education. At the same time he freed the boy's father and brother, who were also among the prisoners. The father, on returning to the United States, reported that he was delighted with his son's prospects. Shortly thereafter, on the occasion of Santa Anna's saint's day, June 13, 1842, the remaining prisoners were released. The United States Minister wrote: "I regard this act of President Santa Anna as one of generosity and magnanimity in every way honorable to him."

This brings up the whole matter of mercy, vengeance and generosity as characteristics of the President. In the heat of battle, or to a rebel who had personally offended or insulted him, Santa Anna could be entirely ruthless. Often this was a deliberate policy to discourage rebellion but at other times it was a purely personal matter. If no policy was involved and if his passions were not disturbed, his natural inclination was to magnanimity. This was noticeable in the cases just mentioned, in his treatment of Bustamante and on numbers of other occasions. In short, the Dictator was a man of high emotions, and his treatment of enemies was usually harsh as

10. L. U. Spellman, "Letters of 'Dawson Men' from Perote Prison," *Southwestern Historical Quarterly*, XXXVIII (April, 1935), 266-67. See also Frederick C. Chabot, *The Perote Prisoners*.

the times were held to justify. On the other hand, if the individual once had his case raised to the personal basis, he might expect either extreme of treatment; he was very seldom a mere prisoner of war.

As has been clearly indicated, the basis of the Dictator's power was the army. He tried to placate the federalists by appointing Francisco García, lately leader of the rebels in Zacatecas, to a position in his cabinet, but even so there were numerous insurrections. Even the foreigners who made sport of the equipment of the Mexican soldier highly valued the influence of the officers on politics. Santa Anna fully appreciated that influence and determined to retain it for himself. Colonels were said to have been made by the hundreds, and eleven new generals were made in the division of Paredes alone. The Dictator's motto was cynically but shrewdly described as: "The Nation for the Army; the Army for Santa Anna."

In all this, Santa Anna practically ignored one very important person, Paredes. He had carefully rewarded Paredes' officers and had cultivated Valentín Canalizo, the leader of Bustamante's troops, but Paredes (who with Valencia had been the kingmaker) went back to Guadalajara largely unrewarded. Here he organized a strong army, and slowly but surely allied himself with the federalists who were powerful in all the western and northwestern sections of the country. By May, 1842, the correspondence between Santa Anna and Paredes had become so acrimonious as to indicate that a break was imminent.

Meanwhile another complication had arisen. March 5, 1842, was the date for the election of deputies to the new congress which was to perform the important duty of making a constitution. In spite of the efforts of the army men, there was a clear majority of *sansculottes,* or federalists, deputies elected. Many thought the new delegates would not be allowed to assemble, but on June 10 they came together determined to organize a federal republic in spite of the known desires of the executive.

[182]

For a time the disagreement became more and more serious till in October Santa Anna made a mistake. He resorted to his old trick of retiring to Manga de Clavo to watch developments. On the plea of his wife's ill health permission was granted, but this deceived no one. Bravo, the President of the Council, took charge of affairs. The agent could not work with the assurance and skill of the Master, and so affairs went slightly less well than before, and Santa Anna received the full blame anyway. The Minister of War, Tornel, whom many considered as the spokesman of Santa Anna, openly said the proposed constitution was a "code of anarchy." The *Mosquito Mexicano* had written on December 6: "The Constitution of 1824 was bad, that of 1836 worse, and that of 1843 is going to be the worst."

The deadlock soon became hopeless and Bravo, obviously working under instructions, dissolved Congress on December 19, 1842. Of course there were the usual appeals to the people while the deputies insisted that armed force had prevented the people's representatives from performing their duties. Whatever may be said of the wisdom or folly of the course of Santa Anna, it was clear to all that the master had thrown off the mask and had once more become the dictator.

The foregoing events show Santa Anna as an administrator facing national problems, but no picture of the man is complete that leaves out the social and personal events of his life. He was tremendously and energetically social; and as the years passed the craving grew to the proportions of a passion in itself.

His family life occupied little of his attention, and, though he always showed the most sincere regard for his wife he had a number of children born out of wedlock. So far as is known, these were freely and frankly recognized by him at all times. Not only are five of them mentioned in his last will and testament, but, on July 7, 1842, he wrote from his office, as President, the following typical family letter to one of his natural children:

[183]

"My dear Pedro:

Answering your letter of the 5th inst., I want to say that you did wrong in not making an estimate of the repairs on your house before you began them. I am not able to furnish you with $800.00, because I have obligations to meet for the payment of the Encesco [Encero?] Hacienda, which I bought. I have not received a cent of the salary due me, and furthermore, I had to furnish the General Treasury with $30,000.00 urgent expense for that garrison, which amount the Treasury still owes me. I have not a cent to spare you.

With regards to Augustina,

Your father, who loves you, and is at your service.

A. L. Santa Anna."[11]

In Mexico City every act of the Dictator's family was a matter for public interest. Sra. Santa Anna was a deeply religious woman and greatly admired by all. When she fell sick from pneumonia in May, 1842, special prayer services were held all over the city for her recovery. All hope seemed to be abandoned, so the Archbishop headed an enormous parade of clerical, lay and military dignitaries, said to have been accompanied by twenty-thousand people carrying eight thousand candles to perform the last rites of the Church. In spite of the excitement and turmoil, the crisis passed and the lady was spared for a short time longer.

A few days later, Santa Anna ordered all Government offices to be closed for three days so that the employees could go with him to the great festival at St. Augustine. There the scenes varied from the tragic to the ridiculous. While the banker blandly presided over the tables, there could be seen the barefoot man, with matted hair, haggard eyes and livid face, watching with the intensity of despair while the chips fell. With success would come some food and clothing for the equally ragged and despairing wife and family in some hovel, plus an orgy of drinking and debauchery. With failure, there would be a patient or pathetic shrug of the shoulders and, with no appreciable change of countenance, one man

11. Wharton, *op. cit.*, pp. 87-88.

[184]

would leave the celebration and some nearby gang of brigands probably receive a new recruit.

At the cock-pits, similar scenes were enacted. As at the gaming tables, certain pits were reserved for the gentry where only silver, and in some cases only gold, wagers were accepted. The Master of Ceremonies opened the event with his cry: "Hail, most pure Mary, the cocks are coming (*Ave Maria purissima los gallos vienen*)." There was no confusion or loud talking; all was done decently and in order. According to one description:

"As far as the company went, it might have been the House of Representatives in Washington; the ladies in the gallery, listening to the debates, and the members in the body of the house surrounding Messrs. ——— and ———, or any other two vehement orators; applauding their biting remarks and cutting saracasms, and encouraging them to crow over each other. The President might have been the speaker, and the corps diplomatique represented itself."[12]

The birds did not last long, for each was armed with strong steel knives in place of spurs. And when birds were trained to jump and slash with these, every few minutes one of them would go down in a pool of blood and after one or two pathetic jerks would lie still. The United States Minister recorded that it was omnious to him to note that the applause was greatest when the President's bird was killed.

The President himself was now at his physical prime. Waddy Thompson wrote of his "finely proportioned person" five feet, ten inches tall and said: "I do not know that I have ever seen a more striking and finely formed head and face." Then he added: "I have seen no countenance except that of General Jackson, whose range of expression was so great, where there was so great a difference between the quiet expression of the face when at rest and in a gentle mood, and its terrible ferocity when highly excited. The mildness of the lamb and the fierceness of the enraged tiger would not much too strongly express this difference. Such is his character, by

12. Madame Calderón de la Barca, *op. cit.*, p. 206.

nature kind and affectionate...."[13] He looked every inch the ruler and had ample private funds with which to play the part. In addition, all army contracts were made through him, so that substantial perquisites were available if needed.

The whole government service was under detailed instructions as to the uniforms of all public officials. When the President left the Palace, he was accompanied by an elaborate cavalry escort. At his formal dinners, members of his staff stood in constant attendance to properly impress the carefully selected guests. Balls at the Palace, however, were another matter. "In fact, I saw few of the ladies belonging to the aristocracy; but very many others who had no business there," wrote Waddy Thompson. "If a corporal, who has married the daughter of the washer-woman of the regiment, has risen to the highest station in the army, his wife cannot be slighted with safety—and such cases have occurred."[14]

Flatterers, sycophants and hangers-on vied with each other in their attentions, so it was not surprising that this boy, reared without the balance-wheel of either family background or training, should have committed that glaring *faux-pas* which was to pillory him with ridicule throughout his country's history. Just as he was about to leave for Manga de Clavo, a splendid ceremony was planned by which the people would remember their hero. On September 27, the leg which had been amputated near Veracruz was to be interred in a magnificent monument especially built for the purpose.

With the hero present, there was first a great military demonstration followed by a spread-eagle oration by Ignacio Sierra y Rosso. In vain did the orator declare that "the holy and terrible Place" of this interment caused his soul to "burn with the fire of enthusiasm" as he contemplated the pride of the nation, the Hero of Veracruz, the martyr, who had devoted his leg to his country. One or two rapscallion punsters seized the opportunity and broadcast anonymous skits making sport of the whole performance. One of these pictured an assemblage of the dead holding a solemn protest

13. Thompson, *op. cit.,* pp. 66-68.
14. *Ibid.,* p. 161.

[186]

meeting and signing a petition to their congress to refuse to accept this leg into their midst for fear it still carried some revolutionary germs that would disorganize their happy country. That would be bad enough, they declared, but it would be an unspeakable catastrophe if the revolution should be successful and as a result they should find themselves ruled over by a leg as yet unjoined by the rest of its body.

Yes, Santa Anna, the Master, had become the Dictator. However, his strength of character and his alarming weaknesses, his determination and his foibles, resulted in the juxtaposition of the sublime and the ridiculous. To the discerning there were already indications of cross currents and shoal waters ahead.

DESPOT

WHILE the complications just noted were becoming more and more serious Santa Anna was down on his estate enjoying his hobby of raising fighting cocks. According to one foreign visitor the owner watched every detail of the training and feeding of his chief pets. When the visitor specially admired one beautiful bird, the host at once said that if he won his fight he would be given to the guest. Of the fifteen that entered the shambles, this bird was the only one that won, yet the visitor had scarcely reached New York on his return home when the fowl arrived safely with Santa Anna's compliments.

It should not be supposed, however, that the magnitude of national events or the pettiness of cockfighting absorbed all of Santa Anna's energies. He cared little or nothing about the details of ranching or farming, but the Clove Spike Hacienda had absorbed so many neighboring properties that practically the whole region from Jalapa to Veracruz was under the same owner. His chief desire was that his power should be recognized and his success admitted: if he owned an hacienda, it must dominate the countryside. But, after all, just at this time the estate and chickens were only avocations to the man, who was shrewdly watching and guiding events through the medium of the procession of visitors who put up at the inns of Jalapa, or who stayed at Manga de Clavo for periods varying from a few hours to a day or so. To keep closer to public affairs, he spent a part of his time at the hacienda of Pacho, the property of his friend, the Prefect of the District, Sr. José J. Gutiérrez. This was just a few miles from Jalapa and saved many hours of weary climbing up and down the edge of the plateau for the couriers from all parts of the republic.

Up in the Capital, meanwhile, Acting President Bravo promptly carried out orders and, on January 2, 1843, the Assembly of Notables came together. Four days later, the body was organized in the salon of the old congress and, acting under instructions, assumed the duties of the dissolved constitutional convention. General Valencia was elected president of the body which at once settled down to work.

By the end of February, it was obvious that all was not well and that the Master in person was needed in Mexico City. This did not please him at all as could be seen from the querulous note in a letter sent to Paredes on February 20, 1843. He said that he was having to go to Mexico City, thanks in part to the awkward position in which he found himself because of the varying conduct of Bravo and others. "My health is not good"; he added, "but I realize that it is necessary to sacrifice it, and this I shall not fail to do for my native land, even though it should mean my life."[1]

On March 5, he made his usual splendid entry into the city, having been duly escorted all the way from Puebla by those who wished—or were forced—to do him homage. A brilliant comet appeared in the heavens just at this time, and was pointed to as a most auspicious omen even though the treasury was bare and foreign nations were clamoring for sums of money long overdue to their nationals.

So far as the northern boundary was concerned, there were numerous possibilities to be considered. Great Britain and France would have been greatly pleased with Texas as an independent nation while Great Britain would have liked a foothold in California. On the other hand, the United States hardly felt in a position to intervene in Texas or California at the time, but certainly did not approve of European intervention. A local element in the situation was the number of Texans held as prisoners at Perote. One of these was ex-Lieutenant Governor, James W. Robinson.

While Santa Anna was on his hacienda a part of the prisoners had attempted to escape. When they were recaptured orders were issued that they be decimated by way of intimi-

1. Genaro Garcia, editor, *El General Paredes y Arrillaga* . . ., p. 79.

dation against further attempts at flight. Just after this Robinson wrote to Santa Anna at Manga de Clavo, suggesting that an armistice be agreed to and that he be allowed to go back to Texas to discuss certain terms which he suggested for a treaty. These included recognition of the sovereignty of Mexico with essential independence for Texas on all local questions. Santa Anna forwarded this letter to the Minister of War and Acting President and suggested its careful consideration. Bravo promptly left the matter in the hands of Santa Anna, who talked things over at Manga de Clavo with Robinson. The Texan had secured his chief objective, freedom, and so gleefully proceeded to his home. When he got there, Houston, the Texan President, refused to approve the tentative arrangement but was willing to consider the armistice.

Meanwhile, the Texan representative at London reported Great Britain was anxious for peace, but was convinced that Santa Anna was simply stalling for time; that he wished to settle the Yucatán troubles and that he would then act forcibly as to Texas.[2] In June, Santa Anna had decreed a merciless war against Texas, including the treatment of all foreigners as pirates, but, as he probably expected, it was impossible to go ahead with the campaign. The armistice proposed was therefore agreed to in September so as to discuss matters further.

By the following spring, England sent word that if Texan independence were granted by Mexico, England and France would try to prevent annexation of the rebels to the United States. Santa Anna pounced upon this idea with delight, and proceeded to twist it to his own ends. He told one of the deputies, "I shall send this communication to the Congress,—show them that England will stand by us,—and they must now give the money" for an active prosecution of the war. "The English Government say we must either conquer Texas or grant its independence—what will Congress say to that?" The British Minister vigorously protested at such a misuse of meaning of the proposal and prevented the transmission of

2. Garrison, *op. cit.*, Smith to Jones, II, 1094-95.

Santa Anna (Napoleonic pose)

the communication to Congress. When word of all this reached London, the clear cut answer came:...."if the President, contrary to our hopes and beliefs, were to take the rash step of invading Texas with a view to its forcible reconquest, and if, by so doing, he should find himself involved in difficulties with other countries, he must not look for the support of Great Britain in aiding him to extricate himself from those difficulties."[3] This did not permit misunderstanding.

As might have been expected, the armistice with Texas did not last long, and the breathing of fire and brimstone continued with constant threats of invasions and the issuance of drastic orders for the conduct of a campaign—always just in the future—that would proceed by sea and land. Of course, this did not go very far. For one thing, the clergy, who knew they would have to pay most of the bills, objected; and for another, the almost certain intervention of the United States on the side of the Texans had to be considered. Thus the time passed with stalling and dickering, and the making of political capital out of the whole question. By the maintenance of a truculent attitude, Santa Anna could the better justify necessary payments on United States claims and the liberation of the Texan prisoners, at the same time that he secured appropriations for a large army.

The money question was demanding more and more attention. As a matter of fact, the national income, according to a treasury report rendered in 1844, had reached well over 29,000,000 *pesos* but expenditures were still more than that. Import duties had been raised a flat 20 per cent, while additional pieces of property had been confiscated here and there, several of them at the expense of the clergy. To raise the cash for the claims payments due the United States in the latter part of 1843 a large number of landlords were asked to the office of the Secretary of State. Thirty men appeared and were "invited" to help raise money for the payment unless they preferred the alternative of a forced loan. They made up eighteen thousand *pesos* only, so a total loan of 2,500,000 *pesos* was announced of which the clergy and landlords were to

3. E. D. Adams, *British Interests and Activities in Texas*, pp. 169-86.

pay 270,000,000 *pesos* in four days. When any individual failed to pay the sum arbitrarily imposed, his property was taken by force and "coaches, pianos, and fine furniture" were taken out and placed on sale for the first buyer.

As for the clergy, they were more and more subjected to a paternal despotism by the government. For fairly obvious reasons, no real property of the Church or jewels from the temples could be sold without government permission. On the other hand, the clergy were also the beneficiaries of the new despotism and, in June, 1843, there was issued a decree that permitted the reintroduction of the Jesuits into Mexico; in September, the decree of six years earlier refusing entrance to foreign regular clergymen was repealed; and in October, the Sisters of Charity were allowed to enter the Republic. The permit for the readmission of the Jesuits was explained by the great need for active missionary work to control the Indians in the northwest, but taken in connection with the other decrees it became part of the definite Church program of the dictatorship, i.e., to foster Church organizations but to demand—or take—liberal contributions from them.

Internal improvements proceeded apace especially around the Capital. The Dictator laid the cornerstone of a new military hospital and ordered a number of bridges to be built. Fairs were encouraged and, in 1843, the famous old Parian (a ruinous group of buildings owned by the Town Council of Mexico City and rented to numerous leading dry goods merchants) was ordered demolished to make way for the beautification of the city. The protests of the City Fathers who were losing thirty thousand *pesos* a year rental, and of the merchants who were given only fifteen days' notice before they had to vacate the buildings, were of no avail. The city was beautified and the masses could see how powerful their ruler was.

So the *léperos,* as the masses of the country were called, did their petty stealing and had their love affairs by night, and came out by day to shout "vivas" for any idol of the bull-ring—either animal or man—or any political or military hero, yet in the midst of rascality their grimy fists would tightly clutch copper coins to be spent for a candle to be offered as thanksgiving at some shrine or for the repose of the soul of some departed one. Back on the street once more, the problem was to acquire actual bread without work. This just now seemed most available through the Despot, but they were always quite ready to drop all work to admire some beautiful flower, to flirt with some pretty girl, or to yell a few "mueras" ("death to" the opposite of "viva," meaning "long life to") for the same man of whom they had appeared to be so enamored a few days or hours before.

No one knew the psychology of the masses better than Santa Anna who fed them with such a variety of activities and news that there was little time for any one to pall upon them. Sometimes it was a gala performance at the great new Santa Anna theatre seating eight thousand people; sometimes the news that he had arrogated to himself the right to grant all licenses to practice law, medicine, or the other professions (he who had scarcely been to school in his life); sometimes that his hangers-on had bestowed presents worth thousands of *pesos* upon him on his saint's day; sometimes that orders had been issued for his portrait to be hung in the public buildings of every town in some Department, or that some splendid new statue was to be unveiled in his honor. One such statue was unveiled in the Capital June 13, 1844, and showed the hero stretching out his arm toward the north and aspiring to the reconquest of Texas. The irreverent snickered to themselves on noting that this grasping hand was yearning towards the national treasury, which was directly to the north of the statue. At the unveiling, a minor incident delayed the ceremonies when the cord, holding the curtain in place, failed to work properly and got caught around the neck of the statute—a clear indication, said the evil-minded, that the original was to be hung for his many rascalities.

Santa Anna knew that he was dealing with masses, each of whom with equal whimsicality, would divide his last tortilla with a mangy starving cur or who would bind its jaws so as to watch in safety while prying open its sores and torturing it to death to find out just how much pain it could stand. He knew that respect and fear were closely akin, and so never let them forget that he could strike with the force of a god and with the devastating completeness of a devil.

Explanations to such people were superfluous, he felt, for they were hardly likely to criticize his pleasures except by way of indicating their own envy. His letter to Tornel, written May 8, 1844, was to answer the rising criticism among the classes. In it, he said that word had come that he was wasting his time on cock-fighting when he should have been doing other things. His answer was: "every man can enjoy himself as he pleases, provided he maintains a proper dignity and does his gambling with gentlemen and, as I do, for entertainment and not for speculation; entertainment is very necessary for a man isolated in the country as I am where the spectacles, dances and promenades of the capital do not take place."[4]

The sum and substance of this criticism, however, was derived from something more serious than cock-fighting. Reports came out constantly that the idea of being a dictator had so gone to his head that all others were looked upon as lackeys. His ministers found themselves called upon for the service of menials and even Sr. Lucas Alamán, with his proud family background for generations and his education and bearing which would have made him welcome at the court of any European sovereign, was startled and speechless on being addressed as a servant and told to bring the Dictator his hat. Also there were constant mutterings among the better informed at the princely haciendas recently acquired by the leaders of the government. The servant was generally felt worthy of his hire, but could all this be classed as hire?

In national affairs no one could deny that Bravo had labored well in the interests of the Dictator, so it was not surprising that he became tired of the position of puppet even though he held the title of Acting President. As a result, Santa Anna returned to power early in March for a seven months period.

So far as obvious politics were concerned, all seemed to be going reasonably well. The Assembly of Notables, acting as

4. Méndez, "Santa Anna, el anormal," *Todo,* April 10, 1934.

a constitutional convention, carried out their instructions and by June, 1843, had produced the *Bases Orgánicas* as the instrument of government for the nation. In brief, this provided that: the departments were at the mercy of the central government on all important questions; and that the franchise was limited to those with an annual income of two hundred *pesos*, while deputies and senators were required to have incomes of twelve hundred and two thousand *pesos* respectively. Also the special privileges and *fueros* of the Church and army were definitely guaranteed.

On June 12, Santa Anna duly took the oath under the new constitution, which was officially proclaimed the next day. In its honor an amnesty was declared for all political offenders. There was the *Te Deum* and the public oath of support by the clergy and officials, followed by the inevitable military review. The Dictator graciously threw into the crowd five hundred *pesos* of twenty-five *centavo* pieces, but observers noted that there was little spontaneity in the applause. As a spectacle it was about up to the average, but the hero had done nothing heroic for several years and the hero worshippers were beginning to forget and to indulge in vague talk about "liberties" and "rights." Few knew what they meant by the words, but it was a well known fact that the peoples' own representatives had not been allowed to meet and that the new constitution was the product of the Dictator's friends.

After a few months, however, the old story was repeated and there was little in the Capital to entertain Santa Anna. As soon as he had satiated the keen edge of his appetites the gayeties of the great city meant little to this man who craved stronger stimulants. There was some work to be done in patching his political fences for the election about to be held under the new constitution but this was work for menials and he preferred not to appear in it personally. That the work was done rather skillfully is obvious from the account of C. M. Bustamante, who by this time was a severe critic of the Dictator. He recorded that he was invited on July 22 to become a member of Santa Anna's Council at a salary of four thousand *pesos* per year plus certain other perquisites. He declined, commenting: "that salary is paid in three installments,—late—partially and never." He then added: "in reality it [the Council] is nothing but a tea party (*tertulia*), and to maintain it sixty-eight thousand *pesos* are spent annually. Out with such a drove of asses! The Count of Santiago has been named in my place. 'He is as tasteless as chocolate,' as one old woman said."[5]

Meanwhile the people must not hear the wrong things. On September 27th, there was to be a great celebration of the entrance of the revolutionary Army of the Three Guarantees (the popular name for Iturbide's army after the announcement of the Plan of Iguala) into Mexico City. A well-known orator, J. M. Laragua, had been selected to grace the occasion, but, when the time came, the speaker could not be found and the program fell flat. Word finally circulated to the effect that the proof of the speaker's address had not pleased the censors for it reflected unpleasantly upon the dictatorship. Hence the gentleman was in prison "incomunicado."

As just said, this kind of work was far better done by subordinates for "an eagle does not peck at flies." To keep up such nagging supervision might easily weaken the Dictator's position on the eve of the election, so he again asked to be relieved of his onerous duties. The man selected for the *ad interim* appointment was Valentín Canalizo, a man of some force but one who was entirely devoted to the interests of the Dictator. His selection was readily approved by the Ministers—whom Santa Anna could remove from office at will.

To keep the record straight and make sure of due appreciation the retiring executive issued a proclamation to the nation. This reviewed his accomplishments in solving the copper money troubles, in improving the educational system, in the building up of business, and in the defense of the national honor. Then, on October 5, he set out for Jalapa and by easy stages continued through his vast estates till he

5. Alvarez, *Carlos María de Bustamante*, pp. 159-60.

reached Veracruz a month later "where he was received as a monarch."

As word began to come in from the elections, it was obvious that all was not going well. Department after Department, in spite of the elaborate electoral machinery, was understood to have reaffirmed its stand of a year before in selecting anti-Santa Anna delegates. When the legislators met in January, 1844, Canalizo greeted them with an able address on the success and accomplishments of the administration. In his official response, the President of the Senate struck a new and somewhat surprising note when he stated that the Executive was mistaken for the national commerce had been destroyed; that the new tariffs had doubled and quadrupled earlier prices though manufacturers were not paying proportionately increased rates; that agricultural production was declining and the mines producing less; that the national debt was rising and the executive wanting still more money to spend. Such a direct challenge was truly alarming.

Early on the morning of January 2, 1844, the galleries were crowded as the members of the two houses slowly gathered in joint session to open the departmental votes on the presidential election. Amidst poorly suppressed excitement, the final vote was announced as nineteen votes for Santa Anna to continue in office for five years, and only two votes for other candidates. The publication of the election returns deceived no one; it simply meant that the opposition was as yet in the sniping stage and was unorganized. A few days later, a test case arose when Senator M. Gómez Pedraza introduced a resolution that Canalizo be removed as Acting President. At once the galleries roared their applause even though the senators rejected the suggestion.

Santa Anna was now truly indisposed—mentally if not physically. It was difficult to tell where the situation might lead, so he reported himself as unable to go up to the city for the inauguration. Meanwhile the vast bulk of the army was concentrated in the region between Veracruz and the Capital, so he could march forward in case of need. A month after Congress first met, United States Minister Thompson still reported that Santa Anna's strength lay in the factionalism and lack of leadership of the opposition. "The army is in his interest and so are the clergy generally. The former, as in all similar cases, of which history informs us, will remain faithful, as long as he can pay them, which it seems to me impossible that he can do much longer, without encroaching on the property of the latter. So that I think there is good ground to believe, that before very long he must lose one or the other. It is hard to say which of the two (the army or the Church) is the strongest."[6]

After two months of aimless talking and criticism Congress adjourned. It "began by proposing to annul many of his [Santa Anna's] decrees; but adjourned without doing so in any one instance." Even such restrictions as were urged upon his indiscriminate use of power were emasculated by his friends in the legislative process and were then ignored after passage.

Out in the west the situation was becoming critical for Paredes y Arrillaga was reported to have joined the federalists. That meant he must have special consideration so he was called to Mexico City and placed on the legislative Junta. To lull suspicions further he was given the important position of Commanding General of the Department of Mexico. After this, the blow fell. He was suddenly accused of insubordination, arrested and then placed in charge of an expedition to far-off Yucatán. On May 23, 1844, Santa Anna wrote him a letter deploring his questionable conduct and telling him that all had been arranged for him to come to the Capital as Acting President when the rumors concerning his treachery became so flagrant that the national government would have been stultified by calling him to that high office. Whether the letter was disingenuous or real, the fact remained that the support of an influential army man now had been lost permanently.

Having shown his independence and a willingness to flout both Congress and the high office to which he had just been elected, the Dictator made his tardy appearance in Mexico

6. *Mexico, Despatches,* Thompson to Secretary of State Upshur, February 2, 1844, XI (Thompson, No. 40).

City late in the afternoon of June 3. There was the usual reception with salvos of artillery, bell ringing, and a parade of one hundred and fifty coaches, mostly filled with those who had "axes to grind." Congress soon learned the cause of the return when it received a request for an appropriation of four million *pesos* and thirty thousand men to carry on an active campaign against Texas. Many were convinced that both men and money were wanted for domestic purposes and that the Texan question was simply the proverbial "red herring" though some troops had been secretly—but not too secretly—despatched to the north.

Congress was in a quandary. A special committee presented a "long and singular" document stamped with dread of the extraordinary powers of the executive. However, it did not blame the Dictator but employed the old trick and constantly complained of his ministry. They recommended appropriating one million *pesos* only and declared that the regular army must be left as it was though local militia might be called out if the "national independence" was in danger. These, in turn, were only to be used outside of their home communities by express permission of Congress. Santa Anna refused to allow this report to appear in *El Diario* (the official organ) but it was published by *El Siglo XIX* anyway.[7] When Congress approved the committee report the issue was squarely joined, with editorials in *El Diario* and other government papers openly denouncing Congress for its flagrant lack of patriotism. Of little avail now was the unveiling of a great gilded bronze statue in honor of the Dictator.

In August, Santa Anna called for the presiding officer of the Chamber of Deputies and read him a two hour lecture on the duties and position of various members of the government. Promptly the word was passed on to the Chamber as information. By the end of August, plots were rife in the Capital. Gómez Farías, in New Orleans, received the following code letter describing events:

7. For a discussion of the relations of Santa Anna and Congress see *Mexico, Despatches,* reports of Ben E. Green to J. C. Calhoun, June 7, 15, 21, 1844, XII.

"Mexico, thirty-first of August, eighteen hundred and forty-four. friend never have the affairs of your country been in such a condition as today; santa anna is obliged to leave the capital; he is threatened with assassination from one moment to the next; the troops which are in tacubaya are under arms day and night, the cannon loaded, the horses saddled, and all the troops in barracks. The destruction of the congress is rumored, but all the forces on which he [Santa Anna] relies are going to rebel, no one can talk to him because he fears everyone; within four days he is leaving for vera cruz. Senor herrera remains as president for two weeks while canalizo comes from san Luis, and in place of canalizo general arista [one of the rebels] is going to take command of the troops which are found in san Luis potosi. In short a revolution is going to break out at any moment, certainly within two weeks, but it is certain that the man is going from this act to the gallows....people are asking for you and even individuals who were your enemies in the year thirty-three have said they recognize their mistakes and confess that you are the only man who is suitable to control....all that I write you is heard openly on the streets....and public places.... It is said that some correspondence which you sent to olaguibal has been captured and has reached the hands of Santa ana. I would regret exceedingly his securing any letter from me since there have been those who have told me that I was in correspondence with you as a result I have prepared (*fingido*) a letter as though it had been sent by you to me and I have showed it to some so that Santa Anna will order me to let him see it."[8]

While the foundations of his government were thus trembling, a tragedy had happened in Santa Anna's personal family. Doña Inés could stand the strain no longer. She died in Puebla on August 23 at the age of thirty-three, just when she should have been entering into life at its fullest. Her life had been a strenuous one. Born January 21, 1811, she was married in August, 1825, when little more than a child and began

8. The original of this letter, in code, was found by the author in 1924 in the *Gómez Farías Papers*, García Collection.

a life of constant physical and nervous activity. She was never a strong woman and one imagines that her glamorous lord and master was rather a strain upon her nerves to say the least of it. As has already been noted, Santa Anna mentions four children in his will: two boys, Antonio (who died as a child), and Manuel; as well as two daughters, María Guadalupe and María del Carmen. In addition, there are the drifting accounts of the child whose mentality was somewhat impaired and of whom the father was said to be so much ashamed that he did not wish him to appear in Mexico City. The mother, as noted above, was reported to have been devoted to the unfortunate one, and to have stayed on the hacienda for long periods of time because of him.

The whole nation held Doña Inés in the highest esteem, and, regardless of what slurs and attacks were hurled at the husband, none was directed at her. Also, her husband, though often unfaithful to her, never referred to her except in terms of the highest respect and commendation both as a manager and as a wife.

Her death took place at 6:30 P.M. on Friday, whereupon couriers dashed off to Tacubaya and notified the Dictator at 1:30 the next afternoon. On Monday the sumptuous funeral services began in the Cathedral of the Capital. The music was furnished by a band of sixty pieces and the Archbishop officiated in person. Santa Anna had a thousand masses said in the chapel of the cathedral, and thus eased his own feelings and made a royal display for the edification of the nation.

Details of the life and character of Doña Inés are scant, but this sketch from the pen of a modern Mexican biographer, while doubtless overemphasizing her economy and personal labor, is well worth considering:

"I lack further information concerning Doña Inés García; but I imagine her as a lady who on marrying turned over her life to her husband (certainly a domineering person and given to polygamy) and to her children. A woman of the coast, affectionate and simple in actions, prompt and early about her duties in the morning dew and under the stars still

[201]

in flight in the warm coastal dawn; with hands hardened by the milking of cows; clothed in cheap cloth; with mind strong to manage mayordomos or peons; often mounted on a side saddle in the style of the time on her favorite horse. Disinclined to interfering in his political strife, she must have been for her centrifugal husband as a soothing drink to which he could resort after his harsh experiences in the Palace, in war, or in his turbid amours."[9]

Shortly after her death, the Dictator asked Congress for permission to go to his estates to mourn with his children. Unfortunately, he had hardly shown himself a sufficiently ideal husband for this request to be taken at face value by a skeptical congress. The two committees on Constitutionality and Internal Affairs (*Gobernación*) met, considered the request, and reported that they considered the motive satisfactory and that his absence would not injure the country. Congress was, of course, well aware of the rumors that Santa Anna desired to place himself at the head of his troops either to dash up to Texas, or to overthrow the government, but it finally gave the permission in secret session by a vote of forty to fourteen.

On September 12, without waiting for the arrival of his regular substitute, Canalizo, the Dictator dumped the executive shadow (he kept the substance) upon the shoulders of José Joaquín Herrera, the President of the Council, and promptly set out for Manga de Clavo. All indications are that the man was "at sea." He did not know just what to do, or how to do it. He wanted time to think and plan—many would say to scheme and plot.

9. Méndez, *op. cit., Todo,* July 3, 1934.

COLLAPSE

WHEN Santa Anna reached El Encero, his new hacienda close to Jalapa, he found it lonesome and dreary. It needed the guiding hand of a woman to enable it to cater to a man's needs in the fullest sense of the word. Doña Inés had been far from well for months, so her spouse had had plenty of time in which to consider possible candidates for her place. To be considered, the applicant must be pretty, she must be vivacious, she must be young, and she must be of a reasonably good family, for Santa Anna was in a position to choose and he was a conoisseur of feminine charms.

The candidates had obviously been considered, and the winner notified before the grief stricken husband left for Jalapa, though, for the sake of the proprieties, nothing was made public. Finally, Santa Anna's impetuous love could stand the strain no longer, so he ordered the period of official mourning to be curtailed and the nation notified to rejoice with him in his great good fortune. The winner as announced was Señorita María Dolores Tosta, a young lady of fifteen years, who was generally known as something of a beauty, if somewhat headstrong and impetuous.[1]

The bride-to-be had no intention of marrying an old man of fifty in some out-of-the-way provincial capital. Poor girl, well might she gather roses while she could, there were to be many thorns on each stem, and the price high indeed. Little did she dream that the future whispering in corners as she passed

---

1. It is interesting to note that Santa Anna in his will refers to the death of Doña Inés as having taken place in April, 1844, but mentions no day of the month. This was clearly a misstatement of the facts and was doubtless a gesture at self-vindication in an effort to make it appear that there was a greater interval between her death and his remarriage. The will also gives the date of the second marriage as October 8, another misstatement.

was to be largely that of pity and malice satisfied and seldom indeed that of envy. The date for the ceremony was set for October 3, 1844, at the National Cathedral, with all the pomp and circumstance of a royal wedding. The bridegroom could scarcely afford to make the trip so soon after his departure, so Juan de Dios Cañedo graciously assumed the double rôle of master of ceremonies and bridegroom by proxy. Canalizo graced the occasion, the bride was given a carefully staged ovation, cannon roared, public buildings were illuminated and there was much noise. On the eleventh, the bride reached Jalapa while the nation expressed its grave disapproval of the violation of the canons of decency and respect which they considered should govern the conduct of all. Sport might be made of the living, but the memory of the dead was held sacred.

In his will, Santa Anna declared that he gave his new wife as a dowry two houses in the Capital: one on San Augustine Street, valued at fifty thousand *pesos;* and another on Vergara Street worth twenty thousand *pesos,* as well as jewelry and other items. But the girl was not destined to see much of Capital society with herself as the First Lady. On arriving at Jalapa, she was escorted to the hacienda of El Encero, some ten or twelve miles distant on the Veracruz road.

The hacienda buildings were on the top of a hill about a third of a mile to the right of the highway. After passing a group of peon huts the traveler entered through a massive stone arch and portico to see the very pretty chapel.[2] Twenty-five yards farther on was the main building, which faced east like the chapel. Two long galleries supported by massive stone arches gave a view over hills and valleys to the east and north, where grew oranges, bananas, coffee and mangoes at the whim of either nature or man. The house was rather small for such an estate and contained only about a dozen rooms though it was substantially enlarged on the south and west by two walled-in areas, that might be called *patios* or

2. In 1934 it had been broken open, its altars desecrated and the building defiled by farm animals wandering in and out.

court yards, to be used for the business and pleasure of the owners.

Here, under his own vine and fig tree,[3] the Dictator passed his honeymoon, listening to the chatter of an active little stream that furnished the place with water as it ran within a few yards of the back of the house. Doña Dolores was probably quite voluble and enthusiastic about the rustic and bucolic beauties for a time, but soon let it be known by acts and words that she had not married to be buried on a country hacienda when there were all the bright lights of Mexico City to be enjoyed.

It might be noted here that there were no children by this marriage. In no place in his writings does Santa Anna criticize his second wife, but his outspoken praise of his first wife in his will, written twenty-three years after her death and while Doña Dolores was still living, leaves the implication that the gay social butterfly had hardly filled the place of her predecessor in the respect and regard of the husband of the two. In fact, acquaintances of the family have handed down the tradition that, as financial and political reverses followed fast upon each other, the new lady of the household became more than a little grasping and shrewish in her disposition.

The honeymoon idyl was soon harshly interrupted. Early in November it was understood that Paredes, at the head of two thousand men had launched a rebellion. This was something definite. Inactivity was over. Now for a ringing call to battle, a wild dash to the front, victory and hero-worship once more!

The British Minister was notified that Mexico would recognize the Republic of Texas in return for a cash sum, with the northern boundary of Mexico to be guaranteed by Great

3. In 1934, in the center of the western courtyard were to be seen two fig trees, said to be of the banyan variety. They had been planted close together so that they had grown into one single trunk some four feet through at a distance of five feet from the ground, while the combined trunks. were nine or ten feet through at the same height. The branches arched out to a radius of forty-five feet with their twists and turns festooned with native orchids. Tradition has it that part of Santa Anna's treasure is hidden beneath these trees, but digging in recent years has only unearthed the skeleton of some poor departed soul.

[205]

Britain and France. Seven thousand infantry, one thousand five hundred cavalry and twenty cannon were at once mobilized and set out for the Capital under the personal command of Santa Anna. Congress was asked for "necessary means to enable the Government to put down the revolution," but United States Minister Shannon was sure that this would not be granted for a majority of Congress hoped the revolution would succeed. He wrote that there were also serious complications down in the south. "The officers of the Government charged with the daily collecting contributions have in many instances been arrested, their right hands cut off and in other respects cruelly treated. Large military forces have been sent by the Gov't. to restore order and enforce the collections of the contributions."[4]

On November 18, Santa Anna reached Mexico City, and, after a formal entrance and *Te Deum* at the shrine of Gaudalupe, took up his residence in the home of Canon Corona in the village of Guadalupe. Here Canalizo promptly paid his respects while the next day most of the senators and deputies were invited to foregather with the Dictator. The session was an eye opener and lasted four hours while Santa Anna listened calmly to many bitter truths. He was made to realize that he must make concessions to secure congressional support and so offered to annul many of the most dictatorial of his acts and to give an accounting to the Congress for his administration. This conciliatory attitude came so late that it availed little with a thoroughly skeptical group of men.

Three days later, on November 22, he set out for Querétaro on his way to try issues with Paredes. Congress forthwith moved to impeach the Minister of War in what was really an attack on Santa Anna. The Constitution provided that the President could not command the army and, though Santa Anna was not in active charge of the office, Congress claimed that his present appointment was unconstitutional unless the approval of the legislative body was secured. The Minister justified his acts, saying that Santa Anna was not the actual

4. *Mexico, Despatches,* Shannan to Calhoun, November 12, 1844 (Shannon, No. 4).

executive and that he was in charge of the army only, hence was not violating the law. The defense was greeted by cat-calls, hooting and whistling in the galleries so that Congress had to continue the discussion in secret session. When the deadlock continued Canalizo dissolved the legislative branch on the twenty-ninth and took over full war powers. Congress promptly retorted by declaring Canalizo ousted from office and issued formal pronouncements which declared the con-duct of Santa Anna that of a rebel.

The situation was further aggravated by events in Querétaro. On approaching the city on the twenty-fifth, Santa Anna or-dered the departmental junta to meet and officially withdraw its pronunciamiento against him within twenty-four hours. It not only declined to do this, but added insult to injury by reaffirming its former stand and by daring him to try to carry out his threat of having the members of the junta sent as prisoners to the Castle of Perote.

The kaleidoscope that was Mexico now whirled rapidly. While Paredes hastily looked for cover in the shape of some good stronghold in which to meet the onslaught of the greatly feared Santa Anna, events were suddenly taken out of his hands. On December 2, the Chamber of Deputies, by a vote of forty-five to ten (nine others later joined the majority) formally protested against the dictatorial conduct of the ad-ministration and of Santa Anna. This was approved by the Senate. Canalizo in retaliation ordered all officials to take an oath to support the administration, but the Supreme Court by publicly refusing to do so on the 3rd added fuel to the flames. The next morning an amused and half fearful populace found the recently erected statue of Santa Anna with a hang-man's halter around its neck and an enormous fool's cap on its head. Two days later part of the troops in the city an-nounced they had joined the Congress in its opposition to the Dictator and the masses poured by the thousands into the square in front of the National Palace.

Canalizo ordered the rest of the troops to march against the rebels. They refused. The mob, out of hand, rushed to the Plaza del Volador, pulled down the statue of the erstwhile hero, and dragged it through the streets, while the Santa Anna Theatre was broken into and badly abused. To save the building from further attacks, the authorities speedily changed its name to the National Theatre. Congress met and placed Canalizo under arrest in the National Palace and named José Joaquín Herrera as executive. No pasquinade was too bitter or diatribe too scathing for publication now if it were directed against the fallen mighty. The leg, so magniloquently buried, was dragged through the streets by the howling mob. At night, the city turned to cock-fights and public rejoicing as though for some great national holiday, with only occasional tearing down of park gates and similar acts of petty vandalism to express the exuberance of the joy of the rabble.

Herrera promptly formed a cabinet, while Santa Anna was making his plans to retreat from Querétaro and was slowly awakening to a realization that he was fighting an outraged nation. On December 17, the Chamber of Deputies formally proclaimed the deposition of the Dictator. He answered them three days later by a proclamation from Querétaro. Speaking in the name of the military, this pledged the army to the *Bases Orgánicas* as the constitution of the country and to Santa Anna as the constitutional president. Now a new three-ringed circus was in full course: Parades in Guadalajara, the Congress and Herrera in Mexico City, and Santa Anna in Querétarto. He announced that he was going to return to the Capital with an increased army to wreak vengeance on the traitors. To Herrera he wrote: "I regret extremely that you have so far forgotten what is due to our old friendship, our pleasant relations, and what I think I am entitled to as first magistrate of the Republic, as not to have thought fit to write me to give information of the events which have placed you for the time being at the head of the administration. I do not know what to think of this silence on your part, although indeed I seem to see in it a kind of hostility towards me personally which I do not think I deserve in any view of the case...."[5]

5. Rives, *The United States and Mexico*, I, 675.

By now the whole country was rising. In Veracruz, the citizens gathered in front of the government building, clamoring for the portrait of the Dictator. When they secured it, it was publicly outraged and burned in the Plaza. The leading friends of the Dictator were driven from the city, while the old hatred of Veracruz for Santa Anna was fanned anew. Similar scenes were taking place in the Departments of Oajaca, Morelia, Zacatecas, San Luis Potosí and Guanajuato.

Broadsides with screaming headlines appeared on the streets of the Capital. One, under the caption of *General Santa Anna's High Treason,* printed the provisions of the secret treaty with the Texans and his farewell to the Texans of June 1, 1836. General Gabriel Valencia publicly explained in another that ill health had prevented his joining the movement earlier but now begged the Mexicans to be worthy of the status of free men. Another broadside pled with its readers to consult their consciences to determine if it were not true that *The Crimes of the Tyrant are Demanding his Head.* Poets vented their spleen in satiric verses to the statue of the Dictator and even his new bride was not exempt from their "serves you right" remarks. The documents of the old forgery charges of 1813 were published in the daily papers. The Litany of the Church itself was parodied in this flood of long pent-up bitterness that had all the characteristics of "snake venom and prussic acid." The *Testament of the Year 1844* listed the following satiric bequests of the year about to depart:

"1st. I bequeath my skeleton to General Santa Anna, who has picked off all the flesh, and I ask that it be shrouded with the mantle of the fatherland, first used in Zavaleta, and that the largest mill stone in the country be tied to it and the whole cast into the midst of the sea. This is my wish."

"5th. I declare that I have a step-father named Antonio López de Santa Anna, who with my sons [above mentioned supporters of Santa Anna] has robbed my large estate and has left my nephews, the Mexicans, without a shirt on their backs...."

"11th. I leave the widows, those retired from active life and my employees, dying from hunger, since their properties were stolen by General Santa Anna."

"14th. I leave the cathedral of Mexico and the convents and monasteries without a single *real* in their treasuries, all their wealth being transported to Manga de Clavo."

"25th. I leave the Mexicans in a state of misery."

"26th. I leave the hacienda of Manga de Clavo and its equipment to the stock-brokers, so that the foreign debt may be paid from the proceeds."

Etc., Etc.

In short, every political act for which the Dictator had once been praised was now classed as treason to some special faction: first, he had been a traitor to Spain; second, a traitor to Iturbide; third, a traitor to the triumvirate; fourth, a traitor to the federation in 1828; fifth, a traitor to the legitimate government in 1832; sixth, a traitor to the federal system in 1835; seventh, a traitor in 1842 to the second constitution, and finally a traitor to Congress and the Constitution in 1844.[6]

Santa Anna was reported as suffering from a renewed attack of that scourge of the coastal country, dysentery, while in Querétaro. Whether true or not, he soon set his troops, rapidly dwindling from desertion, in motion against the Capital. He was still striving with might and main to make political allies if possible, but realized that the prospect was dark indeed. His nephew, Francisco Castro, was sent with letters asking D. Joaquín Lebrija and the Archbishop, "both debtors and friends of mine," to represent him before the Congress in trying to reach an agreement. He offered to resign the presidency and go into exile "for the only and noble" object of avoiding civil war. The government in return was to pay him his salary, and restore his statues to their old places [the pride of the man when his very life was at stake!] and to promise not to penalize the men in the forces still loyal to him. To this plea, the Government of Herrera turned a deaf ear.

Mexico City was now defended by an army of eight thousand men led by Bravo and Valencia; with Paredes and his

6. Anonymous, *Biografía del Gral. Santa Anna*, pp. 25-26.

four thousand men from the west, and old Juan Alvarez in the south, both reported to be on the way to help crush Santa Anna. To try to take the city was to invite disaster, so the ex-dictator in the last days of the year turned his men toward the Valley of Puebla. This city too refused to receive him, so he opened fire on January 2, 1845, and with an army still reported at from eight thousand to ten thousand men captured several outposts. The resistance, however, refused to crumble and word soon came that Paredes and Alvarez were on the way from Mexico City with reinforcements.

Santa Anna knew that the morale of his men was gone. He was likewise bewildered and could not make up his mind. Instead of his rapid decisions and marches to strike an enemy whose forces were divided, he now hesitated, fearing to be caught between the attack of foes on two sides. He lifted the siege of the city and allowed his enemies to unite. Some of his followers urged him to continue the contest, but this was absurd. Instead, he advised his men to submit to Herrera and then turned to the coast accompanied by a few cavalrymen only. To his men he issued this farewell:

"Companions in arms! With pride I sustained the loss of an important member of my body, lost gloriously in the service of our Native Land, as some of you bore witness; but that pride has been turned to grief, sadness and desperation. You should know that those mortal remains have been violently torn from the funeral urn, which was broken, and dragged through the public streets to make sport of them.... I know your astonishment and that you will be ashamed; you are right, such excesses were unknown among us. My friends! I am going to leave, obeying destiny. There in foreign lands I shall remember you. May you always be the support and ornament of your nation.... God be with you!"[7]

When he reached Las Vigas, near Jalapa, he asked General José Rincón for a safe conduct to allow him to proceed through Jalapa to Veracruz, and so on to exile. This was refused, for Rincón determined to capture the fugitive. The latter separated from his men on the night of January 13 and, with

7. Santa Anna, *Memoirs*, p. 55.

three companions, set out for the coast. The party was to skirt the sides of the towering mountain, Cofre de Perote, and then use trails down the precipitous edge of the plateau to the south of Jalapa. The night was bitterly cold as the party tried to find its way through the thick forest and across the barrancas with few other sounds reaching their straining ears than the eerie note of the coyote on the hunt. Soon after daylight, the weary party stopped beside the trail for breakfast and were greatly perturbed to see a man approach. In these wilds a group of men on horseback usually meant bandits so after one glance the fellow dashed off into the woods and was seen no more.

The companions were alarmed and wished to change their route, but Santa Anna was confident that his disguise would get him through. Before setting out, he had secured the outfit of one of the numerous muleteers of this section, with a wide brimmed hat and jacket with embroidered sleeves. His companions, likewise, had divested themselves of all military insignia and had dressed the part of country gentlemen. Due to heavy rains, the roads were especially bad so that progress was slow indeed. By nightfall they were just drawing near the little town of Xico, about eight or ten miles to the south of Jalapa. Suddenly shots were fired from ambush by some Indians of the neighborhood who then rushed out, shouting and firing to seize the small cavalcade.

In the confusion, the mules broke and fled. The guide and Santa Anna's companions jumped from their horses and dived into the heavy growth of weeds and bushes by the roadside. From there they ran into the forest and escaped. Santa Anna could not follow them because of his wooden leg so he quietly sat on his horse, hoping that he could face the matter out and not let his lameness be known. Whether he was led into the ambush by the guide who had been bribed, whether the man who had sighted them in the morning spread the report that led to the attack, or whether it was all pure accident is not certain, but the Indians now had a prisoner.

When they asked who he was, the response was that he was a merchant on his way to the low country. Strangely enough he had given up the character of a muleteer, possibly because he thought he might buy his freedom from these Indians and it would hardly be in character for a muleteer to be carrying much money. The answer only aroused the cupidity of his captors, who forced him to dismount. His lameness was then noted; his wooden leg discovered; questions arose; then suspicions; then conviction. Word had already gone out that the hated owner of the whole countryside hereabouts was trying to escape. They had "El Gordo" ("The fat one," the grand prize in any lottery).

The captive was carefully taken to the Indian settlement and a weird scene enacted. Instead of holding him for a reward, these one-track Indian minds decided on a ceremony of their own. The idea was somewhat crude, but appealed tremendously to their sense of humor, their long suppressed desire for vengeance, and to their idea of essential justice to be meted out to the hated aristocrat. They secured a huge pot or earthenware cauldron and sent out into the nearby fields for specially selected banana leaves, meanwhile emptying their huts of chiles and peppers. The plan was to boil the victim till he was quite dead, but to leave the flesh firm and sound. Then properly spiced, he was to be wrapped in banana leaves and presented to the authorities, who were so eager to secure him, as a huge *tamal*. Under the circumstances, the Indians felt certain their little practical joke would be fully appreciated.[8]

At this point the local priest stepped in to spoil the fun. Fearing the enthusiasm of his charges, he first went to the church and rang the bell with no uncertain strokes. This could always be relied upon to act as a decided sedative upon ebullient spirits. Next he seized the holy vessel containing the Host and, with this in his hands, came out and demanded that the life of the victim be spared. These simple minds could not defy the holy man, so they sullenly agreed to cease

8. *Tamales* are a choice Mexican dish, composed of chopped and highly spiced meat, covered with a layer of hand ground corn meal, the whole wrapped in corn husks and boiled or steamed.

their sport and to surrender the ex-Dictator to the regular authorities of the nation.[9]

On the fifteenth, Santa Anna was taken as a prisoner to Jalapa where his wife and other members of his family were awaiting him. After his recent experiences he was in a particularly bad temper and quarreled with the commander of the guard for not showing him proper respect. Next he administered a good tongue lashing to a badly scared guard because his tramping back and forth on post annoyed the illustrious prisoner. A peremptory message was sent to General Rincón ordering that officer to report to the prison, but the response came back that the General had a stomach ache and could not come. After retiring at 10:00 P.M., Santa Anna was up and pacing his quarters at 3:00 A.M. and calling for writing material. Throughout the ensuing day, he ate little or nothing, but occupied himself for hours in writing. In one of these letters he addressed the Minister of War and complained bitterly that he was treated as a nefarious criminal with guards standing over his bed, who made such a racket that he could not sleep. He said he had no servant to wait on him, and that his family could not visit him, in short: "My situation is worse than when I was a prisoner of war among the Texan soldiers of fortune."[10]

Soon the captive was hustled off to Perote for safe keeping, while the authorities made up their minds what to do. Should he be tried for treason as a President who had violated the constitution; or as head of the army for attacking the legitimate government; or would it be the wiser course to let him slip out of the country into ignominious exile? His property was placed under an embargo, but, beyond that, Fermín Gómez Farías (son of Valentín Gómez Farías) expressed the general uncertainty when he wrote to a friend: "Who knows

9. This incident is related here and, though it is so bizarre as to border on the incredible, it is referred to briefly in various Mexican histories. An account in English is noted in Bancroft, *History of Mexico*, V, 277 note. Then, while in Jalapa in 1934, the author had the pleasure of hearing an Indian women from Xico, herself entirely illiterate, relate the tale as told to her by her grandmother, who witnessed the episode.

10. *Boletin de Noticias*, Supplement to No. 22 (January 20, 1845).

what they will do with this bird (*pájaro*): there are so many opinions on the subject that one cannot form any definite idea of what will happen."[11]

The Minister of War had blandly answered Santa Anna's letter of complaint, saying that he had issued orders for the person of the captive to be properly respected, but he upheld his agents for subjecting Santa Anna to strict imprisonment. As for the request that the prisoner be allowed to leave the country, he replied that that had been "referred to Congress."

At once Santa Anna petitioned Congress, under date of January 28, 1845, asking to be allowed to go into exile. This body assumed the duties of a grand jury to examine the case, and, on February 24, in joint session voted ninety to seven in favor of the indictment against: "His Excellency, Señor General don Antonio López de Santa Anna, constitutional president of the republic, for having attacked the system of government established in the *Bases Orgánicas;* for dissolving the Departmental Assembly of Querétaro, arresting its officials and suspending its Governor, for his co-operation in the issuance, publication and carrying out of the decree of November 29 of the preceding year; and for his rebellion with armed force against the constitutional government re-established in the Republic."[12]

At Perote, the time dragged by slowly. Friendship for the fallen mighty was dangerous, so there is little wonder that outgoing correspondence stressed friendship while that incoming stressed bills and debts due. Even the Town Council of Jalapa now hastily presented a bill for 1229 *pesos* for work done on the hacienda of El Encero over a period of thirteen months by the local chain gang. This incidentally was approved by Santa Anna, who drew a draft on Sr. Barcena for the amount. After some delay the draft was honored or bought

11. *Gómez Farías Papers,* Letter to Rafæl de Fuentes, February 21, 1845. García Collection.

12. C. M., Bustamante, *Apuntes para la historia del Gobierno del .... Santa Anna,* p. 435.

It is interesting to note that on this occasion Guillermo Valle, the youth whom Santa Anna had educated, ably defended his old patron before Congress. Prieto, *Memorias, 1828-1840,* pp. 86-87.

for 780 *pesos,* though in time it was probably collected in full from the Santa Anna estate.

A series of five letters written between April 28 and May 26 to Santa Anna's friend, Sr. José Julián Gutiérrez, who was also the business manager of his estates, gives an excellent insight into the prisoner's thinking and business affairs at the time. The first letter was a vigorous protest against neighboring ranchmen, who had been feeding their stock on Santa Anna's estates, and urged Gutiérrez to see to it that his local foremen were strongly urged to "watch their step" and prevent further incursions. The writer further stated that he was not interested in selling his real estate and, under no circumstances, would he sell to such thieves. The last paragraph struck a philosophical note:

"In short, it is not possible to get inside the human heart to know men. I have taken a great risk judging by appearances; nor is it possible to free onesself of the bonds of the hypocrite and the traitor. The events that have just taken place are not even in the realm of the imagination. My confidence arises from the tranquility of my conscience. I have served our Native Land well, at least as far as my abilities permitted, and I was resting quietly in the domestic circle, far distant from the calamity which befell me. I have been betrayed, and persecuted in a most barbarous manner; and to God I owe nothing more, short of becoming a complete victim. Divine Providence has protected my days and given me health, and I can almost hear the Heavenly Voice saying to me: 'wait, be patient, you will be vindicated before the world, your innocence will become famous and your enemies be confounded.' "[13]

On May 19 he wrote again, complaining bitterly of the abuses reported from his estates, and agreeing with his agent that the city authorities were probably none too anxious to interfere on behalf of a discredited owner. He also said that he understood that the embargo on his property was about to be raised so he asked Gutiérrez to see about renting or selling

13. These letters are in the keeping of Sr. Alberto Gutiérrez J. of Jalapa, Veracruz, who kindly allowed the author to use them.

his holdings. Three days later, he wrote that his wife was leaving for Jalapa the next day, and that he expected to follow soon for his passport was about ready.

On the twenty-fourth, he wrote describing the hacienda of El Encero as having the dwelling, chapel and tenant houses on a property of more than twenty "sitios de ganado mayor" (about 88,000 acres). He said the tenants paid rentals of about one thousand *pesos* annually, with other sums (listed in reasonable detail) amounting to two thousand five hundred *pesos*, which he said could easily be increased to three thousand *pesos*. There were pens to fatten two thousand calves, over two thousand breeding cows, some three hundred horses, and various other equipment. In all he stated that he had one hundred and forty thousand *pesos* invested in the estate, but that under the circumstances he would take one hundred thousand *pesos* for it. If no buyer appeared he would rent the whole as it stood for eight thousand *pesos* yearly rental, paid annually in advance on a lease to run not less than three nor more than nine years. He then urged that the agent raise some cash for immediate needs and added that his new coach "of exquisite construction" was also for sale at fifteen hundred *pesos*, "bearing in mind that it cost more than that," and that he would sell his litter at any price it would bring.

Two days later, he wrote placing the haciendas of Manga de Clavo and Paso de Varas on the market. The former he said he would sell for one hundred thousand *pesos*, "though it was worth two hundred and fifty thousand *pesos* since it has twelve thousand, or more, breeding cows" with other animals in large quantities and contained fifty "sitios" (nearly 220,000 acres) of land with a rental and income from the sale of livestock amounting to twenty thousand *pesos* annually. Paso de Varas contained forty sitios (about 175,000 acres) of land and a "magnificent house at the Puente" Nacional. This estate he valued at one hundred and fifty thousand *pesos*, but would sell for the bargain price of eighty thousand *pesos* even though it yielded an income of from five thousand to six thousand *pesos* net a year.

The property is listed in some detail for the fanciful state-

[217]

ment of Santa Anna's will is frequently taken as fact when he stated that his property was worth one million three hundred thousand *pesos* in 1844. Yet here, in 1845, he listed the same estates as in the will and offered to sell them for two hundred and eighty thousand *pesos,* and did not even pretend that they were valued at more than five hundred and forty thousand *pesos.* The will, it is true, mentioned three houses in addition to the haciendas, which at those high valuations were listed at eighty-three thousand *pesos.* After deducting for the value of the houses and allowing a quite generous sum for personal property, the total value of the estate is brought to just about half the figure so generally accepted, and it is obvious that he was willing to close out his haciendas in 1845 for more nearly one-fourth that figure.

There still remains the question as to whether the Dictator had funds deposited abroad. Possibly so, but the present author has no proof of it. In his will, Santa Anna categorically denied this, though few would consider such denial as proof in itself. In the same will he stated that he gave each of his daughters a dowry of fifty thousand *pesos*—and that was quite possible. Large sums of cash had been passing through his hands as Dictator and he spent lavishly on all sides. However, the fact remained that these extensive estates, his permanent investments, were not in a wealthy section of the country. They contained neither the mineral wealth of many districts nor the population and agricultural value of the valleys such as Puebla, Mexico and Cuernavaca. From the standpoint of military and political strategy, they were well placed between the Capital and Veracruz, but they had comparatively little intrinsic value. Santa Anna loved to do things with the "grand air" of the country gentleman and delighted to "lord it over" wide flung estates. He was no miser, however; money for him was something with which to make a show and to be enjoyed.

Meanwhile the court had been taking depositions and slowly proceeding with the case against him. The question was plainly: what verdict did the political conditions indicate as advisable? The Santanistas were still a faction to be con-

Very rare copy of cartoon printed on loose sheets in 1845 (reproduced from Litografía en Méjico en el Siglo XIX, by courtesy of La Biblioteca Nacional de Méjico)

sidered, so it was not at all surprising that on May 24, 1845, Congress passed a law granting amnesty to all rebels except Santa Anna and his ministers. The indictment against Santa Anna was to be dropped if he left the country at once and forever. He was to be allowed to keep his property and to receive half-pay as a general from the government. In return, he was to agree to renounce the presidency, to satisfy all debts accrued against him, and to go into exile in Venezuela.

On June 3, 1845, he, with his pitiful girl bride who had so recently been dreaming of a queen's position, and other members of his family sorrowfully boarded a packet boat at Veracruz. The first stop was to be Havana. Before sailing he published a broadside or proclamation of farewell from the Castle of Perote with the date of May 26.

He begged his fellow countrymen to examine his political conduct. He admitted mistakes of judgment, but insisted: "When I had all power, I did not raise scaffolds for politic offenses; I banished no citizens to foreign lands, to eat bitter bread and to weep in exile. No one was despoiled of his property nor oppressed by arbitrary imprisonment. Generosity and clemency were my program." Then, he concluded:

"Mexicans! in my old age and mutilated, surrounded by a wife and innocent children, I am going into exile to seek a resting place among strangers. Mercifully forgive the mistakes I made unintentionally; and believe me, in God's name, that I have labored sincerely that you should be independent, free and happy. If I have not succeeded in fulfilling your desires blame only my lack of ability. In whatever strange place, wherever I may end my days, I shall raise my humble petitions to the Eternal for your success in any way that may be most suitable to your best interests, that you may live in peace, the beginning of all good, that you may raise your native land to such a degree of prosperity that it may be listed among the leaders and with the happiest of the nations of the earth."

Thus closed the morning with its long work period. A pause ensued as though man enjoyed his siesta while a cloud passed over the sun and all nature paused pending the outburst of the fast and furious activity of a summer afternoon.

III

AFTERNOON
[1845-1855]

A combination of good and bad qualities; with very real natural ability but without either moral or intellectual training; a spirit with initiative, but without a fixed purpose or definite objective; with both energy and a disposition to rule but handicapped by grave defects; skillful in making general plans for a revolution or campaign, but most unfortunate in directing a single battle....Santa Anna is without doubt one of the most notable characters which the American revolutions have developed....

—ALAMÁN, *Historia de Méjico.*

EXILE AND CHICANERY

As has been seen, the revolution in Mexico City in December, 1844, had placed José Joaquín Herrera in the president's chair. This he occupied with increasing discomfort for a year. The truth was that the opposition to Santa Anna was fairly general but it was far from united in support of Herrera. Some manuscripts found on the person of the Dictator at the time of his capture indicated that he had been negotiating with Great Britain for the sale of the Californias to that country. These documents were eagerly seized and submitted to Congress, but were published also so as to make political capital for the administration. By stressing this sufficiently it was hoped that the ultra-liberals, headed by Gómez Farías, might be prevented from combining with that other persecuted (hence sympathized with) faction, the Santanistas.

It is true that Fermín Gómez Farías, son of Valentín, had written on March 3, 1845, bitterly denouncing the tyrant who was still in prison in Perote, but it was equally true that as early as February 13, M. C. Rejón had written to Valentín Gómez Farías from Havana that many of those who thought the idea of federalism was about to be successful were "seeking the aid of Don Antonio." "But," he continued, "keep this a profound secret since it is advisable to work with the greatest circumspection. The only thing I ask of you is that the newspapers you control neither praise nor blame the said Don Antonio."[1] Thus, before Santa Anna even left Mexico both his friends and one time enemies were scheming to put him back in power, for all knew that where McGregor sat, there was the head of the table.

1. *Gómez Farías Papers*, García Collection.

Meanwhile the long pending clash with the United States was coming measurably closer. Herrera would have liked to negotiate with the Colossus of the North, but the Mexican people had been pumped full of gasconade for so long that the slightest suggestion of giving up Texas even for a cash consideration met with vociferous objections.

In the United States also were political wheels within wheels to be considered. After President Harrison died, Tyler soon found himself a man without a party as the violent quarrels broke out between him and the Whig leaders. Practically everything he proposed, including the annexation of Texas, was balked by those who were supposed to be of his own political faith. This deadlock continued until Polk, the Democratic nominee, in the election of 1844, seized upon the idea of annexation and made it the heart and center of his generally aggressive platform. The country was in a mood for action and so swept Polk into office. Due to the long hiatus between the November election and the March inauguration, Tyler was president for three and a half months after the people at the polls had endorsed the program of annexation. He, now gloating over his popular vindication, joyously pushed through the joint resolution (two-thirds of the Senate not being in a mood to ratify a treaty) providing for the annexation without waiting for the new administration to take office.

Mexico had declared that such action would mean war, but Herrera was so reluctant to engage in hostilities that he actually agreed to discuss terms with a special commissioner to be sent by the United States. When John Slidell arrived with full powers, however, Herrera realized that Mexican public opinion would not endorse any negotiations so he took advantage of a technical interpretation of the wording of Slidell's commission and declined to treat with him.

By this time the location of the southern and western boundaries of Texas was assuming a position of importance. Mexico insisted, with a good deal of justification, that the Nueces, if not the San Antonio, was the stream which marked the recognized limit of its old province. It insisted furthermore that the agreements entered into by Santa Anna as a prisoner in

Texas were null and void both because he had no authority to negotiate and because of duress applied to his person during the negotiations. The Texans, however, and now the Polk administration, clamored for the enforcement of the terms agreed to by Santa Anna and for occupation of all territory north and east of the Río Grande.

At this juncture, both Mexico and the United States sent their troops, under Mariano Arista and Zachary Taylor respectively, to the border to hold their country's property and to prevent invasion. No war had been declared, but each commander was expected to do all the fighting he would or could within the maximum claims of his country. The result was inevitable: "American blood has been shed on American soil and cries for vengeance"; "Mexican blood has been shed upon Mexican soil and cries for vengeance." Thus pent-up and pumped-up emotions found relief in action in the early months of 1846.

But what of Santa Anna while these events were happening? In his *Memoirs* he stated, with an obviously inaccurate date, that after he had left Veracruz to go into exile he was so courteously received by Captain General Leopoldo O'Donell of Cuba that he decided to disembark there instead of going on to Caracas as he had originally intended. However, Cuba was in direct contact with Mexico and a far better point from which to stage a come-back than far-off Venezuela. It has been reported that the exile's chief interest in his new home was in the use of his gamecocks to fleece the gullible Cubans of thousands of *pesos*. He was doubtless glad to let this appear to be the case and he certainly knew gamecocks, but the really vital interest of the man was obvious to close observers whenever a packet-boat was due to arrive from or leave for any Mexican port.

The lack of popularity of Herrera and the occasional sporadic outbreaks in various places, such as the one in Mexico City proclaimed *Federación y Santa Anna,* provided excellent copy to his correspondents and ample food for thought for the exile. Gómez Farías, in spite of the negotiations in progress with Santa Anna, was still notifying the ardent federalists, who remembered too well the days of 1833 and the death of Mejía, that "General Santa Anna will have no part in the struggle that is about to be begun, and which will be purely national and truly patriotic."[2]

On July 7, 1845, M. C. Rejón wrote Gómez Farías from Havana. This was a communication of nearly one thousand words, obviously inspired by Santa Anna. Rejón ably urged the cause of the ex-Dictator and said that the old hero was sick of politics and would not even consider acting as executive, but, that with him at the head of the armies and Gómez Farías in charge of civil affairs, Mexico would have an unbeatable combination with which to face its enemies.[3]

Herrera soon became suspicious and the friends of Gómez Farías were much concerned for his safety. The old liberal was a past master at this game though and later in October boasted: "In the months I have been under suspicion I have gone from house to house without the Government knowing for sure up to the present time, where I have been or where I am, in spite of the fact that a multitude of friends have visited me."[4] In this letter, he mentioned the fact that he had just received word of an attempt to assassinate Santa Anna. This he condemned in no uncertain terms, attributing it to Gómez Pedraza.

Bustamante claimed that the whole story of the attempted assassination was a pure fabrication to work up sympathy and interest.[5] This, of course, was possible but if so it was certainly well done. There were numerous proofs advanced, even to the capture and confession of the would-be assassin. Santa Anna's enemies tried to scoff at the whole affair and said that it was merely another of the old charlatan's efforts to appeal to another group: to be "a man to all women and a woman to all men." If it was mere propaganda it worked

2. *Gómez Farías Papers*, García Collection. Farías to General José Vicente Miñon, May 20, 1845.
3. *Ibid.*
4. *Gómez Farías Papers*, García Collection. Letter in handwriting of Gómez Farías to Manuel Gonzales Cosio, October 25, 1845.
5. Bustamante, *Nuevo-Bernal Díaz del Castillo*, Tomo I, p. 63.

for his sympathizers were becoming more and more numerous.

At the same time the Government was steadily becoming weaker. W. S. Parrott, of the United States Legation, reported to Secretary of State Buchanan on October 11 that the Government was in actual penury and had not been able to negotiate any part of a projected fifteen million *pesos* loan. The troops in the Capital were represented as suffering for actual necessities, while the police were such a farce that robberies and assassinations were "a nightly occurrence." To complicate matters further, he said the recently elected congress was composed of a centralistic Senate and a federalistic Chamber of Deputies.[6]

Increasing numbers of Mexicans were reaching the conclusion that a monarch would be a "gift from heaven" and the only solution to their troubles, but efforts in this direction were held in abeyance after December 14. On that date Paredes y Arrillaga "pronounced" in San Luis Potosí on the grounds that Herrera was planning to alienate Mexican soil. On the thirtieth Valencia followed suit in Mexico City just as word came that Veracruz also had joined the rebels and had invited Santa Anna to return. Herrera could not stand the pressure and retired, so Paredes took charge to try his hand for the next six and a half months.

In the words of Bancroft: "Anarchy reigned supreme." Slidell reported to Buchanan on February 2 that Paredes had established a government that was such a despotism in fact that the civil authorities were "sullen and unwilling." Two weeks later, he reported that the monarchist sentiment was growing and that there was a strong possibility that Paredes sympathized with the idea.[7] The plans for the organization of the new Chamber of Deputies provided for strict class representation by professions and occupations, while active discussion of possible royal candidates was openly indulged in.

6. Smith, *Notes on United States-Mexican Relations*, García Collection.
7. *House Executive Document No. 60*, Thirtieth Congress, first session, Letters of February 2, and 17, from Jalapa, pp. 57-58; 61-62.

Santa Anna himself was promptly informed of all that took place. He was in a frame of mind to snatch at any opening that occurred, but he could not see any in connection with the calling of some European prince as a ruler of Mexico. United States Consul, R. B. Campbell of Havana, reported January 7, 1846: "On this subject overtures have been made to Santa Anna to obtain his aid and influence, all of which he has as yet firmly repelled .... declaring himself entirely Mexican and resolved not to involve the country in the vortex of European politics."[8]

The fact was that from the vantage point of Cuba, Santa Anna had calmly surveyed the field and had determined upon his course of action. He knew that the idea of a monarchy in Mexico was anathema to the United States but that the northern republic was anxious for a solution of the boundary dispute. At the same time, the liberals in Mexico were so terrified at the possibility of a European prince that they were constantly bidding for his support. Great Britain, too, was none too enthusiastic about the idea of a Spanish or Spanish controlled prince on a Mexican throne.

Now, how could the old schemer work all these threads into a single pattern that would harmonize with Mexican political contingencies? His first problem was to convince the Mexican liberals that he had never approved of despotism except as a paternal step in a program to bring about the welfare of his people. To gain the support of the two sturdy old patriots and liberal leaders, Gómez Farías and Juan Alvarez, however, it was necessary to denounce consistently the United States and its aggression. This, at least, was easy for it was in line with his pronouncements for the past fifteen years.

M. C. Rejón continued as laison officer. On January 9, 1846, he wrote under the name of Florentino Gómez to Gómez Farías and asked that all correspondence be sent addressed to this assumed name and enclosed in envelopes directed to the British Consul General at Havana. By March he wrote that

8. *Consular Despatches*, Havana, Campbell to Buchanan, January 7, 1846, Vol. XXI.

all knew the sturdy principles of Gómez Farías, whom Santa Anna considered to be the key man in the situation.[9]

By this time, however, Santa Anna began to take matters into his own hands and to write in person. Gómez Farías kept a personal copy of a long letter addressed to one "Sor. D. Manúel Feulet" in which Santa Anna, invoking the principles of 1832, cordially and whole heartedly endorsed federalism and the idea of a government by the people. He only asked to be allowed to subscribe to the constitution and to fight for the Republic against foreign foes.[10] This letter further contained a detailed plan, with the exact wording he would approve for a pronunciamiento by the garrison at Veracruz. This was to denounce the existing government and all monarchial movements; demand a return to the constitution of 1824; provide for the election of a new congress, yet "guarantee the existence of the army, caring for it as the well deserving (*benemérita*) military class of a free people deserves."

But Santa Anna was not yet in a position to announce openly his conversion to federalism. For one thing he was in Cuba, a Spanish colony, and could not afford to antagonize the pet project of the local officials who wished to establish a Spanish prince in Mexico. So skillfully did he work that the Captain General of the islands remained friendly to him and when a messenger on his way from Santa Anna to the mainland was ousted from a British packet boat for not having a passport from the Mexican Consul, the Captain General of Cuba promptly placed a Spanish brig of war at his disposal to convey him to his destination.

At the United States end of the line, President Polk was as much infatuated with "ways that are dark and .... tricks that

9. *Gómez Farías Papers*, García Collection. Rejón to Gómez Farías, January 9, 1846; and Rejón to Crescencio Boves, March 8, 1846.

10. Strangely enough United States Consul Black in Mexico sent a copy of the important paragraphs of this letter, though the receiver's name was not given, Secretary of State, James Buchanan (*House Executive Document No. 4*, Twenty-ninth Congress, second session, pp. 37-39). It would not appear to be a rash assumption to suppose that Gómez Farías kept a copy and gave the original to Black. If this were not done by Gómez Farías, the original receiver—possibly more in the confidence of Santa Anna than Gómez Farías—saw that Washington was duly informed.

are vain" as Santa Anna. Also, the United States Consul in Havana was reported to have paid unusual courtesies to the exile as soon as he landed in Cuba. These private advances were cordially met by the Mexican but an invitation to an Independence Day dinner on July 4, 1845, was promptly declined. Such a public appearance would have been most impolitic and would at once have been adversely commented on by the many Mexican liberals who so bitterly hated the United States.

By February, 1846, one Colonel A. J. Atocha appeared in Washington. He was a Spaniard by birth, but a naturalized United States citizen, who had been driven out of Mexico a year before because of his supposed connection with Santa Anna. He skillfully whetted Polk's appetite by saying that he came from a visit to Santa Anna, who favored a treaty with the United States which would sell to the northern republic all territory north of the Río Grande and the Colorado of the West for $30,000,000. Other company was waiting to see the President so the envoy displayed the bait, made a few pertinent remarks about Taylor on the border, and retired saying there was much more he would like to talk about. That the bait was tempting is obvious from the fact that Polk did not wait for further details, but the very next day discussed the affair with his Cabinet. He suggested the advisability of sending an agent to see Santa Anna, even remarking on the man he would like to select.

The next day Atocha reappeared and conversations went a bit further though Polk frankly confided to his diary that the visitor appeared to be a man who "would betray any confidence reposed in him, when it was his interest to do so." However, Polk told the stranger that the United States would be glad to consider any proposal made by the proper authorities in Mexico. Atocha promptly replied that no Mexican government could make such propositions and remain in power; that Santa Anna felt the United States must use enough force to appear to coerce the authorities by a three fold program: first, by sending Taylor to the Río Grande; second, by sending a strong naval force to Veracruz; and third, by withdrawing Slidell from the country as minister or agent. For immediate expenses the United States was asked to advance $500,000.[11]

The United States Consul at Havana meanwhile had been unable, partly through lack of knowledge of the Spanish language, to find out much about Santa Anna. As late as June 9, he merely reported that Santa Anna's activities "are generally confined to the cock pit, except upon the arrival of a steamer or other vessel from Vera Cruz," though he did think a steamer would soon leave for Mexico.[12]

Polk did not like Atocha well enough to take matters up through him, but he did send an agent of his own to Cuba. This was Commander Alexander Slidell Mackenzie, nephew of the John Slidell, who had just returned from his abortive mission to Mexico. After a personal interview with the President in which he received verbal instructions Mackenzie set out and reached Havana on July 5, 1846. He called on Santa Anna the next day and was closeted with him for three hours on the morning of the seventh. At this time he read a long statement of Polk's wishes which he had committed to paper after seeing the President.[13] This denounced the Paredes government and stated that Polk would be glad to see Santa Anna in power and "has already given orders to the squadron blockading the Mexican ports, to allow General Santa

11. Quaife, M. M., *Dairy of James K. Polk,* Vol I, various.
Father Mariano Cuevas, *Historia de la Iglesia en México,* Tomo V, pp. 252-53, thinks that Gómez Farías and not Santa Anna sent Atocha. It does seem probable that the liberal leader knew more or less of what was going on, but if Gómez Farías sent the man he certainly deceived Polk by remaining in the background when he could gain little by this but stood to have matters badly confused by going through other hands needlessly.

12. *Consular Despatches,* Havana, Campbell to Buchanan, June 6, 1846. Vol. XXI.

13. Quaife, *op. cit.,* III, 290-92. Polk later complained that Mackenzie had greatly exceeded his instructions in putting anything on paper which could be interpreted as a message from the President. He claimed that Mackenzie was only to see Santa Anna as a matter of secondary importance and that his chief purpose was to inquire about reported commissioning of privateers by Mexico. If this were the case, Mackenzie certainly misunderstood the whole purpose of his mission as may be seen by reading his reports. His only reference to privateering was to the effect that Santa Anna said no such vessels had been authorized to cruise on behalf of Mexico.

Anna freely to return to his country." The United States was pictured as willing to negotiate with the new administration promptly if it could secure a treaty that would settle all claims and boundary disputes, being willing to offer an "ample consideration in ready money" for lands ceded to the United States.

This was a game the old pastmaster of chicanery thoroughly understood. He graciously inquired about the various men in public life in the United States and expressed his high regard for them. For information he casually added that if Mexico either became a monarchy or remained in anarchy he expected to go to Texas, and become a United States citizen! At the same time he also casually referred to the Nueces as the boundary of Texas. Mackenzie hastily set him straight on the fact that the United States would at least demand the Río Grande together with territory to the west including San Francisco.

Santa Anna had a formal statement drawn up in which he warmly endorsed "republican principles" and "an entirely liberal constitution" for Mexico. Mackenzie reported him as saying that if the United States would "promote his patriotic desires, he offers to respond with such a peace as has been described." He also advised that Taylor advance to Saltillo, a good military position, instead of staying at the much weaker Monterrey: in fact, he was willing for Taylor to advance to San Luis Potosí. At the same time Veracruz and its fortress of San Juan de Ullo should be taken by the Yankees who would find it a simple procedure to land three or four thousand men and take the city "whose walls are not strong." Also he urged that Tampico be captured promptly saying that the whole coast was healthy from October to March. At the same time Yucatán should be left alone as Santa Anna could depend upon it and an attack there would stir up needless opposition and complications.

In a second letter, dated July 11, Mackenzie added significant details showing that he had practically ignored the United States consul at Havana in the negotiations. His further comment on Santa Anna was most enlightening. He said that the Mexican was on friendly terms with both the English and Spanish representatives. In fact, as late as July 6, Santa Anna had visited the British brig *Daring* and had been received with a salute, while rumors were rife that he was planning to leave on it for Mexico "from the circumstances of his having given away his game-cocks." The Commodore continued:

"If General Santa Anna be, as he is represented, either intriguing, and faithless, and as such disposed to keep terms with, and make use of all parties, the question occurs, when and with whom if any [*sic*] is he in earnest? This may perhaps be best answered by another question: What country has the most power to forward or thwart his views for his own aggrandizement by having [*sic*] a predominant control on the destinies of his country? Undoubtedly the United States, by their proximity, by their power, and by the war, commenced by Mexico which they are successfully waging against her. He may be an honest, though not wholly disinterested republican from a belief that only a republic is possible in Mexico. He may well as a Mexican loving his country, as the subtlest and most interested doubtless do, be honestly opposed to a war with the United States, because he has the wisdom and experience to know that a war with the United States will be more calamitous the more it is prolonged. He may have discernment to foresee that these views will ere long become those of other Mexicans, and that a peace party will develop itself among them, and blend itself with the republican party to oppose the monarchists and those who are for war with the United States. Whatever therefore may be his personal sentiments towards us the very subtlety ascribed to him must enable him to comprehend that it is the part of wisdom in his present position rather to endeavor to guide the irresistible progress of events for his country's good and his own advancement, than to be overwhelmed in the attempt to oppose them.

"For these reasons even more than the evidence of earnestness which his manner strongly conveyed, I believe in the entire sincerity of his views and his intentions as imparted in his note to the President."

After urging that some "inspired" propaganda in the United States press play up Santa Anna as a skillful administrator, who knew Mexican needs and had its best interests at heart, [14] Mackenzie added:

"It may not be wholly without interest for the government to know that General Santa Anna appeared in excellent health and condition, strong and active, notwithstanding his mutilation, and capable of enduring great fatigue. He had the air of a man of forty well preserved; though the length of time that he has been active in Mexican affairs, makes it probable that he is much older."[15]

Meanwhile, so far as Mexicans could see, Santa Anna was consistently playing the rôle of a patriot. He sent funds to Mexican prisoners in New Orleans and made constant efforts to unite Yucatán more closely to the Mexican union. Even in the light of recent research many consider that Santa Anna was frankly using Polk's cupidity in order to get back into power, and that it was a plain case of "diamond cut diamond" with the Mexican proving the sharper stone of the two. Zamacois states that if Santa Anna had defects, lack of patriotism was certainly not one of them when it was a question involving some foreign country.[16] Over in England the *Daily News* in an editorial of July 7, 1846, frankly referred to Mexico as the "Poland of the West" now being divided up by the United States, while *The Times* on July 15 considered Santa Anna as the hope of his country.

Plans for Santa Anna's repatriation were progressing steadily. A number of the old liberals were fearful of the self-seeking and unprincipled Santanistas, but his return seemed their one chance to avoid extinction and they reluctantly fell in

14. It is interesting to note that Waddy Thompson's, *Recollections of Mexico,* directly conveyed these very ideas though the present writer has no proof at all that they were inspired by the above request.

15. A copy of the letter of June 7th is to be found in Reeves, *American Diplomacy under Tyler and Polk,* pp. 299-307, though so far as the present writer is aware, the letter of the eleventh has never been published.

16. Zamacois, *Historia de Méjico,* Tomo XII, p. 507.

line. At the same time, the exile began to feel quite sure of himself and was more and more inclined to dictate the terms for his return. He did not hesitate to send word that various suggested proclamations would have to be modified or withdrawn in favor of his own ideas. By April 26, the United States Consul John Black reported from Mexico that "a very great majority" of the people were dissatisfied with conditions and that all plans had been made for Veracruz to pronounce on the first, but that local quarrels had prevented it. In spite of the delay, Juan Alvarez had gone ahead and demanded a triumvirate to be composed of Santa Anna, Herrera and Rincón.[17]

So much plotting had naturally attracted the attention of the Government, and on May 29 Fermín Gómez Farías wrote that between May 13 and 17 many of the conspirators, including his father, had been arrested. Their movement had made such headway, however, that he could add: "The revolution of the South [that of Alvarez] is growing daily. Guadalajara has pronounced and the triumph has been complete, Mazatlán has done the same, and according to reliable information, Zacatecas, Durango, Guanajuato and Puebla will quickly join in."[18]

By the time Mackenzie had reached Havana, Santa Anna was writing that he had just received word from Yucatán that was entirely favorable and that he would soon be in Campeche to head the movement there.[19] This plan was probably changed by events growing out of the Mackenzie visit. It was one thing to risk running the blockade into Veracruz and quite another to know that the following order had been issued:

17. *House Executive Document* No. 4, Twenty-ninth Congress, second session, pp. 34-35.
18. *Gómez Farías Papers*, García Collection. This is the first draft of a letter to Santa Anna. In the *Gómez Farías Papers* many such are found. They were kept as copies and, together with letters received, give an excellent idea of developments.
19. *Gómez Farías Papers*, García Collection, letter of July 9, 1846, to Fermín Gómez Farías.

"[PRIVATE AND CONFIDENTIAL]
NAVY DEPARTMENT, May 13, 1846.
Commodore: If Santa Anna endeavors to enter the Mexican
ports, you will allow him to pass freely.
GEORGE BANCROFT
Commodore DAVID CONNER,
Commanding Home Squadron."[20]

As conditions became worse, many suggested that Paredes
go to the front. The British Minister urged him to stay at his
post in the Capital, but the pressure of some of his friends
and those who wanted him out of the way was finally successful. On July 29, he left affairs in charge of General Bravo
and advanced to San Luis Potosí. Certainly he could not plan
very extensive military operations because of the rainy season
but the British Minister thought it was possible that at the
head of the army he could negotiate more freely with the
United States.[21] Since the northern republic was in agreement
with Santa Anna though, this all meant the end of Paredes
as executive. Many of his imprisoned enemies were given
their liberty in honor of the President's birthday in order to
give the impression of a rising spirit of confidence, but this
only hastened his downfall.

On the last day of July the long talked of "pronouncement"
was issued from Veracruz. This supported the Guadalajara
proclamation and called for Santa Anna to return and take
charge. On August 4 General Mariano Salas, in command of
the Ciudadela, the chief barracks in the Capital, denounced
the Government and called for federalism and Santa Anna.
This was the end. The Paredes administration promptly collapsed and Salas became Acting President pending the return of the recently anathematized Hero of Tampico. It was
too late now for conservatives to talk about the incongruous

20. *House Executive Document No. 60,* Thirtieth Congress, first session,
p. 774.
21. Bankhead to Aberdeen, June 29, 1846, No. 88, F. O. Vol. CXVII.
This despatch, together with others from the British archives and numerous
clippings from newspapers of the British Isles were graciously furnished the
author by Professor E. T. Bonn of the History Department of the University
of South Carolina.

alliance of Gómez Farías and Santa Anna, the federalist and the despot.

Santa Anna's own account of his decision to return to Mexico was naïve, to say the least.[22]

"In the city of Havana, In August, 1846, I received the invitations which were addressed to me through a commission, *for me to return to my country to take charge of its defense.* My wound, which broke out periodically, had me in bed: my good friends and my personal interest advised me to remain in retirement, but I could not resist an invitation of this kind, nor forget that I was a Mexican soldier, and I determined to accept it."

On August 8, Santa Anna applied for and after some delay secured, a passport from the Cuban officials. He then took passage on the small British steamer, the *Arab*. The vessel had some engine trouble and was soon overhauled by the *Medway*. When the latter came within hailing distance the Captain of the *Arab* asked to tranship four passengers, but the officer of the *Medway* declined as soon as he knew who they were. One of the passengers reported: "We had a good view of Santa Anna, and his pretty young wife, who, on hearing our decision, stamped her little foot on the deck, and turned poutingly to some of her suite."[23]

Santa Anna later denied any knowledge of Polk's order to allow him to enter the country and insisted that he tried to dodge the blockade by entering the port at night. This, he said, the Captain of the *Arab* asked to tranship four passengers, but The facts seem to be that the *St. Mary's,* a United States sloop of war, overhauled the small boat and sent an officer on board, to the great alarm of the Mexican adventurers. The officer was invited to the cabin where Santa Anna was said to be confined by an "indisposition." "He received the American officer with great cordiality, and handed him a note,—upon perusing of which, the officer took his leave—and the *Arab* proceeded to the blockaded port."[24]

22. Santa Anna, *Apelación al buen criterio* . . . , p. 14.
23. George F. Ruxton, *Adventures in Mexico* . . . , p. 11.
24. *Niles Register,* LXXI (September 26, 1847), p. 49.

Commodore Connor, commanding the United States blockading squadron, reported: "I have allowed him [Santa Anna] to enter without molestation, or even speaking the vessel, as I was informed by the senior English naval officer here, Captain Lambert; she carried no cargo, and would not be allowed to take any in return. I could easily have boarded the *Arab,* but I deemed it most proper not to do so, allowing it to appear as if he had entered without my concurrence."[25]

On shore, active preparations had been going forward for the reception of the returning exile. Both Fermín and Benito Gómez Farías, sons of the old liberal, were at Veracruz several days in advance, trying to reconcile factions and complete all arrangements. At 9:00 A.M. August 16, 1846, the Eleventh Infantry repaired to the dock where they marched around for a couple of hours and finally formed in two lines facing each other. "A most discordant band screamed national airs, and a crowd of boys squibbed and crackered on the wharf, supplied with fireworks at the expense of the heroic city." While the castle fired a salute, Santa Anna walked between the files preceded by his wife on the arm of an officer. The troops "saluted individually and when they pleased, some squibbing off their firelocks, and others, not knowing what to do, did nothing." "The Señora, a pretty girl of seventeen, pouted at the cool reception, for not one 'viva' was heard.... The General was dressed in full uniform, and looked anything but pleased at the absence of any thing like applause, which he doubtless expected would have greeted him."[26]

Thus the hero returned. Could he with this inauspicious beginning hope to do anything for himself or for Mexico?

25. *House Executive Document* No. 60, Thirtieth Congress. first session, For a further discussion of this episode see Rives, *The United States and Mexico,* II, 241 note.
26. Ruxton, *op. cit.,* pp. 17-18.

PATRIOT

IT must not be thought that such an unusual procedure as a nation deliberately allowing its enemy's outstanding political and military leader to go through its blockade would pass unnoticed. In the United States all kinds of newspapers commented freely, and some of them in very uncomplimentary terms on the whole affair. Some felt that the idea was to introduce a discordant element into Mexico, while others shrewdly connected Mackenzie's visit to Cuba with a tentative bargain between Santa Anna and Polk. To calm the discussion and direct sentiment, Polk informed Congress on December 8 that he had sought to weaken the enemy by fostering internal friction in Mexico.

As early as August 4, Polk had sent a confidential message to the United States Senate, asking for an appropriation of $2,000,000 to be used in negotiating a treaty with Mexico, the sum to be used, if necessary, as a payment before the Senate ratified the treaty. Four days later, a similar request was sent to the House of Representatives. This was just at the time Santa Anna was going to Mexico and, Senator Thomas Benton insisted, was for the purpose of carrying out plans made with the Mexican to help replace him in power.[1]

News of these events reached Europe simultaneously. *The Morning Chronicle* (London, September 15) considered it all part of an effort to buy peace, with Santa Anna and Polk "to settle the moralities of the transaction between them." *The Globe* (London) of the same date had much the same idea. *The Nation* (Dublin, September 19) remarked "It is .... possible that an understanding has been come to between the government at Washington and Santa." The *Leeds Mercury* (September 26) referred to Santa Anna's return as "connived at by

---

1. Thomas H. Benton, *Thirty Years View*, II, 681-82.

Commodore Connor." *The Glasgow Herald* (September 18) considered the Mexican corruptible, and that his return to Mexico was the result of "American intrigue." The *Manchester Guardian* (September 16) probably summarized British opinion rather well when it commented: "the probability seems to be, that there is an understanding between him [Santa Anna] and the American government; and we should not be surprised to hear that he has been furnished from Washington with the funds which have doubtless been used to corrupt the Mexican troops. In that case, most probably, the price of his restoration to power will be a treaty of peace, advantageous to the United States...."

Unfortunately for Santa Anna, this same opinion was entertained by people in Mexico. The British Minister Bankhead stated that "he was rather inclined to support" the idea that Santa Anna had "entered into some secret agreement" with the United States authorities, but that confirmation was lacking. He also commented: "The return of General Santa Anna [who is supported only by the Army] is most unpopular in the Country; hitherto his progress has drawn forth no enthusiasm. At Vera Cruz it was marked by strong dislike.— Each party suspects him of Treachery...."[2]

In Veracruz, in fact, there had been an ugly little incident when the people gathered before the City Hall, demanding that the authorities ask Santa Anna for guarantees. Not receiving satisfaction, the crowd selected a tinsmith to go directly to Santa Anna to demand the removal of undesired soldiers from the city. According to the accounts, this representative presented his desires, prefaced by a blunt reminder that Santa Anna had just been in exile for failing to carry out the wishes of the people.

Meanwhile, Juan Alvarez, J. M. Mora, the Gómez Farías family, M. C. Rejón, J. N. Almonte, and numerous others were working with might and main to create a more sympathetic atmosphere. Santa Anna himself proceeded to his estate on his way to Mexico City after issuing an address to

2. Bankhead to Aberdeen, Nos. 120 and 121, August 29, 1846. F. O. Vol. CXCVIII.

his countrymen on August 16. He explained that he had always believed in the will of the people, and that he had changed his views of government in the 1830's because he honestly thought the people had changed theirs. He unsparingly denounced monarchy as utterly unsuited for the Mexicans because of the "intensity and energy" of their democratic principles. He continued: "Fascinated by the example of a nation not yet a century old, and which, under its own government, has attained a degree of prosperity and advantages not enjoyed by those of the old world, notwithstanding their antiquity, and the slow progress of their political systems, our republic aspires only to the management of its own affairs, either by itself, or through representatives, in whom it has confidence.... Was this for the purpose of sounding out the attitude of Mexicans towards the United States? To leave no doubt of his position he added: "The slave of public opinion myself, I shall act in accordance with it; .... subjecting myself .... entirely to the decisions of the constituent assembly, the organ of the sovereign will of the nation." "Allow me again to take it [the enviable title of soldier of the people], never more to be given up, and to devote myself, until death, to the defense of the liberty and independence of the republic."[3]

After a short stay on his estate, Santa Anna went on to Jalapa, where he was received with real cordiality on September 5. Further good news arrived to the effect that Guadalajara was delighted with the whole situation, and that increasing numbers were making up their minds to accept conditions as they found them. It is true that individuals who tried to reason things out were puzzled and one querulously wrote: "What do you think of the manifesto of Santa Anna? I read it, I re-read it and do not understand it."[4] But such seemed few.

In Mexico City, the friction in Salas' cabinet grew worse even though few paid much attention to Salas anyway. He

3. *House Executive Document* No. 60, Thirtieth Congress, first session, p. 781.
4. J. F. Ramírez to Francisco Elorriaga, August 22, 1846, in Ramírez, *México durante su guerra con los Estados Unidos*, p. 134.

was just an interlude and all eyes were now turned in fear and joy to the Veracruz turnpike as people joined in the bustle of preparation. The National Theatre hastily resumed its old name of the Santa Anna Theatre, while statues and portraits so recently in hiding were hustled out to be refurbished and displayed in reception rooms. Painters busily replaced the name of the hero on numerous street signs from which it had been removed while carpenters erected triumphal arches, one of which proudly flaunted the legend: "The well deserving of his country: the immortal savior of the Republic: the hero of Tamaulipas." At night crowds paraded the streets yelling *vivas* for Santa Anna and *mueras* for the monarchists, till desiring more active sport they occasionally stoned the homes of Herrera and his friends. Truth to tell, it is probable that much of this enthusiasm came from a judicious distribution of cash so that the rabble could indulge in pulque.

> Liquor divine!
> Angels drink it
> When they dine.[5]

On September 15, 1846, Santa Anna reached the Capital. Acting President Salas went out to meet him. The returning parade carried four tableaux in as many carriages showing liberty; union of the people and the army; America; and fame. The real feature of the parade, of course, was Santa Anna and Gómez Farías in an open carriage with Santa Anna "democratically" dressed and prominently holding a copy of the Constitution of 1824. Liberals, or "Reds," of 1828-1832, were loudly acclaimed in spite of the fact that Tornel, the great friend of Santa Anna, had cynically referred to them as "cruel and intolerant demagogues."

The "libertine" and the "anti-ecclesiastic" now proceeded to work fast. Both realized that any immediate cash sums

---

5. Chorus of popular drinking song of the day:

> ¿Sabe que es el pulque?
> Licor divino-o!
> Lo beben los angeles
> En el sereno-o.

must come from the clergy, but all was to be done decently and in order. Salas promptly called for the election of delegates to a new congress to meet December 6. Under the existing conditions, the majority were sure to be ultra liberals. Other plans were hastily agreed upon while Santa Anna, with his old time energy, prepared to take the field. Thirteen days after reaching Mexico City, on September 28, he set out for San Luis Potosí to start new military operations against Taylor. This satisfied his own craving for the excitement of the campaign and, as he knew, was the surest way to reach the hearts of his people. One prominent Mexican historian commented that he was now justified in proudly repeating the boast: "I am the nation."

Whatever may have been the intentions of Santa Anna when he landed at Veracruz, he soon realized that the temper of the Mexican people demanded war with the United States, and that to open immediate negotiations would be to throw away all support. He now put forth an honest effort to raise an army and prepare for a campaign in the north. Here was Santa Anna at his best: his flare for publicity, his tremendous personal energy and his powerful personality enabled him to perform wonders with revolution-torn and morale-broken Mexico. After so much talk, the people actually believed in the words of their spokesman: "The war is a necessity of immediate importance; every day's delay is an age of infamy," and here was the leader for the occasion.

Of course the question of Santa Anna's motive may still be debated. Did he desire to defeat Taylor and win the war? Did he plan to be defeated by Taylor after an apparent effort, thus proving to Mexico the necessity for negotiations? Did he simply wish to do his best against Taylor, having the preliminary negotiations with Polk to fall back upon in case of need? The last possibility seems the most logical for no one can doubt the sincerity of his effort who reads the accounts of the northern campaign.

He set out from Mexico City on September 28, 1846, at the head of three thousand men. His supplies and cash were sufficient for a week only, but that was a minor matter apparently. All was glamor and enthusiasm. When he reached Querétaro, the Commander sent forward a proclamation to the Potosinos urging them to forget the unfortunate events of 1823 when he had been so unpopular in their midst. He asked that they look upon him as a Mexican soldier on his way to the frontier to offer his body once more to enemy bullets so as to maintain the integrity of his native land.

On October 14, he arrived at San Luis Potosí to find about four thousand troops gathered there from those who had been defeated by Taylor at Monterrey. The inhabitants greatly feared that their city would be the next point of attack. So, partly through fear, partly through curiosity, and partly through love of a military pageant and hero, the city folk gave a warm and vociferous reception to the troops from the south. Santa Anna immediately rushed the building of defenses for the city and issued calls for men, money and all kinds of supplies.

An undoubted handicap lay in the general dislike of Santa Anna all through the liberal north. Durango, when asked for aid, said its hands were full with Indian troubles, Michoacán did little better, and Zacatecas once more under García, its governor who had been so severely defeated by Santa Anna in 1835, even tried to form an alliance of states against Santa Anna. This kind of feeling was offset in part and troops began to come in from Guanajuato, Jalisco and other points till approximately twenty thousand men were on hand. The quality of the men secured was another matter, however. Some were prisoners sent to the front, while most of them were frightened raw recruits who hardly knew what it was all about. To secure more men the National Guard had been called out while all males from sixteen to fifty had been ordered to enlist, on pain of forfeiting all political rights.[6]

At this point one of Santa Anna's weaknesses developed. He was so busy with his propaganda to secure men and supplies that he paid little attention to the actual training of the troops in camp. They were seldom drilled in battle maneuvers and saw little of the ranking officers who were to lead them

6. Bancroft, *History of Mexico*, V, 414-15.

into battle and in whom no confidence had been built up. Santa Anna was fine for conceiving the general scheme, but he sadly needed a drillmaster to take care of the essential details for which he did not have time and in which he was so little interested. Occasional grand parades or reviews seem to have been about the extent of the organized training that large numbers of the men received.

The most serious problem was how to secure funds. Zamacois estimated that the cost of an army in Mexico in 1846 was a *peso* a day a man. Though there were only thirty-five thousand men in the whole army, this meant over a million *pesos* a month. To raise such a sum at a time when all customs duties were cut off by the blockade was a stupendous undertaking. Then, of course, there was the cost of outfitting men for active service, plus the expenses of active campaigning against a well equipped enemy. The efforts in San Luis were pitiful, though inspiring it is true, and go to show how far Santa Anna had created a local enthusiasm. Four collection offices were opened where people could bring supplies of "corn, beans, rice, wood, meat, lead, copper, money, etc., etc." When there was a fair amount of these gifts collected at any one point, they were carried through the streets in a popular procession in "wagons, carts or even baskets."

But such gifts were a mere drop in the bucket. On November 9, the Commander wrote the Minister of War that he absolutely had to have one hundred and fifty thousand *pesos* at once. By December 7, he was nearly desperate and complained bitterly that the last remittance had been for twenty thousand *pesos*, "not enough to secure supplies for his local troops for two days." On December 30, he reported that he had received one hundred and seventy-five thousand *pesos* out of an expected four hundred thousand *pesos*.[7]

To handle the situation better, he was attempting to concentrate his men, drawing them in from Chihuahua and other exposed points, including Tampico. At once a storm of dis-

7. These letters and others of similar import may be found in Smith, *Letters of General . . . . Santa Anna,* American Historical Association's Report, 1917.

approval broke out. Many said that the surrender of Tampico was part of the nefarious agreement suspected to have been made with the United States, and was proof of Santa Anna's treason. Present day military students, however, are inclined to consider the move a wise one from a tactical standpoint and regardless of the interpretations placed upon it at the time.

The truth was that as 1846 closed, the ghosts of the past were arising to curse Santa Anna and, with their intangible tentacles, were weaving a mesh of complications that was to prove his undoing. As the weeks passed in Mexico City, it became obvious that there was serious danger of the old lines of cleavage of 1832 developing once more. The Gómez Farías papers contain any number of letters carrying professions of loyalty to the old Liberal coupled with serious reservations as to Santa Anna. These correspondents took little stock in the fact that he had declined executive office in September, when he wrote to Almonte, Minister of War: "Your Excellency will at once perceive how great an error I should commit in assuming the supreme magistracy, when my duty calls me to the field, to fight against the enemies of the republic. I should disgrace myself, if, when called to the point of danger, I should spring to that of power!"[8]

The feeling of distrust was aggravated when it was rumored that Santa Anna was trying to side-track Gómez Farías. In the Capital, even more than in San Luis, the raising of funds was the major problem of the government. Forced loans on various classes, one directly applied to the clergy, brought in very little. As a matter of fact the issue was not squarely joined for some time for all wanted the elections over before a program was adopted.

The wisdom of this course was seen when Congress met on December 6 and counted the ballots. For President, Santa Anna received eleven departmental votes only, while Elorriaga received nine. For Vice President, Gómez Farías received eleven to eight for Ocampo and one for Elorriaga. Gómez

8. Brantz Mayer, *Mexico, Aztec, Spanish and Republican*, I, 361.

Farías at once took office as the Acting President, while Santa Anna continued with his military duties. He had repeatedly stated that he would not engage in political matters, but his letters from this time on acquired a more and more dictatorial tone.

After the middle of November, he gave advice and directions freely to the treasury officials, and threatened to publish a "solemn protest" in the newspapers unless more cash was forthcoming. There were those who hoped for just such a step and in Mazatlán, the garrison declared for Santa Anna as dictator. This he declined, saying it would only complicate a difficult situation. On the other hand, his enemies were busy spreading the rumor that he had entered into a treasonable arrangement with the United States. To combat this, the Government sent a circular to the state governors on November 27 expressing its entire confidence in the General, and flatly branding the rumors as malicious and treasonable.

By the time the new executive took office it was quite clear to all concerned that little more cash could be secured through the regular methods or even by further discounting future income through the sale of importation permits. The clergy had not contributed very freely as yet, so even many conservatives were agreed that pressure should be applied—a task thoroughly congenial to Gómez Farías who had advocated just this for nearly a score of years. To him the war provided a golden opportunity to accomplish his life's work, Church reform, and, at the same time to raise funds for the defense of the country he so passionately loved.

There were many to warn the Vice President that Santa Anna could not be relied upon, but the letters received from army headquarters contained only pleas for money and cordial endorsement of plans proposed. The Commander wrote Rejón on January 2 and argued at length for a forced loan on the clergy for twenty million *pesos,* referring to clerical aid offered the governments of Spain and other countries in time of need. He added that he had heretofore refused to touch Church property, saying he would rather cut off his hand first, but that now conditions had changed. He also

[247]

wrote to Gómez Farías endorsing the idea on the grounds that there were no other funds available.

On January 8, Congress started debate on the proposal to raise fifteen million *pesos* on the security of Chuch property. By 11:00 P.M. those favoring the measure were dominating the roll calls by votes of forty-four to forty-one and forty-three to forty-one—a dangerously narrow margain. On hearing that the bill had passed, Santa Anna warmly congratulated the leaders of the movement in letters written by him on the fourteenth. On the day before, he notified the Minister of War that there would be no disorders in the army as a result of the new law and added: "If anything is attempted, I will take the necessary steps and prevent its effects."[9]

Santa Anna's letters to Gómez Farías carried open endorsement of the new bill and pleas for cash coupled with only thinly veiled threats if money were not provided.[10] In a letter of January 18, the General took note of the opposition that had developed and said: "Opposition to the law from that class of persons [the ecclesiastical cabildo] was to be expected, but now that the government has sanctioned the law, it is essential that it be enforced, conquering all obstacles that are offered to it with the greatest energy." What the General failed to mention was that he had sent a personal representative, Basadre, to the Capital to meet with such conservatives as Pedraza and to talk over ways and means with them.

This may have been just a sea anchor cast to windward in anticipation of an approaching storm. It certainly placed his loyalty to the administration in considerable doubt, though there is little to reflect on his patriotism to the nation at the time. Colonel Atocha was still scuttling around between the United States and Mexico, but the Gómez Farías administration seemed to give him scant encouragement, and there is no reason to think that he was making any effective contacts with Santa Anna. On the contrary, when the arch in-

9. Numbers of these letters may be found in the transcripts of the García Collection, or in the *Gómez Farías Papers*. Also see Escudero, *Memorias con Documentos*, p. 40.

10. *Gómez Farías Papers*. See letters of January 2, 4, 7, 14, 16, 18, and 26.

triguer, Moses Y. Beach, was going to Mexico with his schemes to organize a national bank with which to tie up the finances, and to assist the opposition to Gómez Farías which hoped to place Santa Anna in undisputed possession of the president's power, it was Santa Anna himself, who wrote a "confidential" note carrying a distinct warning to the Minister of War on January 22, 1847. He said that he had word that Beach was editor of the New York *Sun* and came as an agent to bring about peace; that he had no official commission, but full powers and would spare no money. "His mission is prejudicial to the interests and honor of the Nation."[11]

To secure the absolute essentials for his men, Santa Anna ordered that ninety-eight bars of silver in the mint at San Luis Potosí be seized and offered his own property as security. He also issued drafts in his own name so that the sum collected on his private endorsement or with his property as security reported as one hundred and eighty thousand *pesos*. Later the government assumed the obligation, but there is no doubt the man was putting forth every effort. The Government, on its part, was having serious trouble with the forced loan from the clergy. Zacatecas, Oaxaca and other sections warmly endorsed the idea, but the holy fathers in Puebla, Mexico City and the points from which most of the cash was to be raised opposed a stubborn resistance.[12] They strenuously denied having any funds and refused to cooperate. Exasperated and in desperation, the Government ordered troops to break into the clerical strong boxes. With ample warning, the clergy had long since hidden their cash, so that the sums secured were pitifully small though a terrible storm of popular rage was aroused at such sacrilege.[13]

Meanwhile the senseless popular demand for an immediate

11. Smith, *op. cit.*, p. 409.
12. G. M. McBride, *Land Systems of Mexico*, pp. 68-69. The first installment of 10,000,000 *pesos* was to be raised as follows:

Archbishopric of Mexico	5,000,000 *pesos*
Bishopric of Puebla	2,000,000 *pesos*
Bishopric of Guadalajara	1,250,000 *pesos*
Bishopric of Michoacán	1,750,000 *pesos*

13. For a discussion of this whole question, see Callcott, *Church and State in Mexico, 1822-1857*, p. 183 ff.

advance would have been hard to withstand in any event. Now it was far worse because of the sinister whisperings and constant reports of Santa Anna's duplicity. Consequently, goaded by popular clamor, the Commander decided on a forward movement against Taylor even though this was the worst possible season of the year. One comforting consideration may have been that word had reached Mexican headquarters that Taylor's forces were being weakened as men were drawn off for the Scott expedition. At such a time one of Santa Anna's swift moving expeditions stood a chance of gaining a victory even though the men were wretchedly equipped and scarcely organized, and even though desertions running into the thousands had already become a problem.

On January 28, 1846, the start was made as Santa Anna, in his chariot and eight mules, surrounded by a brilliant staff, set out. The army of upwards of eighteen thousand was swelled by large numbers of women, both for the officers and men. In truth, the woman of the common soldier did a great deal of the foraging, the cooking and general camp work, though so much can scarcely be said for the wanton crowd maintained by the officers from Santa Anna down the line.

As usual, there was the grandiose proclamation to his men, but scarcely had they had time to hear it read when they faced the desert—and scant comfort did fine words provide there. A two hundred and fifty mile march across the district from San Luis Potosí to Saltillo would be serious for the best equipped troops, but for these ragamuffins, in the month of February, it was terrific. For the first time, many of these troops saw with a growing feeling of uneasiness that the mountain slopes were becoming more and more bare, for vegetation withered and died as they entered the desert.

On the fifth of February, the weather was rather cold, but the next few days were so hot that the sweat poured off the bodies of even those poorly clothed hosts. Then, on the tenth, the elements turned loose their full repertoire. First there was that awesome sensation as though all nature was brooding and hushed. There was a vague uneasiness among the pack

[250]

animals and livestock as the south wind gradually died away and a short calm ensued. Then the clouds seemed mysteriously to thicken and become ominous till the surprised and weary troops saw the blackened masses hurled back and then start rushing southward under the impact of unseen, unheard and unfelt gales high overhead. Far in the north appeared, next to the horizon, a thin white streak that rose with startling rapidity. Here was the fury of the storm incarnate as it crashed forward dealing its staggering blows of wind and drenching rain, that rapidly turned to driving sleet and snow. Next followed the piercing cold of the "blue whistler" which knifed to the very center of a man's being as the storm tore down the valleys between the long mountain ranges which now served to concentrate the fury of the elements upon the shuddering and demoralized troops. This, the first battle, cost Santa Anna's army "more than four hundred men in sick and dead."

The march continued with constantly increasing desertions and scanty supplies more and more depleted. Through the able services of some Texas Rangers serving as scouts, Taylor was warned of the Mexican advance and withdrew his forces to the position at Angostura. To reach this point, the Mexicans advanced nearly fifty miles in the last twenty-four hours with very little in the way of either water or food on the march. On February 22, there was light fighting as the two forces felt each other out and assumed their positions.[14]

The next day was one long and bloody contest, with the tide of battle ebbing and flowing from point to point over the battle field of Buena Vista. In the opinion of Smith, one finds "the two armies not unevenly matched."[15] Santa Anna

14. A. C. Ramsey, *The Other Side*, p. 126. One explanation of the proposed truce which the Mexicans were said to have suggested, with the result that the United States troops ceased firing and sent an emissary for a parley only to be met by continued firing by the Mexicans is: One Lieutenant José María Montoyo found himself among the United States troops after one of the Mexican charges. He did not wish to be captured and so pretended to be an emissary who had been sent to ask for a truce and parley. In this way he got back to his own army, but wisely disappeared till after the discussions were over.

15. Smith, *War with Mexico*, I, 396.

himself was at all points, urging on his men with complete disregard of the personal danger involved. One horse was killed under him, but he mounted another and continued to encourage his men and to reinforce points of danger with his presence. When night fell, the contest could well be described as a drawn battle, worthily fought. The total United States casualties were 723 killed and wounded and 23 missing; while Santa Anna, in his report to the Minister of War, stated: "We have lost in killed and wounded about one thousand." This was doubtless a substantial underestimate which should properly be increased from 50 to 100 per cent for the Mexicans were on the offensive most of the time.

The bravery of the Mexicans was all the more remarkable in view of the fact that they were raw recruits for the most part, and were actually short of food and had been suffering heavy privations for weeks. Bancroft agrees with the Mexican claim that on the morning of the twenty-second the troops had only one ration left, and that they went into battle that day and fought through the twenty-third without any more food.[16] Even though this may be a slight exaggeration, there can be no doubt they suffered a very real food shortage. Beyond question, the men were ably led and had a fanatical belief in this commander who so recklessly exposed himself.

But, when the reaction set in in the night hours, what then? Santa Anna stated that there had been considerable desertion during the day and that the outlook for the morrow was dark. At a council of war, practically all officers said simply that men and horses were hungry and could not be relied upon for a third day's fighting.[17] The next morning, when Taylor was fearfully making preparations for a retreat of his

16. Bancroft, *op. cit.*, V, 419 note.

17. Santa Anna later claimed that the determining factor in deciding to retreat was the report that had reached him of revolution in Mexico City, together with orders for him to return at once to protect the government. This argument seems a little weak when one considers the distance involved and the fact that his return one day earlier could mean little in Mexico City, especially when that day if spent in the north could easily mean the difference between his own army victorious, or demoralized by a retreat after a "claimed victory" only.

own, there came the joyful news that the Mexican forces had left their lines and were headed back across the desert.

The Mexican retreat indeed was ordered soon after nightfall. "At first the march was like a funeral procession, except that dead men appeared to be celebrating their own obsequies." The groans of the wounded and dying made the weird light of the thin moon all the more unearthly. To retrace the route already scoured clean of all food supplies meant still more of hunger and suffering in the wintry weather, so it was not surprising that the men deserted by scores and hundreds. Here was the real defeat of the Army of the North as dysentery, typhus and other diseases aided hunger in complete demoralization of men and officers. The army was so completely shattered that less than half the number who set out from San Luis Potosí ever returned through that gateway to their old homes.

DEFEAT

EVENTS in Mexico City were moving rapidly while Santa Anna was in the north. Gómez Farías, with a crusader's zeal, had determined to apply in full the forced loan on Church property, but found the opposition as zealous as his own support. Before long there were both clerics and laymen to say that force should be met with force and on February 27 active rebellion broke out. M. Peña y Barragán at once wrote to governors of several of the states, proposing as a solution that Santa Anna be placed in direct charge of affairs.

After nine days of fighting, the rebels and their clerical friends were about to lose heart and give up the contest for Gómez Farías was presenting unexpected resistance, and had a much firmer grasp on the situation than had been expected. At this point, however, the chicanery of Moses Y. Beach began to have results. In spite of Santa Anna's warning that he was a secret agent of the United States the man had been able to pose as a sincere friend of Mexico in its hour of need. He actually secured the approval of a plan for a national bank by which he would have been able to control the national finances in large measure. But before this could be organized the revolt in Mexico City provided a quicker means of demoralizing affairs than the bank plan afforded. When the rebels faltered he provided the wherewithal to enable them to continue the contest. He later stated that since Scott was just landing he considered "almost any outlay would be justified. The rebellion was therefore kept up, until the sudden appearance of General Santa Anna closed the affair." He boasted that this occupied five thousand men and "all the arms, munitions of war and means of the government in the City of Mexico for twenty-three days."[1]

Meanwhile Santa Anna had left the field of Angostura and was hastening southward ahead of his straggling forces, carrying only a few captured standards and guns as proof of his "victory" over Taylor. On March 6 he wrote to Gómez Farías, lamenting the misfortunes of his country, but saying that he was approaching to protect the government. Four days later, he wrote saying that both sides must agree to a truce until he could arrive for both reason and humanity were "impiously outraged" by this shedding of Mexican blood by Mexicans when all should be fighting the invader.

The change in the tone of these letters was obvious and ominous to the Liberals. From the wording of the first letter they might confidently expect aid, but in the second they were referred to in much the same terms as the rebels even though Santa Anna was still insisting that he would use "firmness and energy" in putting down the revolt and then would retire from power to his estate or any point where his country needed him.[2]

After a few days in San Luis Potosí, the General continued southward once more. Scarcely a day passed but that some delegation or commissioner arrived to pour out a tale of woe or to make a good impression on the man who held the balance of power. Gómez Farías sent liberal apologists, while the conservatives sent their agents. Santa Anna shrewdly kept his own council while weighing possibilities, ways and means. The great essential was cash. How get this with the least opposition? To support Gómez Farías would provide a record of consistency but very little money.

At last came the suggestion that the adventurer was so eager to hear. The clergy would provide two million *pesos* cash if

1. Smith, *War with Mexico*, II, 331 note. See also *ibid.*, pp. 11-12. A discussion of Beach's plan for a national bank may be found in Callcott, W. H., *Church and State in Mexico, 1822-1857*, pp. 192-93.
2. Letter of March 6 in *Documentos Relativos a Santa Anna* (transcript) in García Collection; letter of March 10 in translation in *Niles Register*, LXII (April 17, 1847), p. 102; letter to Gómez Farías of March 9 in *Gómez Farías Papers*.

the obnoxious laws were repealed. This was more than could be secured by trying to enforce the liberal laws and would mean clerical support instead of opposition. As though to make action all the more imperative came word that Scott had landed at Veracruz. This latest invasion provided a more serious danger than that from Taylor who had always been separated from Mexico proper by the deserts of the north.

Self-interest and patriotism now urged the same course. Why worry about consistency and the support of Gómez Farías when here were new and powerful friends, who promised greater personal and national advantages? Was it not the patriotic thing to take the course that provided the best chance of saving the nation even at the cost of sacrificing a few ardent liberals?

On arriving at Mexico City, Santa Anna took over the executive's office and quickly gave the city the greatly desired peace. He had Congress place both power and discretion in his hands: it authorized him to raise twenty million *pesos* from the Church authorities, but gave him the right to repeal the obnoxious laws of the two preceding months if he saw fit. This was a real weapon to bargain with, so the clerical "offer" was accepted.[3] Again he became the hero of the Church and the nation.

He was widely acclaimed by the people but hardly dominated the situation completely for Congress showed unexpected independence and yielded to the new program reluctantly. It well remembered the old feud between its predecessors in the legislative halls and this dictatorially inclined military hero. Its members insisted on thinking for themselves and only after a great deal of pressure had been brought to bear were Santa Anna's desires enacted into law on March 31 by the scant vote of thirty-eight to thirty-five. The new program suppressed the vice presidency; repudiated Gómez Farías; allowed the President to head the army in the field; and

---

3. Cuevas, Mariano, *Historia de la Iglesia en México*, Tomo V, p. 263, comments that the clergy provided 2,500,000 *pesos* in the name of patriotism, but that they raised the sum only by the most serious of personal sacrifices.

authorized the selection of a provisional president to take the executive chair.

Santa Anna, simultaneously with the passage of the bill legalizing his program, issued a proclamation to the people and announced that he was going to the front to meet Scott. Comparatively few knew how much pressure had been needed to secure the selection of Pedro María Anaya as provisional president, and that several of Santa Anna's nominations for military promotions had been rejected outright by Congress. The masses simply heard:

"I am resolved to go out and encounter the enemy."

"My duty is to sacrifice myself, and I will know how to fulfill it! Perhaps the American hosts may proudly tread the imperial capital of Azteca. I will never witness such opprobrium, for I am decided first to die fighting!"

"Mexicans! You have a religion—protect it! You have honor—then free yourselves from infamy! You love your wives, your children—then liberate them from American brutality! But it must be action—not vain entreaty or barren desires— with which the enemy must be opposed."

"Mexicans! your fate is the fate of the nation! Not the Americans, but you, will decide her destiny! Vera Cruz calls for vengeance—follow me, and wash out the stain of her dishonor!"[4]

Promptly he set out for the eastern front, leaving the Capital on the afternoon of April 3. As the people crowded around his coach applauding their hero, he, with a husky voice made one of the greatest oratorical appeals of his career with the simple statement: "Union, Mexicans, union, union!"

On the fifth, Santa Anna reached his hacienda of El Encero, located just east of Jalapa. This became his headquarters while he threw himself with all his magnificent energy into the task for which he was so well fitted; that of organzation of an army. He ignored the lukewarmness or actual disaffection of General Gabriel Valencia and the National Congress and worked day and night to obtain supplies. The source

4. *Senate Executive Document*, No. 1, Thirtieth Congress, first session, pp. 259-61.

made little difference; forced loans from the state of Vera-cruz; sale of public property for what it would bring; cajolery, bombast, appeals to patriotism; or any other means that occured to his fertile mind, were employed. He reported on April 7 that there was not a single grain of powder at Perote or "in the army," though this was probably one of those exaggerations which he later frankly admitted he was willing to make on behalf of the national welfare.[5]

While *El Republicano* was spreading the rumor that there was danger of a dictatorship he was driving live stock from his own haciendas to the slaughter pens to feed his men and doing his best to raise the morale of his forces. A description of the kind of troops he was able to collect has been left us by a traveler, who records his impressions thus:

"The marching costume of these heroes, I thought, was peculiarly well adapted to the climate and season—a shako on the head, whilst coat, shirt, and pantaloons hung suspended in a bundle from the end of the firelock carried over the shoulder, and their cuerpos requiring no other covering than the coatings of mud with which they were caked from head to foot, singing, however, merrily as they marched.

"Night now came on, and pitchy dark, and the road was almost impassible from the immense herds of cattle which literally blocked it up. The ganado [live stock] all belonged to Santa Anna, whose estate extends for fifty miles along the road, and bore the well-known brand of A. L. S. A.—*alsa*, or forward as the Mexicans read it, which are the initials of the General Antonio Lopez de Santa Anna."[6]

In order to overlook no possible aid guerrilla troops were authorized to prey upon the invaders. This, of course, meant that any band of highwaymen or marauders could now be patriots—or felons—as occasion demanded or opportunity afforded. The only reasonable deduction to be made from all this activity is that Santa Anna was using every means at his disposal to raise an effective military force and to harass the enemy. Later events would indicate that he was still

5. Santa Anna, *Apelacion al buen criterio . . . .*, p. 41.
6. Ruxton, *Adventures in Mexico*, pp. 21-22.

willing to negotiate secretly, but he was just now determined to reinstate himself in the good graces of the Mexican people. If he could only defeat Scott soundly, the United States demands would be much less exorbitant, and he would be the unquestioned national hero and patriot, who could do about as he wished with his country.

Scott, meanwhile, had approached Veracruz by sea and found it very poorly defended. After some light fighting, the fortress of San Juan de Ulloa and the city were captured, but this only meant the beginning of a hurried march to the plateau. The dreaded hot season had not yet begun but, even so, it was highly inadvisable to leave troops from temperate regions on that coast line for a long period. On April 8, the advance began with the Mexicans offering no resistance. In fact, General Canalizo was so panic stricken that he fled from the National Bridge, leaving his artillery behind. When Santa Anna heard of the retreat he sent orders to Canalizo to go back and get the guns—and there was still time to do it before the enemy arrived!

After considering various possibilities, the Commander-in-chief determined to make his stand at Cerro Gordo, just east of El Encero. It is true that some of his engineers disapproved the selection of the battle ground because of the poor water supply, because it might be attacked by a flank movement, and because another hill overtopped the Mexican works. These criticisms Santa Anna brushed aside, saying that water could be obtained, that a flank movement through the tropically wooded barranca or ravine was out of the question, as was the idea of any troops being able to scale the heights of the neighboring hill, which, he said, even rabbits could not climb. Further protests brought the scathing remark that "cowards never felt safe anyway."

In a cyclonic twelve days, a ditch or canal of three leagues in length was constructed to bring water into camp, fortifications were thrown up and upwards of forty cannon placed, as an army of about eight thousand men was thrown together. Serious criticism of the Commander's plans can be made, but his activity and accomplishments were nevertheless astonishing. Scott's troops advanced and made contact with the Mexicans on April 17. The talked-of movement through the barranca went forward that night as Michigan lumberjacks wielded their axes to carve a way through the tropical vegetation. Legend has it that a sentry reported the sound of chopping but that the officer who disturbed Santa Anna to tell him of it was scoffed at. A second report to the same effect was answered by threatened disciplinary action for spreading alarming rumors. The Yankees likewise outclimbed Santa Anna's mythical rabbits so the untrained Mexican troops found themselves attacked from front, flank and overhead. They quickly broke and fled: the defeat became a rout and three thousand prisoners were captured, as well as forty-three pieces of artillery and numerous other supplies.

Seeing that the battle was lost, the Commander fled to El Encero, thinking that Canalizo and his cavalry were there. Canalizo had sought safety well beyond this point though, so Santa Anna, closely pursued by the Yankees, turned southwestward across country to Orizaba. After following trails and paths for hours, the fugitives reached the hacienda of Tuzamápan about 5:00 P.M.

The dynamo of his energy had run down. Santa Anna was spent physically and mentally and descended to the depths of despair. His old wound was troubling him seriously and this flight, on the heels of the catastrophe, left him aching from head to foot. He spoke to no man, was too sore to move, and simply sat huddled in his seat, a picture of dejection and misery. At 11:00 o'clock at night a rumor came in that a searching party of Americans was near by. A few scattering shots confirmed the report, so the cripple half scrambled and was half lifted onto a horse. With an Indian guide, the pursued passed single file into the night along the trail across the treacherous mountainside.[7] On the second day, the little band reached Orizaba, where General Tornel and other officers had some troops. Stragglers from Cerro Gordo were also

7. An unconfirmed local legend has it that the night was so cold that Santa Anna and a companion killed a horse, and removed the intestines so that they could crowd into the carcass for warmth.

picked up and a force of some three thousand slowly assembled.

The morale of the troops was so sadly shaken, however, that there was no other idea in the minds of the leaders than that of retreat. The United States troops marched into Jalapa, passed on up the old Royal Road through "La Hoya, a terrible pass," as Scott called it, and took over the old fortress of Perote with its sixty-six guns. In short, their chief obstacles were heat, sand, disease, lack of supplies and danger from guerrillas: the Mexican army itself was at this time hardly to be classed as an active menace.

In the Capital all kinds of rumors were afloat. Santa Anna was denounced bitterly for inefficiency and cowardice, while the even more sinister old rumors as to his treachery began to circulate once more. Congress did not dare to depose him for he was clearly the best organizer in the country. Yet they were determined to forestall any danger of treason. On April 20, just as news of Cerro Gordo reached Mexico City, they gave him "unlimited" power, but at once proceeded to limit it. He was given absolute authority over domestic questions but was strictly forbidden, on pain of being classed as a traitor, to enter into any communication or negotiation with the United States government.

The Commander meanwhile retired from Orizaba to Puebla as the next possible point of defense. However, the City of the Angels knew quite well that Scott's troops were only a few hours behind the Mexicans. Santa Anna himself reported that he was greeted on his arrival by copies of instructions in which the authorities had advised the people what to do when United States soldiers took over the city. He insisted that the populace received him enthusiastically, but the facts are that he was none too popular in Puebla. He at once levied the customary forced loan, but had to be content with a mere one-third of the thirty thousand *pesos* demanded. Some state that out of chagrin he confiscated valuable Church jewels and vessels, but the proof seems insufficient. Beyond doubt, the Poblanos did not wish to fight, and in truth there was little or no time in which to prepare a defense. After mutual recriminations, Santa Anna continued on his way while the city prepared to receive the invader.

Scott moved in and settled down for nearly three months to consolidate his holdings, acclimate his men, prepare for the grand march to the Capital—and to negotiate. Periodically the shadowy figure of Atocha had continued to appear in Washington or in Mexico, endeavoring to weave some kind of a pattern into the international cloth then on the loom. Possibly he himself was none too sure of what was going on, but there were others closer to the directing powers. Polk, in April, 1846, had asked Congress for a million dollars "(to be accounted for of course) that I might be able to settle our Mexican difficulty speedily." Polk had also authorized the sending of Nicholas P. Trist as commissioner of the State Department to accompany Scott. He was to negotiate a treaty with Mexico and was authorized to use a sum up to $3,000,-000 for the purpose.[8] After their widely advertised preliminary bickering and suspicions, Scott and Trist seemed to agree upon a method of procedure.

Soon after Puebla was captured the negotiations opened stealthily, but with very definite purposes in view. Certain British residents and officials were apparently the go-betweens. All understood that this was not covered in the rule books, but felt that the end justified the means. Scott called upon his secret service funds for an advance payment, reported to have been $10,000, "to overcome the resistance of members of [the Mexican] Congress" to anything Santa Anna might propose. The real payment, reported to be a million dollars, was not included in the terms of the treaty, but was to be made privately to Santa Anna. When rumors of such negotiations reached the public in the United States, Polk indignantly repudiated the very idea, and agreed that Scott ought to be recalled immediately if he had entered into such an agreement.

The official investigation conducted later showed that some such arrangement was made. Scott, with considerable asperity,

8. Quaife, *Diary of James K. Polk*, I, 317; *Senate Executive Document* No. 52, Thirtieth Congress, first session, p. 108.

refused to give names and facts except to the President or one of his Cabinet. His attitude was apparently well summed up in his letter of February 6, 1848, to the Secretary of War when he wrote:

"Sir: I have not reported on the subject of secret disbursements since I left Jalapa. First, because of the uncertainty of our communications with Vera Cruz; and, second, the necessity of certain explanations which, on account of others, ought not to be reduced to writing. I may, however, briefly add that I have never tempted the honor, conscience, or patriotism of any man, but have held it as lawful in morals as in war to purchase valuable information, or services voluntarily tendered me."[9]

In brief, it would seem that Santa Anna was to "persuade" his Congress to agree to terms while Scott advanced slowly into the Valley of Mexico. Then the Mexican planned to use the cash to consolidate his power, pending the payment of sums provided in the published treaty. Santa Anna had honestly done his best to protect his country from the invader and had failed. Now he turned to trickery and the secret negotiations that had been a possible alternative all along. So far as his personal attitude was concerned, it is probable that he felt that he was working for the best interests of his country. Indeed most people can rather easily convince themselves that what is best for themselves is best for their nation.

Meanwhile the defeated leader crossed over the mountains into the Valley of Mexico. The malcontents in Congress had numerous supporters by this time, and it was generally known that Santa Anna and President Anaya were in serious disagreement over the appointment of General Valencia (whom Santa Anna had disciplined for alleged insubordination some months before) and others to important military posts. On May 18, Santa Anna was at Ayotla, less than twenty miles from the Capital. From there he addressed a letter to Congress in which he stated that there was imminent danger of a revolution, and that this would redound to the advantage of

9. *House Executive Document* No. 60, Thirtieth Congress, first session, p. 1085.

the enemy. He contended that this was aimed at him so that he was glad to forestall it by sending in his resignation as President of the Republic and as Commander-in-Chief. At once Tornel and others rushed to convince him of his mistake. They shrewdly appealed to his vanity and insisted that his resignation was playing directly into the hands of the rebels, whose greatest desire was to get him out of the way. As a result, he reconsidered his action and wrote Congress a second letter on the same day. In this he said that he had been so impressed by the immediate and overwhelming protests that had reached him that he withdrew his resignation.

His enemies clearly lacked either the strength, or courage, or both, to force an acceptance of the resignation once it was in their hands. Likewise they refused to take any responsibility for affairs. Days and weeks passed without a quorum appearing in Congress for the transaction of business, so that Santa Anna again became an essential dictator, being the only one with the combination of initiative and courage willing to take responsibility. So far as he was concerned, he was now in the position of having all to gain and nothing further to lose, so he plunged into the maelstrom.

Once more all was activity. Plans earlier discussed were partially carried out to encourage the desertion of Irish Catholics from the United States army. Proclamations went out to the people, declaring that the Capital would never be surrendered, that the President would die first. On pain of severe penalties, all private citizens were ordered to surrender their arms to the government, while each issue of the *Boletín Oficial* carried a list of names of those patriots who were contributing cash, meat, or agricultural products for the cause, though seldom did the value of these individual gifts, as reported, pass the twenty *pesos* mark. If substantial funds or supplies were located elsewhere, they were promptly acquired regardless of the owners' protests. In this fashion, funds belonging to the Academy of Fine Arts and other institutions were seized, while forced loans were promptly clapped on those who were suspected of ability to pay.

As June and July passed, it became obvious that no effort

was to be made to prevent the United States troops from entering the Valley of Anahuac. There were several points along the route over the mountains between Puebla and Mexico where the road seemed to defy the laws of gravity as it hung to the sides of the precipices. A few tons of gunpowder placed in mines under the road could have blown it to atoms, while a few hundred men could have held thousands at bay. However, the road was left intact and the few hundreds of men not placed in position. This all lent strong circumstantial evidence to the charge that a definite agreement had been reached with the invaders. When they actually menaced the Capital it was felt that even the most dense could see that terms had to be granted. Then, once the peace was arranged, some of the surplus cash of the United States would flow into the hungry maw of Santa Anna and his government, and all would live happily ever after!

This was, at least, plausible reasoning, and Scott duly made his appearance in the month of August. The trouble was that the populace had been so fed upon rumors of treachery that the slightest suggestion that Santa Anna was interested in anything but war to the death brought demands for his displacement. His energies had not flagged and though the defense of the road from Puebla had been neglected, all possible steps were taken to raise troops to defend the Capital. All men from sixteen to fifty were required to take up arms. Special brigades were organized by various professions in the city till the armies lost in the north and east were replaced by a third horde of twenty to twenty-five thousand men. Many of them had seen no military service, but all of them were filled with fervor at the thought of defending their city and their homes from pillage and destruction. Arms and ammunition were manufactured or imported from nearby points and, all in all, it began to appear as though the Americans might have a rather rough time of it.

Scott's plan was to advance early in August at the head of about nine thousand five hundred troops. On July 25, and again on the thirty-first, Trist reported to Secretary Buchanan that Santa Anna had secretly notified him that the United

States army should advance to El Peñon, a strongly fortified point about nine miles from Mexico City and that he would then endeavor to make the peace he was so desirous of securing.[10] Congress continued to avoid responsibility for decisions by the simple expedient of refusing to provide a quorum for the transaction of business. Another complication was the fact that General Gabriel Valencia returned to Mexico City the end of July, and once more injected all his personal hatred of Santa Anna into the situation. Unfortunately for Mexico, he had so many friends and admirers that it was felt a place must be made for him. Far better to have kept one of the two and let the other go.

Scott duly advanced, but found the direct road so strongly fortified and El Peñon so well defended that he decided to swing around and approach from the other side of the city, in spite of the difficulty of campaigning through the lakes and swamps. He seemed to follow the Puebla agreement to a certain point but was not willing needlessly to jeopardize his men by frontal attacks on fortified positions. In early August, Santa Anna had inspired editorials placed in the Government organ (the only paper allowed to be published) which indicated possibilities of negotiations. Trist reported: "Last night, a letter was received from the intended recipient of the million, showing that the business is rapidly and satisfactorily maturing."[11] But, by this time, Valencia and his friends had done so much judicious—or injudicious—talking that Santa Anna did not dare openly to propose peace even as a military necessity. He had been so successful in assembling the raw material for an army that the people believed he had a perfected military machine available. Now he had to try to use it and it must be admitted that he was far from being averse to doing so. He was always a gambler at heart, and he well knew that Scott was badly outnumbered and in a position where a defeat could easily become a catastrophe.

The United States forces advanced promptly and sharp en-

10. *Mexico, Despatches,* Vol. XIV.
11. Smith, *Notes on United States-Mexican Relations,* see letter of August 14, 1847.

gagements took place at Contreras and Churubusco. At this time, Santa Anna was the personification of energy, and won praise from all. As usual, Scott was successful though he was losing valuable men. At Contreras (or Padierna) there occurred a most unfortunate incident for the defenders of the Capital. Valencia, fully convinced that he was the great man of the country, was in charge of this part of the defense. The United States troops had attacked his position but found it stoutly defended. A hurry call to Santa Anna for reinforcements brought that General himself to the section menaced, but it was now 5:00 P.M., and a drenching rain was falling. Santa Anna insisted that he could not cross the intervening ravine and that he soon realized the only thing to do was to send Valencia orders to retire during the night.

Valencia, however, thought that he was the victor and was rapidly assuming, in his own eyes, the importance of commander-in-chief. He flatly refused to retreat and violently condemned Santa Anna for failure to support him, openly saying that the Commander-in-chief was a traitor. The next day Valencia's dreams of glory faded as the United States army delivered its smashing attacks, and his forces, in their exposed position, were cut to pieces. At Churubusco, it was estimated that Scott lost about one thousand men, while ten times that number of Mexicans had been eliminated by death, wounds, capture or dissolution of their units. Valencia's insubordination had been punished, but at what a price![12]

Now surely all could see that peace was a necessity. Santa Anna told the Spanish *Chargé d'affaires* that he was going to take matters into his own hands, while he notified Trist that he was planning to secure a quorum in Congress by appointing men for the vacancies caused by chronic absentees. Scott, meanwhile, seemed to think that this was a good chance

12. *Senate Executive Document* No. 65, Thirtieth Congress, first session, pp. 416-53. The rivalry and hatred of these two men now became common talk over the city as is amply shown by a large number of private letters captured by Scott and published. It might be said that Santa Anna actually started to the reinforcement of Valencia the next morning, but that he was too late and on approaching the field was met by a flood of panic-stricken fugitives.

to follow up earlier negotiations. At any rate, he agreed to an armistice, which would give the demoralized Mexicans valuable time in which to reorganize, while he could scarcely hope to be much stronger in the near future. He said that he did this so that he might not "scatter the elements of peace."

According to the terms of the truce, neither side was to strengthen itself during the period and pending the outcome of the negotiations. As a matter of fact, both generals seem to have done what they could in the way of reorganization and strengthening of their outfits, if not of their positions. In the negotiations, Trist foolishly made his maximum offer to begin with. No Mexicans—and few other diplomats for that matter—could conceive of such a thing, and so promptly countered with proposals that would have ceded the United States little indeed except Texas. Thus, the negotiations languished while some United States troops, who had gone into the city for supplies in accordance with the terms of the truce, were set upon by the crowd and narrowly escaped serious manhandling. Mutual dissatisfaction over observance of the terms of the armistice brought it to an end on September 7, fifteen days after it had been agreed to.

Santa Anna now notified the people that the terms, as offered by the United States commissioners, involved dishonor for Mexico in that they would have essentially reduced the southern nation to the position of a colony of the northern republic. "To such audacity we could oppose nothing but our firmness and our valor." Then followed a plea for all Mexicans to protect the altars of the country, their wives and their daughters from violation and insult. This was the end of the hopes of Santa Anna for any arrangement that would secretly provide him with foreign gold. Gamboa's bitter and circumstantial narrative attacking Santa Anna's whole career had just been published and added strength to Valencia's claims that Santa Anna was a traitor.[13] The only thing left was to fight to the bitter end.

Once the armistice was broken, Scott's advance was prompt and involved heavy fighting at Molina del Rey and other

13. See Santa Anna, *Las Guerras de México con Tejas y los Estados Unidos.*

points. By his own account, these engagements of September 8-14 cost him 1,651 men in killed, wounded and missing. Santa Anna, too, engaged in feverish activity. He took advantage of the anniversary of the surrender of the Spaniards at Tampico, September 11, to hold a review of his troops and to attempt to stir up flagging patriotism. Two days after the anniversary, General Terrés was driven back from Belen Gate by the United States troops. Santa Anna arrived with reinforcements just as the survivors fled. When he met Terrés, he berated him as a coward, struck him in the face, tore off his insignia and ordered him under arrest.[14] On the heels of this came the fall of Chapultepec, the home of the Viceroys of old Spain and a fortress overlooking the city. Bravo, the old hero of Independence and the boys of thirteen to fifteen, who were in the lower grades of the national military school (all others had joined the regular army) offered a gallant resistance. These lads died at their posts like heroes to provide a rallying cry for Mexican patriotism through the ages. With the fall of this point, the war was over and it was only a matter of time till Scott would take over the city.

A council of war was called, and it was decided to abandon the city. The "Immortal Three-Fourths" (as the wags were now calling Santa Anna in reference to his mutilation) wearily withdrew to Guadalupe. During the evacuation of the city the jails were opened and some two thousand criminals were released. Some have attributed this to orders of Santa Anna, but proof has never been advanced. In fact, his most severe contemporary critic, Gamboa, simply accused him of not taking proper precautions to prevent the escape of the renegades.

Scott was too weak to organize control of the city and to undertake a pursuit of the fugitive simultaneously, so Santa Anna remained just outside of the city for twenty-four hours. He started to leave once, then returned to the suburbs on hearing that the populace had risen against the invaders. When he saw that this was not the case, the little flicker of

14. A court martial exonerated Terrés in 1849, but the incident has long provided material for controversy among Mexican annalists.

hope died, and he turned toward Puebla, leaving the proud Capital of the Montezumas to the somewhat poorly organized and irregularly clad fighting devils from Yankeedom.

Santa Anna now resigned from the presidency, and named the President of the Supreme Court, Peña y Peña, as the president *ad interim,* though he was to be associated in the executive power with General Herrera and Sr. Alcorta, former Minister of War. The President's right to name the executive triumvirate was challenged, but his response was that he was going to fight to the death and must be at a distance from the new seat of government about to be established at Querétaro.

The Commander's new plan was to cut Scott's communications at Puebla and was a quite feasible one. Santa Anna's name, however, no longer carried magic with his men and they deserted by scores and hundreds. To appeal to their loyalty, further service was placed on an entirely voluntary basis—more left for home. Probably action would lift their minds out of despondency so the march began—over a thousand more left the ranks. He reached the outskirts of Puebla and, boasting of his numbers, summoned Colonel Thomas Childs to surrender the city, saying he outnumbered Childs eight to one. The Colonel responded on the same day, September 25, with a flat refusal.

For the ensuing ten days a desultory siege was kept up, but on October 7 word came that the Acting President, M. de la Peña y Peña, on behalf of "public morality" and "military discipline" found it necessary to ask His Excellency, General Santa Anna, to surrender the control of his troops to his old rival, General Manuel Rincón. Pending Rincón's arrival, General Juan Alvarez was to take over the command. The fallen hero was graciously permitted to select any place of residence he desired, "with the approval of the government." At such a place he was to wait, under pledge of his word of honor, the appointment of a court martial to consider his military conduct during the war.

This was the death knell of his hopes. He was again plunged into the depths of a profound melancholy. On the sixteenth, he issued a proclamation in which he protested against the rank injustice with which he had been treated, but urged his men to devote themselves to the service of the nation. The document closed thus:

"Soldiers! be faithful servants of your country!—Let no misfortune intimidate you. Perhaps the moment is not far distant when conducted by another more fortunate chieftain, fortune will be propitious to you."[15]

15. *Niles Register,* LXXIII (December 4, 1847), 217, contains a copy of this farewell address.

FLIGHT AND RETURN

MANY military men and some others still felt that Santa Anna was their one hope of being able to return to power.[1] He listened for a time to the voice of these sirens, but soon lapsing back into melancholia and hopelessness retired to Tehuacán, about seventy-five miles southeast of Puebla. From here he was forced to witness the consummation of some of the great events of his country's history while he was a mere onlooker. The treaty of peace was signed—and he was not a beneficiary or even consulted as to its provisions. From the depths of wounded pride and chagrin, he issued a few proclamations such as that of October 22, in which he pled: "Mexicans! I am a man, and I have defects, but never have I sinned against my country; never has my breast harbored anti-national sentiments. A good name to leave behind me has been the aim of my ambition. I have earnestly longed for everything which is great and glorious for Mexico, and to obtain it I have not spared my own blood. You know this and you will do me justice."[2]

But the hurricane of events sucked his words into the air and they were gone.

Soon rumors began to spread to the effect that the old General wished to escape from Mexico to Guatemala. If he had such an idea in mind, it was forestalled by Benito Juárez, Governor of Oaxaca. When Santa Anna took up his residence in Tehuacán, he asked that Oaxaca give him command of the state troops. As commander of these forces, he would have free access to the southern coast and would be quite close to the southern republic. Of course, it is possible that the rumors of his projected flight arose from this request of a man whose

1. *Mexico, Despatches,* Trist to Buchanan, October 25, 1847, XIV (Trist, No. 18).
2. *Niles Register,* LXXIII (December 4, 1847), pp. 215-16.

whole purpose may have been to continue the war against the United States from the southern fastness that had fostered so many Mexican forlorn hopes. On the other hand, Santa Anna may have planned an escape from a court martial controlled by his enemies. Whatever the cause which inspired the request, Juárez flatly vetoed the suggestion and refused Santa Anna the right even to cross the borders of Oaxaca. Juárez explained to his legislature the following July that he feared the entrance of the deposed commander into the State would be the signal for a revolution which had been threatening for some time.[3]

The Mexican army had now practically disintegrated and Scott proceeded to free his captives while he carefully fostered the growing peace party. The Santanistas were classed as friends of peace, but their leader could only injure the cause by espousing it. Hence he remained silent or continued to cry for vengeance.

Santa Anna's beautiful, if sharp-tongued, young wife, who had stayed in Mexico City with one Sr. Atristain during the time when her husband was facing Taylor, was now with her husband at Tehuacán. Their whereabouts reached the ears of Colonel Jack Hays, of the Texas Rangers. He secured permission from Scott to try to capture the Mexican, so a group of three hundred and fifty men were selected and set out. Inflamed by their hatred, smoldering ever since the days of the Alamo massacre, the Texans and their comrades rushed over the hills and the valleys, reaching Tehuacán the morning of January 23, 1848. Santa Anna had just two hours warning of the impending raid, so horses were called for and in a swirl of excitement and fear a few personal possessions were thrown together as the family fled. Sra. Santa Anna and a daughter of the General left in a coach while he followed on horseback.

3. In his *Memoirs* Santa Anna insisted that the Indian Governor had been inspired by a desire for petty vengeance because of the fact that, in 1828, when Santa Anna was visiting Don Manuel Embides, Juárez had waited on the table as a barefoot Indian lad, and that his pride had hurt him ever since. Obviously, the two men had nothing in common and their antagonism arose both from personalities and principles.

Finding their quarry gone, the raiders made huge sport of opening the numerous chests and trunks filled with the possessions of the family of the ex-President. His coats loaded with gold braid, his walking cane with handle ablaze with diamonds, sapphires and emeralds, and numerous bric-a-brac were divided as spoils. The ladies' garments were thoroughly examined and duly marveled at, but were forwarded to Sra. Santa Anna with the compliments of the captors. In his *Memoirs,* Santa Anna characterized the raid as an attempt at assassination—and it must be admitted that had the Texans laid hands on him, the chances are that he would have been reported as "killed resisting arrest."

There was no longer anything to be gained by staying in Mexico so Santa Anna asked permission to be allowed to go into exile once more. At this very time the states were casting their ballots for the presidency, but he did not await word from the complete returns for of the first twelve states reporting, only two favored the fallen hero. Strangely enough, Peña y Peña was ignored likewise in spite of the fact that he had tried to clear his own skirts of association with Santa Anna by declaring that he had assumed office by virtue of the constitutional provisions and not because of Santa Anna's decree in his favor.

The new executive, Herrera, found his hands more than full in trying to reach an agreement with the invaders and in persuading the Mexican people that the terms should be accepted. Under the circumstances, the leaders wisely concluded that the best thing to do was to let Santa Anna leave as quietly and quickly as possible. They relied upon the fact that he was so discredited as to be harmless abroad, though he would be a constant source of irritation if he remained in Mexico. The request was granted and on March 17, 1847, a safe conduct was issued by Colonel George W. Hughes, Military Governor of the Department of Jalapa, allowing Santa Anna, "his family and personal armed retainers" to pass through the United States lines to Veracruz.

Just after leaving Perote, Santa Anna, his wife and daughter were graciously entertained at a banquet by Colonel Hughes, who showed the Mexicans numerous courtesies. The meal was abruptly interrupted by the unceremonious entrance of the Ranger Colonel, Jack Hays, who, with a number of his men, had come to have a look at the Mexican, and to see what could be done about such an unheard-of procedure as that of entertaining the reprobate whom the Rangers had so long sought. Hughes' aide, Major Kenly, skillfully placed the affair on a social basis by introducing the Texan to Santa Anna and his women folks. The rough old Colonel gasped but rose to the situation, and reluctantly returned to his men to insist that they might wait to see Santa Anna leave only provided they remain in strict military formation.

It was a tense party who left the scene of the banquet soon after. With Major Kenly on horseback leading the way at a hand gallop, the Santa Anna coachman whipped up his horses to a run and the coach rocked and swayed as the party ran the gauntlet through the lines of the half-amazed, half-indignant Texans who had to be content with muttered, ribald remarks on seeing their quarry escape. At Jalapa, Santa Anna was received with military honors as a general of division and escorted by a company of United States cavalry out to El Encero. Here the Mexican returned the courtesy of a few days before and lavishly entertained Colonel Hughes and officers of the escort with a dinner in their honor. Probably it was here also that the finishing touches were put on his proclamation of farewell, which was dated March 24, but which gave Tehuacán as the place of writing in the document itself. This was a not unskilled summary of his contributions to Mexico, and carried an appeal of real force.

"Mexicans! One of the leaders of the Revolution for Independence; the one most passionately devoted to your good name; he who had the glory of offering trophies torn from foreign enemies to the Republic; he who has struggled with them conquering a thousand difficulties; he who has shed his blood in the maintenance of your rights; in short, your most loyal friend, addresses to you his last farewell."[4]

4. Santa Anna, *Las Guerras de México con Tejas y los Estados Unidos,* p. 197.

A few days later, the refugees went down to the coast to the small port of Antigua, a few miles north of Veracruz. Here they embarked on April 5 for the British Island of Jamaica. Santa Anna's *Memoirs* briefly state that the authorities received him well and that he was pleased with life there. However, the language and customs were strange to all of them and his daughter, then about fifteen or seventeen years of age, and his wife only a few years older, soon became dissatisfied. There were no small children to occupy either of them and these women, who had been reared to lead social functions, were bored and ill at ease among the British matrons and debutantes of the island.

This must have been a period of disillusionment and bitterness for Santa Anna. Word reached him that Leonardo Márquez had "pronounced" in his favor in February, 1849, but at once came the further news that the movement had been easily crushed. Gamboa had already published his philippic denouncing the career of Santa Anna from his birth through 1847, so there was small room for surprise when Congress, on hearing of the Márquez revolt, hastened to entertain a resolution that Santa Anna must never return to Mexico unless express permission had first been secured from that body. In vain had his apologist, Suárez y Navarro, asked if Mexico was so weak and afraid that it would resort to injustice against one man. He insisted that no court had passed sentence of banishment and that Santa Anna only wanted his rights as a Mexican. The immediate response of Congress was to order that the presentation of Suárez y Navarro be returned to him so that it might be worded in "respectful terminology." He changed a few phrases to secure its reception, but Congress adopted the resolution of banishment anyway.

It was bitter food for thought for the exile, no longer young, to realize that the thinking classes of his nation considered his name as a symbol of anarchy, and furthermore that it was synonymous of efforts to foment anarchy for private ends. It was scant comfort to feel that he had honestly tried to protect his native land against the invader and had been misunderstood. To add to his discomfort was the disappointed, childless and sharp-tongued young wife only one-third the age of her husband. Hardly a restful or happy home!

After some months of discussion, it was decided to leave for New Granada and to start life anew there. In March or April, 1850, the family sailed for Cartagena, but found that walled city terribly hot. The town was enjoying unusual prosperity in connection with the shipment of supplies for the building of the Panama Railroad, but mere business held no more attraction for the old exile now than it had had for the merchant's apprentice in 1810. Instead he looked around and found the little town of Turbaco, some fifteen miles away, that was noted for its delightful climate.

Santa Anna was not suffering from any shortage of funds, and soon located a house with the very background and reputation that he desired: the great hero of South American independence, Bolivar, had once lived there. In addition, he acquired an ample estate and threw himself into the career of a gentleman planter with all the energy he had recently displayed in fighting the Yankees. Most of his land was devoted to a large cattle ranch while he raised some tobacco and introduced the cultivation of sugar cane on the lowlands. But his pride was a small mountain which he turned into a coffee finca. The local church and Priest's house were rebuilt and the whole community taught to look up to him as the "patrón" with that respect which must have been a queer mixture of fear and love. He obviously felt that he was through with Mexican affairs for good and all and even went so far as to have a tomb built in his new home where his remains could rest.

An acquaintance of the time pictured him as rather tall than short, but admirably proportioned. His face was not attractive, but of a blackish tint and rather grim and harsh, with the lower lip hanging. The teeth, white and even, were offset by a heavy and vulgar nose. The forehead was wide and spacious, the eyes beautiful, and the hair somewhat curly. When he was sitting down or walking around he was handicapped by the loss of his leg for he never got used to the

[277]

artificial limbs made for him, but when he mounted a horse, he was once more a splendid figure, lending himself with ease and grace to the movements of the animal.

Ordinarily his voice was "heavy, harsh and imperative" as that of a man accustomed to be feared and obeyed; but he knew how to soften it when he wished to use some of those phrases with which he enthralled subordinates and the masses. "I have reached the conclusion," wrote V. Salado Alvarez, "that perhaps all of his prestige lay in the fact that he knew how to use phrases that sounded well to the ears of those people who had been taught to esteem words rather than contents and to devour the brilliant and attractive skin of the fruit, leaving the pulp of strong flavor and ill aspect."[5]

From time to time, various and sundry reports came from Mexico: the army was being reorganized; cholera was sweeping the nation; numerous sections were suffering from Indian outbreaks; the monarchists were gaining strength, or Mexican bonds were selling to London for $25\frac{3}{4}$ per cent to $27\frac{1}{8}$ per cent of face value. But the doings of this whole republic of eight millions of people were dim and distant—merely echoes from a previous existence. More interesting, but still from the academic standpoint only, were reports of progress such as might be seen in the queer innovation of the post office department which now was carrying any letter dumped upon it anonymously if the sender simply attached a stamp to the envelope in lieu of the old cash payment system.

On the other hand, conditions in Mexico were as turbulent and restless as when Santa had been present to fan the flame of discontent. The national income was showing a slight improvement, but this was far from sufficient to care for the needs of the day. From Vera Cruz to far away Guadalajara roads were so unsafe that any traveler, who had to use them for as great a distance as two hundred miles, considered himself fortunate indeed if he neither had the experience of picking himself up from an overturned coach, or of seeing at least one dead man, the victim of bandits, hanging by the roadside.

5. Salado, *De Santa Anna a la Reforma*, I, 178.

The "mild-mannered but honest" government of Herrera closed with the hectic election of 1850. In this, the opportunist, General Marino Arista, was elected as a liberal over his opponents Almonte and Santa Anna, who as usual was proposed by his adherents. Arista commanded little respect at his inauguration in January, 1851, and speedily lost most of that little. Simultaneously, strangely disquieting reports and letters began to reach the old warrior down in Turbaco. Just as he had decided to give up political ambitions, it appeared that important coalitions were being formed in his favor. Far be it from him to discourage them! Accustomed as he was to discount partisanship and estimate political possibilities, the yapping treble chatter of the professional disturber of the peace was readily detected and considered for its real value only by this wary and experienced campaigner. But when the rich diapason tone arose from the landlords, the merchants and peaceful folk in general, and the clergy it meant cash, publicity, and propaganda. This was something else again. The adventurer listened carefully and found that his old attitude toward centralism had acquired astounding popularity.

The clerics were properly fearful of the opportunist liberal Arista, and the army longed for the good old days of dictatorship. These facts were not surprising or anything new to be excited about, but there was also the report that the wealthy landlords and merchants longed for a strong central government that would give them peace and protection. All recognized the old Dictator's ability and even those who detested his despotism were forced to admit that he seemed the only man who could control the situation. They simply hoped that he had learned his lesson. As for the charges of treason during the recent war, they were largely forgotten. The experience had been a nightmare for all Mexico, and now that it was over it was obvious that Santa Anna had risked as much as any of them and had lost far more than most. Having failed, had he not returned to voluntary exile instead of having remained to dabble in local political issues?

By the latter part of 1852, matters were fast becoming critical. While Congress was busy discussing internal problems such as the opening of transportation across the Isthmus of Tehuantepec, a serious revolt was again brewing out in Guadalajara. In this western provincial capital, the local representatives of the central government were unpopular on general principles and especially because of the recent reorganization of the local militia. Among the disgruntled was one José María Blancarte, a hatmaker, who had been ousted from his rank (he had been elected by his own men, hence was obviously popular) of colonel. Somewhat later, he had "beaten up" one policeman and wounded another in petty brawls.

Knowing that he would soon be called to account, Blancarte headed a popular movement and seized the local government. Discontent was so general that the movement grew surprisingly and the local hatmaker found himself talking in big terms which involved the deposition of Arista and the issuing of a call for the return of Santa Anna. By the end of September, General José L. Uraga, who had been sent out to crush the movement, was proclaimed its leader with the duty of calling a special congress to form a federal constitution and select a president. Thus the movement catered to all the discontented elements, federalist or centralists, and became truly formidable.

The President's cabinet resigned, Indians were ravaging the frontiers, adventurers from California were invading Sonora, Guatemala had re-invaded the province of Soconusco, foreign creditors were pressing for their interest and principal payments, and three-fourths of the country was in revolt. The *coup de grace* was given by the revenue producing ports. Tampico joined the rebels in December and reduced its import rates so as to attract trade from Veracruz. This meant ruin for the Veracruz merchants so they met the competition by pronouncing for federalism and Santa Anna and by lowering their own custom rates.

Arista realized that the situation was hopeless and resigned January 5, 1853, while the Chief Justice, Juan Bautista Ceballos, took charge for a month. The new executive hardly knew

[280]

Cartoon appearing in Calendario Caricato *for 1856 (reproduced from* Litografía en Méjico en el Siglo XIX, *by courtesy of* La Biblioteca Nacional de Méjico)

what to do. Political prisoners were freed as a gesture of conciliation, but a concrete program was lacking. Congressional support weakened so Ceballos dissolved that body amidst serious disorders. The members ignored the order and tried to meet later to select a president, but were forced to disperse. Now various and sundry suggestions were made until prominent leaders met at Arroyozarco, near Querétaro, and empowered Uraga to appoint a junta of notables. This, in turn, was to select a dictator to act for not more than a year while a new congress was drawing up a constitution. The Mexico City authorities finally agreed to this, provided the state legislators (or state governors, if no legislatures existed) were to select the dictator, and provided that a citizen *not in the country* might be voted for. Ceballos so disapproved the modifications that he retired from the executive's office on February 7. Forthwith the leaders of the movement chose Manuel María Lombardini to carry on as executive till a dictator could be selected.

The new "Depository of the Supreme Executive Power of the Republic," as Lombardini was called, owed his position largely to his association with various families of prominence. Of a good family himself, he was well educated and kindly inclined to his fellow men, but he was represented as a walking cartoon with nose "thin as a knife," mustache "drooping like flags that the wind does not stir" and all of them pointed to the bulging and insubordinate stomach which protruded so far that it made his head appear as a postscript uncertainly appended to his body. The caricature was further embellished by an amazing army of medals and decorations which covered the great expanse of his front, and a deep reverberating and "brandy-soaked" voice.[6] He well knew that he was in office to "hold the fort" merely, so he took the surest way to temporary strength by encouraging education and religion, granting numerous military promotions and by such hints of what was to come as the gift of lands in Lower California, Sinaloa, and Sonora, to the extent of about 210 square miles to the heirs of Iturbide.

6. Prieto, *op. cit.*, pp. 397-98; Salado, *op. cit.*, I, 156.

But what of Santa Anna? A committee of three hastened to notify him of events and to inquire his pleasure as soon as Veracruz revolted. At first, he cannily received their statements as information, but refused to commit himself. Should he again risk the goddess of chance, who had already proven so fickle? The very nature of the man himself and the socially disappointed young wife clamored "yes." So he allowed himself to be persuaded and indicated his willingness to again "sacrifice himself" and his interests for his nation.

When the ballots were opened on March 17, the Hero of Veracruz had received eighteen out of twenty-three state votes. In the South, staunch old General Alvarez was calling for loyalty in his section, referring to Santa Anna as the "only man who could lead the country from its painful situation," while Lucas Alamán lent the powerful support of the finest of the old conservatives. With integrity above suspicion even in the turmoil, Alamán wrote to Santa Anna on March 23 and offered his support in a plain spoken, manly letter that carried nothing of flattery, but was a splendid summary of conditions as they existed, and of the writer's political ideas. He approved full government support for the Roman Catholic Church; a strong government carefully controlled by definite principles; the abolition of federalism and popular elections, this to be assisted by the formation of new political units so that the old state loyalties would be forgotten; a strong army; and a strong executive (Santa Anna) aided by the advice and support of a small, but able council. Aláman honestly believed such a government to be the best for the country, and had reached the conclusion that Santa Anna had so learned his lesson that the Conservatives could hold him in line.

When word came that the vindicated hero was returning again to head the government, there was a very fever of preparation. Every section of society felt that it had to be represented, while political organizations sent their commissioners, agents, or "ambassadors" to welcome the old hero. Veracruz swarmed with military men, clergymen, politicians, dealers in government supplies, custom brokers, and plain adventurers, as well as those who aspired to each of these classes, pending the arrival of the great dispenser of patronage. Such men as aloof Lucas Aláman, chief of the delegation from the Ecclesiastical Cabildo of Mexico City and probably the most powerful political figure in the nation, might keep national welfare as their watchword, but others like Antonio Haro and Manuel Escandón were only awaiting an opportunity to quarrel like adolescent schoolboys over the control of the tobacco monopoly or the farming of the customs duties.

On April 1, the guns of San Juan de Ulloa announced the arrival of the Hero. All stores were closed while the people crowded to the docks to witness the landing. The Military Governor presented the keys of the city, then the General and his wife marched through the center of a double column of troops, amidst the roaring of cannon, the clanging of bells, the blaring of bands, and the hysterical shouting of the people. After passing under an arch of triumph there came the regular *Te Deum* followed by a military review. The first chance to rest came at 5:00 P.M., but who wanted to rest? Not the feverishly gloating old man nor his panting social-climber of a wife, who, at last, seemed in a fair way to secure that for which she had married years before. After a short interval, there were official congratulations which lasted till time to grace the evening festivities that made even outdoors brilliant with twelve hundred lights on the palace and public buildings.

The next day, Saturday, was spent in hearing reams of carefully prepared oratory and reports from all sections. Finally arrived the delegation from Puebla, headed by the somewhat hesitant and timid little lawyer, Joaquín Ruiz. His first words were harmless, but the ears glutted with fulsome flattery soon detected a new note. Boredom changed to mild interest, incredulity, and forthright indignation. Was the man beside himself? Hear him: "This pomp and exaggerated enthusiasm which surrounds you, Sir, hide the real truth. The nation really does not believe in you who have always sacrificed it to your ambition and caprice." Efforts to silence the little man were in vain. "I have been sent to tell your Ex-

[283]

cellency the truth. Your Excellency does not have any political principles, you are the tool of the disgraced (*relajado*) clergy and the prostituted military men."[7] At last he was silenced and hustled out of the room. It was just an episode, but it indicated that some still remembered the past, and that it would be well for the new administration to be circumspect. Unfortunately, once the fellow was banished, the incident was apparently forgotten as preposterous.

On the night of the third, there was a splendid dinner and ball presented by the élite of the city, and two days later the royal party moved on to El Encero. Here Lombardini had two battalions of troops waiting to act as escort of honor. After a short rest on his old property the triumphal procession continued through the country preceded by flattering notices on all sides. The expected proclamation was properly vague, general and patriotic; most of those who sought favors received promises—all they could expect as yet; and the general approval was capped by the news that Santa Anna had modestly declined the title of "Captain General," which had been especially created for him, and that he had granted amnesty for past political offenses.

On April 16, the escort reached the outskirts of the Capital at Santa Anna's favorite shrine of Guadalupe. Again there was a great ovation, which the recipient acknowledged with regal gestures. That he might not fail to savor the last atom of the applause, he ordered his aides not to attempt to keep back the crowds, who promptly seized the equipage, unhitched the mules, and dragged His Excellency's carriage to the Colegiata. Here was sung the usual *Te Deum*, Santa Anna prayed devoutly at the sacred shrine, and then was accompanied by the Archbishop and the clergy of both the Cathedral and the local church to the residence prepared for him.

After three days of final preparations, he was ready to advance to the Capital for the inauguration on the twentieth. Shrewd observers detected a coolness and a "feeling of dis-

7. Guillermo Prieto, *Memorias . . . . 1840-1853*, pp. 401-2.

trust for the future" among the "best informed men here,"[8] but this was generally covered up by noise and brilliance as civil authorities, the military and the clergy vied with each other to do honor to, and "make time" with, the key man of the country. In a regal ceremony which included the conferring on Santa Anna of the Grand Cross of Charles III (which had been granted by Doña María Cristina six years before, but had never been delivered due to the vicissitudes of fortune), the new executive took the oath: "I, Antonio López de Santa Anna, swear before God to defend the independence and integrity of the Mexican territory, and to promote the well-being and prosperity of the nation, in accordance with the bases adopted by the Plan of Jalisco and the convention agreed to by the combined forces the sixth of last February in this Capital." Then the new executive retired to the chief saloon of the Palace, where the Provisional President surrendered to him the great chair of the presiding officer, and, in a loud voice, proclaimed: "Today, the twentieth of April of the year eighteen hundred and fifty-three, His Excellency Señor Captain General don Antonio López de Santa Anna takes possession of the Presidency."

8. *Mexico, Despatches,* United States Minister Alfred Conkling to Secretary of State W. L. Marcy, XVII (April 22, 1853), No. 33.

MOST SERENE HIGHNESS

PROBABLY at no other time in his whole career was it more important for Santa Anna to decide calmly whether he would be guided by principles or by personalities; by a program or by opportunism. The way seemed reasonably clear for the adoption of a definite program based on principles. The three great elements of the conservative faction were all ready to be welded into a compact unit behind an announced plan that would provide for essential one-man rule. The landlords and the clergy longed for this, and only asked that they be told what to expect and that they be given an opportunity to provide advisers at court as liaison officers. These moneyed classes also would have been glad to provide the cash with which to satisfy the army and to employ it in suppressing Indian outbreaks and banditry.

Of course, such a program would have antagonized the diehard liberals, but many of them were of the professional and merchant classes and would have been willing to stretch their political principles in order to acquire security. European courts would have been delighted at such an administration, and Washington, D. C., would have hesitated long before expressing more than mild disapproval now that the rising clamor of the slavery issue claimed national energies, and since the recent intervention in Mexico was chiefly remembered by many because of its aftermath of scandals and court martials, new boundry disputes, and an enormous national debt.

The first weeks after the arrival at Veracruz, Santa Anna quite properly listened to varying reports. No clear cut plans were announced though all felt that indications pointed to his following the logical course. When the name of the new cabinet ministers were announced, the great old conservative,

Lucas Alamán, was the Minister of Foreign Affairs; and his associate, Manuel Diez de Bonilla, was the Minister of Gobernación, or Interior. On the other hand, a disturbing appointment was that of the liberal, Theodosio Lares, to the important post of Minister of Justice and Public Instruction. The clergy were nonplused and soon realized further that they could draw small comfort from the balance of the cabinet roster. That tall, pale impeccably dressed literary man, J. M. Tornel, nicknamed Lorenzo the Magnificent, was Minister of War. Though he was the "quintessence of courtesy," he was generally classed as a mild liberal but primarily as a Santanista. The wealthy concession hunter, A. Haro y Tamariz, was Minister of the Treasury—another disconcerting selection, for he also was a Santanista and a mild liberal. The Minister of Public Works (*Fomento*) was the non-party scientist, Joaquín Valáquez de León.

After the first surprise, however, it was felt that the appointments were not so bad for it was fairly certain that Alamán would dominate the situation, and, so long as that was the case, the Church was safe and reasonable consistency could be expected. Haro y Tamariz also proved an agreeable surprise in that he promptly launched a reform program, which insisted on substantial economies and the elimination of graft.

At this point, misfortune overtook the administration when Providence struck down Alamán, who died June 1, 1853. United States Minister Conkling reported: "He was by far the ablest and best informed man in the present cabinet, if not in the Republic; though not popular I think he was universally believed to be honest and patriotic."[1] Diez de Bonilla at once took the vacant position, and Ignacio Aguilar became Minister of Interior; this left the cabinet sadly weakened. A general relaxation was felt and in a short time ugly rumors began to circulate to the effect that the old gang of 1841-44 was surrounding the Dictator. The cabinet members found that when the old cronies got together others were kept waiting for appointments and treated with scant courtesy.

1. *Mexico, Despatches,* XVII, No. 43, Conkling to Marcy, June 2, 1853.

They feared to protest and dared not resign because of the retribution they knew would follow. Only Haro was an exception. He publicly resigned and then hastened into hiding to publish a biting denunciation of the financial abuses being allowed. To weaken the administration further, the able and prominent Tornel died of apoplexy on September 11. Now all restraints were gone. The new appointees were spoilsmen and henchmen of the Dictator.

These changes seriously weakened Santa Anna with his ablest supporters, and only one of them brought even a measure of support from any one group. Haro's resignation had been precipitated when he proposed a forced loan guaranteed by clerical property, so now the clergy were a little better satisfied but it was increasingly clear that the administration was to be the old personal dictatorship whose guiding principle would be opportunism and the whims of a corrupt clique at court.

The personal element rapidly surged to the front as the primary motive behind most acts. When so prominent a man as Mariano Riva Palacio was suspected, he was forthwith arrested and plans made for his banishment. No less a person than the staunch old liberal Indian of the South, Juan Alvarez, sent a protest. But in spite of Alvarez's prestige and power, which was commonly said to be so great that no leaf of a tree moved in all the southern area without his permission, still the Dictator declined the request that Riva Palacio be freed. Was not Alvarez simply an ignorant old Indian, seventy years of age, who could be ignored when he ceased to be of use? Needless to say, the old Indian soon became openly antagonistic to the administration which he had first endorsed.[2]

2. Santa Anna's bitterness toward Alvarez is seen in his *Memoirs* where he referred to Alvarez as the "Panther of the South," and repeated the story that he had Negro blood in his veins. He then said that Alvarez was bitterly opposed to the appointment of Alamán to the cabinet, and left it to be inferred that this was the cause of the Indian's disaffection. This would seem to need more proof, however, in view of the fact that Alvarez appeared to be definitely loyal until well after the death of Alamán.

Even before this José López de Santa Anna,[3] a son of the President, was ordered to capture Juárez, the liberal Indian Governor of Oaxaca, and take him to Veracruz. After an imprisonment of a few days in the fortress of Ulloa, the captive was placed on board an English vessel sailing for Havana in June, 1853. From there, the hated Zapotec made his way to New Orleans to foregather with other refugees and to plot revolution. The exiles were in such poverty that Melchor Ocampo was working as a potter, José María Maza was a waiter in a restaurant, while the future President and sturdy bulwark of his nation, Benito Juárez, was securing such a meager pittance by his trade of cigar making that, at times, he was actually short of food.

Honest criticism was now of importance only for the purpose of identifying an enemy. Opposition journals were summarily banished though at times one would be called to the dictatorial presence and ponderously informed that the great man "had many pairs of breeches (*calzones*)" and so could stand an ample rawhiding. When one young journalist, Guillermo Prieto, dared to agree with the lecturer and ruefully remarked that he suspected Santa Anna had more than he (the journalist) did, the Dictator lost his temper and declared he would teach the insolent upstart a lesson. He raised his cane and advanced to administer a thrashing when the young man threw open a side door and took to his heels.[4] Thus, in one way or another, there passed temporarily from the scene such men as Guillermo Prieto, Ponciano Arriaga, Miguel Buenrosro and Melchor Ocampo.

Not all of Santa Anna's political acumen had been lost, however; men of political significance were frequently given positions of importance. For instance, Ignacio Comonfort was made customs' collector of Acapulco, June 10, 1853, at an annual salary of six thousand *pesos*. Likewise, Lombardini

3. This would seem to be son of one Doña Rafæla Morenṣa. He is mentioned in Santa Anna's last will and testament as one of two natural sons, the other being named Angel José later fled to Cuba on his father's overthrow, and married there.

4. Guillermo Prieto, *Memorias, 1840-1853*, pp. 409-10.

had made the initiator of the rebellion, Blancarte, a general. Now Santa Anna appointed him Commanding General of the wealthy state of Guanajuato. Blancarte asked to be excused, saying that he was not a military man by profession, but Santa Anna insisted that he enjoy the lucrative office at least for a time.

The prominence of personalities in this, the last administration of Santa Anna, is further seen in accounts current about him. As late as 1934, men then in their eighties and early nineties still insisted that Santa Anna was a loyal friend. His imperious aspect was said to cover a "soft and sweet" (*suave y dulce*) disposition which was freely displayed to his friends. On the other hand, there is still current in Jalapa the story that on passing through the streets of the city the Dictator's litter was delayed by some peons loitering and playing in the thoroughfare. The litter was abruptly ordered to stop while its occupant made note of the names of the men. Afterwards instructions came back, ordering the arrest of those who had delayed the imperial passage so that they could be sent as slaves to the dreaded plantations of Yucatán.[5]

The celebration of the saint's day of the Dictator became an occasion to startle even the easy going society of Mexico City. Business houses were closed while all indulged in the fiesta. Friends, the ever fearful concession hunters, and hangers-on vied with each other in presenting all kinds of gifts that would be distinctive or amusing. In 1853, these amounted to tens of thousands of *pesos* in value, and included a calash and four with full equipage, a magnificent ring and scores of other presents. With the full possibilities of the occasion thus advertised, all forthwith began to rack their brains to make the celebration of 1854 a real one, Again the presents ran the gamut from the sublime to the ridiculous— but all costly—while newspaper editors and favorites published editorials or delivered orations in which they flourished

---

5. This may be another version of the same incident referred to in the gossipy account of Salado (*De Santa Anna a la Reforma*, I, 283) when he says that on December 10, 1853, an order was issued that nine residents of Jico should be sent to military service for eight years because they had the audacity to desecrate the General's person when he attempted to flee in 1845.

the adjectives and phrases they had been hoarding and privately savoring for twelve months. *El Universal* declared:

"General Santa Anna is not only the father of our people, he is our savior .... In him the great military glories are personified, the national flag remained pure and stainless in his hands .... he came to kill the monster of anarchy and to shed the magic power of his conciliating words amidst our dissensions; he saved us from ignominious ruin and gave us the peace we longed for; he re-established our credit before the world and placed us on the path where are to be found our happiness, our future and our glory. Therefore, the country has confided to him its powers, has delegated to him its sovereignty and has entrusted to him its honor and its independence." Etc., etc.[6]

On November 12, 1853, there was published the decree re-establishing the Order of Guadalupe, originally instituted by Iturbide. This had been one of the "trappings of monarchy" with which the first emperor had surrounded himself, so the implication was obvious. Santa Anna became the Grand Master, while the descending ranks of the Order provided places for all and sundry, whether taken from the ranks of the clergy, the military or mere civilians. The uniforms, hats, sashes, and jewels authorized for the separate ranks were fearfully and wonderfully made: the Dictator himself spending long and anxious hours discussing the advisability of using red, green or yellow, silk, wool or fustian, for the lining of this, that or the other sash, cape or coat. Among the men, the heart burnings and bitterness were extreme as the rivalry for the more coveted ranks became keener, while the remarks of the spouses of the less fortunate recipients of the order must have been choice morsels of effective Castilian speech.

For days and weeks, all were a-twitter with expectancy as the lists were being prepared. At last, in the early days of November, the letters of nomination were sent out by Minister Bonilla. Sr. Juan B. Ceballos, former president of the Republic and Chief Justice of the Supreme Court, answered on November 4th with the astounding statement that he declined the

---

6. Zamacois, *Historia de Méjico,* Tomo XIII, pp.780-81.

honor because of his "profound conviction" that there was no place for such an institution in a republic. One Marcelino Castañeda also declined the honor because he stated that the expenses were so great that his small fortune could not defray them. On the twenty-sixth, Bonilla responded to Ceballos in a letter in which he congratulated the newly founded Order in not being handicapped at the begining by a man who would seriously injure its standing by his political principles, "if, indeed, you have any." Four days later, the Dictator acted and abruptly notified Ceballos that he was undesirable as a member of the Supreme Court and was to consider himself dismissed since the national welfare demanded unity of sentiment among its leaders. Because of the extremely unhealthy climate, Ceballos wisely went into exile for a time. This whole affair was simply a public illustration of a fundamental principle of the government as expressed in writing an order sent to the Commanding General of Veracruz the preceding August: "A public official must close his ears and work without thinking for himself."

Meanwhile the year for which the dictatorship had been authorized was rapidly drawing to a close and something had to be done about it. Those in charge of affairs well knew that the doggerel written by a man, observing the mass of Santanistas waiting for the arrival of their chief from exile, still held true:

> This mass of Santanistas whom you see
> Who with so great eagerness await Santa Anna,
> If a king would satiate their ambition tomorrow
> Would forthwith become monarchists.

> Do you know what they were yesterday? Federalists.
> And will become something else if profit beckons;
> Those who today worship Don Antonio
> Tomorrow will adore Don Demonio [the devil].[7]

---

7. Rivera, *Historia de Jalapa*, Tomo IV, p. 388 note.

Este monton que veis de santa-annistas
Que con tanta ansia esperan á Santa-Anna,

For a time it did well enough to throttle the press and banish recalcitrant editors, meanwhile exiling dangerous opponents who could not be attached to the dictatorship by such rewards as sent Uraga to Berlin and Almonte to Washington as ministers. Towns having less than ten thousand inhabitants had their local governments suppressed entirely, while larger places were dominated by the military appointments of the Dictator. But this was repression and terrorization. How build up actual and permanent support? The first step was to strengthen the army till, in July, 1853, it included seventy thousand men with an addition of more than twenty thousand more soon thereafter. Special units of "crack" troops were formed whose treatment in food, pay and uniforms guaranteed effective and steady support.

However, this still emphasized force, and some voluntary agents were advisable, if not essential. Naturally the finest possible agents were the clergy and the way to secure their aid was in line with the Dictator's inclination as well as his policy. The Jesuits were readmitted to the country in September, 1853, with a splendid ceremony, while the Archbishop and bishops had been declared honorary councillors of the nation. In addition, every effort was made, and with apparent success, to maintain cordial relations with the Holy See. The results were truly gratifying though it must always be remembered that Santa Anna retained in his own hands the final power over things political. By his decree of September 5, 1853, the ecclesiastical *fuero* was specifically refused recognition in all cases of treason. This was insisted upon in the case of the execution of at least one curate, Manuel Gómez. Not only did the higher clergy fail to protest this invasion of what they might have considered to be their rights, but they were themselves anxious to have the Dictator assist the Papal

---

Si un rey les sacia la ambicion mañana
Han de volverse todos monarquistas.

¿Sabeis que eran ayer? ¡Federalistas!
Y mas serán si al oro le dan gana;
Y los que adoran hoy á D. Antonio
Adorarán mañana á D. Demonio.

Nuncio and the Archbishop at the investiture of their highest officials.

Thus the machine was oiled and primed. Surely before long someone would take the hint and initiate a movement to prolong the dictatorship, which had been scheduled to run for one short year from the date of accession of Lombardini. One observer wrote concerning official business: "Patience will be necessary: for at this time The President and the cabinet: think and dream only of the Dictatorship, with the Empire: which is to follow."[8] Finally the eagerly awaited suggestion was made in Guadalajara in November, and was promptly seconded in Guanajuato, Aguascalientes, Mexico, San Luis Potosí, Puebla, Michoacán, Querétaro and Zacatecas. Such a logical and sensible proposal was duly considered, approved and made official in a decree of December 16, which set forth that the exigencies of the situation were such that the executive would continue to exercise discretional powers as he saw fit. In addition, he was even given the right to name his successor in office; the name of said individual to be deposited in a sealed envelope in the Ministry of Relations, there to be available in case of need.

Various and sundry titles for the ruler had been suggested by this time, but it was finally agreed that Most Serene Highness would be best. This the Dictator accepted as the appropriate title for the head of the nation and not for himself alone. At the same time, he greatly added to his popularity by again declining the title of Captain General and the salary of sixty thousand *pesos* that was offered him.

But there still remained the ever pressing problem of raising cash. The army had to kept satisfied, and the exorbitant expenses of the court as well as a thousand and one other details were clamoring for funds and more funds. Once more Santa Anna's thoughts turned to the overflowing coffers and the acquisitive instincts of Brother Jonathan. He well knew that to alienate Mexican soil carried grave danger, but the lure was too great. As early as May 2, 1853, word went to Wash-

8. *Mexico, Dispatches,* XVIII, No. 15, Gadsden to Marcy, December 4, 1853.

ington[9] that Alamán and Santa Anna would both favor making a treaty for the opening of the Tehuantepec Isthmus for trade. When nothing came of this proposal in which both were interested, attention again turned to the northern border.

The United States was anxious to shift responsibility for restraining Indian forays all along the boundary, as had been required by the treaty terminating the war. Also a survey had shown that the simplest way to iron out existing boundary troubles would be for Mexico to cede to the United States that block of territory which the northern republic was so anxious to secure for the purpose of building a transcontinental railroad from New Orleans and San Antonio to the west coast. On June 20, Conkling was informed that the lowest figure Mexico would consider for such a cession was $20,000,-000—incidentally this was a larger figure that the whole annual revenue of Mexico. The territory involved had little or no actual value to Mexico, so it was largely a matter of negotiation and dickering.

To all suggestions for a cession of the Río Grande Valley, Santa Anna returned a flat negative for his people would not stand for more than a boundary "adjustment," and there was no possible dispute over the lower Río Grande which could even theoretically be invoked. The negotiations proceeded slowly for Santa Anna was clearly critical of the United States, and the new United States Minister, Gadsden, was strongly pro-liberal and outspoken in his disapproval of the Dictator. On October 18, the Minister wrote to Marcy under the special caption of "Private":

"This is a Government of *plunder* and *necessity*—We can rely on no other influence, but on an appeal to both—We can afford to be liberal in our offerings to the first—but the acceptance all depends on our not losing sight of the last—As sensitive as the *Supreme Government* is to Castilian honor when they affect to believe that it is threatened: they are more or equally yielding to a demand which is backed by the power to execute." He then advised that troops be sent to occupy "every pass and crossing place" along the Río Grande,

9. *Mexico, Dispatches*, XVII, No. 34, Conkling to Marcy, May 2, 1853.

with an ample naval force placed conveniently on the Mexican coasts. Again he wrote: "The President though absolute has no head to pursue or maintain a policy—He is as uncertain as the winds and currents which distract him—To maintain his power is his sole end and aim."[10]

Gadsden's objective, however, was to get the territory and Santa Anna's to get money, so personal antipathies were suppressed and the negotiations advanced to the point where a treaty was signed by which the United States was to pay $15,000,000. This was amended later and the document as ratified provided for $10,000,000 as the sum involved.[11]

His Most Serene Highness recounted the incident in his *Memoirs*:

"The boundary question with the United States was serious and demanded preferential treatment. The Government in Washington, with knife in hand, was planning to cut still another piece from the body it had just mutilated so horribly, and was threatening another invasion. In the deplorable condition of the country a break with the colossus seemed like a catastrophe to me, so I adopted the measure which patriotism and prudence dictated: a peaceful settlement."

When the treaty was ratified there was cash in hand at last, the army was built up and the dictatorship continued indefinitely. The lid was off! The sky was the limit! Reprisals and banishments continued in increasing numbers and, at times, on mere suspicion. Anyone who spread alarming rumors, or spoke disrespectfully of the authorities, was subject to arrest under a decree of July 29, 1854, and anyone who failed to report those known to be guilty was subject to a two hundred *pesos* fine or two months in prison. A year after this, the United States Minister reported: "Luciano Mateo

10. *Mexico, Despatches*, XVIII, Gadsden to Marcy, October 18, 1853, and October 31, 1853.
11. The distribution or use of this money would be an interesting study. The Mexican agent in Washington retained a generous fee of some 70,000 *pesos* for his labors in handling part of it. In his last will and testament Santa Anna refers to $232,000 as having been paid to him for back salaries and damage to his property during the war with the United States. His opponents, however, claimed that the sum paid him reached the fantastic figure of 700,000 *pesos*.

the African resident at Minatetland [*sic*]: though relieved
from the military incarceration to which subjected is still held
to bail for trial on charges for having spoken disrespectfully
of His Serene Highness, in violation of a Decree that to mention irreverantly [*sic*] the name of that functionary; or to de-
mur to his acts, is Treason."[12]

When Sra. Santa Anna arrived at the Capital on July 26,
1853, there was an elaborate reception costing twenty-five
thousand *pesos,* with salvos of artillery of twenty-one guns
each. But this was when the hangers-on were novices at the
entertainment game. As the months passed, it was well understood that no one was to be allowed to wound the vanity
of the Dictator by overshadowing him in any way or on any
occasion whatsoever. Brilliant receptions to the Spanish poet
José Zorilla were quickly stopped when His Most Serene
Highness "considered it a matter for shame" that so much
attention should be paid a foreigner.

Probably the outstanding private entertainer of the day
was the Count of Cortina, who lavished presents of fantastic
value upon the Dictator on his saint's day. At one of the
Count's balls, one thousand five hundred guests paid Santa
Anna and his wife regal honors in a palace whose halls and
staircases were lined with mirrors, reflecting torrents of lights
from massed chandeliers. The building was stifling with the
aroma of thousands of flowers, which were only less brilliant
in their fanciful colors than the elaborate dress of both women
and men. The Apostolic Delegate, the diplomatic corps, the
wealth, youth, beauty and much of the talent of the nation
were there to do honor to the occasion and to partake of the
magnificent supper prepared.

More and more, the cloying fumes from the heady wine
of power befuddled the wits of the Dictator. Increasingly his
personal whims and appetite got the better of his judgment.
It was well known that he had never restrained his appetites so
now the man of sixty felt that he must prove that he was
still in possession of all his physical powers by leading his
court as it plunged from one excess to another.

12. *Mexico Despatches,* XIX, No. 66, Gadsden to Marcy, July 3, 1855.

At the great festival of St. Augustín, the Dictator casually placed his bet of five hundred ounces (presumably of silver) and watched it disappear, and then with studied nonchalance carefully flicked the ashes from his cigar so that they would not scatter on his clothes. More successful at the cockpits, he scrupulously collected his winnings and then gallantly scattered them to the singers, dancers and entertainers of the occasion.

His own palace at Tacubaya was dazzling with tapestries, rugs, mirrors, and all kinds of costly furnishings. Magnificent and dignified functions were held without number, but there were also other occasions which ended in disgraceful orgies where human appetites held undisputed sway. The Dictator was still most abstemious with regard to liquor, but he gloried in his succession of mistresses. In fact, he considered himself quite a connoisseur along those lines due to his long and extensive practice and to his present position which enabled him to choose from the most attractive. Seldom did the selected ones consider themselves poorly paid, though it is true one mercenary little Louisa rejected—for a time—the advances of that "indecent old peg-leg." Lacking a modern press agent, the poor girl had to arrange her own publicity, but proved something of an adept at the game. According to the reports, her chance came after a few nights at the palace so she collected the Dictator's set of magnificent decorations which included specimens from Venezuela, New Granada, Brazil, Ecuador and Spain, as well as numerous Mexican decorations, topped by that of the Grand Master of the Order of Guadalupe. With these she joyously paraded the city and only allowed them to be redeemed on payment of the round sum of a good thousand *pesos*.

Thus affairs. Conditions were undoubtedly corrupt in the extreme—and were, of course, suspected of being worse. Notoriety and fame were hard to distinguish and the real efforts that were made to improve conditions (and such efforts were fewer in number than in the early 1840's) were completely overshadowed by the spectacular and the infamous. What magnificent energies going to waste!

[298]

ALL IS VANITY

IN spite of his interest in playing the emperor in the hectic society of the day, Santa Anna was well aware that the position of foreigners in Mexico was of great importance to his career. During 1854 only about 1200 immigrants in excess of emigrants reached the country, but still there were upwards of twenty-five thousand residents of Mexico who owed allegiance to foreign powers. Of these, over half were from Spain, nearly one-fourth from France, and about five or six per cent each from Great Britain, Germany and the United States.

Naturally, however, the most important foreign relations of 1853 were still those with the uncomfortable northern neighbor. For one thing, William Walker was engaged in his escapades in Central America and after Mexico's experiences with United States adventurers in Texas and California, it was inevitable that Walker's activities in the South should be greatly feared. With his collapse and execution, however, the Mexican Government seized some small credit for itself on the ground that his decline had been effected in part by its own policy of rigid regulation of shipments of arms and supplies to the area involved. Soon after this came the Mesilla sale to the United States, so, on the whole, all seemed to be going well.

Quickly, though, another complication developed in the far northwest. Large numbers of Frenchmen had gone to California with the gold rush of 1849. Soon many became discouraged and began looking for new homes. One Charles de Pindray led a band of them as adventurers to Sonora in 1851. He was shot in some mysterious fashion, but the idea of filibustering and gold hunting in northwest Mexico developed, and the affable and accomplished scamp, G. R. Raousset-

Boulbon became deeply interested in it. The official French attitude was one of general interest in "foreign markets, commerce, and interests" but probably involved no specific plans for expansion in this far away and little known province.[1]

Meanwhile, there had been some talk of a coalition of the states of Chihuahua, Durango, Jalisco, Coahuila, Zacatecas, San Luis Potosí and Tamaulipas for mutual protection against the Indians. In addition to the clear implication that the home government was neglecting the area, there was the common understanding that the United States was encouraging the idea. As a result, the Mexican authorities were glad to foster non-United States immigration, such as that of the French, to the district. Raousset capitalized this feeling and entered into a contract to protect the frontier mines which were controlled by the French banking house of Jecker, Torre & Company with Frenchmen drawn from California. His expedition landed at Guaymas, Sonora, with some two hundred and fifty men. Santa Anna's satellite, J. M. Giménez, was sent to represent the mining company whose properties were to be protected. The local officials speedily lost interest in the affair, probably due in part to fear of the French adventurers but also to the pressure brought to bear by the powerful Barron, Forbes & Company, "financial lords of Mexico's west coast" who resented this invasion of their mining monopolies. For a time the newcomers were somewhat at a loss as to how to proceed, then captured Hermosillo, a city of twelve thousand people, but hardly knew what to do with it, and finally gave up the place and dropped the whole affair.

The next step was for Raousset to go to Mexico City to see Santa Anna. He arrived in July, 1853, and offered to colonize six thousand men north of 31° north latitude. Most of these were to be unmarried and were to come from California and France. As opposition developed to his scheme, he reduced the number of the proposed expedition to five hundred military men who were to fight the Apaches and develop mineral resources. His proposal was substantially revised by Santa

1. An excellent study of this subject is: Wyllys, R. K., *The French in Sonora,* which has been used for much of the sketch given here.

Santa Anna at about sixty

Chapel at El Encero (August, 1934)

Old breastworks (August, 1934)

Anna and his council, both of whom feared the Americanized Europeans and insisted on retaining an equal share with Raousset in all minerals found, though in return they expressed a willingness to help finance the expedition. These proposals Raousset rejected. The two adventurers, the Mexican and the Frenchman, like two wary old tom cats, had cautiously circled each other, but were so suspicious they had refused to come to terms.

Raousset now returned to California to act on his own account. His relations with William Walker and John C. Fremont are uncertain, but his chief desire was obvious enough. It was to get a thousand men to north Mexico under his own control. After a typical Arabian Nights' expedition that included the capsizing of his vessel and two weeks spent in salvaging supplies and turning the ship right side up, the Frenchman reached his destination and organized several hundred men, only to have his plans again foiled when the authorities definitely turned against him. In a last battle in July, 1854, the French lost 48 killed, 78 wounded and 313 taken prisoners. Among the prisoners was Raousset, who was executed, though his men were treated with considerable leniency.

The victorious commander, Colonel José María Yañez was hailed as a national hero. This seemed to wound the vanity and ruffle the serenity of his Most Serene Highness so the *Diario Oficial* promptly gave the hint to other periodicals by severely criticizing Yañez for inefficiency. Soon the too popular commander was removed from his post as Governor and Commanding General of Sonora and ordered to appear before a court martial to explain his conduct. The immediate prevalence of rumors of a revolt which would involve the northwestern states showed the wavering of sentiment as the army began to lose faith in the man who no longer took the field himself, and who failed to award credit where it was due.

Though danger of an immediate advance by the United States was apparently eliminated, Santa Anna was gaining comparatively little credit personally and his position was clearly weakening. Gadsden wrote October 19, 1854, saying that Santa Anna was dealing with a Venezuelan adventurer, and continued "Possibly S[anta] A[nna] realizes he cannot carry out his plan in M[exico], partly due to U[nited] S[tates] opposition so he is thinking of transferring his attentions and intentions to Ven[ezuela]." Four months later, Gadsden realized the Dictator was thinking little of Venezuela but reported that he seemed to be setting himself up as the exponent of absolutism in the New World in an effort to offset Monroe's republicanism as sponsored by the United States.[2] As a matter of fact Santa Anna periodically denounced the "American Gothic Aggression" but this was chiefly for home consumption for he was in desperate need of money and had no intention of allowing announced principles to stand in the way of a chance to secure a little more of the Yankee's cash. In July, 1855, he again approached Gadsden to discuss possible terms of another land sale to the northern republic. The result was a series of conferences extending over several weeks, but the Dictator's political ship was sinking and the negotiations languished.

On the whole, European diplomatic representatives were generally felt to endorse Santa Anna and to desire his permanence in power. Each of them was to be conciliated and courted; his anger must be placated if aroused, and harmony must be maintained if at all possible. The British Minister, Doyle, was frequently the spokesman of the group and was outspoken in giving advice to the Dictator, to the end that further United States expansion must be opposed in every way possible. The power of these ministers was shown just after Santa Anna assumed control. The Spanish Minister served notice that certain damages, which Mexico had agreed to pay to the Mother country, had not been forthcoming, and that he would leave Mexico if an arrangement was not made. The threat was sufficient and the damages paid.

Just at the return of Santa Anna a most interesting intrigue started with the European powers, but one little dreamed of by Mexicans even of the court circles. Lucas

2. *Mexico, Despatches,* Gadsden to Marcy, marked "private," October 19, 1854, XVIII; also *ibid.,* Gadsden to Marcy, February 19, 1855, XIX.

Alamán, the head of the Council, was a monarchist at heart and strongly favored a Spanish prince for the Mexican throne, so it is probable that the suggestion was his. Be that as it may, within a month after reaching Mexico City, Santa Anna had opened negotiations through the Prussian Minister for a corps of several thousand German troops. This was not endorsed at Berlin, so a still more significant step was taken. The idea was to secure a tripartite intervention of Great Britain, France and Spain in Mexico in order to place a Spanish prince in power. Also, immediate aid was solicited against the activities of William Walker in Lower California which was felt to be a United States invasion.

The British foreign office showed little or no interest so Santa Anna's agent, J. M. Gutiérrez Estrada, pressed his scheme at the Spanish Court where Queen Isabella was an eager listener. The United States Minister pointed out that Spanish officers and men were being added steadily to the Mexican army, where they would be of great value if the plans materialized.[3] Just as all seemed to promise success, however, revolution broke out in Spain and a ministry assumed power that refused to consider the project. Probably this was just another "sea anchor" to steady the faltering craft of the new administration and Santa Anna was relieved to know that Alamán's scheme was not likely to succeed when there was still a chance of his retaining power himself. However, as late as July 1, 1854, he commissioned Gutiérrez Estrada to carry forward the discussion of plans at the courts of London, Paris, Madrid or Vienna. In Mexico, there was complete silence on the subject. In fact, the cabinet as a whole and even Tornel remained in entire ignorance of the negotiations which were to come to fruition long after they could be of any help to Santa Anna. One last effort to secure foreign support was an attempt to raise a force of three thousand Swiss mercenaries for service in Mexico. This too came to naught so Santa Anna was left to the vengeance and ambitions of his disgruntled countrymen.

In the realm of home affairs, likewise, there was a cred-

3. Perkins, *The Monroe Doctrine*, p. 326.

itable beginning which had an equally ineffective culmination. Substantial reforms in the judicial system were projected and a commercial code that has been called the first intelligent reform of the kind after Independence from Spain was promulgated in 1854. Along literary lines, the opera and the theatre were encouraged while a substantial prize was offered for the best composition for a national anthem. The winner was announced on the anniversary of the battle of Tampico, September 11, 1854, when the composition was officially proclaimed as adopted.

Along more practical lines were the efforts to remove the aqueducts from the streets of the Capital; the grant to a Mr. Richards to construct a railroad from Veracruz to Mexico City, and the law to encourage colonization. The tragedy of the situation, however, lay in the fact that these were simply good intentions with which Santa Anna's road to ruin was paved. There was little or no chance, and in truth not too much effort, to carry them into execution.

Whether for good or ill, the army was substantially improved and public works connected therewith received marked attention. Certainly highway robbery and public disorders showed a decline over previous years, and one would be inclined to praise the efforts made had not the accompanying corruption and abuses been so great as to lead directly to the horrors of the Three Years War which followed the fall of the dictatorship.

The one permanent and constructive reform in governmental organization was the introduction into the Cabinet of the Ministry of *Fomento* (Public Works). This department had control of roads, bridges, and all kinds of internal improvements. It encouraged railroad building and the construction of telegraph lines, and fostered agriculture, mining and commerce. So popular did it become that even the liberals, who overthrew the dictatorship and despised all it had accomplished, nevertheless retained the office as a definite part of the governmental machine.

The Dictator was popular with the masses but even there an element of discontent was noticeable after the middle of 1853.

[304]

In spite of the hero worship accorded him and the glamor surrounding the military establishment, there was an ever present fear of the *sorteo* (the drawing of lots for military conscripts) in all sections. The poor folks would shout their *vivas* for the hero and gloried in bands and parades but had such a haunting fear of the press gang that dragged men off to the cantonments that they fled by scores and hundreds as soon as word went out that the local community was to furnish a new quota for the service.

To add to the unrest was the suppression of anti-administration newspapers. Even the powerful *Monitor Republicano* fell a victim, to say nothing of the minor ones that were swept out of existence when they dared to speak critically of those in power. To the thinking classes and the potential liberal leaders, this was a serious matter. To help nip opposition in the bud the Minister of War developed an extensive spy system. This brought about anonymous arrests, violent imprisonments, and "drum head" court martials, and so controlled civil trials that they were looked upon as little better than judicial assassinations by the liberals. As might have been expected, the spies felt that they had to justify their existence and so there was the ever present temptation to prove their efficiency by numerous arrests. The results were to be seen in the working off of old grudges and in trumped-up charges based on mere suspicion. As the public began to murmur there was an attempt to justify the espionage on the grounds that it was directed against traitors and annexationists, who were in league with the dread northern colossus.

Then there was the undoubted fact of increased restlessness. Even the liberals had respected Alamán and most of them had a real regard for Tornel, but after the deaths of these leaders such men as Juan Alvarez, Ignacio Comonfort, Valentin Gómez Farías, Benito Juárez and many others seriously began to consider the most effective ways of protecting their rights from the ever encroaching dictatorship. Here were the real leaders of the masses and, for the most part, men of sincere principles. Many of them would have foregone their extreme ideas of democracy if they could have been reassured as to executive consistency and steady national development. True enough, many of Santa Anna's desired reforms were in line with their wishes, but when the proposals had filtered through a machine composed of opportunists so much time had elapsed and the reforms had been so emasculated as to be almost unrecognizable as steps on behalf of national welfare. Likewise the position of self-respecting and constructive liberals was so misinterpreted to Santa Anna by the spies, toadies and place hunters that all too often the sincere reformers were looked upon by the Dictator as actual or incipient traitors.

In February, 1854 all plans were made for his Most Serene Highness to go down to his favorite resort, Jalapa. The place was refurbished and new furniture purchased. On the twentieth, the telegraph announced that he was leaving that day, but, before he could get out of the Capital, word came that Alvarez was in rebellion in the south. Much as Santa Anna affected to despise the old Indian he really feared him so much that this Jalapa trip was postponed for a time. A month later, the gorgeous new furniture was sold and it became well known that the revolt was spreading fast.

The formal *pronunciamiento* of Ayutla was issued on March 1 by one Florencio Villareal, who had been willing to act as the tool of Alvarez and Comonfort because he was disgruntled with Santa Anna over military appointments. This in itself was significant for it showed that the men actually fighting for a principle could now use the opportunist and place seeker against the Despot who had gone into power with the almost unanimous support of the adventurer class. The tragedy of the situation for the Dictator lay in the fact that consistent support of any one definite program would have given him a real organization with which to work, but now the liberals were antagonized and in open rebellion; the army leaders deserting when not coddled and bribed; the masses were fearful; the old conservative landlords uncertain, and even the clergy were not too enthusiastic in their support.

The Plan of Ayutla demanded that Santa Anna be ousted from power and that the general-in-chief of the rebels appoint one man from each state and territory to select a temporary president. He in turn was to have almost dictatorial power at first, but was to call a constitutional convention within fifteen days to draw up a republican form of government. Ample guarantees were given to the army—for obvious reasons—and General Nicolás Bravo, Juan Alvarez and Tomás Moreno were invited to lead the revolt.

In spite of the fact that Comonfort joined the rebels and the southern port of Acapulco was quickly captured, the whole affair was officially laughed at as preposterous—just a matter of some "old cats climbing up where folks could hear them squall," said the hangers-on at court. On March 14, Alvarez issued a ringing call to his *"pintos"* ("painted ones," Indians with brown splotches on their skin due to a peculiar disease) and the lovers of independence of the southern mountains. This too was scoffed at as the babbling of a seventy year old imbecile in his dotage. But just the same, Santa Anna cancelled his trip to the country. Troops and more troops were mobilized in Mexico City, and the laughter and scoffing held a more and more self conscious and nervous note.

The Dictator may have softened somewhat of late years, but he could still recognize danger. Also he knew quite well that nothing would help him as much as a military victory. In the olden days, he was ready to set out one, three or five days after receiving news of rebel activities, but now four weeks passed by and the Dictator was not ready to take the field before March 16. Once it had been his pride and boast to travel light and fast, with himself in the van directing the activity of the scouts, but now the dignity of His Most Serene Highness precluded anything of the kind. Even a few years before, every energy had been bent to wipe out the acknowledged foe but now the foe had to be more or less incidental to a glorious triumphal march during which every village and town were to have time to prepare ovations and entertainments for the great man. The Minister of War announced that the southern "tour" would last a month, and was for the purpose of investigating conditions in the south!

[307]

All started off well. Cuernavaca staged a magnificent reception, while further south at Iguala, the Commander was tendered numerous courtesies, among them the presentation of four thousand *pesos* cash and private gifts in the form of the crucifix and mass book used by the Liberator on taking the oath after signing the Plan of Iguala. Incidentally—ever so incidentally—all rebel leaders who were captured were promptly shot. As a matter of fact, the rebels were presenting little organized resistance, but petty raids, ambushes and sniping were of constant occurrence. More serious was the fact that this army from the plateau was now down on the lowlands and the climate began to get in its deadly work.

On reaching Chilpanzingo the end of March, there was another great reception. Following this, Santa Anna called on General Bravo, who was sick at his home in the town. The old hero of Independence was suffering from age primarily and had declined to join the rebels with whom he was thought to sympathize. He had great influence in the region, however, and Santa Anna was anxious to secure his public endorsement and support. After a seemingly friendly interview, the Dictator left an army surgeon to care for the old man. A very few days later, both Bravo and his wife suddenly died on the same day. At once it was reported that they were victims of a double poisoning at Santa Anna's orders because Bravo had not openly and enthusiastically endorsed the dictatorship. Positive proof of either guilt or innocence seems lacking though the facts as reported are not above suspicion.

Soon Santa Anna was before the rebel stronghold of Acapulco. The month allowed for the southern "tour" passed and the Capital wondered and murmured. It was only known that the Dictator was so far down in the southern wilds that his couriers were intercepted from time to time. Inevitably rumor factories indulged in an orgy of speculation. Some of the superstitious were whistling to keep their courage up and eagerly repeated the tale that a magnificent eagle, of the variety called Imperial, had circled over the troops and finally lit near the Commander, allowing him and him only to approach and touch it. Such tales were too old, however, to gain much credence even among the *léperos* (the poor city dwellers or inhabitants of the slums).

By the middle of April, the national troops were badly demoralized by lack of victories, the constant sniping and the deadly effects of the climate. The Commander realized that his army was hardly in condition to settle down to a long seige of Acapulco and that it was in such a frame of mind that a frontal attack on the breastworks of the city would be equally futile. Where was the old romantic appeal with which he had driven his men into battle against Taylor for two days on scarcely more than a single meal? Gone! Gone forever!

On the twentieth, Santa Anna sent a commissioner to demand that Comonfort surrender the city. When the rebel promptly refused, it was suggested that "arrangements" might be made whereby Comonfort could recoup all his investments in the revolution so far "and live happily ever after." In fact, the sum of 100,000 *pesos* was casually mentioned. This too was flatly declined. With matters thus deadlocked, Santa Anna ordered a direct attack of nine hundred men on the city held by its five hundred defenders. A sharp repulse. Then what? Oh, well, it was foolish to waste good men on a heavily fortified place! Simply retire, cut the enemy to pieces throughout the countryside and let the city go for a time. A new philosophy for the man who had so impetuously and recklessly forced his way into the Alamo at all costs!

The country was now ravaged with a vengeance: by the rebels to keep supplies from the government troops and by the latter for the sake of revenge. A price was placed on the heads of the leading rebels and the "tour" again turned northwards. Garrisons were placed in the towns and word sent back to Mexico City that the south had been pacified. The victor was returning in triumph and had simply left a bit of routine "mopping up" for his subordinates to complete.

On May 16, His Most Serene Highness reached the Capital. The reception had much the aspect of a Roman triumphal entry: there was music, fireworks, the opera, bull fights, salvos of artillery; oratory and a great arch of triumph. This was surmounted by a statue of the Dictator, clad in his robes of the Order of Guadalupe, and holding the national flag in his hand. On the arch was written:

> While the sun sheds its burning light
> Life will not be lacking in nature;
> Thus, also, while Santa Anna lives,
> Mexico will enjoy peace and happiness.

Five days later, a fierce storm, in some accounts called a hurricane, blew down the arch and broke the statue. Was the old Indian god of war and storms, Hurakán, indignant at this travesty committed in the name of war?

Those who closely observed the Dictator on his return commented that he was pale, nervous and distraught, in spite of an obvious effort to be urbane and gracious. The experience had been a bitter one and His Most Serene Highness had lost his serenity. It is clear that he realized the danger and was sending cash abroad. As he admitted in his will, it was about this time that he exported the 232,000 *pesos* on which he claimed that he lived for the next twelve years.

Disorders increased and nerves were strained, yet still the man was capable of a generous act. One Enrique Angón was arrested in the southern part of the State of Puebla and promptly condemned to be shot as a conspirator. He begged to be allowed to see his wife and children. The permission was granted and the officials supposed they had seen the last of their prisoner. At three A.M., however, they were awakened by the returning condemned man, who simply thanked them for their courtesy and placed himself at their disposal. The act was reported to Santa Anna by telegraph who immediately ordered that the sentence be suspended and the prisoner released.

On October 2, Gadsden wrote: "In the glory of his [Santa Anna's] displays he has invoked the Feasts and festivals, the abominations and revelries of debauchery and of banquets, until the handwriting of an abused and insulted people, has reappeared on the wall."[4]

As a gesture, Santa Anna claimed that he wanted to know

4. *Mexico, Despatches,* Gadsden to Marcy, October 2, 1854, XVIII, No. 44.

[310]

exactly what the people thought of him. He ordered a plebiscite to be held on December 1, in which the people would indicate if they wished him to remain in power. The voting consisted of each man personally signing the affirmative or negative book placed at the polls. Signatures amounted to a categorical approval or disapproval of the administration while it was generally felt that a negative vote was equivalent to a request for execution, or banishment at least. On the first day of the voting in Mexico City, the ballot stood 12,452 to 1. But some men such as Porfiro Díaz dared to sign the negative book. When the returns were in, few were surprised at this order:

"With surprise and indignation His Most Serene Highness has seen that some recalcitrant individuals, boasting of anarquistic ideas, have voted for the rebel Juan Alvarez for president of the nation. In view of this, His Most Serene Highness orders that all those who thus voted be arrested and tried as conspirators, in as much as they have shown their sympathy for the revolt.

God and Liberty

Blanco, Minister of War.

Mexico, December 11, 1854."[5]

Disorders now sprang up on all sides. In the south a few hundred government troops were captured at Huetamo after the rebels had maintained an organized siege of a week. By the end of February, 1855, only Chilpanzingo remained of the Santa Anna garrisons established, and Alvarez was advancing to attack that point with several thousand troops. On the twenty-sixth, the Dictator quietly left the Capital at 4:00 A.M. for the south. The *Diario Oficial* explained his leaving by saying His Most Serene Highness was taking a trip for his health. Of course, this deceived no one.

The question was: had the old dynamic military leader once more reasserted himself? No, those days were gone. Sixty years had passed and taken their toll—and the last twenty-two months had been far from conducive to physical

5. E. Galarza, *The Roman Catholic Church . . . . in . . . . Mexico*, pp. 97-98.

fitness. The old ruthless orders for the destruction of life and property of the rebels were given, but it was the son, Colonel José López de Santa Anna, who was entrusted with the active work of rebel chasing. On March 10, the old man quietly re-entered Mexico City. It was late in the afternoon and orders had been issued for no special reception. The Cabinet, City Council, Supreme Court, and other officials went out to greet him, but the artillery salutes, the bell ringing, speech making, etc., were wisely eliminated.

Reports from the south were more and more depressing. The troops were decimated by the climate and were deserting by the scores and hundreds. Orders were issued to reward local authorities for the capture of deserters at the rate of five *pesos* per head, while, if deserters were found in their localities, the authorities were to be fined twenty-five *pesos* for the first offense, fifty *pesos* for the second, and impressed into military service for the third.

Money, money, money was the crying need. As has been seen efforts to sell more territory to the rapacious northerners came to naught. All payments to foreign citizens were suspended "including even conventional agreements to France, Great Britain and Spain."[6] New duties were hastily levied while merchants who would pay import duties in advance were given special reductions and concessions. The extremity to which the administration was reduced may be seen from the fact that men from Yucatán were being sold by Santa Anna as contract laborers to Havana. Giménez, who acted as agent for Santa Anna strenuously denied later that these men were sold into slavery and advanced a sample contract as proof.[7] Considering the mentality of the victims and their position in society, however, one can only sympathize with their fate as "voluntary" laborers.

The military conscience of the old warrior would not let him rest. He still felt that he must be in the field, so the

6. *Mexico, Despatches,* Gadsden to Marcy, May 5, 1855, XIX, No. 63.
7. *El Pájaro Verde,* May 12, 1874.

middle of May he again left Mexico City. This time, he went directly to the west, for the southern rebels were coming up in that direction. He had a well organized force and again marched through the country with little opposition. In Morelia, he was given a cordial reception and was extended many courtesies by D. Pelagio de Labastida, bishop elect of Puebla. The rebels were keeping out of his way, so he decided to force matters by attacking Comonfort at Ario. No sooner had the new expedition set out than the fury of the elements broke with "tempests, cloudbursts and snowstorms." Exclaiming that he had come to fight the rebels and not the elements, the weary old man retraced his steps, finally reaching Mexico City on June 8.

The far north was now joining the rebel cause with pronouncements in the Departments of Nuevo León and Tamaulipas. The end was in sight so the Dictator wisely concentrated his troops so as to hold the still fairly loyal east; the south, west and north were in revolt. To the east lay Puebla and the important port, Veracruz. Also, to the east lay the route to a possible—if not probable—exile.

On June 25 the Dictator called the members of the Council of government in special session. He asked their opinion as to whether a republic should be established and, if so, by what body? He also asked if they thought he should resign. Their own fate depended upon his, so they promptly answered "no" to the last question, but on July 13 said they thought a republic was advisable.

Anonymous broadsides began to appear. One sample was as follows: "Mexicans: the moment of vengeance has arrived: the tyrant, who from the height of his power insults the people with his magnificence, must fall bathed in blood beneath the poniard of the same people. His infamous courtiers, his wicked ministers, must perish. No flight, no pity. Flight means that he will return to oppress us some day; pity will stultify us before the world; it is necessary to erect a scaffold on every street; it is necessary to bathe yourselves in the blood of those rich ones who are swelled with pride over

[313]

their own splendor. The ministers of the tyrants must be dragged through the streets."[8]

All through June and July there were constant rumors that Santa Anna was preparing to flee. When his wife started for Veracruz, it was understood that much of her husband's personal belongings were in her baggage. Then came word of rebellion in the Department of Veracruz. This might cut off all chance of reaching the coast, so on August 9 Santa Anna left to put down the revolt—or thus it was reported. Before he left Mexico City, he selected a triumvirate to take charge of affairs till the nation could organize itself. The names of the men chosen were placed in a sealed envelope which was entrusted to the ministers.

On the twelfth Santa Anna issued a proclamation from Perote saying that the collapse of his government was due to the rebellion aimed at his personal administration. In view of this, he gladly resigned for the sake of peace and prosperity for his country. Before copies of the document could reach the Capital, however, the city had declared in favor of the Plan of Ayutla, and early in the morning of the thirteenth the Alameda was crowded with a singing throng shouting *vivas* for the new era.

Flight was now the Dictator's main preoccupation. On the sixteenth, his family boarded the *Iturbide* in port at Veracruz, and at 5:30 A.M., the next morning, he joined them. Shortly after midday the anchor was raised and the vessel sailed. Slowly the outlines of the city and of the great fortress of San Juan de Ulloa faded into the dusk and into the distance as the old cripple wended his way once more to Havana. From thence, he went to Cartagena and later to St. Thomas as his stormy spirit hungrily sought some slight thrill in change.

For Mexico a period was closing. Santa Anna had symbolized military ambition, but, at heart, loved his native land. True, he had confused its well being with his own, but withal he had loved it. More consistency might have enabled him

8. Zamacois, *op. cit.*, Tomo XIV, pp. 45-46. Copies of similar broadsides are found in the García Collection.

to have been a Porfirio Díaz, but his blood and background were different to that of Díaz. With or without him, his country would have gone through a stormy period. Given the conditions, plus his tempestuous character aggravated by a training in the school of frontier warfare, the result was inevitable except in the case of a genius. And the Almighty, in His wisdom, had seen fit to bless this child of destiny with a marvelous personality, tremendous energy and a facile brain, but, for some inscrutable reason, had omitted the balance wheel and left him an opportunist.

IV

DUSK
[1855-1876]

What future bliss, he gives not thee to know,
But gives .... Hope to be thy blessing now.

—ALEXANDER POPE, *An Essay on Man*

HOPE SPRINGS ETERNAL

AFTER a short stay in Havana, Santa Anna continued on his way to his properties near Cartagena. Here a warm and cordial welcome was awaiting from the simple country folk who still considered him their "patrón." Once more he settled down to a quiet routine that must have made the hurly-burly of the last few years seem the dim recollection of a dream world.

Apparently it was here that he started writing his memoirs which, in many ways, are such a naïve production as to leave the reader wondering. No special effort was made to publish them and certainly that could have been done easily by a man of wealth. They can hardly, then be classified as propaganda, but rather as the private apology of the man. They contain numerous historical inaccuracies, if not actual perversions of fact, which can be noted by even the casual investigator. As a result, it would seem that they are simply an old man's mental picture of his career in which the harsh and unattractive was forgotten or explained as a matter of necessity. Here was shown a passionate lover of Mexico at all times; a man who fought for his country's independence; who was a liberal in principle, but who became convinced that the only way to make his people happy was through conservatism.

It was well for the Exile that he had sent funds abroad for his enemies were determined on vengeance. The old Indian, Juan Alvarez, acted as President for a time and was then followed by Ignacio Comonfort. He, on January 9, 1856, ordered the Supreme Court to take charge of the Santa Anna properties pending such a time as the owner should appear before the national courts to face an indictment for abuse of power in connection with the Mesilla sale, and to justify his conduct of the war in the south against the liberals. If the former Dictator did not appear before the courts his property was to be used to pay damages inflicted on others by Santa Anna, and to reimburse the national treasury for sums squandered by him. At the same time, the Town Council of Veracruz was authorized to repossess itself of the *"fincas"* of which the Dictator had despoiled it. The property of El Encero, the pride of his later years, was finally sold to an Agricultural Society, while Paso de Obejas and the old home estate of Manga de Clavo were sold, presumably for a tithe of their value, to a private individual.[1] Some few of his holdings were apparently not confiscated for in a list of urban properties in Veracruz in 1858 appears one, No. 112, with a valuation of 17,200 *pesos* when the value was estimated on the basis of the annual rental being six per cent of the whole.[2]

Such political reports from Mexico as reached the Exile were bewildering. The victorious liberals had launched an astonishing program. Decree after decree, law after law, was promulgated which wiped out every vestige of the conservatism that had been undoubtedly popular a few years before. The clergy were held to have been the mainstay of the dictatorship, so they had to bear the brunt of the reforms. When clergymen protested, they were frequently exiled from the country, if a worse and more sudden fate did not befall them. The elections were so effectively "managed" that the Constitutional Convention was entirely in the hands of the liberals. With monotonous regularity, this body proceeded to write into the Constitution the earlier laws and decrees of the reformers. It swept far ahead of President Comonfort in its actions, and determined to destroy forever the political power of the clergy and to break up the large estates in the hands of either ecclesiastical or lay corporations for the benefit of the masses.

Special investigating committees (*comisiones de inquisitiva*) were appointed for each department of the government so as to lay forever the spectre of Santa Anna's despotism. These reported weekly on decrees and acts of the dictatorship which

1. *Monitor Republicano,* May 29, 1874.
2. Lerdo de Tejada, Miguel M., *Apuntes Históricas de ....Vera Cruz,* III, 155-81. This document gives a list of Veracruz real estate.

they thought needed nullification or revision. On one occasion the Committee on *Gobernación* reported that it was useless to revise the Dictator's decrees dealing with public lands since they had already been superseded by decrees of Alvarez. The Congress took violent exception to the report and insisted on driving another nail into the ghost's coffin by reversing the report seventy-nine to three, the three being the members of the committee. On another occasion, the Congress by a unanimous vote of the eighty-one delegates present refused to recognize the validity of the extension of the dictatorship beyond the one year for which it had been first authorized. This, of course, automatically nullified the legality of all acts of government for the last year and a half that Santa Anna had been in office.

On the promulgation of the new constitution in 1857 there broke out the tragic, fanatical Three Years War. On the one side was ranged conservatism with the open financial support of the clergy, and on the other the liberals of the nation led by the indomitable Benito Juárez. Here was another fullblooded Indian to take up the mantle of the weary Juan Alvarez and Valentín Gómez Farías. He was a man who simply did not know when he was defeated: compromise was not in his makeup. Whether at the head of thirty men and fleeing for his life, or at the head of the nation as President, he was the same. Phlegmatic, calm and emotionless, he fought through the Three Years War and came out victor. With all his work undone by the European invasion, he calmly, as a fugitive, continued fighting and returned to power with the overthrow of Maximilian. A greater contrast to Santa Anna could hardly be imagined. No wonder the glamorous old Exile despised him.

The contest from 1857 to 1860 was the first real civil war based on principles in Mexican history. Families were divided, thousands killed and tens of thousands made homeless; quarter was seldom given or expected. Here was a situation which would have appealed irresistibly to Santa Anna as a younger man. But the country patriarch of Turbaco had almost learned his lesson, and in spite of recurring waves of yearning for the

[321]

old excitement, he stuck to his ploughshare and pruning hook for a time.

Naturally, some of his old friends and supporters still hoped that he would return and there were a few movements such as the abortive revolt in February, 1856, in San Juan de Ulloa. This is said to have been incited by Juan Lagarde and José L. L. de Santa Anna, who were being held in the fortress as prisoners. For the most part, however, his one-time friends were now very quiet indeed or were, like Giménez, trying to secure contracts from the new authorities, and were quite indignant when their newly professed loyalties were questioned.

After about a year, country life again began to pall on the Santa Anna entourage and apparently the old man began discreetly to "sound out" European powers to see if they might now be interested in his earlier suggestion of intervention. A rumor of these schemes was published in a Spanish paper in New York, only to be promptly denied by Santa Anna's son, José, and Sr. Vidal y Rivas, his Father-in-law, who spoke for him in Cuba. On May 16, 1857, the United States Consul General in Cuba wrote, saying that Spain was about to despatch a fleet to reinstall Santa Anna in Mexico, and that both Great Britain and France approved the move.[3] This very emphatic despatch is entirely too circumstantial to be without some foundation in fact. Also, it should be noted that these rumors dovetail with the proclamation scattered through Mexico in June, 1857, and which was understood to have been written by Santa Anna. This flattered the army and blamed Alvarez and other liberal leaders for having brought about the recent troubles with Spain. Incidentally it strongly advised friendly relations with foreign powers, but, of course, offered the services of the author in order to repel foreign aggression from the sacred soil of Mexico.

Though the old adventurer still had a few friends in the country, this feeler fell upon deaf ears for the most part. The so-called "better people" who of necessity would form

3 *Consular Despatches, Havana*, Vol. XXXVI, A. K. Blythe to Lewis Cass, May 16, 1857.

the nucleus for any conservative move such as this, had been so disillusioned that they felt they could not afford to entrust power to him again. If he were brought back, it would mean approval of an expensive court and the clergy knew that they would be called upon to support it. If a dictatorship must be installed, many felt that Comonfort, who of late had been wabbling as a liberal, would be a better selection for it was obvious that he would respond to pressure.

Before long Comonfort actually made a bid for this very conservative support but was so hesitant that his move failed and the Santanistas again took courage. It was at this point the United States Minister, John Forsyth, reported that had the Assembly of Notables, called to select a President, been fairly constituted, Santa Anna would have had an even chance to have been selected for sentiment was again veering toward him because of the dearth of satisfactory leaders. He continued:

"While all admit that Gen. Santa Anna was the greatest plunderer the Nation has ever owned as a ruler, all unanimously agree, that apart from this, he was the best ruler of the Nation. In his character of acquisitiveness, he only differed from his predecessors in degree, for it is not doubted that *all* gain much more than their salaries;—while, as a firm and energetic magistrate, causing his Gov't. to be feared and obeyed, no other President has approached him. During his administration—everybody says—the roads are free from robbers, commerce is secure, & rogues & enemies of Society are condignly punished. It is a common remark here, that he never permits anybody to compete with him in preying upon the public. Many Mexicans hold, that the Public treasures which he notoriously absorbed, were more than compensated by the energy of his administration, and the order & safety which existed under it.

"I may remark, in passing, that *I* should have stronger hopes of making a favorable Treaty with Santa Anna, than I have with the present Gov't. Santa Anna *will* have money, & he

[323]

is not afraid to sell Territory if that be necessary to obtain it."[4]

Thus among the conservatives there was a rising sympathy and support for the Exile. At the same time, he was beginning to attract the active interest of the European powers, coupled with the tacit approval of the United States Minister. European support to prevent United States expansion and the endorsement of the United States Minister, who felt that Santa Anna's accession to power would mean the sale of more territory to the United States! A master diplomat in whom Machiavelli would have gloried!

Early in 1858, a revolution broke out in and near Cartagena but now that the Mexican situation was "warming up" it would never do to become involved in local politics. So, once more Santa Anna and his family got out their traveling equipment and sought new homes. Their immediate destination was Havana. There, arrangements were made with his local financial agents, and the party continued to the island of St. Thomas "where he acquired a splendid estate and held a sort of small court .... his residence on the island may be compared to the position of one who eagerly scans the world from a watchtower, in order to seize any favorable movement for again trying his luck."[5]

On April 22, 1858, a formal proclamation was issued. This was really a long apology for his last administration. It pointed out the desperate conditions when he assumed power, showed how order was brought out of chaos and how the long standing and dangerous boundary disputes in the north had been solved in a way that redounded to the credit of the nation at home and abroad. Emphasis was laid on the rebuilding of the

4 *Mexico, Despatches*, Vol. XXI, No. 71. John Forsyth to Secretary of State Lewis Cass, March 18, 1858.

5. Egon Cæsar Corti, *Maximilian and Charlotte of Mexico*, I, 22.

It was in connection with this residence in St. Thomas that E. G. Swann published the volume, *Santa Anna's Ghost*, in which the old man is pictured as the almost demented victim of remorse because of having killed a young girl and her lover in the 1840's when the girl repulsed his lecherous advances. The whole tale is so out of keeping with the career of the man as to demand little credence until supported by proof of a type which, up to the present, is entirely lacking.

fortifications at Veracruz, Perote and in the Capital so that the program of his administration was said to have been "The preservation of Mexican Nationality at all costs" on the basis that "If you love your country, prepare for war." He declared further: "It is the army, and the army alone,.... that can conserve the heritage which we ought to pass on to our children." Though a long list of internal improvements and other contributions to the country were cited, the proclamation constantly adverted to the fact that the army had been the basis of his government, and that peace and prosperity had been the result. The reading of this left not the slightest doubt that if this man ever returned to power it would be with the definite intention of establishing a military despotism.[6]

As the Three Years War progressed, the wheel of fate revolved and temporarily placed Miguel Miramón in the presidency. He tried to cater to the various conservative factions, and restored to Santa Anna his rank as a general in May, 1859. However, the Exile was not to be tempted from his retreat without a definite understanding. He had obviously reached the point where he had ceased to act first and explain later; he had thought the matter over and had a fairly definite plan of action in mind. This did not mean that his ethics had changed for it soon became obvious he was still ready to play the opportunist, but simply that age and experience had made him more cautious.

Juárez, meanwhile, was still fighting for the cause of democracy but was in desperate straits at times. He even went so far as to try to raise money by the MacLane-Ocampo Treaty for the cession to the United States of transit rights across the Isthmus of Tehuantepec. Though the cash was not obtained because the treaty was not ratified, slowly the liberal cause triumphed and the Exile was left in amazement at the success of the stolid old Indian who had become Presi-

6. Luis G. de Vidal y Rivas, *Biographie du General Antonio López de Santa Anna*, p. 46 ff. Extensive excerpts from this proclamation may be found in the biography written by his Father-in-law who acted as his Cuban agent for several years.

dent of Mexico. Even now Juárez made no effort to conciliate opposition but doggedly pursued his reform program. Opponents were promptly sent from the country even though as highly placed as the Apostolic Delegate and the Ministers of Guatemala and of Spain.

As the financial stringency became greater, payments on foreign debts were suspended in June, 1861. This, of course, was the cue for which Napoleon III, the new adventurer of the French, had been so eagerly waiting. He got in touch with the Mexican exiles in Europe who had been hoping for a Spanish prince to lead them back to peace and plenty and let them know that he would consider placing a prince on the Mexican throne under French protection. One of the leaders of this group was Gutiérrez de Estrada, who had long been a Santa Anna agent and admirer. But, unfortunately for the old adventurer, the group also contained such pursuasive men as Hidalgo and Almonte, who feared him and considered him unreliable and a trickster.

On October 15, 1861, Santa Anna wrote to Gutiérrez de Estrada, saying that Mexico "cannot have peace without a radical cure and that cure must be the substitution of a constitutional emperor for that farce called a Republic." He added that the European rulers could select the prince they wished and said: "today, more than ever, am I resolved to carry out this idea, and I shall work for it without ceasing." Six weeks later, he again wrote warmly endorsing Maximilian of Austria as the proposed prince, saying that the selection was the best possible. He announced that he intended to go to Mexico soon, and that he was anxious to take part in the important work of establishing the empire.[7]

Abroad there was still power in the old name of Santa Anna as was seen in December when Archduke Maximilian and his brother, Emperor Francis Joseph, of Austria, met in Venice and made plans for the Mexican venture. These provided:

7. García, editor, *Correspondencia secreta de los principales intervencionistas Mexicanos, 1860-1862*, pp. 40-41; Zamacois, *op. cit.*, Tomo VIII, p. 431 note.

"A provisional regency of as short a duration as possible, was first to be set up in Mexico, consisting of three persons, of whom, by Gutiérrez's advice, one was in any case to be Santa Anna, and one a bishop. The regency should only issue decrees subject to the express reservation of the Emperor's future assent. Santa Anna was to receive thirty-six thousand scudi, the same sum as when he was President, and, if he so desired, the title of Duke of Vera Cruz, or Tampico, and he should accompany the new Emperor upon his entry into the capital."[8]

How the news of this must have warmed the heart of the adventurer. Here was glorious vindication. And if from the regency he could not step into a position of primary importance in the kingdom he would have lost his touch and skill indeed! By the way, just what was the court dress of a Duke like? And which title was the better; that of Tampico, which carried an implication of military victory over the Spaniards, or that of Vera Cruz, which could be skillfully applied to his successes at that port, and also would carry more meaning abroad because of the prominence of Veracruz trade? Yes, probably the latter would be the better. Thus the old man thought, wondered and dreamed.

Unfortunately for him, however, Hidalgo and Almonte were working with might and main to discredit him. Each had his own pet schemes which Santa Anna would not be likely to further. In addition, the old man's record was so long and so varied that it took little initiative to paint a drab sketch of the man when he was at such a distance that his own personality could not be brought to bear.

On December 6 Gutiérrez urged Santa Anna to go to Mexico so as to be available on the ground and lead the movement in person. Santa Anna responded on the last day of the month saying that the proposal to land eight thousand men would never do, for Mexico could put twenty-five thousand in the field to oppose them. Thus he frankly anticipated serious opposition. On January 15, 1862, he wrote that he still had not left for Mexico because he was "ill." In other

8. Corti, *op. cit.*, I, 141.

words, he was apparently waiting to see what developments would take place. Meanwhile he was confident of his position with Maximilian and had lost his appetite for campaigning.

The situation that was his undoing, however, was developing in Europe. Almonte had gained the confidence of Napoleon III and the Emperor of the French was the man to provide the sinews of war for Maximilian. He was paying the piper, hence called the tune—and Maximilian duly danced by changing his plans for the membership of the Regency. January 14, 1862, Napoleon wrote Maximilian:

"This letter will be handed to you by General Almonte. He is a very excellent fellow, and, what is more, a very capable man who is highly esteemed. I think Your Imperial Highness will do well to give him full powers, and choose him as the center of action and your principal agent."

Almonte was wise enough to act slowly, at first tentatively approving Santa Anna as a member of the Regency, but privately determined to sidetrack both Gutiérrez as agent in Europe and Santa Anna as a competitor in the new empire as soon as he felt secure in his own position.

Meanwhile the fleets of Spain, Great Britain and France had reached Veracruz on their ostensible mission of collecting claims. When the French landed forthwith and prepared for a more or less permanent occupation, their associates retired and left them to their own devices. Napoleon's men then marched into the country and proceeded to convince the Mexicans how eagerly they had awaited the invasion. Unfortunately for Santa Anna, just as his agent was being over-reached in Europe, he was losing out in the New World by not being in Mexico in person. Almonte it was who scurried over from Europe to accompany the troops—and gather the plums for himself. Clearly, this Santa Anna is far different to the man of twenty years before whose activity had been the dread of his enemies.

By June, the French were ready to call for a junta to "select" a Regency and Assembly of Notables. In spite of the urging of Santa Anna's friends, the old general still remained in Cuba and Almonte's schemes began to bear fruit. He,

Archbishop Labastida and General Mariano Salas were announced as the members of the Regency. Almonte hastened to consolidate his position and ordered that Santa Anna should be treated merely as a private individual if he came to Mexico. The Exile wrote bitter strictures to Gutiérrez haughtily stating that he would await the call of his Emperor.[9] Once more he assumed the rôle of the modest maiden who expected to be sought after, but unfortunately his charms had been so frequently displayed as to become those of a bedraggled wench indeed.

The plain fact, however, was that Maximilian had begun to suspect that Santa Anna's party had disintegrated. The power of the new emperor might have helped to restore him before the public, but Maximilian was looking for those who could offer him active support, and not damaged reputations which he might be able to repair. *La Orquesta* of January 17, 1863, published a full page cartoon, showing a lone figure on the sea shore. The caricature was supported by one peg leg, had its rather scant hair painfully brushed forward to hide a growing bald spot, a big nose obviously meant to be red, and a poorly restrained corpulence. Over his shoulders was a robe labelled "Grand Master." With his finger to his ear the man was straining to catch the sounds from across the waters. On the other side was a bell labelled "*Venid, Traidores* (Come Traitors)," but a man was holding the bell clapper and the ringing could not be heard. The title of the whole was: "One old man with a bell can make Santa Anna come." A few suggestions of this type, together with the constant innuendoes of Hidalgo and others, and Maximilian had begun to lose interest in the broken down old Exile.

As soon as it was known that the formal selection of Maximilian had been made, Santa Anna hastened to write him under date of December 22, 1863, assuring him that not a mere party but the great majority of Mexicans eagerly awaited their sovereign. His letter closed thus: "May Your Most Illustrious Highness recognize in the Dean of the Mexican

9. The correspondence referred to in the last five paragraphs may be found in García, *op. cit.,* or Corti, *op. cit.*

Army a supporter and disinterested friend, and your most obedient servant who wishes you the greatest happiness and who attentively kisses the illustrious hands of Your Most Illustrious Highness."[10]

It was perfectly true that the outlook was not too promising but it was obviously a case of now or never. Maximilian and his beautiful young wife were about to embark for their new home, so Santa Anna decided to cast the die. His estates were the first major ones on the route from the coast to the Capital. Almost anything might be done if he could play the host to his Emperor and entertain the embyro court with the enchantments of Jalapa in spring time.

In January and February, 1864, all was bustle and excitement as the household on St. Thomas prepared for the new adventure. To add to the anticipation was the knowledge that this was to be contact with royalty sanctioned by the centuries-old aristocracies of Europe, and not with a parvenu or pseudo home product.

As hopes and anticipations waxed in St. Thomas, so increased Almonte's uneasiness. Were all his scheming and work to go for naught if this meddling old man arrived? He used his position as chief of the regency to the full and inspired the French General Bazaine with his own fears. Hence it was not surprising that when Santa Anna reached Veracruz February 28, he and his son Angel were required to sign a statement, pledging their support to the French Intervention, the monarchical theory of government and to Maximilian as Emperor of Mexico. Furthermore Santa Anna had to agree to act as a simple citizen and to abstain from all political activity.

The reception extended to the old man was surprisingly enthusiastic as balconies and roofs of the port were crowded by those who sought to do honor to him they already looked upon as the first Duke of Veracruz. On this same day there appeared in Orizaba a proclamation over the old and familiar name, Antonio López de Santa Anna. Though the General

10. Romero, *Correspondencia de la Legación Mexicana en Washington,* Tomo VII, pp. 191-92.

insisted that his friends published this without his authorization the argument was specious. The document called attention to the fact that Santa Anna had led the movement for democracy, then added: "But the illusions of youth are passed and in the presence of the great disasters brought about by that system [democracy], I do not wish to deceive anyone; the last word of my conscience and of my convictions, is a constitutional monarchy."

The motives back of the issuing of this proclamation are hard to fathom. Was it possible that he was still trying to reinstate himself in power? Was it just an old man (now seventy) who could not forget the past? Probably this last explanation is the better—always remembering that there was a lurking hope that he might be able to demonstrate enough actual popular support to give him a stronger position at court. Whatever the reason, the fatal blunder was committed for this violated his pledged word and placed him entirely at the mercy of his enemies. The next day, he wrote pledging his allegiance to the Regency, but Almonte flatly ignored the letter and hastened gleefully to point out to Bazaine that Santa Anna was a dangerous and most disturbing element; that he was trying to build up a following in opposition to the French, and had already broken his solemn promise. Forthwith orders were issued for the old man to be shipped back into exile. Almonte had won!

Though the town council of Jalapa and others sent best wishes and congratulations on his happy return, Bazaine peremptorily ordered Santa Anna to re-embark at once. The order was delivered at 10:00 o'clock in the morning and it was only by the most insistent explanations and ample guarantees of his friends that time till 4:00 P.M. was allowed in which to pack and make preparations. In truth, the old man was quite weak from an attack of his old complaint, dysentery, which had kept him in bed four days just after landing and at the time the blow fell he had only been on his feet for two days. In a letter to Bazaine, dated March 12, Santa Anna vigorously protested against the new order of banishment saying that he did not understand French, and did not realize

[331]

that he had signed an agreement to issue no proclamations. This explanation was about as weak as were the grounds of complaint in the first place. The expressed reasons, however, were not the real ones. It was plainly a contest for power in which initiative, energy and activity still decreed that youth must be served. But alas for don Antonio another now represented youth.

Again the weary return to St. Thomas! Then an appeal to Maximilian, who had already been amply "prepared" by Bazaine and Hidalgo. Maximilian naturally supported his subordinates, and probably never realized that he was losing a possible adherent of some actual value.

Soon the new Emperor arrived and was in the midst of the mælstrom of events. Not a broad minded man, he relied upon the strength of the French, who had agreed to supply him with twenty thousand men through 1867, and upon the suggestions of his advisers. Though debts piled up alarmingly and Juárez continued with his persistent and annoying opposition, the Santanistas were snubbed on all sides in spite of the fact that this was just the time when the glamor of the Empire was wearing off and relations were becoming critical with the clergy. The worldly wise advice of Santa Anna, at this juncture, would have been worth careful pondering. He wrote to his old friend Giménez on November 15, 1864:

"If I could have talked to the Emperor, as I desired, I would have told him without beating about the bush: that he should adopt the religious principle as the basis for his throne, the support of the conservatives and landlords, together with that of the Clergy and Army, uniting in the latter the old veterans and the best youth of the country. But the events of the 12th of March (the expulsion from Veracruz) which you witnessed, separated me from the Monarch, and my noble desires were frustrated."[11]

Here was Santa Anna's calm estimate based upon his lifetime of experience. By repeated trials, he had found out where actual elements of strength for any Mexican government

11. Santa Anna, *Mi historia militar y política, Annex* XII, p. 248.

[332]

of the time lay. But the new Emperor blundered on and tried to adopt a half-way course between the French liberals and the conservative clergy. By this he hoped to keep French support and weaken Juárez, while not actually breaking up the hierarchy. Due to complications in Europe and pressure from the United States the French troops were recalled; likewise, the Juárez liberals steadily became stronger while the Empire was weakened by a rupture with the Papal Nuncio. Even the support of the broken reed, Santa Anna, was gone. In his eyes the one unforgivable sin was committed when the Emperor took no steps to soothe the pride so brutally abused by the new order of banishment. Such an injury could only be wiped out by vengeance.

DREAM—OR NIGHTMARE

NEITHER Maximilian nor Santa Anna was ready for an immediate break, so when the old General sent in his claims for military pay in January, 1865, they were approved, From this point the story for the next six months is told in the letters of the time. Even when the application for back pay was pending before the authorities of the Empire, Angel Santa Anna was severely criticizing the Emperor's appointments to office and clearly indicated the possibility of a rupture.[1]

By March 15, Santa Anna himself was writing to his nephew, Manuel, to be very cautious for conditions were likely to change quickly, and to be sure to burn all incriminating correspondence as soon as he had read it. The same day, he wrote Giménez, saying the Confederate War was about over in the United States and that there was real danger of the combined United States and Confederate armies invading Mexico for additional territory. A month later, he sent his son, Manuel, to Jalapa to take charge of the family property, but wrote to his nephew: "You tell me nothing of conditions, when it is so necessary to be abreast of events. When you write me, do it in detail on matters of interest."

In May, he was feeling more confident and wrote to his old friend Giménez not to accept any position or office under Maximilian, and a month later Angel Santa Anna wrote to his cousin that his Father had changed, that all Mexicans were to be considered brothers now that independence was in danger. The foreigner must be driven out of the country and

---

1. The letters referred to in this and in the ensuing three paragraphs are found in García, *La Intervención francesca . . . . segun el archivo del Mariscal Bazaine,* seventh, eighth, or ninth parts; or in García, *Correspondencia secreta de los principales intervencionistas,* third part.

the old "Veteran of Independence, the Hero of Tampico" was ready to offer his services.

Shortly before this, Giménez had written that he was tired of it all. He stated that, after sixty-seven years he had very little to show for his life, and that he was quite sure his old chief would applaud his determination to go to Jerusalem where he planned to join the Franciscan Fathers who were caring for the Holy Sepulchre. A few months earlier this idea might have been approved, but now new plans were on foot and every supporter was needed. Santa Anna answered:

"I do not approve the journey to Jerusalem. Stay quietly in your retirement. It is not necessary to go to a convent at so great a distance in order to dedicate one's heart to God. I believe that you were suffering from hypochondria and that you were not feeling well when you last wrote me.

"Continue sending me all the news as it happens, and take good care of yourself. Command as you wish your sincere servant and friend who wishes you all happiness and who kisses your hand."

The dream—or nightmare—had begun.

The poor old man still thought he was a great power in the land. Again appeared the inevitable proclamation under date of July 8:

"LIBERALS AND CONSERVATIVES! Let us forget our fraticidal contests and go forward! Let us unite against the common enemy. One single flag covers us, the flag of liberty; one single thought animates us, that of war to the death against the invaders who destroy our towns and kill our brothers. Eternal hatred to the tyrants of our Native Land!

"Fellow citizens! On the memorable 2nd of December, 1822, I took as a motto these words: *Down with the Empire! Long Live the Republic!* Now from the foreign soil on which I find myself, I repeat it with the same enthusiasm."[2]

Most Mexicans smiled at this, but it was no joking matter for Maximilian whose Empire was already staggering to its

2. Santa Anna, *Memoirs,* Appendix XX, pp. 278, 280.

fall. Rumors began to go the rounds that the old man might attempt to land at Acapulco and co-operate with the old followers of Alvarez in the south. Then again, the newspapers said that he was supposed to be co-operating with the liberal supporters of Juárez, who had headquarters in New York. The Imperial Government itself answered the proclamation by ordering the immediate confiscation of the Santa Anna estates.

Any efforts to arouse the Mexicans by one who had been out of the country for ten years were absurd on the face of them, to say nothing of the fact that in this case they were the work of a man who had frankly endorsed the Intervention, and who now denounced it. The leaders of all groups dismissed the matter as absurd unless the glamor surrounding the old name were capitalized in an appeal to the masses. But there was, in actual fact, a situation developing in the north that might be able to make just this kind of an appeal.

The United States had crushed the Confederacy, but many, like General U. S. Grant, were convinced that the task of the Union army would not be complete until Maximilian was driven from Mexico. As the recently rebellious states of the Union were organized under military control, the young, successful, audacious and efficient General P. H. Sheridan was put in charge of the states of Louisiana and Texas with an astonishingly large number of men. Most of these troops who were theoretically sent to control the recent rebels were actually placed along the Río Grande, hundreds of miles beyond the center of population.

Carefully fabricated rumors skillfully reinforced by pretentious troop movements on the northern bank of the river at the psychological moment convinced the Imperialists that the United States troops were about to advance to vindicate the Monroe Doctrine. The United States Secretary of State, W. H. Seward, was convinced that hostilities were inadvisable, but brought all possible diplomatic pressure to bear to secure the withdrawal of French support from Maximilian. Thanks in part to this mixture of military and diplomatic pressure, and in part to the arising European complications,

Napoleon was rapidly losing interest in Mexico, and was persuaded to consolidate his military strength by recalling the expeditionary forces from Mexico.

It did not take Santa Anna long to realize that the United States was holding Sheridan as the sword of Damocles over the head of the Empire while it brought diplomatic pressure to bear. In October, he authorized one Lisandro Lameda to open negotiations with President Johnson and Secretary of State Seward of the United States. No results were secured, but about the end of December he again sent letters to both officials. He pledged himself to secure the freedom of Mexico, and begged for the co-operation of the "Great Sister Republic" while he, "The Founder of the Mexican Republic" invoked the Monroe Doctrine for its salvation.[3]

On December 30, 1865, Mr. Seward left Washington for a trip to the West Indies. It has been suggested that the announced voyage for his health had as an additional objective the acquisition of West Indian possessions for the United States. The Russian Minister, Baron Stoeckle, however, at once reported to Romero, the Minister of the Juárez government, that he had it on good authority that Seward was going to St. Thomas "with the purpose of reaching an agreement with D. Antonio López de Santa Anna for the organization of a government in Mexico on the exit of Maximilian."[4] The only reasonable conclusion would seem to be that Seward much preferred to use diplomatic pressure, but that he was not sorry to have Sheridan on the border as an alternative, and that he wanted to look Santa Anna over as another possible string to be added to his bow.

A week after sailing, Seward was in St. Thomas. On arriving, he received an invitation to call upon Santa Anna, who sent his regrets for not calling on the Secretary on board his vessel but excused himself because of his lameness. This invitation was accepted and an unusual interview took place.

3. The two letters of December 31, 1865, are found in the State Department Archives, *Miscellaneous Letters, 1865,* part II; also see *House of Representatives Executive Document, No. 17,* Thirty-ninth Congress, second session, pp. 2-3, for still another letter.

4. Romero, *op. cit.,* Tomo VII, p. 5.

The Secretary of State took pains to explain his conduct as a courtesy call on "a fallen enemy" though he made note of the fact that Santa Anna was well preserved and anxious to demonstrate his patriotism and his hatred of Maximilian. Mr. Seward also admitted that he showed enough interest in Santa Anna to catechize him as to his support of the Empire two years before. To this, he said, Santa Anna responded that he withdrew his support when he realized the seriousness of the French Intervention, and that he had never countenanced any loss of Mexican autonomy. Mr. Seward then stated that the Mexican "seemed to him a man of very good understanding, with a very firm will and of good abilities as the leader of a party."[5]

Santa Anna reported the interview quite differently in his *Memoirs*. He said the Secretary called upon the Governor of the Island and then on him:

"The unexpected visit of this personage made me wish to know his object, but in half an hour of conversation, I did not secure an explicit answer: half expressions (*palabras cortadas*) in a low voice as of one who wishes to speak and who restrains himself .... In spite of the mysterious conduct of the diplomat I understood his intentions, we agreed *as to the expulsion of the French,* and he offered me *protection.* On taking leave of me with a significant look and a strong handshake he said to me: 'General, to Mexico.' On the following day I was preparing to return Mr. Seward's visit when his vessel sailed."

Just how much Seward said or implied is uncertain, but the old man, hungering for a return to power, took the whole affair very seriously indeed. The account quoted above was probably affected by his later disappointment, but it should also be recalled that Seward's account was one given by him to explain his conduct to the friendly Mexican Minister at Washington who was bitterly antagonistic to Santa Anna. A week after the interview the old Exile wrote to a friend saying that Seward had assured him that the United States would never recognize Maximilian, and that it was bringing pressure to bear on Napoleon in the name of the Monroe

5. *Ibid.,* pp. 89-91.

Doctrine. He continued: "He [Seward] thinks that Napoleon will be obliged to withdraw from Mexico, or that the Government of Washington will not be able to prevent the soldiers *camped on the Río Grande* from helping the Mexican patriots."

To Giménez, he wrote the same day saying that he would endorse the government in Mexico, regardless of who occupied the presidency and provided only that the government was purely national. "Today I say with the old woman: 'Long live the old hen even if she does have the pip' (*Viva la gallina y viva con su pepita*).[6]

Maximilian was obviously concerned and tried to discredit Santa Anna by publishing his earlier offers of support. Meanwhile, Romero consistently refused to give the slightest encouragement to Santa Anna or to any proposal that might result in co-operation with him. Thus, though Seward was obviously impressed by the Exile, he could hardly use the old man while co-operating with Juárez, the head of the Liberal party in Mexico. Also, the need for him was less since the pressure exerted on the north Mexican border was having results. Sheridan wrote: "During the winter and spring of 1866 we continued covertly supplying arms and munitions to the Liberals—sending as many as 30,000 muskets from Baton Rouge arsenal alone."[7] But as Juárez grew stronger and more and more likely to succeed, Seward had less and less use for Santa Anna.[8]

Now ensued for the perennial adventurer a period of anxious waiting. Agents dispatched to Washington met with a more and more frigid reception. However, it occurred to one of these worthies that it would be a simple matter to fleece

6. These last two letters found in García, *Correspondencia secreta*, tercea parte, pp. 127-30.

7. Sheridan, *Memoirs*, II, 224-255.

8. In Mexico, *La Orquesta* of April 2, 1866, carried a page of cartoons to show how fleeting a thing is glory. Artistic and literary glory was shown as a bubble which bursts. The glory of actors was shown by a sketch of a theater, showing the peanut gallery crowded, but orchestra, dress circle and balcony empty. Military glory was represented by an old man with a peg leg and head bandaged; the background was a field of corpses, while beside ,him stood a gamecock with foot in a sling and head wrapped up. The reference was obvious.

the gullible old man out of some cash when he was so eager for good news. A letter over Seward's forged signature notified the anxious Santa Anna that the House of Representatives had approved a loan of fifty million dollars for Mexico, and that the Senate's approval was certain. Of this sum thirty million were earmarked for Santa Anna's enterprise, and he was urged to start for Washington at once.

So much for the ground work; now for the scheme: Santa Anna's agent, Dario Mazuera, had full powers to act in the name of his chief so he leased a ship in the United States. This he took to St. Thomas, telling the old Mexican that he had bought it for the movement signing Santa Anna's name to notes aggregating $250,000. The victim did not like the looks of things, but did not want to block so fine a beginning, and so actually advanced substantial sums to the crooks, which he claimed amounted to over $35,000. By then selling the notes, the rascals apparently realized further sums so that the victim was fleeced of some $70,000 to begin with.

He was now panting to be off for New York, where the $30,000,000 was supposed to be on deposit awaiting his disposition. On May 4, the *New York Herald* published a proclamation of Santa Anna's in Spanish and English. On the twelfth he arrived in person, and received considerable attention from the press, which was quite interested and, on the whole, friendly. On the other hand, the Anglo Saxons were strangely remiss: there was no representative from the State Department to receive the party; the guns of the harbor did not fire salutes as Mazuera had promised, and the cash was not at once available. However, the old man could not speak English, so he was put off with one excuse and another. His appeals to fellow Mexicans in New York for co-operation met little response, and that little was mostly hostile on account of Romero's open antagonism. On the other hand some of the plans were thriving for supplies were being assembled quickly if one could judge from the bills presented for payment. In truth, Santa Anna's authorizations to Mazuera and others to act for him had been freely used in contracting debts which were clamoring to be paid.

A letter was dispatched to Seward to pay the respects of the Mexican general and to offer to co-operate in full with the United States and Juárez in driving Maximilian and the French from Mexico. The Mexican Minister, however, had publicly repudiated Santa Anna, and Seward declined to meet the Mexican's representatives or to have any dealings with him or them. The Mexican Club of New York denounced the adventurer and scathingly reviewed his career, advertising his inconsistencies and weaknesses for all who would read.

Complications now rose thick and fast; suits and counter suits were brought before the courts with regard to the notes issued in the name of Santa Anna, the fraud connected with the so-called sale of the *Georgia* to Santa Anna, and for various and sundry other affairs, large and small. One suit was actually instituted in the name of his landlady whose charge set forth that she was afraid he would leave without paying the board bill of $350.50 for himself and his staff.[9]

Word arrived that Maximilian had confiscated Santa Anna's property and this raised the adventurer's stock somewhat for it increased his importance as an enemy of the Empire, but Seward remained in a quandary. Juárez still looked like the best bet so the Secretary of State kept in touch with Romero and notified him each time he had declined to see Santa Anna or had put him off with an evasive answer. Thus passed July, August and September, while Santa Anna finally became convinced that, in spite of all of his pleas and explanations, the Juárez government would not even accept his proffered co-operation. This was obviously what kept Seward from having anything to do with him.

Litigation expenses were becoming serious by this time for his lawyer's fees, alone, amounted to $30,000, if Santa

9. Another one of the worthy rascals surrounding Santa Anna employed a rather novel scheme to fleece the old man. Santa Anna held his note for $5,000, but the friend asked that this be returned, promising, on his word of honor, to pay later, but saying he was about to marry a rich Cuban heiress and needed all his available funds to maintain appearances until the ceremony was over. The victim agreed to assist Cupid at the time but later had to sue for his money and attempt to recover his losses in the United States courts.

Anna's own statement is correct. The old man began to get restless and to plot actively for a direct invasion of Mexico in his own name. Efforts were made to raise arms and supplies, as well as to secure volunteers. On October 8 he addressed a Fenian celebration in New York just when that organization was causing trouble in Canada. Dressed in full uniform as a Mexican general, he praised the quality of the Irish troops that had joined him in the Mexican War, and was clearly making a bid for the support of such as might be interested. He ordered a set of bonds, amounting to $950,-000 to be engraved and prepared for issuance in order to meet the expenses of the expedition. For redemption of these bonds he pledged his personal estates in Veracruz, Turbaco and St. Thomas. It is doubtful if any quantity of these were sold but a few were apparently put out to see what they would bring.[10]

Meanwhile, Santa Anna's nephew, who carried the same name, began to suspect that his uncle was being victimized. He wrote directly to Seward on November 7, 1866, asking point blank if the United States had entered into a treaty or agreement to support his uncle as that gentleman so firmly believed. In reply, Seward stated plainly "this government has not recognized any other Mexican authority, or held correspondence, or entered into negotiations, with any other than that of President Don Benito Juárez."[11] This reply was enclosed in a letter to United States Attorney S. G. Courtney, New York City, who was to entrust it to the mails only after verifying the fact that the nephew was actually in the city. The attorney reported that the man was actually there and that he had mailed the letter.

10. The Mexican Minister reported constant interviews with the State Department in which every action of Santa Anna was carefully reviewed. On the other hand, Santa Anna was bombarding all concerned with letters and protests on every occasion, but to follow all this would require a long technical discussion of little value here. The State Department Archives at Washington contain quite a number of Santa Anna letters and Romero, *op. cit.*, devotes several hundred pages to this subject.

11. *House of Representatives, Executive Document No. 17,* Thirty-ninth Congress, second session, pp. 52-53.

If this communication reached the uncle, he ignored it for in November he was still writing to President Johnson. A letter of the thirtieth complained of the treatment he had received in the United States, and stated that he would have returned to St. Thomas but for the fact that a commission of Mexicans had arrived in the name of the clergy and conservative party, of the chief military officers under Maximilian, and even from the Archduke himself. These, he claimed, placed a fund of 5,000,000 *pesos* at his disposal to act as mediator, saying that otherwise the place hunters of Miramón and Márquez would seize control of Mexico. He asked the endorsement of the United States Government, saying that he would, if it desired, turn all power over to Juárez, or to any other person selected in Mexico by the people. He then asked Johnson to see him to receive "information which I wish not [to] trust to writing." The only answer was a notice from Seward saying that all correspondence on official Mexican affairs must go through the regularly constituted officials. "Under these circumstances you will perceive that the correspondence which you have opened cannot be continued."[12]

It was soon quite certain that there was little to be accomplished in the United States. Everything was different: the people, the climate, the customs, the food. Only avarice remained common to all peoples, so far as the old Exile could see, and with his handicaps as a foreigner he was always the victim. His personal fortune wasted away and the only ray of hope lay in the meager reports from the homeland. As spring came on, these indicated the end of the Empire was near. It was obvious that Juárez would be the favored son, especially since he could count on United States support, but still there were a few who felt that Santa Anna would have a chance and who plotted for his return.[13]

12. Copy of letter to Johnson of November 30, 1866, in State Department Archives, *Miscellaneous Letters, November, Part II, 1866*, Response of Seward, dated December 8, in *House Document No. 17, op. cit.*, p. 55.
13. It appears that his wife was in Mexico most of this time. Also there was much general correspondence back and forth.

Finally, tired of trying to buy propaganda, of appealing to deaf authorities, and hungering for the old country, the adventurer determined to go direct to Veracruz to see what he could do in person as Maximilian's empire crashed. Before leaving he, General of Division, Well Deserving of his Country, Grand Master of the Spanish Order of Charles III, Grand Cross of the Red Eagle of Prussia, General-in-chief of the Liberating Army of the Mexican Republic, etc., etc., etc., commissioned one Gabor Naphegyi as Minister to Washington with power to sell Mexican bonds of $10,000,000 or more, as needed, bearing seven per cent interest. The grand old phrases of the grand old days! Interspersed in the document were seductive suggestions that he would soon be at the head of the Liberating Army or the provisional president of his country.

On March 22, the little band set out on board the *Virginia* from New York after taking elaborate precautions to conceal their plans lest the now suspicious United States officials prevent their sailing. Even the captain of the vessel was reported not to have known the identity of his passengers. The plan apparently was to seize Veracruz for a conservative republican movement, thus shrewdly gathering the maximum of supporters from the old Santanistas, the real conservative republicans and desparing imperialists who would prefer this to the radical government of Juárez.

Four days after he set sail, the city of Tamaulipas formally recognized Santa Anna as head of the Mexican armies and as president *ad interim*. On June 3, the *Virginia* reached Veracruz.

Santa Anna immediately repaired to the castle of San Juan de Ulloa and plunged into the schemes which he hoped would lead him once more to Mexico City as master. The next day, a proclamation was issued to the nation which was especially calculated to flatter the Veracruz area and recalled the fact that there the writer had "planted the tree of liberty" and had later "watered that tree" with his blood. However, there was lacking the old ringing call to arms, instead the proclamation was a plea for peace—of course, with himself as the understood mediator.[14]

Meanwhile, all were assured that the new movement had the endorsement of the United States Government. United States Consul E. H. Saulnier, felt this to be impossible and asked Commander F. A. Roe, of the U. S. S. *Tacony* to try and prevent Santa Anna from landing because there was real danger of trouble if he did so. He said there was no doubt that many in both fortress and city were eager for the General to land while others were as vigorously opposed to it.

On the seventh, Commander Roe went on shore and found the city greatly disturbed. He talked matters over at the British Consulate and decided to prevent Santa Anna from landing that night when the proposed movement was scheduled to take place. At his request, the cutter of Captain Aynsley of H. M. S. *Jason* was made available and the two naval officers proceeded to the *Virginia* with the flags of Great Britain and the United States sewed together side by side and flying from the same flagstaff on the boat. They boarded the *Virginia* and promptly asked for Santa Anna. When he approached Commander Roe somewhat abruptly informed him that he was to spend the night on the United States war vessel. Vigorous protests brought threats to use force; the Captain of the *Virginia* later testifying that the British captain actually suggested the use of more moderate language to his companion officer. A friend of Santa Anna testified that he protested against the use of force, saying that Santa Anna was a cripple, but that the response of Commander Roe was he "would take him if he had to break the other leg of the damned old scoundrel."[15]

On reaching the U. S. S. *Tacony*, the prisoner was treated with real consideration and given excellent accommodations in the Captain's own quarters. The next morning as the *Virginia* was sailing from the port, it stopped and took Santa Anna on board from the warship, though the *Tacony* fol-

14. A copy of this in English translation may be found in *Senate Executive Document No. 20*, Fortieth Congress, first session, p. 114.
15. *Ibid.*, pp. 108-11.

lowed her for many miles to sea to be sure that she continued on her outward journey and did not attempt to return with the disturbing passenger to Veracruz.[16]

It is evident that the immediate cause of the failure of the adventurer's latest scheme was the conduct of the United States Consul and Naval Commander, who knew that their Government was endorsing Juárez. To an impartial observer, it is incredible that Santa Anna after all these years could have mustered anything like a following with which to have opposed the phlegmatic Juárez with his able supporter, the hard fighting Pórfirio Díaz. However, to the embittered passenger on board the *Virginia* this was simply one more instance of the northern Republic wrecking his plans and injuring his native land.

The *Virginia* continued on her way to Yucatán where the next scene in the somewhat farcical and turbid drama was to be laid. On the afternoon of the eleventh, the ship reached the port of Sisal before proceeding on its way to Cuba. Santa Anna promptly sent ashore the inevitable proclamation, recalling the days forty years before when he was military governor of the province. It was a plea for peace with the statement that he hoped to bring this about.

The next morning a Mexican officer and file of soldiers boarded the *Virginia,* and, with gunboats strategically placed

16. The *Diary of Gideon Welles* (United States Secretary of the Navy), III, 115-16, under date of June 21, 1867, has this entry:

"I took to the Cabinet and read a strange despatch from the Commander Roe of the Tacony, who, under the advice of the American and British consuls, took upon himself to seize Santa Anna, place him on the ship in which he came to Veracruz, escort him twenty miles to sea, and forbid his return. It was an extraordinary proceeding and I made it a point to read the whole despatch in Cabinet. Seward said, 'That was all right,' and asked me to send him the dispatch, or a copy, for he wanted to keep the record. No one else seemed to trouble himself about the matter except the President, who remarked that the Mississippi and the levees were giving us much trouble by the overflow, and he thought it might be a blessing if the waters would go and drench Mexico and wash out her faithlessness. I regret that Roe should have permitted himself to be a tool of the consuls, though I doubt not his intentions were right, but I apprehend that some exceptions would have to be taken to Roe's conduct, and that I might have to recall and take action in the case. As it is, I think the Admiral must give his attention to Mexican affairs."

nearby, "invited" Santa Anna and his private secretary father-in-law, Vidal y Rivas, to land. Captain John Deaken, of the *Virginia*, protested vigorously by saying that he was instructed by Commander Roe not to allow Santa Anna to land on Mexican soil. The invitation was so "pressing," however, that Santa Anna was promptly landed and held as a prisoner of war.

Santa Anna's agent in New York protested vociferously to the State Department about the whole affair as an insult to the United States flag. Seward promptly sent for Minister Romero and "appeared greatly surprised" as one "who had just been rescued from an awkward position" to be informed that the *Virginia* was definitely in the territorial waters of Mexico at Sisal, and that force had not been employed but that the arrest of Santa Anna had taken place after he had landed. Seward at the same time urged Romero to reassure the public that Santa Anna had not been shot. Two days later, he told the Mexican "unofficially" that the report that the United States was sending the warship *Susquehanna* for the purpose of returning Santa Anna to the United States was all a mistake, though it probably was not advisable to contradict the rumor publicly at the time.[17]

After a few days, the prisoners were taken to Campeche where several hot weeks dragged by. By order of Juárez, now in control of the Capital, Santa Anna was finally transferred to the famous old castle of San Juan de Ulloa, whose walls he had so many times trodden as an ambitious young soldier, a proud commander or—just recently—as a fearful and anxious conspirator. Here he was treated reasonably well and obviously was not plunged into the noisome dungeons of such evil repute, but, even so, little could be done to make San Juan pleasant in August and September.

In truth, the fear displayed by the prisoners was no idle matter for other adherents of the Empire had received short shrift from the conquering Liberals. It was here, with the firing squad as an imminent possibility, that Santa Anna's last will and testament was drawn up and signed September

17. Romero, *op. cit.*, pp. 60-61, 82-83.

27th.[18] It was a long document with forty-nine provisions. The introduction was a devout expression of faith followed by the first provision, entrusting his soul to God. The second provided that all debts should be paid and that a donation of twenty-five *pesos* was to be made to "libraries and public instruction." Then followed a jumble of statements, justifying his public career and disposing of his remaining property. He referred to a residence in Turbaco and to properties in St. Thomas, "all of which cost 73,000 *pesos.*" With his Mexican property confiscated, and expenses now piling up, this was not much with which to face the future. Considerable sums were claimed to be due him, but there was obviously little chance of collecting them.

Among the debts recognized as owed by him was the one found in provision No. 30, that throws considerable light on the general condition surrounding the prisoner:

"I declare likewise that I owe to D. Pedro Ballestado of Campeche, an Inn-keeper, a Spaniard, the sum of 775 *pesos,* which he charged me [this doubtless included Vidal y Rivas also] for food which he gave me in the month and a half of my imprisonment in that city. Although the sum which he charged me is excessive, let it be sufficient as a consideration that he gave me to eat at that time when no one else remembered the services that I had rendered to my country. For this reason, it is my will that he be paid."

He named as general or "universal" heirs his children, María Guadalupe and Manuel, and his granddaughter, María Carolina Maillard, daughter of his daughter María del Carmen who had predeceased her father. His own two children were made joint executors. He then included the following provisions which must be taken to indicate a desire to do justice and extend recognition:

"No. 41. I declare that the following are my natural children: Doña Paula Santa Anna, daughter of María Cesarea; Doña Merced and Doña Petra Santa Anna, daughters of

18. A copy of this document is available in the García Collection of the University of Texas.

[348]

Doña Amada Sandoval, the first of these last being the widow of Arrillaga and the other still unmarried (*de estado honesto*).

No. 42. I declare likewise that I have, as natural children Colonels D. José María and D. Angel López de Santa Anna.

No. 43. It is my wish that when all my property has been collected and liquidated and that the debts due under the laws, have been paid, that the value of one-fifth of my properties be divided in equal parts between my five above mentioned children in the two preceding provisions. May they receive this portion with God's blessing and with mine."[19]

Another interesting feature of the will is the steady and high praise that he extends to his first wife for her thriftiness, housewifely qualities and loyalty. True to the instincts of a gentleman, there was no expressed criticism of any woman, but the inference can hardly be escaped that his second marriage had fallen somewhat short of entire felicity.

But the trial was coming on rapidly. The date had been set as October 7 before a military tribunal. When the court was called to order the prosecuting attorney read letters showing Santa Anna's complicity with the Imperialists and made an impassioned plea for the death penalty that brought a storm of applause from the excited spectators. The attorney for the defense, Joaquín M. Alcalde, arose with the words: "Crucify him! Crucify him! thus shouted the Jewish rabble." He skillfully presented Santa Anna's sweeping denials of having endorsed the Intervention; protested that a military court had no jurisdiction during time of peace; and reviewed the very real services and contributions of the defendant on behalf of his country throughout his long career, not failing to include his last efforts which had been so misunderstood and misrepresented.

The court considered the evidence, it is to be presumed, and passed sentence most wisely indeed for the administration. The death penalty would have been very foolish when the

19. Inhabitants of Jalapa insist that he had other natural children, the sons and daughters of pretty Indian girls of the neighborhood. However, given the conditions, it would have been unusual indeed for them to have been recognized.

United States was already none too pleased about the method of capture employed at Sisal. A continuation of the exile for the septuagenarian was far wiser than a death penalty, for the adventurer was now fully discredited and the Grim Reaper could be relied upon with reasonable certainty to make a fairly early appearance. So thought the jurists.

On November 1, 1867, the English packet boat set off for Havana and once more carried the old commuter into exile.

DARK
[1876]

So fallen! so lost! the light withdrawn
Which once he wore!
The glory from his grey hairs gone
Forevermore!

Oh! dumb be passion's stormy rage,
When he who might
Have lighted up and led his age
Falls back in night.

. . . .

Scorn! Would angels laugh, to mark
A bright soul driven,
Fiend-goaded, down the endless dark,
From hope and heaven!

Then, pay the reverence of old days
To his dead fame;
Walk backward, with averted gaze,
And hide the shame!

—JOHN GREENLEAF WHITTIER

RETURN AND DEATH

THE annals of history provide few instances indeed of men who paid, as did Santa Anna, with such long neglect and bitter loneliness for having prostituted great talents to the whims of a time-server impelled by a driving ambition.

After a short stay in Havana, the disillusioned wanderer was informed that the authorities of the island wanted him to leave. He then proceeded to Puerto Plata for a year, and finally to Nassau, in the Bahamas, where he settled down. It is not surprising that his bitterness and especial hatred were directed towards Juárez. In fact, he childishly wrote Father Fischer and urged him to secure arms and supplies from Europe in order that he, Santa Anna, might lead a new movement against the Liberals.[1] Of course, no one took the proposal seriously except a few deluded rebels, such as a small band in Jalapa, or one or two old followers, such as Giménez.[2]

In 1870, the Juárez administration found itself strong enough to grant a general amnesty to political offenders. However, Santa Anna was specifically excluded as being unfaithful and a traitor to his country. This hurt the Exile tremendously and his writings of the next few years reeked with an absorbing and incoherent hatred of "that obscure

1. Corti, *op. cit.*, II, 824.
2. Giménez, *Memorias*, p. 211. Giménez himself was in desperate financial straits. He wrote to his old master offering to come and stay with him if the latter would send transportation. Santa Anna declined with thanks, saying that his own finances were badly depleted and he hardly knew his own plans. By the end of July, 1868, Giménez applied for help to the Canon D. José Mariano Mesa, of the church at Guadalupe. The cleric found a lodging for the derelict with three respectable ladies, who gave him lodging, food and cared for his clothing for thirty-five *pesos* per month. "Ah, what a situation for a man accustomed from youth to enjoy all the good things and pleasures of life, and to give alms instead of to receive them!"

Indian, the cursed Juárez." One broadside he had printed was especially childish in its querulous, babbling inaccuracies.

And, in truth, what was left for the man? Little but memories. Only an occasional visitor lightened the tedium of the days as they turned into long weeks, monotonous months and dreary years for him to whom excitement, variety and change had been as the very breath of life. Thus passed 1871, 1872 and 1873. There were still his game cocks, but even these had lost some of their attraction. How many times the old man, now rapidly approaching fourscore, must have lived over the events of his picturesque career.

Among the fond memories was the cadet full of ambition and hope. Then came quickly the proud young cavalry officer in the north of Mexico who dashed clattering at the head of a handful of men into some peaceful village, while men, women and children, scattered like frightened chickens from their sociable market place as the ribald, haughty and fun-loving soldiery recklessly upset their wares and continued down the street with no pause except to snatch an article which attracted them, or to exchange bold glances with some flirtatious wench.

Quickly the scene faded and there appeared the face of some stolid Indian, with his age-old, impassive countenance, staring at his horny feet as he sat in the sun at the door of his one-roomed hut. His pyjama-like garb was as simple as the hut itself which was frequently no more than five by seven, or at most eight by ten, feet in size. The frame and corner poles were the cut spikes of the flowering century plant and the sides and top made of layers of grass which formed a thatch, bound in place by fiber from the century plant. The humble roof of four to six feet in height gave the whole an appearance not unlike that of a rather ambitious dog kennel built for the numerous mangy members of the canine tribe scurrying about on all sides. These, it is true, appeared to be welcomed as bed fellows, in most cases so as to add their skinny heat to that which might be conserved by the ragged clothing of their masters in the clear and piercing mountain air.

In the never ending procession of memories were the glories of past triumphs, the military entries to the Capital, the state receptions with foreign ministers and churchmen in official robes, the ceremonies in cathedrals and palaces, and the wistful faces of half-forgotten sweethearts. Then there was the life at the Clove Spike and El Encero; the wild beauties of the Plateau's edge; the buzzards with wings outspread and coasting to a hopping stop, like airplanes making a bumpy landing, on the housetops of Jalapa or Veracruz; the country sports; the Indian girls; lavish meals, and the old schemes and plots for a new ascent to power. Through it all Santa Anna had been the hero, the central figure on a really big stage. Now—memories only!

Ever and anon came letters or reports from Mexico, telling of things truly astonishing. Overshadowing all others was the unbelievable fact that Juárez remained in power. Little less incredible was the report that foreign countries considered his government stable and that North Germany, Italy and Spain had actually extended official recognition between 1869 and 1871. Reports also had it that Mexico City now had a gas lighting system and that the railroad the exile had long before supported was rapidly nearing completion.

Mingled in the reports were occasional meager crumbs of comfort that were interpreted to show that the Liberals were absolutely ruining the country. For instance, they were allowing emissaries of Protestantism to preach their heretical doctrines in the land. Also, all this ridiculous talk of public school education for all children which was the height of absurdity. Even more fantastic was the recent movement for the installation of *colegios* (upper schools) for women. Such was ruinous in itself for it could only result in foolish notions for those not able to understand or use them. And to think that such institutions were to be found (by 1874) in seven of the states as well as in the federal district!

But such ideas held only a fleeting interest. Some of the time was still taken up in completing his *Memoirs,* which he now frankly offered as recollections, saying that part of his records were destroyed by the United States troops when they invaded Mexico, and that others were lost with his baggage in New York. This last part of the *Memoirs* provides few material facts to the reader, but gives insight into the man's thinking. The signature was attached in Nassau on February 12, 1874 (just nine days before he was eighty years old), and shows the childish old man heroizing his earlier career. Two short extracts will suffice to illustrate the tone of the whole:

"Short, very short is the life of man, imperfect his works, insufficient his ability, insatiable his desires, lively his hopes, sure his suffering....

"Very few lines remain to be added to this inaccurate writing after making obvious the injustice and ingratitude of my enemies in attacking my reputation as a soldier and ruler of my native land; it being sufficient to merely mention my opportune and important services in the War of Independence, in the establishment of the Republic and in struggling against invaders even to the shedding of my own blood. But before laying down my pen I wish to record also: that I defended the Apostolic Roman Catholic Religion (the only one in which I believe and in which I must die) without being careless of the properties belonging to the Church which no one dared to touch while I was in power. Consequently I did not wound my conscience and honor by enriching myself with the spoils of the churches or the goods held in *mano muerta.*"

By this time, the hand was trembling badly and the eyesight was growing dim as cataracts slowly shut out the light.

As the last paragraphs were being written splendid news had just arrived, for now Juárez was dead, the old feud was ended and the Liberals actually extended amnesty to the old Exile.[3] Again a flurry of preparation, but how few and simple the contents of the boxes and trunks this time! On February 27, the packet boat reached Veracruz and Santa Anna immediately landed to be quietly received by a few

3. President Juárez died on July 18, 1872. At once Chief Justice Sebastián Lerdo de Tejada qualified as president, and a few months later was regularly elected to office.

House where Santa Anna died

Indian woman of Xico

old friends. The next day he took the train for Orizaba which was half way up the plateau and a good place for a man of eighty to stay for a few days in order to acclimate himself after spending his time at sea level in the tropics for practically eighteen years.

Probably it was a relief to the old man that the railroad did not go through Jalapa for then there would have been the nerve racking process of traveling for hours through country that had once been his pride, to say nothing of passing by his old homes at the National Bridge, Manga de Clavo and El Encero. On Saturday, March 7, the party again boarded the cars and were jerked along to the plateau. The peering old eyes could see little of the glories and majesty of nature on all sides, but blood, long thinned by life in the tropics and by the passage of time, felt the bracing tingle of the almost cold air as the octogenarian complainingly asked for a military great coat but petulently rejected a woolen shawl as beneath his dignity.

At 9:30 P.M. the train brought the weary party into the Buenavista station at the Capital. Some members of his family, a few of his old adherents and a small crowd of the curious were there to see the arrival. But here was no pageantry, just a slightly bewildered old man, who was still a bit afraid of trains. One or two sporadic *vivas,* counteracted by a few murmurs, and all was quiet! This was not acclaim; merely curiosity expressed before the crowd drifted off by twos and threes.

A coach was waiting, so the party got in and rattled away to No. 6 Calle Vergara right in the heart of the city.[4] The newspapers of the day reported the arrival but considered him as a relic of the past and not as having intrinsic interest for the present. The *Monitor Republicano* of March 4, 1874, commented: "In the hour of pardon and forgetfulness, Mexico does not remember the great political errors of the man who so long controlled its destinies.... The Republic today

4. This is now known as Bolivar No. 14 and only a block and a half from the famous House of Tiles (Sanborns), and two blocks from the Alameda in the direction of the Zócalo.

stands with majesty on the throne of peace, and can forget mistakes and open its doors to the one it kept in exile so long." The Church organ, *El Pájaro Verde,* was about the only newspaper that considered his doings of sufficient interest to warrant occasional news items in the ensuing few weeks.

This time there was no proclamation: experience had kept its school and the pupil had at least learned his lesson. Unfortunately, some of his friends were not so wise and a week after his arrival *El Pájaro Verde* referred to a move to try to secure a pension for the "Hero of Independence." Those who visited the limited quarters inhabited by the old General quickly realized that the once large fortune was dissipated and that actual want was in the offing.

But the social amenities must be observed and early on Monday the ninth, a note was sent to the President's palace asking when Lerdo could receive the former President. When word came back that that evening would be suitable there was much brushing up of the old uniform and painfully the trip was made. No record of the interview seems to be left, though from a newspaper account one judges it was a mere formal affair.[5] Eagerly the old friends watched and hoped for a repayment of the call, but the courtesy was not forthcoming: President Lerdo had his hands full and had no extra strength to lend to a broken reed.

A week later, a visit was made to the Shrine of Guadalupe, which Santa Anna had always held in especial veneration and had always shown a particular interest in. Giménez asserts that the neighborhood prepared to receive its old friend with music and rockets, and only desisted at Giménez's urgent representations that this might injure Santa Anna with the authorities.

Meanwhile a physician began treatments which he asserted would restore the failing eyesight. Old friends dropped in at No. 6 as did numbers of the merely curious, who called on various pretexts, but who helped to create a general air of excitement, stir and bustle. The Zócalo, Alameda, Chapultepec, and other scenes of past triumphs and glories were to be

5. *El Pájaro Verde,* March 12, 1874.

visited and mused over. Thus several weeks passed pleasantly enough.

By May, a movement was in full swing to secure the return of the confiscated estates and back military pay for the General. Hs old weakness of listening to flatterers and hangers-on arose to do him a final serious injury. The sentimental Mexicans were rather sorry for the old wreck and it was quite obvious that there would be little opposition to granting him a pension in memory of his past services so as to make his closing days comfortable. However, inspired by the old crowd, he would have none of it and insisted that he would be satisfied with nothing less than the return of the vast estates that had once been his. This aroused all the old hatreds and the *Monitor Republicano* declared that it was time to recall the record of this "pariah" who had so injured his country. It insisted that the confiscation of 1856 was "in order to pay damages to third parties who had just claims against Santa Anna, and to repay the quantities taken from the national treasury during his administration."[6]

El Pájaro Verde acted as the spokesman of Santa Anna, claiming that his property had never been actually confiscated under the laws, but had only been deposited with the Supreme Court. The months of May and June saw a long series of articles on the subject. These reviewed the early career of the fallen hero and were in the general tone of:

"THE ILLUSTRIOUS AND WELL DESERVING GENERAL SANTA-ANNA

And against whom, sirs, [is the attack made]: against the strong? No, against the disarmed athlete, against the eagle chained for nineteen years, against the weak but worthy old man, tormented in every way by an evil fate...."

The *Voz de México* echoed the articles of *El Pájaro Verde*, but it was all a case of shouting against the wind. The bill was lost in a Congress of Liberals, who were inclined to agree

6. *Monitor Republicano.* See three column editorial on front page of issue of May 6, 1874; another article on May 29, 1874; and others extending through June.

with the *Monitor* that "he is now an example of human life: a criminal who still walks the earth bearing in his conscience the mark of remorse." The writer admitted that the old general was entitled to pity, but did not think the nation could do more than pardon his crimes, lift his banishment and open the doors of his native land to the exile, who had betrayed it, bathed it in blood and left it to be tortured by the flames of civil strife.[7] Thus it was that in December Congress approved pensions for all veterans of Independence "who had in no way lent services or aid to the Intervention or the Empire."

Meanwhile an even more direct insult was aimed at the old man by the Administration. On August 23, there were elaborate exercises to commemorate the Battle of Churubusco. The President and his Cabinet took part, but the old Commander-in-chief who had led the Mexican army on that occasion, was left to his bitter ruminations in the Calle Vergara. The next day *El Pájaro Verde* gave half its front page to a letter of Santa Anna in which he lauded his own activities in the battle. It would have been a kind act if some friend had suppressed this boastful letter of a plaintive and scarcely responsible person. Such action would, at least, have left him the dignity of silence.

Now, more and more, Vergara No. 6 was deserted for days at a time. On occasions, such as his saint's day, numbers would gather to pay their respects and a few simple presents would arrive—but how pitifully few and how pitifully simple now that the flatterers knew there was no chance for him to get back his estates. Occasionally a flash would return to the once eagle eye, but as one observer noted: "the toothless, decrepit old lion had even lost his claws and the royal personality had lost the grandeur of other years."

The early efforts to restore the failing eyesight were of no avail though one account has it that a Dr. José María Bandera, who had been awarded a prize by Santa Anna when he was a young student, now visited his benefactor. After an examination, he told the general that he could remove the cataracts by an operation. Santa Anna declined saying: "If, being

7. *Ibid.*, May 28, 1874.

[360]

blind, I suffered so many ingratitudes on returning to my home land—what would I see if you again returned my sight? No, I do not wish to see; leave me sunk in darkness, I am more tranquil thus."[8]

Fortunately real destitution was averted by securing 14,000 *pesos* from the estate of Manuel Escandón in payment of notes originally totaling 25,000 *pesos*, which had been given long before in exchange for the sale of the Hacienda Paso de Varas. This removed the actual pinch of poverty, but only momentarily revived a flicker of interest. More and more the old body liked to sit and bask on the sunny side of the courtyard, while the mind dozed or caught a fleeting glimpse of past grandeur reflected from the wavering old memory's silver screen. In an occasional flare of indignation, he would declare that he was going back into exile, but Doña Tosta had no intention of seeing their small funds dissipated in such a fashion and, as though reasoning with a child, changed his mind for him.

Less and less frequently the neighbors saw him venture out for a bit of exercise. On these increasingly rare occasions, they witnessed the dim eyes peering toward the ground trying to find a safe footing for tottering steps made still more uncertain by the worn and splintered peg-leg. The waist-coat was likely to be none too clean, for even an old dandy at the age of eighty-one had trembling hands that sometimes made mistakes in handling soups and chile con carne. As the rattle and clatter of the coach of some parvenu, coming down the cobbled street, reached the pedestrian, there would be one or two hurried, perilous steps to gain the haven of a doorway. There the old eyes would flash and the old back try to straighten—but just for a minute. Suddenly the trembling figure would shrink and the tottering form would once more grope for safe spots on which to place his stick and his worn peg-leg as he realized that he was very weary and needed to be at home to rest.[9]

8. Juan de Dios Peza, *Recuerdos,* pp. 53-54.
9. Juan de Dios Peza, *Recuerdos,* pp. 54-55. At about this time, rumor makes a last reference to the martyred leg. The story goes than an "old man of the people" came one day, carrying a box, and refused to see any but

Giménez gave an account of the personal finances of Santa Anna at this time that has neither been verified or disproved.[10] However, the detail is so specific as to leave a strong impression of substantial authenticity. He stated that Doña Guadalupe, the daughter of Santa Anna who married Sr. Francisco de Paula Castro, contributed 150 *pesos* monthly to her father's expenses and that the son, José, who lived in Havana, added another fifty *pesos*. The daughter feared this would not be enough and asked Sra. Tosta, the wife of Santa Anna, to add to the sum from her quite substantial holdings. The latter, however, bluntly responded that she did not intend to beggar herself, simply to provide funds for the plunderers of her husband. Possibly the barbed shaft was intended for Giménez and his associates, and may account, in part, for his bitterness. Regardless of that, the fact was noticeable that in spite of the meager expenses of the household the fair sum recently acquired from the Escandón estate unaccountably disappeared before the General's death when his wife was apparently the only one who had access to the balance, and failed to account for it if any such balance existed.

As 1875 passed, it was more and more obvious that the end was approaching. A visitor noted that he found the General in an arm chair, crushed by weakness, despondent and carelessly dressed in soiled linens. His Most Serene Highness was now overwhelmed by senility and only aroused himself to wipe his drooling lips from time to time or to interject a guttural ejaculation when some simple pointed statement was made to compliment his conduct in the past. The past was

---

Santa Anna. After recovering from his surprise at his host's decrepit condition, he told the General that he had fought with him at Tampico and Veracruz. When the mob tore down the monument to his leg in 1855, this peasant followed the crowd as one of them till they wearied of their sport, then he secured the bones and hid them. He and his wife had treasured them for years as a sacred trust, but she had died, so now he, at last, had come to fulfil their joint desire and to deliver the remains to their life long hero. Santa Anna, in tears, responded that he could no longer express his appreciation by conferring a military promotion, or even an ounce of gold by way of reward "but I do for you that which is done for a good son," and he embraced the man and kissed him on the forehead.

10. Giménez, *Memorias,* p. 260 ff.

life: the present mere existence with which the old brain had no interest—it preferred to drowse itself away.

Vitality ebbed slowly and a profound melancholy possessed the man though the splendid physique which had for years defied climate and not a few weakening dissipations refused to give up the struggle easily. Winter turned to spring and early summer was at hand before release came. It was 1:30 A.M. on June 21, 1876, that breathing stopped. As it happened, after so long a period of decline, only his wife was present though the news soon spread. The archives of the Ayuntamiento of Mexico contain the death certificate, duly sworn to by Miguel Tosta, a brother-in-law. It laconically recorded Santa Anna's old ailment, chronic diarrhœa, as the immediate cause of death.

El Pájaro Verde and *La Voz de México* immediately published laudatory reviews of his career, praising his abilities and his contributions to the nation. Typical of their attitude is the statement: "If in his [Santa Anna's] moral character there was an inclination to love flattery, and a tendency to impose his will on others, there stood out most prominently of all his respect for Religion, his love of his native land and his passion to improve it and make it great."[11] Most of the Capital city papers carried the death notice promptly and accompanied it by graceful expressions of interest.

Before his death, the embittered old man had asked that the utmost simplicity be followed in connection with the funeral. Friends had rallied around, however, and insisted on a certain amount of dignity and recognition. A lot was secured in the cemetery of the village of his beloved Guadalupe, where was located the shrine of his peculiar devotion. On June 22 the cortege made its way from No. 6 Vergara at 8:00 A.M. to the cemetery four miles away. Though the procession passed hundreds on its way, who respectfully bowed their heads or removed their hats, this was a purely formal mark of respect paid to the passage of a corpse. Few recognized in the small group of twenty carriages, with no government officials or even troops present, the funeral party of

11. *El Pájaro Verde,* June 23, 1874.

one of the most powerful figures in Mexican history. Even the *Monitor Republicano* was inclined to take the government to task for its negligence in overlooking such a simple courtesy to a former president.

At the grave side an eloquent oration was delivered by General Santiago Blanco who summarized the spectacular career of the man who had been elected as president of his country on five separate occasions. The oration was freely commented on by the newspapers of the Capital and several of them printed it in full. Three days after the funeral the abbott and ecclesiastical cabildo at Guadalupe announced the final tribute to the departed. This took the form of a special service held on the twenty-eighth on behalf of the repose of the soul of their "worthy benefactor."

As a whole, public opinion was rather well summed up in the attitude of *El Siglo Diez y Nueve,* June 29, 1876:

"GENERAL SANTA ANNA—The last hours of his life inspire the saddest of reflections: the man who controlled millions, who acquired fortune and honors, who exercised an unrestricted dictatorship, has died in the midst of the greatest want, abandoned by all except a few of his friends who remembered him in adversity. A relic of another epoch, our generation remembered him for the misfortunes he brought upon the republic, forgetting the really eminent services he rendered to the nation. He was as a tree, stricken in years, destitute of foliage, to whose boughs even such parasites as are usually found on dry and withered trees did not cling."

The bitterest of enemies of 1855, in an inspired moment, could hardly have outlined a course of events for the ensuing twenty years as galling to a man of the peculiar nature of Antonio López de Santa Anna as those actually endured by him.

TABLE OF DATES

Birth, Feb. 21, 1794.
Entered army as cadet, June 9, 1810.
Northern campaign, 1811-21.
    Promoted to Second Lieutenant, Feb. 6, 1812.
    Promoted to First Lieutenant, Oct. 7, 1812.
Stationed at Veracruz, 1814-21.
    Bandit chasing, 1814-18.
    Promoted to Captain, Dec. 29, 1816.
    Bandit chasing and village building, 1819-20.
Joined rebels, Mar. 29, 1821.
    Promoted to Lieutenant Colonel by Viceroy, Mar. 29, 1821.
    Promoted to Colonel by rebels, Mar. 29, 1821.
Campaigns on East Coast, 1821-23.
    Promoted to Brigadier General, May, 1822.
    Break with Iturbide, Dec. 1, 1822.
    Plan of Casa Mata announced, Feb. 1, 1823.
Abdication of Iturbide, Feb. 19, 1823.
In the North, 1823.
    Sailed for Tampico, Mar. 19, 1823.
    Proclamation for a Federal Republic at San Luis Potosí, June 5, 1823.
In retirement at Jalapa, 1823-24.
Military Governor of Yucatán, 1824-25.
Country gentleman, 1825-27.
In revolt, 1828-29.
Governor of State of Veracruz, 1829.
Campaign against Spaniards at Tampico.
    Landing of Spaniards, July 16, 1829.
    Capitulation of Spaniards, Sept. 11, 1829.
In retirement, 1830-32.
    Execution of Guerrero, Feb. 14, 1831.
In rebellion, Jan., 1832.
    Triumphal entry into Mexico City, Jan. 3, 1833.
    Elected President as liberal, Apr. 1, 1833.
Turns conservative, early 1834.
    Conquest of Zacatecas, 1835.
    Texas campaign, 1836.
        Battle of the Alamo, Mar. 6, 1836.
        Battle of San Jacinto, Apr. 21, 1836.
Return to Mexico, Feb. 21, 1837.
In retirement, 1837-38.
Wounded at Veracruz by French, Dec. 5, 1838.
Acting President, Mar.-July, 1839.
    Victory at Puebla, Apr. 30, 1839.
Overthrow of Bustamante, Sept., 1841.
Dictator, Oct., 1841-45.
    Bases Orgánicas, June 13, 1843.
    Death of Doña Inés, Aug. 23, 1844.

Remarriage, Oct. 3, 1844.
General uprisings, 1844.
Exile in Havana, June, 1845-Aug., 1846.
Entrance to Mexico City, Sept. 15, 1846.
Northern campaign, 1846-47.
    From Mexico City, Sept. 28, 1846.
    Elected President, Dec. 6, 1846.
    Advance from San Luis Potosí, Jan. 28, 1847.
    Battle of Buena Vista, Feb. 22-23, 1847.
    Return to Mexico City and reorganization of government, Mar., 1847.
Eastern campaign, 1847.
    To the front, April 3, 1847.
    Battle of Cerro Gordo, April 17-18, 1847.
    Back to Mexico City, May 18, 1847.
    Scott entered Valley of Mexico, Aug., 1847.
    Armistice, Aug. 23-Sept. 7, 1847.
    Capture of Mexico City, Sept. 13, 1847.
    Ordered to give up command, Oct. 7, 1847.
Exile, 1848-53.
    To Jamaica, April 5, 1848.
    To Cartagena, Colombia, Mar. or April, 1850.
    Elected President, Mar. 17, 1853.
    Landed at Veracruz, Apr. 1, 1853.
Dictator, 1853-55.
    Inauguration, Apr. 20, 1853.
    Dictatorship officially continued, Dec. 16, 1853.
    Mesilla sale (Gadsden Purchase), 1853.
    Plan of Ayutla, Mar. 1, 1854.
    Southern campaign, Mar.-May, 1854.
    Plebiscite on continuance of Dictatorship, Dec. 1, 1854.
    Western campaign, May-June, 1855.
    Flight from Mexico City, Aug. 9, 1855.
Exile, 1855-64.
    In Colombia, 1855-58.
    In St. Thomas, 1858-64.
    Three Years War, 1857-60.
    French Intervention, 1862 ff.
    Return to Veracruz, Feb. 28, 1864.
Exile, 1864-66.
    Seward's visit, Jan., 1866.
    To New York, May 12, 1866.
In New York, May, 1866-Mar., 1867.
Last Mexican debacle.
    Sailed from New York, May 22, 1867.
    Arrested in Veracruz, June 7-8, 1867.
    Arrested in Sisal, June 12, 1867.
    Back to exile, Nov. 1, 1867.
Havana and Puerto Plata, 1867-68.
Nassau, 1868-74.
    Completion of *Memoirs*, 1874.
    Return to Mexico, Feb. 27, 1874.
To Mexico City, Mar. 7, 1874.
Death, June 21, 1876.
Funeral, June 22, 1876.

DRAMATIS PERSONAE

I

The Family:
Antonio López de Santa Anna Pérez de Lebrón, the man.
Antonio López de Santa Anna, his father.
Manuela Pérez de Lebrón, his mother.
Manuel López de Santa Anna Pérez de Lebrón, his brother.
Doña Inés García, his first wife.
Others in order of significant appearance:
Joaquín de Arredondo, commander of northern campaign.
José Dávila, Spanish commander of Veracruz.
Agustín Iturbide, sponsor of Plan of Iguala, first emperor of Mexico.
José Joaquín de Herrera, rebel leader.
Juan O'Donojú, Spanish Viceroy.
Manuel Rincón, leader of rebel forces and rival of Santa Anna.
Joel R. Poinsett, United States diplomatic agent.
Guadalupe Victoria (Manuel Felix Fernández), patriot leader of revolution and President of Mexico, 1824-29.
José Antonio de Echávarri, Captain General of province of Veracruz.
C. M. Bustamante, liberal supporter and later critic of Santa Anna.
Nicolás Bravo, patriot leader, Vice President in revolt from 1827 to 1828.
Vicente Guerrero, patriot leader, candidate for president in 1828, then secured office by force.
M. Gómez Pedraza, rival of Santa Anna, candidate for president in 1828 and declared elected.
Isidro Barradas, Spanish commander of forces invading Tampico in 1829.

II

Vicente Guerrero, President, 1829.
Anastasio Bustamante, Vice President elected 1828, in revolt Dec., 1829, President 1829-32 and 1837-39.
Joel R. Poinsett, United States diplomatic agent.
Anthony Butler, United States diplomatic agent.
Lorenzo de Zavala, Mexican liberal, later prominent in Texas.
Stephen F. Austin, Texas leader.
M. Gómez Pedraza, cat's-paw of President, 1832-33.
Valentín Gómez Farías, Vice President, 1833-34.
Mariano Arista, conservative victim of Santa Anna in 1833.
Guillermo Valle, youth befriended by Santa Anna.
Miguel Barragán, President *ad interim,* 1835-36.
Juan Álvarez, Indian, patriot leader, liberal.
Francisco García, liberal governor of Zacatecas in 1835, in Santa Anna's cabinet in 1841.
J. Antonio Mejía, filibusterer using United States as a base.

[367]

Martín P. Cos, brother-in-law of Santa Anna, defeated in Texas and later returned to Texas campaign with Santa Anna.

Samuel Houston, commander of Texas troops, later President of Texas.

William B. Travis, Texas commander at the Alamo.

James W. Fanning, Texas commander at Goliad.

José Urrea, Mexican commander at Goliad.

David G. Burnet, President of Texas.

Andrew Jackson, President of the United States.

Juan N. Almonte, aide-de-camp of Santa Anna.

José Justo Corro, President of Mexico, 1836-37.

M. M. Giménez, aide and steady supporter of Santa Anna.

Mariano Paredes y Arrillaga, Santa Anna supporter in 1840, opponent in 1843, President of Mexico, 1846.

Gabriel Valencia, Santa Anna supporter in 1840; severe critic in 1847.

James Hamilton, Texas agent.

José M. Tornel, friend of Santa Anna about 1842.

Lucas Alamán, consistent conservative and eminent historian of period.

Valentín Canalizo, Acting President in 1843-44.

José Joaquín Herrera, Acting President in 1844-45.

María Dolores Tosta, second wife of Santa Anna.

José Julián Gutiérrez, friend of Santa Anna in 1840's.

III

Valentín Gómez Farías, liberal, Vice President, 1846-47.

M. C. Rejón, friend and supporter of Santa Anna.

James K. Polk, President of the United States.

A. J. Atocha, agent of Santa Anna in Mexico and the United States.

A. S. Mackenzie, United States agent sent to see Santa Anna.

Mariano Salas, Acting President in 1846.

Zachary Taylor, United States general in northern campaign.

Winfield Scott, United States general in eastern campaign.

Pedro María Anaya, Provisional President in 1847.

Nicholas P. Trist, United States agent with Scott's army.

Gabriel Valencia, rival of Santa Anna.

Manuel de la Peña y Peña, President in 1848.

José Joaquín Herrera, President, 1848-51.

Benito Juárez, governor of Oaxaca in 1847, liberal leader of 1850's.

Jack Hays, Colonel of Texas Rangers.

Mariano Arista, President, 1851-53.

Manuel María Lombardini, supporter of Santa Anna, President in 1853.

Lucas Alamán, leader of conservatives.

Juan Álvarez, Indian leader of South, opposed Santa Anna after 1854.

José López de Santa Anna, son.

Ignacio Comonfort, liberal, opponent of Santa Anna after 1854.

G. R. Raoussett-Boulbon, French adventurer.

IV

Ignacio Comonfort, President, 1856-58.

Benito Juárez, liberal.

J. M. Gutiérrez de Estrada, Santa Anna agent in Europe.

Napoleon III of France.

Juan N. Almonte, Mexican agent in Europe, anti-Santa Anna.
M. M. Giménez, Santa Anna supporter in Mexico.
Maximilian I, Emperor of Mexico, French puppet.
William H. Seward, Secretary of State of the United States.
M. Romero, Mexican Minister at Washington.
E. P. Roe, officer commanding United States navy in Mexican waters.

V

Benito Juárez, President in 1870-72.
Sebastian Lerdo de Tejada, President in 1872-76.
M. M. Giménez, old friend.
Doña Dolores Tosta, wife.

BIBLIOGRAPHY

The following briefly descriptive bibliography is offered as an introduction to the most readily available Santa Anna material. It gives the chief volumes actually found of value and makes no effort to give the numerous titles having little or no information on the life of the Mexican leader.

The best set of published bibliographies are those in the series *Monografías Bibliográficas Mexicanas*. There are about thirty of these which emphasize certain states of the Mexican republic or special types of material on Mexico.

PRIMARY SOURCES

I. GOVERNMENT DOCUMENTS

A. MANUSCRIPTS

Consular Despatches, Havana, United States State Department Archives, especially Vols. 21 and 36. (Special reports on Santa Anna.)

Mexico, Despatches, United States State Department Archives, Vols. 1-31. (Cover years 1823-1867 and are invaluable.)

Miscellaneous Letters, United States State Department Archives, vols. for 1865-1867. (Several Santa Anna letters and others concerning him found here.)

B. PRINTED

MEXICO:

Ministerial Reports (selected reports giving information on condition of the country and on Santa Anna administrations):

Informe de la administración general de Correos...., México, 1857.

Memoria de la Secretaría de Estado y del Despacho de Relaciones..., México, 1832, and 1844.

Memoria del Secretario de Estado y del Despacho de Guerra y Marina...., México, 1844.

Esposición del Secretario de Hacienda, México, 1849, 1851, 1852, 1853, 1855.

Memoria del Ministerio de Justicia y Negocios Eclesiásticos, México, 1831, 1832, 1833, 1835, 1838, 1844, 1845, 1849, 1852.

GENERAL ITEMS:

Circulares y otras publicaciones hechas por la Legación Mexicana en Washington, durante la Guerra de Intervención, 1862-1867, México, 1868, 2 vols. (Contains number of letters from Santa Anna and correspondence concerning him.)

Dictamen de la comision especial de la Camara de Diputados del Congreso General...., México, 1851. (On Tehuantepec Affair.)

Dublán, Manuel, y Lozano, José María, *Legislación Mexicana Colección completa de los Disposiciones legislativas expedidas desde la independencia de la República,* México, 1867-79, 11 vols. (Excellent for reference.)

[370]

Romero, Manuel, editor, *Correspondencia de la Legación Mexicana en Washington durante la Intervención Extranjera, 1860-1868,* México, 1870-1892, 10 vols. (Much Santa Anna material.)

UNITED STATES:

House of Representatives (scattered material, except as indicated):
Executive Document No. 4, 29th cong., 2d. sess., Washington, 1846.
Executive Document No. 60, 30th cong., 1st sess., Washington, 1848. (Good.)
Executive Document No. 17, 39th cong., 2d session., Washington, 1867. (Especially good.)

Senate (scattered material):
Document No. 21, 33d cong., 2d sess., Washington, 1855. (Slight value.)
Document No. 25, 33d cong., 2d sess., Washington, 1855. (Slight value.)
Document No. 72, 35th cong., 1st sess., Washington, 1858.
Executive Documents Nos. 1, 52, 65, 30th cong., 1st sess., Washington, 1847. (War material, some quite good.)
Executive Document No. 20, 40th cong., 1st. sess., Washington, 1868. (Good on arrest of Santa Anna at Sisal.)
Report No. 355, 32d. cong., 1st sess., Washington, 1852.

II. LETTERS AND DIARIES

A. MANUSCRIPTS

(IN GARCIA COLLECTION EXCEPT WHERE SPECIFIED)

Alamán, Lucas, *Archivo Relativo a su historia de México, 1808-1849.* (About 200 manuscripts—a few on Santa Anna.)

Comonfort, Ignacio, *Correspondence and Papers.* (A large mass of papers and correspondence. Good for period after 1850.)

Gutiérrez, José Julian, Letters of Santa Anna to. (A few excellent letters in possession of Sr. Alberto Gutiérrez J., Jalapa, Mexico.)

Gómez Farías Papers, 1821-1857. (About 4,000 letters and papers; absolutely basic to such a study.)

Manning and MacKintosh Papers, 1847-1852. (Slight value.)

Riva Palacio Papers. (Several thousand papers covering whole period. Valuable.)

Papers of Thomas J. Rusk. (Scant value.)

Santa Anna, Documentos Relativos a A. L. de. (About 75 manuscripts and transcripts. Valuable.)

Smith, Justin H., Papers, 20 vols. (Material collected by Smith for his works on Texas and Mexican wars. Very good.)

B. PRINTED

Adams, Ephraim Douglass, editor, "Correspondence from the British Archives concerning Texas, 1837-1846," in *Southwestern Historical Quarterly,* Vol. XVII-XVIII. (Some good material.)

Aznar Barbachano, Tomás, and Garbó, Juan, *Memoria sobre a conveniencia utilidad y necesidad de origir constitucionalmente en estado de la Confederacion mexicana el antiguo Distrito de Campeche ....,* Mexico, 1861. (Some material.)

Barker, Eugene C., *The Austin Papers,* Washington, 1928. (Several items.)

Bianchi, Alberto G., translator, *Correspondencia de Juárez y Montluc, antiguo consul general de México, acompañada de numerosas cartas de personajes políticos relativas a la Expedición de Mexico, publicada por León de Montluc* . . . ., Mexico, 1905. (Scant material.)

Blackwood, Emma Jerome, *To Mexico with Scott, Letters of Captain E. Kirby Smith to his wife prepared for the press by his daughter*, Cambridge, 1917. (Good for atmosphere.)

Chabot, Frederick C., *The Perote Prisoners: Being the Diary of James L. Trueheart, Printed for the First Time, together with an Historical Introduction*, San Antonio, 1934. (A good diary for this particular subject.)

Chávez Orozco, Luis, *Un esfuerzo de México por la independencia de Cuba, con un prólogo* . . . ., Mexico, 1930. (Several items.)

—————, *La gestión diplomática del Doctor Mora* . . . ., Mexico, 1931. (Scant material.)

Clemente Vasquez, Andrés, *Bosquejo histórico de la agregación a México de Chiapas y Soconusco y de las negociaciones sobre límites entabladas por Mexico con Centro América y Guatemala*, México, 1932. (Effects of revolutions abroad.)

Corti, Egon Caesar, *Maximilian and Charlotte of Mexico*, New York, 1928. 2 vols. (Good.)

Documentos, Merida de Yucatan, 1842. (Good.)

Estrada, Genaro, *Don Juan Prim y su Labor Diplomática en México*, México, 1928. (Slight value.)

Falconer, Thomas, *Letters and Notes on the Santa Fe Expedition, 1841-1842*, New York, 1930. (Scant material.)

Garrison, George P., *Diplomatic Correspondence of the Republic of Texas*, Washington, 1908, 1911. 2 vols. (Good.)

García, Genaro, editor, *El general Paredes y Arrillaga, su gobierno en Jalisco, sus movimientos revolucionarios, sus relaciones con el general Santa Anna* . . . ., *según su propio archivo*, Mexico, 1910. (Quite good.)

—————, *La intervención francesa en México según el archivo del Mariscal Bazaine*, parts 1, 3, 4, 7, 8, 9, 10, Mexico, 1907-1910. 7 of 10 volumes. (Quite good but scattered.)

—————, *Papeles inéditos y obras selectas del Doctor Mora* . . . ., Mexico, 1906. (Scant.)

García y Pereyra, editors, *Correspondencia secreta de los principales intervencionistas mexicanas, 1860-1862*, parts 1, 2, 3, Mexico, 1905-1907. 3 vols. (Good.)

Morse, John T., Jr., *Diary of Gideon Welles, Secretary of the Navy under Lincoln and Johnson with an Introduction* . . . ., Boston, 1911, 3 vols. (Some material.)

Peña y Reyes, Antonio de la, *Algunos documentos sobra el tratado de Guadalupe y la situación de México durante la invasión americana*, Mexico, 1930. (Fair.)

—————, *Don Manuel Eduardo de Gorostiza y la cuestión de Texas. Documentos históricos precedidos de una noticia biográfica* . . . ., México, 1924. (Fair.)

—————, *El Tratado, Mon-Almonte, Colección de documentos precedida de una introducción* . . . ., Mexico, 1925. (Fair.)

—————, *Incidente Diplomatico con Inglaterra en 1843* . . . ., México, 1923. (Fair.)

—————, *Lord Aberdeen, Texas y California* . . . ., México, 1925. (Slight value.)

—————, *La Primera Guerra entre Mexico y Francia* . . . ., Mexico, 1927. (Fair.)

Pola, Angel, *Discursos y manifiestos de Benito Juárez....*, Mexico, 1905. (Fair.)

————————, *Miscelanea. Comunicados, respuestas, inciativas, dictámenes, informes, brindis....*, México, 1906. (Slight value.)

Quaife, Milo Milton, *The Diary of James K. Polk during his Presidency, 1845-1849....*, Chicago, 1910. 4 vols. (Interesting.)

Ramirez, José F., *Memorias, Negociaciones y documentos para servir a la historia de las diferencias....entre Mexico y los Estados Unidos....*, Mexico, 1853. (General.)

————————, *Mexico durante su guerra con los Estados Unidos*, Mexico, 1905. (Pro-Santa Anna.)

Ramsey, Albert C., *The Other Side: or notes for the history of war between Mexico and the United States*, New York, 1850. (Interesting.)

Rincón, Manuel, *El General Manuel Rincón justificado a los ojos de los Mexicanos imparciales de las imputaciones calumniosas y gratuitas que el escelentisimo señor General Don Manuel Gómez Pedraza le hace en su manifesto publicado en Nueva-Orleans el 17 de Marzo de 1831*, Mexico, 1831. (Good.)

Rather, Ethel Zivley, "Explanation to the Public Concerning the Affairs of Texas, by Citizen Stephen F. Austin," in *Quarterly of Texas State Historical Association*, Vol. VIII. (A few references.)

Smith, Justin H., "Letters of General Antonio López de Santa Anna Relating to the War between the United States and Mexico, 1846-1848," in *Annual Report of the American Historical Association for the Year 1917*, Washington, 1917. (Good.)

Thorndike, Rachel Sherman, *The Sherman Letters. Correspondence between General and Senator Sherman from 1837 to 1891*, New York, 1894. (Fair.)

Toro, Alfonso, *La Iglesia y el Estado en México (Estudio sobre los conflictos entre el clero católico y los gobiernos mexicanos desde lo independencia hasta nuestros dias*, México, 1927. (Anti-Church, documents.)

Williams, J. J., *The Isthmus of Tehuantepec*, New York, 1852. (Fair.)

III. MEMOIRS

A. MANUSCRIPTS

Mis Memorias. Escritas de mi puño y letra sin ayuda de nadie, en mi último destierro, in García Collection. (Excellent.)

B. PRINTED

Adorno, Juan Nepomuceno, *Análisis de los Males de México*, México, 1858. (General.)

Alamán, Lucas, *Historia de Méjico desde los primeros movimientos que preparon su independencia en el año de 1808 hasta la época presente*, Méjico, 1849-1852. 5 vols. (Excellent—Conservative.)

Almonte, Juan N., *Noticia Estadística sobre Tejas*, México, 1835. (Good —local.)

Alvarez, Francisco de Paula, *Santa-Anna hasta 1822*, Guadalajara, 1822. (Violent attack.)

Anonymous, *Historia de la revolución de México contra la dictadura del General Santa-Anna, 1853-1855*, México, 1856. (Anti-Santa Anna.)

Arista, Mariano, *Reseña historica de la revolución que desde 6 de junio hasta 8 de octubre tuvo lugar en la República el año de 1833 a favor del sistema central,* Méjico, 1835. (Good.)

Aviraneta é Ibargoyen, Eugenio de, *Mis memorias intimas, 1825-1829,* Méjico, 1906. (Good for special period.)

Benton, Thomas H., *Thirty Years' View: or History of the Working of the American Government for Thirty Years, from 1820 to 1850 . . . .,* New York, 1889. 2 vols. (Some material—special interest only.)

Blanchard, P. and Dauzats, A., *San Juan de Ulùa ou relacion de l'expédition Francaise au Mexique sous les ordes de M. le Contre-Amiral Baudin,* Paris, 1839. (Good for special topic.)

Bocanegra, José María, *Memorias para la historia de México independiente, 1822-1846,* México, 1892-97. 2 vols. (Pro-Santa Anna. Many documents.)

Bustamante, Carlos María, *Apuntes para la historia del gobierno del general D. Antonio López de Santa Anna, desde principios de octubre de 1841 hasta 6 de diciembre de 1844 . . . .,* México, 1845. (Good.)

———, *Cuadro histórico de la revolución de la América Mexicana,* México, 1821-27. 5 vols. (Good.)

———, *El Gabinete mexicano durante el segundo período de la administración del Exmo. señor Presidente D. Anastasio Bustamante, hasta la entrega del mando al Exmo. señor Presidente Interino D. Antonio López de Santa-Anna . . . .,* México, 1842. 2 vols. (Continues *Cuadro Histórico.* Good.)

———, *Historia del emperador D. Augustín de Iturbide hasta su muerte, y sus consecuencias: y el establecimiento de la República popular federal,* México, 1846. (Good.)

———, *Memorias para la historia de la invasión española sobre la costa de Tampico de Tamaulipas hecha en el año de 1829 . . . .,* México, 1831. (Pro-Santa Anna.)

———, *El Nuevo Bernal Díaz del Castillo, ó sea Historia de la invasión de los Angló-Americanos en México.* México, 1847. 2 vols. (Good.)

C(alderon) de la B(arca), Madame, *Life in Mexico,* London, 1843. (Good on political and social conditions of early 1840's.)

Caro, Ramón Martinez, *Verdadera idea de la primera campaña de Tejas y sucesos ocurridos después de la acción de San Jacinto,* México, 1837. (Anti-Santa Anna, by his secretary on the campaign.)

Ciudadano que no Tomó la mínima parte en aquellos acontecimientos, *Pronunciamiento de Perote por el General Antonio López de Sta. Anna, y sucesos de su campaña hasta la derogación de la ley que lo proscribió,* México, 1829. (Possibly written by Tornel. Pro-Santa Anna.)

Dios Peza, Juan de, *Recuerdos de mi vida. Cuentos, diálogos y narraciones anecdóticos é históricos,* México, 1907. (A few early recollections and impressions.)

Escudero, J. A., *Memorias del Diputado por el Estado de Chihuahua, ... con documentos justificativos . . . . para la historia del Congreso Constituyente mexicano del año de 1847,* México, 1848. (General.)

Filisola, Vicente, *Memorias para la historia de la Guerra de Tejas,* México, 1849. 2 vols. in 1. (Many documents—excellent.)

———, *Memorias para la historia de la Guerra de Tejas, por el General de división y actual Presidente del supremo Tribunal de guerra y marina de la República,* México, 1848-49. 2 vols. (Precedes the work listed above—excellent.)

Giménez, Manuel María, *El Conde Raousset-Boulbon en Sonora. Relación inédita,* México, 1905. (Edited by Genaro García. Good for this special topic.)

————————, *Memorias del Coronel Manuel María Giménez, Ayudante de Campo del General Santa Anna, 1798-1878*, México, 1911. (Edited by Genaro García. Pro-Santa Anna, by a close friend.)

Gilliam, Albert M., *Travels over the Table Lands and Cordilleras of Mexico. During the Years 1843 and 1844*, Philadelphia, 1846. (Violently anti-Santa Anna. Some facts of value.)

Grant, U. S., *Personal Memoirs of U. S. Grant*, New York, 1885. 2 vols. (Slight value.)

Kuykendall, J. H., editor, "Reminiscences of Early Texans. A Collection from the Austin Papers," in *Quarterly of Texas Historical Association*. Vols. VI-VII. (Special interest only.)

Lemprière, Charles, *Notes in Mexico in 1861 and 1862: Politically and Socially Considered*, London, 1862. (General.)

Lerdo de Tejada, Sebastián, *Memorias de D. Sebastian Lerdo de Tejada*, Guadalajara, 1911. (Recent period only—general.)

Mora, José María Luis, *Méjico y sus revoluciones*, Paris, 1836. 4 Vols. (Last volume good for early period of Santa Anna.)

Peña y Reyes, Antonio de la, *Comentarios de Francisco Zarco sobre la Intervención Francesca (1861-1863)*, México, 1929. (Little on Santa Anna.)

Poinsett, J. R., *Notes on Mexico, made in the autumn of 1822, accompanied by an historical sketch of the Revolution, and translations of official reports on the present state of that country*, London, 1825. (Good but general.)

Portilla, Anselmo de la, *Historia de la Revolución de México, 1853-1855*, México, 1856. (Anti-Santa Anna.)

————————, *Méjico en 1856 y 1857. Gobierno del General Comonfort*, Nueva York, 1858. (Anti-Santa Anna.)

Prieto, Guillermo, *Memorias de mis Tiempos, 1828 a 1840*, Paris and México, 1906. (Good on general conditions.)

————————, *Memorias de mis Tiempos, 1840 a 1853*, Paris and México, 1906. (Anti-Santa Anna.)

Raines, C. W., editor, *Six Decades in Texas or Memoirs of Francis Richard Lubbock, Governor of Texas in War-Time, 1861-63, A Personal Experience in Business, War and Politics*, Austin, 1900. (A few references of value.)

Ruxton, George F., *Adventures in Mexico and the Rocky Mountains*, London, 1847. (Observations of a shrewd observer.)

Santa Anna, Antonio López de, *Apelación al buen criterio de los nacionales y estrangeros. Informe que el Escmo. Sr. General de División, benemerito de la patria D..... dio por acuerdo de la sección del gran jurado, sobre las acusaciones presentados por el señor diputado Don Ramón Gamboa*, México, 1849. (Santa Anna's apology with documents—valuable.)

————————, *Las Guerras de México con Tejas y los Estados Unidos*, México, 1910. (A collection of documents and manifestos—the work of Genaro García. Most valuable.)

————————, *Mi Historia Militar y Política, 1810-1874*, México, 1905. (Memoirs edited by Genaro García. Excellent.)

Santangelo, Orazio Donato Gideon de Attellis, *Statement of facts relating to the claims of....a citizen of the United States, on the Government of the Republic of Mexico....*, Washington, 1841. (A few letters of Santa Anna included.)

Sheridan, P. H., *Personal Memoirs of....General United States Army*, New York, 1888. 2 vols. (A few interesting facts.)

Sherman, W. T., *Memoirs of General William T. Sherman*, second edition, New York, 1889. 2 vols. (Of special interest only.)

[375]

Smith, S. Compton, *Chile con Carne; or the Camp and the Field*, New York, 1857. (Interesting on period of 1840's.)

Suárez y Navarro, Juan, *Historia de México y del General Antonio López de Santa Anna. Comprende los acontecimientos políticos que han tenido lugar en la Nación, desde el año de 1821 hasta 1848*, México, 1850. (Pro-Santa Anna.)

——————, *Historia de México y del General Antonio López de Santa-Anna*, México, 1851. Vol II of above. Only known copy is in García Collection.)

Smither, Harriet, editor and translator, "Life of Santa Anna" in *Papers of Mirabeau B. Lamar. Edited from the Original Papers in the Texas State Library*, Austin, Vol. VI. (Violently anti-Santa Anna.)

Thompson, Waddy, *Recollections of Mexico*, New York, 1846. (General sketch—Pro-Santa Anna.)

Tornel y Mendivil, José María, *Breve Reseña Histórica de los acontecimientos más notables de la Nación mexicana, desde el año de 1821 hasta nuestros días*, México, 1852. (Pro-Santa Anna.)

Tudor, Henry, *Narrative of a Tour in North America: comprising Mexico, the mines of Real del Monte, the United States, and the British colonies: with an excursion to the Island of Cuba*, London, 1834. 2 vols. (Some good description and observations.)

Vidal y Rivas, Luis G. de, *Biographie du General Antonio López de Santa-Anna*, Paris, 1863. (Pro-Santa Anna, by his father-in-law who also acted as his private secretary in 1860's.)

Ward, H. G., *Mexico*, second edition, London, 1829. 2 vols. (By British *Chargé d'Affaires*. General, a few good references.)

Wilson, Robert A., *Mexico and its Religion, with Incidents of travel, 1851-54*, New York, 1855. (Of general interest—anti-Roman Catholic.)

Winkler, E. W., editor, "Reminiscences of Sion R. Bostick," in *Quarterly of Texas Historical Association*. Vol. V. (Editorial comments—excellent.)

IV. NEWSPAPERS AND PERIODICALS

A. CONTEMPORARY

Boletín, Puebla, 1844-45, scattered numbers. (Anti-Santa Anna.)

Boletín de Noticias, México, 1841-45, broken files. (Anti-Santa Anna.)

Boletín Oficial, México, 1838-60, scattered numbers. (Attitude varied with administration.)

Gaceta del Gobierno Imperial de México, Mexico, 1822. (Some good material.)

Edinburgh Review, Edinburgh, 1832-58. (Occasional reports only.)

La Marimba, México, 1832. (C. M. Bustamante, editor, Anti-Santa Anna.)

Monitor Republicano, México, 1874-76. (Critical of Santa Anna.)

Mosquito Mexicano, México, 1834-43. (Files almost complete. Pro-Santa Anna.)

La Nacionalidad, Guanajuato, 1855-56. (A liberal paper.)

Niles Weekly Register, containing political, historical . . . . documents, essays, and facts . . . . and a record of the events of the times, Baltimore, 1820-48 and Philadelphia, 1848-49. (Some excellent material and documents.)

La Orquesta. Periódico omniscio, de buen humor y con caricaturas, México, 1863-67. (Conservative but anti-Santa Anna—some good cartoons.)

El Pájaro Verde, México, 1874-76. (Pro-Church; pro-Santa Anna.)

Periódicos de Méjico, Diversos. Published from 1820 to 1900. 3 bound volumes in García Collection.

Political Broadsides, mostly for 1830-55, but some later. Nearly all libraries have some of these.

Quarterly Review, London, 1829-51. Continued as *London Quarterly Review,* New York, 1852-67. (Some good items.)

El Siglo Diez y Nueve, México, 1843-45; 1876. (Anti-Santa Anna in 1840's.)

El Telégrafo. Periódico oficial del Gobierno de los Estados Unidos Mexicanos, México, 1833-34.

La Voz de Iturbide, Guanajuato, 1856-1857. (A liberal paper.)

Voz de la Patria, México, 1829-1831. (Edited and written by C. M. Bustamante. Really a history of Mexico in the 1820's.)

Westminster Review, London, 1824-1914. (A few articles of value.)

B. RECENT

Boletín de la Sociedad Mexicana de Geografía y Estadística, México, 1852-1918. (Articles of considerable value.)

Quarterly of Texas State Historical Association—See *Southwestern Historical Quarterly.*

Southwestern Historical Quarterly, Austin, 1897-1935. (Numerous articles of great value.)

The Texas Magazine, Austin and Dallas, 1896-1897. (Contains some excellent material, notably C. W. Raines, "Life of Antonio López de Santa Anna.")

Todo—Semanario Enciclopédico, México, 1934-1935. (Contains articles and documents of much value.)

V. PAMPHLETS

Chiefly Controversial

Anonymous, *La escelentísima señor doña Inés García de Santa Anna, digna esposa del supremo magistrado de la nación. . . . y la Puebla que habría querido inspirale vida, llena de sentimiento vió su muerte el día 23 de Agosto de 1844 . . . .,* no place or date of publication. (Praise of Sra. Santa Anna.)

—————, *La Guerra de Tejas sin máscara,* México, 1845. (Violently anti-Santa Anna.)

—————, *Historia de la Orden Mexicana de Nuestra Señora de Guadalupe,* México, 1854. (Special topic treated—pro-Santa Anna.)

—————, *El Partido Conservador en México,* México, 1855. (Anti-Santa Anna.)

—————, *Tiembla la fación tirana, porque ya volvió Santa-Anna,* México, 1837. (Pro-Santa Anna.)

B[ustamante], C. M., *Carta de un diputado del congreso de la Unión al General Don Antonio López de Santa Anna,* 1832 [?]. (Some material.)

—————,*Invasión de México por D. Antonio López de Santa Anna,* México, 1832. (Anti-Santa Anna.)

Barriero, Miguel, *Resúmen instructivo, que publica el comisario de división del Exército de Operaciones sobre Tejas . . . .,* Matamoros, 1837. (Shows conditions in army.)

García y Cubas, Antonio, *Noticias Geográficas y estadísticas de la República mexicana,* México, 1857. (Statistical—good.)

Haro y Tamariz, Antonio de, *Esposición . . . . sobre la monarquía constitucional,* Paris, 1846. (Shows ideas of the time.)

Pacheco, José Ramón, *Exposición del Ex-Ministro de Relaciones con motivo de la communicación oficial que, acerca de las conferencias tenidas....con el comisionado de los Estados-Unidos....* Querétaro, 1847. (Defense of Santa Anna.)

S[antangelo, Orazio Donato Gideon de Attellis], *The Two or Three Millions. No Appropriation Recommended*, Dated February 7, 1847. (Anti-Polk. One letter of Santa Anna given.)

Sierra y Rosso, Ignacio, *Discurso que por encargo de la junta patriótica pronunció el en panteón de Santa Paula el ciudadano....en la colocación del pie que perdió en Veracruz el Esmo....D. Antonio López de Santa Anna ....,* México [?], 1842. (Beyond comment.)

Un Mejicano [J. N. Almonte], *Breve refutación al memorandum del General D. Ignacio Comonfort, Ex-Dictador de la República Mejicana, y la obra encomiástica de su gobierno, escrita por el señor D. Anselmo de la Portilla ....,* New York, 1859. (A few references of value.)

SECONDARY MATERIAL

I. SPECIAL STUDIES

Adams, E. D., *British Interests and Activities in Texas, 1838-1846*, Baltimore, 1910. (Good for special field.)

Barker, Eugene C., "The San Jacinto Campaign," *Quarterly of Texas State Historical Association*. Vol. IV. (A critical study with valuable documents.)

————, "The Tampico Expedition," *Quarterly of Texas State Historical Association*. Vol. VI. (A valuable critical study.)

Callcott, W. H., *Church and State in Mexico, 1822-1857*, Durham, 1926. (A special treatment of the Church question.)

Callahan, James Morton, "Evolution of Seward's Mexican Policy," *West Virginia University Studies in American History*, Series I, No. 4-6. (Little on Mexico.)

Cleland, Robert Glass, "The Early Sentiment for the Annexation of California: an Account of the Growth of American Interest in California, 1835-1846," *Southwestern Historical Quarterly*, Vol. XVIII. (A few references to Santa Anna.)

Garber, Paul Neff, *The Gadsden Treaty*, Philadelphia, 1924. (Contains some good material for 1853-55.)

Galarza, Ernest, *The Roman Catholic Church as a Factor in the Political and Social History of Mexico*, Sacramento, 1928. (Considers Santa Anna the tool of the Church.)

Galindo y Galindo, Miguel, *La Gran Década Nacional ó Relación histórica de la Guerra de Reforma, intervención extranjera y gobierno del Archiduque Maximiliano, 1857-1867*, México, 1904-6, 3 vols. (A detailed study of the period—a little on Santa Anna.)

Hancock, Walter Edgar, *The Career of General Antonio López de Santa Anna (1794-1833)*, (MS, Ph. D. thesis), University of Texas Library, 1933. (A mass of manuscript on early period.)

Mateos, Juan Antonio, *Historia parlamentaria de los congresos mexicanos de 1821 a 1857*, México, 1877-86. 11 vols. in 5. (Some good material.)

McBride, George McCutchen, *The Land System of Mexico*, New York, 1923. (Good on special field.)

Perkins, Dexter, *The Monroe Doctrine*, 1826-67. (A few good comments on European contacts.)

Rather, Ethel Zivley, "Recognition of the Republic of Texas by the United States" in *Quarterly of Texas Historical Association*, Vol. XIII. (A few good references on Santa Anna.)

Reeves, Jesse S., *American Diplomacy under Tyler and Polk*, Baltimore, 1907. (A few special references.)

Rives, George Lockhart, *The United States and Mexico, 1821-1848. A History of the Relations between the two Countries from the independence of Mexico to the close of the War with the United States*, New York, 1913. 2 vols. (Some good material.)

Smith, Justin H., *The Annexation of Texas*, New York, 1919. (Excellent research on this special topic.)

Turner, F. H., "The Mejía Expedition," *Quarterly of Texas Historical Association*. Vol. VII. (Special interest only.)

Valle, Adrián del, *Historia Documentada de la conspiración de la Gran Legión del Águila Negra*, Habana, 1930. (Special interest.)

Williams, Amelia, "A Critical Study of the Siege of the Alamo and of the personnel of its Defenders," in *Southwestern Historical Quarterly*, Vol. XXXVI-XXXVII. (Good.)

Wyllys, Rufus Kay, *The French in Sonora (1850-1854). The Story of French Adventures from California into Mexico*. 1932. (Special interest—good.)

II. BIOGRAPHIES

Alvarez, Melchor, *Historica documentada de la vida pública del Gral. José Justo Alvarez . . . . de la guerra de reforma*, Mexico, 1905. (Later period.)

Anonymous, *Biografía del general Santa-Anna, y convenio secreto que celebró con el presidente de los Estados Unidos. O sean apuntes históricos para tenerlos presentes el hacer el congreso la elección de presidente de la República*, México, 1847. (Anti-Santa Anna. Pamphlet.)

Barker, Eugene C., *The Life of Stephen F. Austin, Founder of Texas, 1793-1836, a Chapter in the Westward Movement of the Anglo-American People*, Nashville and Dallas, 1925. (Good—special interest.)

Bancroft, Frederick, *The Life of William H. Seward*, New York and London, 1900. 2 vols. (Slight reference to Santa Anna.)

Beals, Carleton, *Porfirio Díaz, Dictator of Mexico*, Philadelphia, 1932. (Slight reference to Santa Anna.)

Bulnes, Francisco, *Juárez, el verdadero, y la verdad sobre la intervención y el imperio*, Paris, 1904. (Slight value.)

García, Genaro, *La autobiografía del Gral. D. Antonio López de Santa Anna*, MS. (Manuscript notes of García for a biography. Excellent. In García Collection.)

Hanighen, Frank C., *Santa Anna, The Napoleon of the West*, New York, 1934. (Very good interpretation.)

James, Marquis, *The Raven, A Biography of Sam Houston*, Indianapolis, 1929. (Special interest only.)

Jones, Charles C., *The Life and Services of Commodore Josiah Tattnall*, Savannah, 1878. (Special interest only.)

Méndez, Lic. Eugenio, "Santa Anna el Anormal," in *Todo, Semanario Enciclopédico*, 1934. (A special interpretation. Several suggestive articles.)

Navarro y Rodrigo, Carlos, *Iturbide*, Madrid, 1869. (Anti-Santa Anna.)

—————, *Vida de Agustín de Iturbide. Memorias de Agustín de Iturbide*, Madrid, 1919. (Anti-Santa Anna.)

Pola, Angel, *Benito Juárez, exposiciones (como se gobierna). Biografía por Anastasio Zerecero*, México, 1902. (Little material on Santa Anna.)

Raines, C. W., "Life of Antonio López de Santa-Anna," *Texas Magazine.* Vols. I-III. (Good. Very little on later career.)

Rippy, J. Fred, *Joel R. Poinsett, Versatile American*, Durham, 1935. (Material for the 1820's.)

Rowland, Kate Mason, "General John Thomson Mason. An Early Friend of Texas, *Quarterly of Texas State Historical Association.* Vol. XI. (Slight value.)

Salado Alvarez, V., *La Vida Azarosa y Romántica de Don Carlos María de Bustamante*, Madrid, 1933. (Good—general.)

Sierra, Justo, *Juárez, su obra y su tiempo*, México, 1905-1906. (Good—general.)

Villa-Amor, Manuel, *Biografía del General Santa-Anna aumentada con la segunda parte*, Mexico, 1857. (A brief sketch—pamphlet.)

Wharton, Clarence R., *El Presidente. A Sketch of the Life of General Santa Anna*, Houston, 1924. (Superficial—some good suggestions.)

Zayas Enríquez, Lic. Rafael de, *Benito Juárez, su Vida—su Obra*, Mexico, 1906. (Special interest only.)

III. GENERAL HISTORIES

Ancona, Eligio, *Historia de Yucatán desde la epoca más remota hasta nuestros días*, Mérida, 1878-80. 4 vols. (Anti-Santa Anna. Special interest.)

Arrangoiz, D. Francisco de Paula de, *Méjico desde 1808 hasta 1867. Relación de los principales acontecimientos políticos que han tenido lugar desde la prisión del virey Iturrigaray hasta la caida del segundo imperio . . . .*, Madrid, 1871-72, 4 vols. (Conservative. Anti-Santa Anna.)

Bancroft, Hubert Howe, *History of the Pacific States of North America: History of Mexico*, San Francisco, 1883-88. Vols. IV-IX. (Excellent.)

—————, *History of the Pacific States of North America: Texas*, San Francisco, 1889. Vol. XI. (Excellent—special interest.)

Cuevas, el P. Mariano, S. J., *Historia de la Iglesia en México*, El Paso, 1928. 5 vols. (Account of an ardent churchman.)

F. L. . . . ., Chevalier de la Legion d'Honneur, *Le Mexique, Études Historiques au Point de vue Politique et Social*, Paris, 1859. (General.)

Foote, Henry Stuart, *Texas and the Texans; or advance of the Anglo-Americans to the Southwest, including a history of the leading events in Mexico . . . .*, Philadelphia, 1841. 2 vols. (Some good documents.)

Herrera Moreno, Enrique, *El Cantón de Córdoba, Apuntes de Geografía Estadística, Historia*, etc., Córdoba, 1892. (General.)

Kennedy, William, *Texas: The Rise, Progress and Prospects of the Republic of Texas*, London, 1841. 2 vols. (Good—special interest.)

Lerdo de Tejada, Miguel M., *Apuntes Históricos de la Heroica Ciudad de Vera Cruz, precedidos de una noticia de los descubrimientos hechos en las islas y en el continente Americano y de las providencias dictadas por los reyes de Espana para el gobierno de sus nuevas posesiones, desde el primer viaje de don Cristóbal Colón, hasta que se emprendió la conquista de México*, México, 1850-58. 3 vols. (Excellent.)

Mayer, Brantz, *Mexico, Aztec, Spanish and Republican*: *A historical, geographical, political, statistical and social account of that country from the period of the invasion by the Spaniards to the present time; with a view of the ancient Aztec Empire and civilization; a historical sketch of the late war; and notices of New Mexico and California,* Hartford, 1853, 2 vols. (General.)

Moore, John Bassett, *A digest of international law as embodied in diplomatic discussions, treaties and other international agreements, international awards . . . , and especially in documents, published and unpublished, issued by presidents and secretaries of state of the United States . . . .* Washington, Government Printing Office, 1906. 8 vols. (Special interest.)

Muro, Manuel, *Historia de San Luis Potosí,* San Luis Potosí, 1910, 3 vols. (Special interest.)

Pérez Verdía, Luis, *Compendio de la Historia de Mexico . . . ,* Paris, 1911. (General.)

Rivera, Agustín, *Anales Mexicanos; La Reforma y el Segundo Imperio,* México, 1904. (General.)

Rivera, Manuel, *Historia Antigua y Moderna de Jalapa y de las Revoluciones del Estado de Veracruz,* Mexico, 1867-71. 5 vols. (Excellent—general.)

————, *Los gobernantes de Méjico . . . . ,* Méjico, 1872-73, 2 vols. (General.)

Sierra, Lic. D. Justo, editor, *México, Su Evolución Social. Síntesis de la historia política, de la organización administrativa y militar y del estado económico de la federación mexicana; de sus adelantamientos en el orden intelectual . . . ,* México, 1900-2. 2 vols. (Good, Anti-Santa Anna.)

Yoakum, H., *History of Texas from it first settlement in 1685 to its annexation to the United States in 1846,* New York, 1856, 2 vols. (Good—special interest.)

Zamacois, Niceto de, *Historia de Méjico desde sus tiempos más remotos hasta nuestros dias . . . ,* 23 vols., Barcelona, 1878-1903. (Good—many documents.)

IV. MISCELLANEOUS

Azcoitia, Francisco X, *Breve Reseña Histórica de la Ciudad de Xalapa,* Xalapa, 1934. (Special interest only. Pamphlet.)

————, *Paginas de la História de Xalapa,* Xalapa, 1933. (Special interest only. Pamphlet.)

Bassols, Narciso, *Valentín Gómez Farías, discurso pronunciado el 5 de Julio de 1933, en la Cámara de Diputados, en ocasión del translado de los restos del Patricio a la Rotunda de los Hombres Ilustres.* México, 1933. (General. Pamphlet.)

Bulnes, Francisco, *Las Grandes Mentiras de Nuestra Historia. La Nación y el Ejército en las guerras extranjeras.* Paris and Mexico, 1904. (Violently anti-Santa-Anna.)

Ferry, Gabriel, *Les Revolutions du Mexique,* Paris, 1864. (General.)

Gómez Farías y la Reforma Educativa de 1833, Mexico, 1933. (Special interest only. Pamphlets.)

INDEX

Bravo, Nicolás, joins rebels, 1822; 42-43; on triumvirate, 48; demands expulsion of Poinsett, 62; in exile, 66; as executive, 164, 183, 189, 194; joins revolt, 210; Plan of Ayutla, 307; death, 308.

Buena Vista, *see* Angostura.

Bulnes, Francisco, on Mexicans, 117.

Burnet, D. G., 142 ff.

Bustamante, Anastasio, Vice President, 81; and Santa Anna, 82; troubles, 88 ff.; returns from North, 94; agreement at Zavaleta, 95; President, 155, 160; to fight rebels, 161-64; fear of Santa Anna, 165; dissatisfaction with, 171; overthrow, 173-74.

Bustamante, Carlos María, joins Santa Anna, 21; proclamation written by, 24; criticism of Santa Anna, 31; on revolution of 1828, 66, 68; on Spaniards at Tampico, 72; on conditions, 1839, 161; cited, 172, 176, 215, 226; on Santa Anna, 1843, 195.

Butler, Anthony, to Mexico, 85; on Santa Anna, 85-86; mentioned, 93; on Gómez Farías, 100; on Santa Anna, 111-12.

Calderón, Gen. José, campaign from Perote to Oaxaca, 68 ff.; campaign of 1832, 90 ff.

Calderón, de la Barca, Madame, on Santa Anna at home, 165-66; on Bustamante, 167; cited, 171, 185.

Callcott, W. H., cited, 249, 255.

Campbell, R. B., 228.

Campeche, 53.

Canalizo, Valentín, President *ad interim,* 196 ff.; trouble with Congress, 206; overthrow, 207-8.

Caro, R. M., on Alamo, 131; cited, 144.

Casa Mata, Plan of, publication, 46; Congress and, 48.

Cayetano Portugal, Juan, 112.

Ceballos, Juan Bautista, 279-80; declines membership in Order of Guadalupe, 291-92.

Cerro Gordo, Battle of, 259-60.

Chabot, F. C., cited, 181.

Chapultepec, battle, 269.

Charleston Mercury, cited, 180.

Chávez Orozco, Luis, cited, 55.

Chiapas, joins rebels, 92.

Chihuahua, anti-Santa Anna, 97.

Chilpanzingo, 308, 311.

Cholera, in 1833, 104.

Churubusco, battle, 267.

Clergy, attitude to Spain, 1821, 18; restrictions, 1833, 100; California missions secularized, 104-5; support Santa Anna, 111-13, 119; *fueros* returned, 113; support Santa Anna, 177; control, 192; oppose forced loan, 248-49, 254; and Santa Anna, 255-56; on Arista, 279; on Santa Anna, 286-87; Santa Anna aids, 293-94; penalized, 320; in Three Years War, 326; Santa Anna on, in last will, 356.

Coahuila, conditions critical, 1812, 10; mentioned, 12.

Comonfort, Ignacio, Plan of Ayutla, 306-7; in West, 313; President, 319-20; conservative, 323.

Concha, Manuel, death, 32.

Conner, David, order to pass Santa Anna through blockade, 235-36, 238.

Constitution of 1857, drawn up, 320-21.

Contreas, battle, 267.

Córdoba, city, joins rebels, 19, 21; Santa Anna retreats to, 26.
Córdoba, Treaty of, framed, 27-28; repudiated, 31.
Corro, José Justo, President *ad interim*, 120, 150.
Corti, Egon Caesar, cited, 324, 327.
Cos, Martín P., brother-in-law of Santa Anna, 124; to Texas, 125.
Country life and sports in Veracruz, 57 ff.
Cuernavaca, conservative, 1833, 110-11.
Cuevas, Mariano, S. J., cited, 231, 256.

Dávila, General José, Governor of port of Veracruz, 13, 17, 25, 26; to San Juan de Ulloa, 29.
Dios Peza, Juan de, cited, 361.
Dúran, General Gabriel, mentioned, 101.
Durango, mentioned, 91, 244.

Echáverri, José Antonio, Captain General of Veracruz, 38; relations with Santa Anna, 38-39.
Elías, Bernabé, clash with Santa Anna, 32-33; clash with Iturbide, 42.
Elizondo, Ignacio, in North, 8-9.
Ellis, Powhatan, on Santa Anna, 150.
El Encero, mentioned, 24, 84-85; Santa Anna to, 203; description, 204-5, 217; headquarters, 257.
England (*see* Great Britain).
Escudero, Manuel, cited, 248.

Fernández, Manuel Félix, *see* Victoria, Guadalupe.
Fanning, James W., surrender, 132.
Fijo de Veracruz, Santa Anna as cadet, 5; attitude of officers, 12.
Filisola, Vicente, cited, 11; on Texas conditions, 134; in Texas, 140-42.
Foote, H. S., cited, 87.
Forsyth, John, 323-24.
France, views on Cuba, 1823, 54; protests atrocities in Texas, 134; Pastry War, 155 ff.; peace, 161; on Raousset, 300.

Gadsden, James, Mesilla Purchase, 294-96; on Santa Anna, 302, 310.
Galarza, E., cited, 311.
García, Francisco, Governor of Zacatecas, 114-16; restless, 171; in cabinet, 182.
Garrison, G. P., cited, 146, 149, 164, 190.
García, Genaro, editor, cited, 189, 326, 334, 339.
Garza, Jaime, loan to Santa Anna, 12, 17.
Giménez, M. M. Raousset, 300-1; in 1864, 332, 334-35; a derelict, 353; on last days of Santa Anna, 361-62.
Goliad, surrender of Fannin, 132; massacre, 133.
Gómez Farías, Fermín, on conditions, 214, 223; conspirators arrested, 235.
Gómez Farías, Valentín, for Vice Presidency, 96-97; fear of, 98; acting President, 98 ff.; rift with Santa Anna, 108; to exile, 110; in touch with affairs, 121; on Texas revolt, 122; return to Mexico, 154; restless, 167-68; in exile, 199-200; approached by Santa Anna, 223, 226; elected Vice President, 246; Acting President, 247 ff.; raising funds, 248-50, 254; repudiated, 256.
Gómez Farías Papers, cited, 36, 38, 98, 99, 100, 101, 121, 215, 223, 226, 229, 235, 248, 255.
Gómez Pedraza, Manuel, mentioned, 61; election as President, 64; overthrow, 69; again endorsed, 92; as cat's-paw, 93-95; as President, 96 ff.; in opposition, 197.

Great Britain, mentioned, 5; on Cuba, 54; protests atrocities in Texas, 134; on California, 179; on Texas, 189-90; and Santa Anna, 1846, 228-29, 233; newspaper opinion, 234, 239-40.
Guadalajara, joins rebels, 1823, 46; in revolt, 1840, 171; in revolt, 1852, 280; to continue dictatorship, 294.
Guadalupe, Order of, organized, 35; re-established, 291.
Guanajuato, anti-Santa Anna, 97; supports Santa Anna, 244.
Guerrero, Vicente, acclaim of Iturbide, 34; joins rebels, 42-43; mestizo vs. creole, 60-61; on masonry, 61-62; election of 1828, 64; victory, 69-70; on Santa Anna at Tampico, 76, 78; support of Santa Anna, 83-84; collapse, 83; capture and death, 86.
Gutiérrez, J. J., mentioned, 188; letters to, 216-17.
Gutiérrez de Estrada, J. M., in Europe, 326 ff.
Guzmán, Valentino, mentioned, 15.

Hamilton, James, on Santa Anna, 164; bribe for Santa Anna, 179-80.
Hancock, W. E., cited, 8.
Haro y Tamariz, A., in cabinet, 287; resignation, 288.
Harrisburg, Texas government in, 134.
Hays, Jack, 273-75.
Herrera, José Joaquín de, rebellion, 20-21; as executive, 202, 208, 223 ff.; resigns, 227; election, 274, 279.
Hidalgo y Costillo, Father Miguel, mentioned, 6, 7, 10, 12.
Hill, John, 181.
Houston, General Samuel, retreats in Texas, 131-34; at San Jacinto, 135-37; and Santa Anna as a captive, 139-46; wounded, 139, 142.
Hughes, George W., 274-75.

Iguala, Plan of, announcement, 19; mentioned, 27.
Iturbide, Agustín, Plan of Iguala, 19; plan for rebellion, 27; Treaty of Córdoba, 27-28; acquires the crown, 29, 31; suspicious of Santa Anna, 30, 33, 39-41; coronation, 35; rebellion, 41 ff.; overthrow, 46-47.
Iturbide, Doña Nicolasa, courtship of Santa Anna, 32, 37.
Iturrigaray, José de, Viceroy, 1803-8, 6.

Jackson, Andrew, on Santa Anna, 146, 149.
Jalapa, name and climate, 3; spirit of independence, 6; Plan of Iguala, 19; forced loan, 22; geography, 22-23; quarrel with Santa Anna, 23, 32-33, 71; defeat of Santa Anna, 45; hails Santa Anna, 105; conservative, 110; Santa a prisoner in, 214; reception, 241.
Jalisco, dissatisfied, 1831, 86, 91; supports Santa Anna, 244.
Jones, C. C., cited, 151.
Juárez, Benito, Governor of Oaxaca, 272; dislike of Santa Anna, 273; in exile, 289; in Three Years War, 321, 325-26; supported by Seward, 341-43; President, 347, 353; reforms and progress, 355; death, 356.

Laborde, Angel, Spanish officer, 73.
Laborers sold to Yucatán, 312.
Lamar, M. B., on Santa Anna, 142-43.
Landero, Pedro, rebel, 1832, 88.
Laredo, mentioned, 10; Santa Anna to, 129.
Lemaur, Francisco, Spanish officer, 38, 44-45.
Lemprière, C., cited, 85.
Léperos, 192-93.

Oaxaca, retreat to, 68; joins rebels, 92; conservative, 110; Santa Anna refused entrance to, 272.
Ocampo, Melchor, 289.
O'Donojú, J., Viceroy, 1821, 27; Treaty of Córdoba, 27-28; death, 29.
Orzaba, city joins rebels, 19-20; forced loan, 21; mentioned, 93; conservative, 110, 118; Santa Anna flees to, 260; proclamation of Santa Anna, 330-31; mentioned, 357.
Orizaba, mountain, mentioned, 3, 85.
Orquesta, La, on Santa Anna, 329, 339.

Pájaro Verde, El, cited, 312; friendly to Santa Anna, 358-60, 363.
Paredes y Arrillaga, in revolt, 171-73; ignored, 182; crushed, 198; revolt, 1844, 205-7; as President, 227; to front, 236.
Parrott, W. S., report, 126, 227.
Peña y Peña, Manuel, President, *ad interim,* 270-74.
Perote, royalists threatening, 24; plans to attack, 27-29; Santa Anna takes, 1828, 65; Santa Anna to, 172; Santa Anna prisoner in, 214.
Picaluga, Francisco, capture of Guerrero, 86.
Poinsett, J. R., on Mexican society, 35-36; on Cuba, 54; and Masons, 61-62; on revolution of 1828, 66; cited, 82; back to United States, 85; criticizes Santa Anna, 108-9.
Polk, J. K., and Santa Anna, 1846, 229 ff.; to Congress, 239; negotiations, 262.
Pope, Alexander, 317.
Portilla, J. M., in Texas, 133.
Prieto, Guillermo, on Mexican army, 154-55; on Lombardini, 281; cited, 284; on Santa Anna, 289.
Puebla, mentioned, 22, 24, 27; attacked by Santa Anna, 93-94; conservative, 110; Santa Anna defends, 162-63; attack on, 211; Scott in, 261 ff.; Santa Anna to. 270.

Quaife, M. M., cited, 231.
Quintero, Cayetano, mentioned, 8, 12.

Raines, C. W., cited, 14, 144, 151.
Ramsey, A. C., cited, 251.
Raousset-Boulbon, G. R., to Mexico, 299; to see Santa Anna, 300-1.
Rebellions, fundamental causes, 116-17.
Reeves, J. S., cited, 234.
Rejón, M. C., Santa Anna agent, 223, 226.
Rincón, José, 25.
Rincón, Manuel, Governor of Veracruz, 30; and Santa Anna, 61; campaign from Perote to Oaxaca, 67 ff.; refuses safe conduuct to Santa Anna, 211; mentioned 214, 270.
Río, Plan del, mentioned, 45.
Río Grande, mentioned, 8, 128, 225; Mexicans to retreat beyond, 140-41.
Riva Palacio, Mariano, arrested, 288.
Riva Palacio Papers, cited, 34.
Rivera, Cambas, M., cited, 4, 21, 98, 292.
Rives, G. L., cited, 208, 238.
Robinson, J. W., 189-90.
Roe, F. A., 345-46.
Romero, M., cited, 329; 347; on Seward and Santa Anna, 337-42.
Ruiz, Joaquín, 283-84.
Rusk, T. J., Texan Secretary of War, 140.
Ruxton, G. F., reception of Santa Anna, 237-38; on soldiers of Mexico, 258.

St. Augustine festival, 184-85, 298.
Salado Alvarez, V., cited, 278, 281.
Saladas, Mariano, Acting President, 236, 243; on Regency, 329.
San Antonio, capture, 1813, 11; Santa Anna to attack, 128; raid by Woll, 179.
San Felipe de Austin, mentioned, 92.
San Jacinto, Battle of, 135-37.
San Luis Potosí, Santa Anna to, 1823, 49-51; mentioned, 93; Santa Anna to, 126; organizing army, 243 ff.

Santa Anna, Antonio López de, birth and parentage, 4; education, 4; cadet, 5; to north, 1811, 7 ff.; promotion and conduct, 8; wounded, 8-9; Battle of Medina, 10-11; forgery, 11-12, 16-17; return to Veracruz, 13; rebel and bandit chasing, 13-16; made captain, 14; town building, 15-16; service record by 1821, 17; attitude to Spain, 1821, 19; joins rebels at Orizaba, 20; double promotion, 20; effort to assassinate, 21; attack on Veracruz, 21 ff.; quarrel with city council of Jalapa, 23, 28, 32-33, 71; decorations, 24; repulse at Veracruz, 25-26; threats against Veracruz, 26-27, 29; Treaty of Córdoba, 27-28; brigadier general, 29, 34; Iturbide suspicious of, 30; to Capital, 32; attitude to Iturbide, 32-38; decoration, 35; character, 37; courtship, 32, 37; military commander of Veracruz, 38; Echáverri, 38-39; break with Iturbide, 39-44; defeat at Jalapa, 45; Plan of Casa Mata, 46; to North, 48; at San Luis Potosí, 49-51; favors democratic government, 50-51; court martial, 51-52; to Yucatán, 53-56; plan to invade Cuba, 54-55; at Manga de Clavo, 56 ff.; marriage, 56-57; children of, 57, 200-1, 348-49; masonic troubles, 61-63; supports Guerrero, 64; decree of outlawry, 65; campaign from Perote to Oaxaca, 67 ff.; return to Jalapa, 70; plans to repel Spaniards, 71; Tampico campaign, 72 ff.; honors, 76-78; personal appearance, 81; and Bustamante, 82-84; retirement, 1830-32, 84 ff.; hankering for office, 87-88; advice to President, 89-90; in revolt, 91 ff.; to Mexico City, 94; at Zavaleta, 95; triumphal entry, 95; elected President, 97; supports Gómez Farías, 97-101; in actual control, 100; captured by own men, 102; ends rebellion, 103; on Texas, 105; and Valle, 105 ff.; turns conservative, 108-10; position and strength, 111-12; program, 113 ff.; to Manga de Clavo, 114; Zacatecas revolt, 114-16; applause, 118-19; and *Siete Leyes*, 120; conditions, 1836, 121; on Texas revolt, 125-26; plans for Texas invasion, 126-27; expedition to San Antonio, 127-30; orders, 129; the Alamo, 130-31; bogus marriage, 131; Goliad massacre, 131-33; excited, 134-35; at San Jacinto, 135-37; captive in Texas, 139-46; negotiations, 140-42; danger and panic, 142-43; trip to Washington, 146-48; and Jackson, 148, 149; return to Mexico, 149-51; in retirement, 151-53; to oppose French, 156-58; wounded, 158; hero, 159-61; President *ad interim,* 161 ff.; Mejía revolt and death, 162-63; to Manga de Clavo, 164-67; powers, 169; "mediator," 172; rebel, 173-74; organizes government, 173-75; inauguration, 175; problems, 175-79; internal improvements, 178, 192-93; bribe, 179-80; Congress obstreperous, 182-83; leg buried, 186-87; in contact with affairs, 188-89; pressure from Great Britain, 190-91; finances, 191-92; in power, 194 ff.; re-election, 197; struggle with Congress, 197 ff., 206; death of wife, 200-1; retirement, 202; marriage, 203-4; to quell revolt, 205-6; riot in capital, 208; nation-wide revolt, 209-11; resigns, 211; effort to escape and capture, 211-14; charges, 215; a prisoner, 215 ff.; property owned, 217-18; to exile, 219; in Cuba, 225 ff.; plans, 228-29; and Polk, 229 ff.; playing the game, 234-35; return to Mexico, 237-38; feeling in Mexico, 240-42; organizing army, 243 ff.; distrust, 246-47, 258; elected President, 246; to meet Taylor, 250; Angostura, 251-52; retreat, 252-53; southward, 255; takes charge, 255-57; to meet Scott, 257 ff.;

Spellman, L. U., cited, 181.
Suárez y Navarro, Juan, cited, 41, 83, 84; still a friend, 276.
Swann, E. G., 324.
Sylvester, J. A., 137.

Tampico, mention, 1811, 7; as Santa Anna de Tamaulipas, 77.
Taylor, Zachary, in North, 243, 250-52.
Texas, in rebellion, 10-12; restless, 85, 105; campaign, 122 ff.; protest and independence, 124-25; Santa Anna invades, 127 ff.; position, 189-91.
Thompson, Waddy, on life in Mexico, 167-68, 186; on Santa Anna, 197-98; referred to, 234.
Three Years War, 321, 325.
Tolumé, Battle of, 91.
Tornel y Mendívil, José María, on Santa Anna, 1822, 45-46, 65; victim, 165; outspoken, 183; supports Santa Anna, 264; in Cabinet, 287; death, 288.
Travis, Col. William B., at Alamo, 130-31.
Trist, Nicholas P., with Scott, 262, 266.

Ulloa, San Juan de, Dávila, retires to, 29; mentioned, 38; plan to attack, 39-40; Santa Anna and Lemaur, 44; French attack, 156 ff.
United States, views on Cuba, 54 ff.; Santa Anna to, 146-48; and California, 179, 189; negotiations, 224-25; blockade of Mexico, 235; on Santa Anna passing blockade, 239; Gadsden Purchase, 294-96; on border trouble, 299; Raousset, 300 ff.; policy on Maximilian, 336 ff.
University of Mexico, closed, 104; opened, 113.
Uraga, José L., 279-80, 293.
Urrea, José, in Texas, 131-33; restless in Mexico, 167-68.

Valencia, Gabriel, mentioned, 162, 171, 189; in revolt, 172, 210, 227; disaffected, 257, 263, 266; clash with Santa Anna, 267.
Valle, Guillermo, 105-7, 215.
Vanegas, Francisco Xavier, Viceroy, 6.
Veracruz, mentioned, 3; Santa Anna stationed at, 13-16; panic in, 21-22, 24; Santa Anna as Military Governor, 38; revolt against Iturbide, 41; forced loan, 72.
Veracruzano Libre, El, 61.
Victoria, Guadalupe, as a rebel, 19; opposes Iturbide, 37; popularity, 41; recognized by Santa Anna, 43; encourages Santa Anna, 45; on triumvirate, 1823, 48; and *Aguila Negra,* 54; mestizo vs. creole, 60-61; opposes Santa Anna, 65.
Vidal y Rivas, Luis G., in Cuba, 322; cited, 325; arrested, 347.
Villareal, Florencio, 306.
Voz de México, 363.
Voz de la Patria, cited, 82, 83; death penalty for political opponents, 86.

Walker, William, 299, 301.
Ward, H. G., cited, 56-57.
Welles, Gideon, 346.
Wharton, C. R., cited, 109, 184.
Wharton, W. H., on Santa Anna, 142; in Washington, 148-49.
Whittier, J. G., 351.
Williams, Amelia, cited, 127.
Wyllys, R. K., cited, 300.

Xico, flight and capture of Santa Anna, 212-14.

Yellow fever, in 1833, 104.
Yoakum, H., cited, 135, 145, 146.
Yucatán, Santa Anna as Military Governor, 53-56;; mentioned, 73; in 1841, 178; laborers sold to, 312.

Zacatecas, dissatisfied, 86, 91, 244; rebellion of 1835, 114-16; restless, 171.
Zamacois, Niceto de, cited, 45, 75; on reforms of 1833, 101; cited, 234, 314; on army costs, 245.
Zavala, Lorenzo de, Governor of State of Mexico, 66; mentioned, 69, 105; to Texas, 86; on Santa Anna, 122; opinions of, 123.